AIR POWER AGAINST TERROR

America's Conduct of Operation Enduring Freedom

Benjamin S. Lambeth

Prepared for United States Central Commar
Approved for public release; distribution

 NATIONAL DEFENSE RESEARCH INSTITUTE

The research described in this report was prepared for United States Central Command Air Forces. The research was conducted within the RAND National Defense Research Institute, a federally funded research and development center sponsored by the Office of the Secretary of Defense, the Joint Staff, the Unified Combatant Commands, the Department of the Navy, the Marine Corps, the defense agencies, and the defense Intelligence Community under Contract DASW01-01-C-0004.

Library of Congress Cataloging-in-Publication Data

Lambeth, Benjamin S.
  Air power against terror : America's conduct of Operation Enduring Freedom / Benjamin S. Lambeth.
    p. cm.
  "MG-166."
  Includes bibliographical references.
  ISBN 0-8330-3724-2 (pbk. : alk. paper)
  1. Afghan War, 2001—United States. 2. Afghan War, 2001—Aerial operations, American. 3. War on Terrorism, 2001—I. Title.

DS371.412.L36 2005
958.104'6—dc22

2005000649

The RAND Corporation is a nonprofit research organization providing objective analysis and effective solutions that address the challenges facing the public and private sectors around the world. RAND's publications do not necessarily reflect the opinions of its research clients and sponsors.

RAND® is a registered trademark.

Cover photo courtesy of Associated Press/Sergei Grits.

Published 2005 by the RAND Corporation
1776 Main Street, P.O. Box 2138, Santa Monica, CA 90407-2138
1200 South Hayes Street, Arlington, VA 22202-5050
201 North Craig Street, Suite 202, Pittsburgh, PA 15213-1516
RAND URL: http://www.rand.org/
To order RAND documents or to obtain additional information, contact
Distribution Services: Telephone: (310) 451-7002;
Fax: (310) 451-6915; Email: order@rand.org

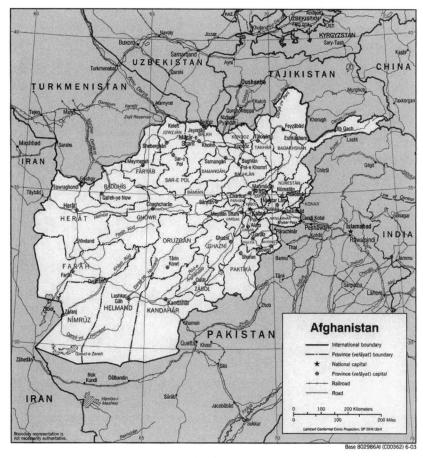

Map of Afghanistan

Preface

The attacks carried out against the United States by radical Islamist fanatics on September 11, 2001, almost instantly thrust the nation into a no-notice war on terror. This sudden showdown against a shadowy but determined foe placed a heightened demand on virtually every resource at the disposal of the new administration of President George W. Bush. The principal ingredients of that war would consist not only of traditional military moves but also of expanded homeland security measures, diplomatic initiatives, efforts to find and embargo enemy sources of financing, and covert intelligence operations. Although the war's initial focus was directed against the immediate perpetrators of the attacks—Osama bin Laden and his al Qaeda terrorist organization—the Bush administration swore that it ultimately would bring pressure to bear not only on that and other terrorist movements around the world but also on state leaders who harbored them.

This book assesses the planning and initial execution of Operation Enduring Freedom, the first U.S. response to the terrorist attacks of September 11 against al Qaeda's center of gravity in Afghanistan and against the Taliban theocracy that provided it safe haven. Since that campaign was largely an air war enabled by U.S. and allied special forces and indigenous Afghan opposition groups, the report focuses predominantly on the air portion of the joint and combined operations that were conducted in Afghanistan from October 7, 2001, through March 2002 by U.S. Central Command (CENTCOM). Its intent is to derive insights of a strategic and operational nature that not only will be of practical use to U.S. defense planners in and of themselves but also will offer a backdrop against which to assess the more complex and demanding Operation Iraqi Freedom that took place a year later to bring down the regime of Saddam Hussein. Although unbeknown to its participants at the time, Operation Enduring Freedom proved in many ways to have been a dress rehearsal for the even more eventful campaign that soon followed.

The research reported here should interest both uniformed officers in all services and civilian members of the defense establishment concerned with strategy and force employment issues raised by the war in Afghanistan. The research was conducted for U.S. Central Command Air Forces (CENTAF) within the International Security and Defense Policy Center of the RAND National Defense Research Institute, a federally funded research and development center sponsored by the Office of the Secretary of Defense, the Joint Staff, the unified commands, and the defense agencies.

For more information on RAND's International Security and Defense Policy Center, contact the director, James Dobbins. He can be reached by email at James_Dobbins@rand.org; by phone at (703) 413-1100 extension 5134; or by mail at the RAND Corporation, 1200 South Hayes Street, Arlington, Virginia 22202-5050. More information about RAND is available at www.rand.org.

Contents

Figures

Summary

The terrorist attacks of September 11, 2001, caught the United States and its leaders completely off guard. They also defined the face of early 21st-century conflict by elevating radical Islamist terrorism to the level of a core threat to U.S. security. The attacks were the boldest hostile act to have been committed on U.S. soil since Pearl Harbor. As such, they prompted a feeling of unity throughout United States perhaps unmatched since the nation's entry into World War II. Although no one immediately claimed responsibility for the attacks, the U.S. government quickly determined that they were the work of the wealthy Saudi Arabian exile, Osama bin Laden, and his al Qaeda terrorist network.

Even as the attacks were still under way, the alert status of U.S. forces around the world was raised to Defense Condition (DEFCON) 3, their highest alert level since the Yom Kippur War of 1973. Moves also were implemented to update plans for combat operations in the most likely areas of possible U.S. military involvement around the world. Within minutes of having learned of the attacks, U.S. commands throughout Europe, Asia, and the Middle East established crisis action teams to enforce heightened force-protection measures and to assess the status of the forces in their respective areas of responsibility that might be committed to action in the looming war on terror.

In crafting a response to the attacks, the first challenge that the Bush administration faced was building the broadest possible international coalition to lend material support and moral legitimacy to the impending war. The second challenge entailed developing a concrete strategy that defined and specified the campaign's priorities and goals. The third was to develop a detailed force-employment plan for meeting those priorities and achieving the administration's most immediate strategic goals. Finally, there was a need to begin fielding and prepositioning the required combat and combat-support assets of all U.S. services for any such action.

Before any of these initiatives could be put into motion, however, the Department of Defense first had to establish an air defense umbrella over the United States to ensure against any further terrorist use of aircraft as weapons. Before the September 11 attacks, the United States had maintained only a token air defense posture consisting entirely of two Air National Guard fighters poised on round-the-clock 15-minute alert at each of only seven bases along the nation's coasts to protect American air sovereignty. Less than a day after the attacks, however, the picture had changed dramatically, with dozens of armed fighters maintaining round-the-clock patrols over more than 30 American cities. In addition, this greatly enhanced nationwide air defense posture, code-named Operation Noble Eagle, maintained an undisclosed number of armed fighters on alert at bases throughout the United States.

Preparing for War

It soon became clear that the U.S. response to the September 11 attacks would consist not just of combat operations but also of diplomacy, coalition-building, heightened intelligence activities, immigration control, enhanced homeland defense, extensive police work, and efforts to identify and embargo al Qaeda's sources of funding. Yet there was no doubt that the initial round would be an air-dominated military offensive to take down bin Laden's al Qaeda network in Afghanistan and that country's ruling Taliban theocracy, which had provided the terrorists safe haven. Within just a day of the attacks, the Bush administration made determined moves to assemble a broad-based international coalition before committing the nation to any military action. For its part, the North Atlantic Council invoked the mutual defense clause in the charter of the North Atlantic Treaty Organization (NATO) for the first time in the alliance's 52-year history. The administration also garnered the support of numerous other countries around the world, including Russia, and pressured Pakistan to provide whatever intelligence and logistical support might be needed to help capture or kill al Qaeda's leaders and assist the United States in retaliating against any countries that may have supported them. Shortly thereafter, Pakistan agreed to open its airspace for the transit of any U.S. air attacks against the Taliban and al Qaeda and to halt the flow of fuel and supplies from Pakistan to Afghanistan.

On the domestic front, Congress promptly granted the administration a $40 billion emergency funding package for conducting counterterrorist operations, with a provision for an immediate release of $10 billion for the White House to use at its discretion. Congress also moved quickly to empower President Bush to take action against the terrorists by issuing a joint resolution that released the White House from any obligation to seek a formal declaration of war in the course of pursuing its options. Within days of the terrorist attacks, the Senate passed a 98–0 resolution authorizing the use of all necessary and appropriate force. Shortly thereafter, the House of Representatives passed a similar resolution by a vote of 420–1.

Next, the administration began building a strategy for carrying out a phased response to the terrorist attacks, starting with a war focused on al Qaeda and the Taliban in Afghanistan but eventually reaching beyond to terrorist movements worldwide with the global reach to harm the United States. At the time of the September 11 attacks, there was no plan in existence for U.S. military action in Afghanistan. Yet in the span of just three weeks, the government pulled together an effective coalition, crafted the beginnings of a serviceable strategy, moved needed forces and materiel to the region, made alliances with indigenous anti-Taliban elements in Afghanistan, laid the groundwork for an acceptable target-approval process, and prepared to conduct concurrent humanitarian relief operations.

To facilitate the impending war, the Bush administration sought and gained the approval of the Saudi government for the use of the

xvi   Air Power Against Terror: America's Conduct of Operation Enduring Freedom

Combined Air Operations Center (CAOC) maintained by the air component of U.S. Central Command (CENTCOM) at Prince Sultan Air Base in Saudi Arabia. Support also was gained from several former Soviet republics in Central Asia for the temporary basing of U.S. aircraft and military personnel slated to conduct combat operations against Afghanistan. A key element of this planning was a determination by the administration to avoid causing any harm to Afghan noncombatants so as to avoid further inflaming anti-American passions throughout the Islamic world. The war plan that emerged accordingly sought to rely to the fullest extent possible on precision-guided weapons.

The United States Strikes Back

On October 7, 2001, CENTCOM commenced Operation Enduring Freedom, a joint and combined war against al Qaeda and the Taliban in Afghanistan. The campaign began at night with strikes against 31 targets, including early warning radars, ground forces, command-and-control facilities, al Qaeda infrastructure, and Taliban airfields. Attacks on the second day also began during the hours of darkness but continued this time into daylight, indicating a determination by CENTCOM that the Taliban's air defenses had been largely negated. During the fifth consecutive day of bombing, mountain cave complexes harboring al Qaeda combatants and equipment were attacked for the first time. After the tenth day, the target list was greatly expanded and discrete engagement zones were established throughout the country to facilitate aerial attacks against Taliban and al Qaeda forces. Although these engagement zones were similar to the kill boxes that had been set up during Operation Desert Storm a decade earlier, they did not allow allied aircrews to attack anything that moved inside them without prior CENTCOM approval because of persistent uncertainties regarding the location of friendly Afghan opposition forces and allied special operations forces (SOF) in close proximity to known or suspected enemy positions. Nevertheless, their establishment did indicate an impending move away from preplanned targets toward pop-up targets of opportunity as they emerged.

The successful insertion of a small number of U.S. SOF teams into Afghanistan after 11 days of bombing signaled the onset of a new use of air power in joint warfare, in which Air Force terminal attack controllers working with SOF spotters positioned forward within line of sight of enemy force concentrations directed precision air attacks against enemy ground troops who were not in direct contact with friendly forces. In this phase of operations, airborne forward air controllers also identified enemy targets and cleared other aircraft to attack them. Thanks to the reduced enemy air defense threat, U.S. aircraft were now cleared to descend to lower altitudes as necessary to attack any emerging targets that were observed to be on the move.

By late October, however, a sense of frustration had begun to settle in among some observers as the war's level of effort averaged only around 63 strike sorties a day, with continuing attacks against fixed enemy military assets and relatively little apparent damage being done to Taliban troop strength. In light of this seeming lack of progress, a growing number of critics began predicting either a quagmire or an outright U.S. failure. These voices of concern naturally put the Bush administration on the defensive in its effort to refute allegations that the campaign had bogged down.

In fairness to the administration, there remained a lack of much actionable intelligence on elusive targets at that still-early stage of the war, and the nearness of friendly indigenous Afghan Northern Alliance forces to Taliban front lines created a constant danger that those forces might get hit by errant bombs. Moreover, although the opportunity for U.S. cooperation with the Northern Alliance had been available and ready to be exploited in principle from the very start of the campaign, CENTCOM was slow to insert SOF teams into Afghanistan to empower the opposition groups because of persistent bad weather. Even after the tenth day of U.S. combat involvement, the latest of CENTCOM's several efforts to insert the first SOF unit had to be aborted at the last minute because of conditions that prohibited safe helicopter operations.

Finally, on October 19, two Air Force Special Operations Command (AFSOC) MH-53J Pave Low helicopters successfully delivered Army Special Forces Operational Detachment Alpha 555 (more commonly known as A-Team 555) to a landing zone in Afghanistan's Shamali plains, which had been marked by a Central Intelligence Agency (CIA) team that was already in place and awaiting its military compatriots. These Army SOF troops, with their attached Air Force terminal attack controllers, would provide the first eyes on target for enabling what eventually became a remarkably successful U.S. exercise in air-ground cooperation.

The Rout of the Taliban

On October 21, Northern Alliance forces began marshaling for an attack on Mazar-i-Sharif, with a view toward eventually moving from there on to Kabul. Two days later, the most intense ground fighting since the start of Enduring Freedom occurred as Northern Alliance and Taliban forces exchanged heavy fire. The Northern Alliance aimed at hastening the Taliban's collapse by striking from all sides. U.S. cooperation enabled the application of opposition-group pressure in the north, while U.S. SOF units sought to organize similar pressure in the south against Kandahar.

The Northern Alliance's full-up offensive commenced on October 28. That day saw ramped-up U.S. air attacks against Taliban artillery positions that were threatening a Northern Alliance supply line. With the intensified use of B-1Bs and B-52s against the Taliban front lines, Northern Alliance leaders who once criticized the bombing now came to praise it and to draw increased hopes of achieving success. The A-Teams were now calling in heavy air attacks against the Taliban's two circles of defensive trenches around Mazar-i-Sharif. Enemy supply lines and communications were cut, hundreds of enemy vehicles and bunkers were destroyed, and thousands of Taliban fighters were either captured or killed or else escaped.

On November 9, Northern Alliance forces took Mazar-i-Sharif. That success was the first tangible victory in Enduring Freedom. Two days later, the Northern Alliance surged against Taliban forces defending Kabul. Then, on November 13, Northern Alliance forces captured Kabul as Taliban forces beat a retreat, creating a strategic breakthrough that silenced critics of the operation who, for a time, had voiced concerns about an impending quagmire.

The capture of Mazar-i-Sharif and Kabul by the Northern Alliance, enabled decisively by American air power working in close harmony with allied SOF teams, was a major breakthrough. Thanks to the rapid accumulation of advances that had been achieved in such short order, the resistance now controlled nearly three-quarters of the country, as contrasted with only 10 percent in the northernmost reaches before the start of the campaign just a few weeks before. With the fall of Mazar-i-Sharif and Kabul, the Taliban suffered a major loss, and al Qaeda forces in Afghanistan were clearly on the run. Although a substantial number of al Qaeda and Taliban combatants succeeded in eluding the campaign's effects, the interim victories that culminated in the fall of Mazar-i-Sharif and Kabul nonetheless foretold the successful conclusion of the hardest fighting by allied forces less than a month later.

On December 1, air attacks on Kandahar intensified as opposition forces moved to within 10 miles of that last remaining Taliban holdout and a loose encirclement progressively became a siege. By that point, the United States had accomplished much of what it had sought by way of campaign goals. The Taliban were in flight; the cities of Mazar-i-Sharif, Herat, and Kabul were in the hands of opposition forces and calm; al Qaeda's terrorist infrastructure in Afghanistan had been all but destroyed or dispersed; and a post-Taliban interim Afghan leadership was being formed.

With the fall of Kandahar 63 days into the campaign, CENTCOM's focus shifted to tracking down bin Laden and his top lieutenants, stabilizing post-Taliban Afghanistan, and addressing humanitarian concerns in the war-ravaged country. Toward that end, the primary thrust of combat operations now shifted to the mountain cave complex at Tora Bora to which many Taliban and al Qaeda combatants were believed to have fled.

The bombing of the Tora Bora mountains continued nonstop every day for three weeks, after which it was suspended for a brief period to allow opposition-group formations to advance on the caves in search of al Qaeda fugitives. Those formations moved in on three sides, forcing the most hard-core remnants of al Qaeda to seek refuge in the higher mountains of eastern Afghanistan. For a time, bin Laden was known to have been in the area. In the end, however, his trail went cold and he succeeded in getting away.

On December 18, for the first time since the war began on October 7, the bombing came to a halt. Although hundreds of Taliban and al Qaeda fugitives managed to escape across the border into Pakistan, the Taliban regime was brought down only 102 days after the terrorist attacks of September 11. By late February 2002, Operation Enduring Freedom had largely devolved from a high-technology air war into a domestic police action as the United States now found itself striving to pacify feuding warlords, protect the embryonic interim Afghan government, and ensure adequate force protection for the 4,000 U.S. troops who were now in the country.

Operation Anaconda

After two months of relative quiescence following the fall of the Taliban and the installation of the interim Karzai government, U.S. ground troops met their fiercest test of Enduring Freedom up to that point in an initiative that came to be known as Operation Anaconda. This push by the Army into the high mountains of Afghanistan was the first and only large-scale combat involvement by conventional U.S. ground forces in Enduring Freedom to date.

The nearby Shah-i-Kot valley had been under surveillance by CENTCOM ever since early January 2002, prompted by reports that Taliban and foreign al Qaeda combatants were regrouping there in an area near the town of Gardez. Over time, enemy forces continued to flow into the area, to a point where it appeared as though they might begin to pose a serious threat to the still-fragile Karzai government. At least two considerations underlay the Anaconda initiative: (1) A desire on CENTCOM's part to preempt the growing concentration of al Qaeda fighters who were assembling and reequipping themselves in the Shah-i-Kot hinterland; and (2) mounting intelligence indicating a conviction by al Qaeda leaders that U.S. forces would not pursue them into the mountains and take them on in winter weather.

Unlike all previous U.S. ground combat activities to date, Anaconda was planned almost from the start to be conventionally led and SOF-supported. It represented the first instance of U.S. willingness to put a substantial number of American troops in harm's way since Operation Desert Storm more than a decade before. In all, some 200 SOF combatants, 800 to 1,000 indigenous Afghan fighters, and more than 1,400 conventional U.S. Army troops were assigned to participate in the operation. It envisaged a three-day offensive whose declared mission was to capture or kill any al Qaeda and Taliban fighters who might be encountered in the area.

The plan for Anaconda fell apart at the seams almost from the very start, thanks to heavy enemy resistance and the lack of adequate U.S. fire support to counter it. Unexpectedly fierce fighting broke out during an attempted predawn insertion of SOF combatants into the high Shah-i-Kot mountains on the operation's third day when those combatants encountered a sudden hail of preemptive large-caliber machine gun, rocket-propelled grenade, and mortar fire from determined al Qaeda fighters who were holed up in the caves there. As a result, fixed-wing air power, which had been all but excluded from the initial Anaconda planning, had to be summoned as an emergency measure of last resort when events on the ground seemed headed for disaster. That air support would prove pivotal in producing what ultimately was a successful, if costly, allied outcome. In all, eight U.S. military personnel lost their lives to hostile fire and more than 50 were wounded, some severely, during the initial conduct of combat operations.

Once CENTCOM's air component was fully engaged in the operation, the CAOC quickly provided additional assets to support the still-embattled U.S. ground troops. By the end of the first week, as allied air attacks became more consistent and sustained, al Qaeda resistance began tapering off and friendly forces seized control of ever more terrain. That said, what was initially expected to last only 72 hours went on for two weeks. In the end, it took the eleventh-hour intervention of CENTCOM's air component in a major way to correct for Anaconda's initial planning errors once the going got unexpectedly rough.

Viewed in hindsight, those who planned and initiated Operation Anaconda failed to make the most of the potential synergy of air, space, and land power that was available to them in principle. Once the air component became fully engaged, the concentration of aircraft over the embattled area required unusually close coordination among the many participants and controlling elements because of the failure of Anaconda's planners to see to needed aircraft deconfliction arrangements in adequate time. That requirement often limited how quickly fixed-wing air power could respond to sudden calls for fire support. Aircraft run-in headings had to be restricted because of the closely confined and congested battlespace, with multiple stacks of aircraft operating and dropping bombs simultaneously through the same block of air and with friendly ground forces in close proximity to the enemy, both of which dictated specific attack headings to avoid fratricide from weapons effects. Moreover, many targets were cave entrances situated on steep slopes, which limited the available run-in headings for effectively delivering ordnance. Fortunately, despite these manifold complications, not a single midair collision or other aircraft mishap occurred at any time during Anaconda, and no further U.S. loss of life to enemy action was incurred.

Distinctive Achievements

Operation Enduring Freedom saw a further improvement of some important force-employment trends that were first set in motion during the Gulf War a decade earlier. For example, precision weapons accounted for only 9 percent of the munitions expended during Desert Storm, whereas they totaled 29 percent in Allied Force and nearly 70 percent in Enduring Freedom. As for aerial warfare "firsts," the war saw the first combat employment of the Global Hawk high-altitude unmanned aerial vehicle (UAV), as well as the first operational use of Predator UAVs armed with Hellfire missiles. It also saw the first combat use of the precision-guided Joint Direct Attack Munition (JDAM) by the B-1 and B-52. (During Allied Force, only the B-2 had been configured to deliver that satellite-aided weapon.)

Moreover, for the first time in the history of modern war, Enduring Freedom was conducted under an overarching intelligence, surveillance, and reconnaissance (ISR) umbrella that stared down constantly and relentlessly in search of enemy activity. This mix of mutually supporting sensors enabled greatly increased ISR input over that available during earlier conflicts. It also permitted a degree of ISR fusion that distinguished Enduring Freedom from all previous air operations.

Perhaps the greatest tactical innovation of the war was the highly improvised integration of Air Force terminal attack controllers with Army Special Forces A-Teams and Navy Sea–Air–Land (SEAL) commando units to produce a SOF-centric application of precision air power against emerging targets that added up to a new way of war for the United States. SOF teams performed three major missions throughout the campaign. First, they marshaled and directed the unorganized forces of the Northern Alliance. Second, they built small armies out of the Pashtun tribesmen in the south. Third, they provided invaluable eyes-on-target identification to U.S. aircrews for conducting precision air attacks.

Far more than during the earlier case of Operation Allied Force, when NATO aircrews toward the end received targeting information on several occasions indirectly from Kosovo Liberation Army ground spotters, Operation Enduring Freedom showed that air power can be more effective in many circumstances if it is teamed not only with forward ground spotters but also with friendly ground forces sufficiently robust to flush out and concentrate enemy forces. What was demonstrated in Afghanistan on repeated occasion, especially early on, was not classic close air support or air interdiction but rather SOF-enabled precision air attacks against enemy ground forces with no friendly ground forces in direct contact. This novel use of air power enabled ground support to air-delivered firepower, yet at the operational rather than tactical level of war. It also made for a doctrinal gray area that blurred the line between "supporting" and "supported" and that featured SOF teams finding, identifying, and tracking targets for an implicit *air* scheme of maneuver in which there was no concurrent friendly *ground* scheme of maneuver under way. Operations were generally so fluid that "supporting" and "supported" command relationships flowed back and forth seamlessly.

The two most pivotal ingredients that made this achievement possible were long-range precision air power and uncommonly good real-time tactical intelligence provided by mobile SOF teams able to operate, in effect, as human ISR sensors. Units from different services with little or no prior joint warfighting experience performed under fire as though they had trained and operated together for years. In all, Enduring Freedom was uniquely emblematic of the quality and resourcefulness of today's American military personnel.

Finally, Operation Enduring Freedom was more than just a SOF and JDAM story. It also featured a mobility component that was no less indispensable for ensuring the war's success. Until a land bridge from Uzbekistan was opened in late November, everything the military used, including fuel, had to be airlifted into Afghanistan because the country was landlocked. The successful execution of the lift portion of Enduring Freedom spotlighted the value of logistics as a weapon system, as well as the fact that effects-based operations entail materiel delivery as well as bombing.

Problems in Execution

To be sure, the conduct of Enduring Freedom was not without inefficiencies and friction. To begin with, almost from the war's opening moments, a tense relationship emerged between the air component commander's operation in the CAOC in Saudi Arabia and the CENTCOM staff in Tampa, Florida. A variety of factors occasioned this situation, not the least being the campaign's uniquely exacting rules of engagement overlaid on an unclear and rapidly changing strategy—the latter owing to the fact that initial planning for Enduring Freedom was essentially a pick-up game in the immediate aftermath of the September 11 attacks. The most important causal factor, however, was CENTCOM's resort to a less-than-ideal initial template for conducting combat operations in Afghanistan.

Adopting a familiar repertoire to which it had been habituated for 10 years, CENTCOM chose to conduct Enduring Freedom using roughly the same procedures as those of the very different Operation Southern Watch (OSW), the enforcement of the no-fly zone over southern Iraq. In contrast, Enduring Freedom was to be a full-fledged war against the Taliban and al Qaeda, in which the goals and imperatives, one would have thought, would naturally be driven by the demands of a fight to the finish rather than those of a UN policing action. It was entirely predictable that problems would develop once CENTCOM opted instead to impose onto the Afghan war an OSW-like operations flow, with the latter's strict interpretation of assigned rules of engagement and stringent special instructions and target vetting procedures, all dominated by heavy senior leadership involvement that exercised not only highly centralized control but also centralized execution.

There also were different schools of thought within CENTCOM with respect to how best to conduct the war. Those in the CAOC during the war's early days were convinced that they were the best equipped to determine the most appropriate force employment options at the operational and tactical levels. They also felt that those at CENTCOM headquarters were animated by a land-warfare mindset that failed to appreciate what modern air power could accomplish if used to its fullest potential. By the same token, at least some key staffers at CENTCOM felt that the most senior Air Force airmen in the CAOC were overly service-centric in their thinking and were seeking, in effect, to fight their own private air war.

All of this was further aggravated by a pronounced geographic separation between CENTCOM headquarters and the CAOC, a distance that covered eight time zones. Unlike the benchmark case of Operation Desert Storm, the overall combined force commander and his air component commander were not physically collocated. Much counterproductive friction between the forward and rear components of CENTCOM ensued as a result of this substantial separation of command elements. In hindsight, one could argue that the combined force commander and his principal staffers should have deployed forward to be nearer the air component commander around

xxvi   Air Power Against Terror: America's Conduct of Operation Enduring Freedom

the clock. Short of that, had the air component commander been collocated with the combined force commander at CENTCOM headquarters and delegated the execution of CAOC functions to his forward-deployed CAOC director or, alternatively, had he been able to provide a senior general-officer representative at CENTCOM as his personal emissary to the combined force commander, perhaps much of the early tension that occurred between the front and rear could have been alleviated—or prevented altogether.

The greatest frustration for the CAOC's airmen, however, was the fact that target selection and the development of the Joint Integrated and Prioritized Target List were done at CENTCOM headquarters rather than in the CAOC. According to joint doctrine, the air component commander oversees a daily air tasking cycle that takes both commander's intent and assigned rules of engagement as points of departure and proceeds from there through a systematic development process beginning with strategy input, moving on to target selection, then to Master Air Attack Plan creation and dissemination, and finally to execution. Yet in the case of Enduring Freedom, a key element of this cycle was preempted by CENTCOM. As a result, the strategy-to-task process was taken out of the air component commander's hands, leaving the CAOC planning staff to be little more than mission schedulers, to all intents and purposes.

In addition, some severe inefficiencies in target approval were revealed. Sensor-to-shooter data cycle time (more commonly known as the "kill chain") in Enduring Freedom was reduced in duration from hours—or even days—often to single-digit minutes. An oversubscribed target-approval process, however, often nullified the potential benefits of that breakthrough by lengthening decision timelines, making the human factor the main source of delay in servicing time-sensitive targets. From the first night onward, the exceptional stringency of the rules of engagement caused by collateral damage concerns led to a target-approval bottleneck at CENTCOM that allowed many fleeting attack opportunities to slip away. The repeated suspected escape of enemy leaders as a result of delays in securing target approval, moreover, was a consequence not only of rules-of-engagement constraints but also of a cumbersome target-vetting process within CENTCOM that had been fashioned after the one used in OSW, with which CENTCOM was both familiar and comfortable, instead of being tailored to meet the uniquely different and more urgent demands of the war on terror.

Many airmen complained bitterly about the seeming stranglehold imposed on their professionalism and flexibility by CENTCOM's seizure of execution authority from the air component commander and what the resultant highly centralized control and stringent rules of engagement were doing to prolong target-approval times. As for the rules themselves, they emanated from the president himself, who was determined to avoid any targeting mishap that might even remotely suggest that the campaign was an indiscriminate war against the Afghan people or Islam. That determination led to an entirely valid requirement for a minimally destructive air campaign using tactics that would not risk alienating the Afghan rank and file, further damaging an already weak Afghan infrastructure, and further inflaming anti-American sentiments elsewhere in the Arab world. These objectives were well understood and embraced by the leadership in the CAOC. Yet the latter wanted to build and execute an effects-based campaign focused on key elements of the Taliban organization rather than to follow the more classic attrition-based approach that CENTCOM headquarters was imposing.

Nevertheless, more than in any previous war, Operation Enduring Freedom saw not just centralized planning, almost uniformly acknowledged by military professionals to be highly desirable in principle, but also an insidious trend toward centralized execution that could yield highly undesirable and even irreversible consequences if not duly disciplined and managed in a timely way. The nation's greatly expanded global communications connectivity not only provided an increasingly shared operational picture at all levels but also enabled what some have called "command at a distance." A downside of the expanded ISR connectivity and available bandwidth that have evolved since Desert Storm is that at the same time they have made possible far more efficient and timely operations than ever before, they also have increasingly enabled direct senior leadership involvement in the finest details of force employment, at least in slow-paced activities like OSW and medium-paced wars like Operation Enduring Freedom with relatively small numbers of sorties and targets to manage at any moment.

Some kinds of wars with exceptionally pronounced political sensitivities, of which Enduring Freedom was emblematic, will continue to require both stringent rules of engagement and centralized execution. However, there is an inherent tension between the imperatives of political control and those of efficient mission accomplishment that senior leaders must understand. Although the American military command-and-control network has now evolved to a point where centralized execution has become routinely possible in principle, decentralized execution remains the preeminent virtue of American military culture because it constitutes the bedrock of flexibility. Doctrine and practice must accordingly seek a way to reconcile this growing dilemma lest the recent tendency toward centralized execution as the rule rather than the exception be allowed, through operator default, to undermine one of the nation's most precious military advantages.

On Balance

In all, Operation Enduring Freedom earned far more by way of deserved accolades than demerits. Never before in modern times had the United States fought an expeditionary war so remote from its base structure. The tyranny of distance that dominated the campaign redefined the meaning of endurance in air warfare and represented an unprecedented test of American combat prowess. One B-2 sortie lasted 44.3 hours, becoming the longest air combat mission ever flown in history. It was not uncommon for fighter sorties to last 10 hours or more. The war saw the longest-range carrier-based strike operations conducted in the history of naval air warfare.

Beyond that, the United States commenced combat operations from a standing start with less than a month's time to plan and marshal forces for the impending war. The campaign saw an unprecedented reliance on SOF, in which a unique synergy flowed from the unconventional enabling of precision air power by SOF and indigenous friendly ground forces. Each force element amplified the inherent leverage of the other, with SOF teams allowing air power to be effective against elusive targets and air power permitting allied SOF units to work more efficiently with indigenous Afghan opposition groups in often close-quarters land combat against Taliban and al Qaeda forces—all with a complete absence of involvement by heavy-maneuver U.S. ground forces.

With respect to tactics, techniques, and procedures, Enduring Freedom offered a laboratory for testing, in a live combat setting, some of the most significant air power advances to have taken place in more than two decades. Its dominant features were persistence of pressure on the enemy and rapidity of execution, thanks to the improved data fusion enabled by new technologies, a better-managed CAOC, more help from space, and smarter concepts of operations. Accurate and timely target information was made possible by linking the inputs of Predator and Global Hawk UAVs, the RC-135, the U-2, the E-8, and other sensor platforms around the clock. This improved connectivity enabled constant surveillance of enemy activity and contributed significantly to shortening the kill chain. Predator and Global Hawk offered a major improvement in that they did not represent national assets like satellites and hence bore no requirement for the CAOC to request tasking. The resultant capability was effective in part because UAVs can now remain on station for a long time, enabling the elusive goal of instantaneous attack by finding a target, matching it with a weapon, shooting the weapon, and observing the resultant effects.

If there was anything "transformational" about the way Enduring Freedom was conducted, it was the dominance of fused information over platforms and munitions as the principal enabler of the campaign's success in the end. That new dynamic made possible all other major aspects of the war, including the integration of SOF with precision-strike air power, the minimization of target-location error, the avoidance of collateral damage, and command from the rear—both for better and for worse. Thanks to real-time imagery and increased communications connectivity, the kill chain was shorter than ever, and target-attack accuracy was truly phenomenal. Throughout Enduring Freedom, persistent ISR and precision attack gave CENTCOM the ability to deny the enemy a sanctuary both day and night. Such network-centric operations are now the cutting edge of an ongoing paradigm shift in American combat style that may be of greater potential moment than was the introduction of the tank at the beginning of the 20th century.

The Enduring Freedom experience also pointed up some new facts of life about likely future American combat involvement. First, it showed that positive target identification and avoiding civilian casualties have become permanent features of the emerging American way of war. Second, it suggested that senior leadership will continue to guard its authority to make strike approval decisions for target attacks that entail a high risk of inflicting civilian casualties. Approval time and time-sensitive target timelines will increasingly be determined by prevailing rules of engagement and target-approval criteria. Accordingly, airmen must get away from the "one size fits all" approach to targeting doctrine. Because quick-response attack against emerging targets has become the new reality, airmen need to create new concepts of operations to accommodate it. They also need to begin forging new ways for managing the downside effects of improved information fusion, including, most notably, such issues as the trend toward centralized execution.

Acknowledgments

This work has been made both richer and better informed by the help of numerous individuals who had first-hand involvement with Operation Enduring Freedom. I thank, first and foremost, the two successive Combined Force Air Component Commanders (CFACCs), Air Force Generals Charles Wald and T. Michael Moseley, for candidly sharing with me their recollections of what mattered most in that operation. Others to whom I am grateful for discussing with me various aspects of Enduring Freedom include General William Begert, Commander, Pacific Air Forces; General Hal Hornburg, Commander, Air Combat Command; General Gregory Martin, then-Commander, United States Air Forces in Europe, and his staff; Air Chief Marshal Sir John Day, Royal Air Force (RAF), Commander, RAF Strike Command; then–Air Marshal Sir Jock Stirrup, RAF, senior British Ministry of Defense representative to U.S. Central Command (CENTCOM) during the critical early portion of Enduring Freedom; Lieutenant General Franklin Hagenbeck, USA, commander of Operation Anaconda during Enduring Freedom; Lieutenant General John Corley, USAF, Major Generals David Deptula and Stephen Wood, USAF, and Rear Admiral John Cryer III, USN, directors of CENTAF's Combined Air Operations Center (CAOC) at Prince Sultan Air Base, Saudi Arabia, at various times during Enduring Freedom; Rear Admiral Mark Fitzgerald, USN, former Commander, USS *Theodore Roosevelt* carrier strike group, whose embarked air wing (CVW-1) participated in Enduring Freedom; Colonel Thomas Ehrhard, USAF, School of Advanced Air and

Space Studies at Air University and Chief of the Strategy Division in the CAOC during the early part of Enduring Freedom; and Air Force Lieutenant Colonels Mark Cline, Pete Gersten, David Hathaway, Scott Kindsvater, and Clete Norris, all assigned to CENTAF's CAOC staff during various portions of Enduring Freedom. For their insights as senior mentors who taught the week-long Combined Force Air Component Commander (CFACC) Course 02B at Maxwell AFB, Alabama, which I was privileged to attend in August 2002 in support of this study, I am grateful to Lieutenant Generals Charles Heflebower and Michael Short, USAF (Ret.). Kathi Jones, the command historian at 9th Air Force, provided me with some much-appreciated documentary assistance.

Finally, for their helpful comments on all or parts of an earlier draft of this study, I thank Generals Hornburg, Martin, Moseley, and Wald; General Charles Horner, USAF (Ret.), CFACC during Operation Desert Storm; then–Lieutenant General Ronald Keys, USAF, Deputy Chief of Staff for Air and Space Operations, Headquarters United States Air Force; Lieutenant General Short; Lieutenant General Victor Renuart, USAF, Director of Operations at CENTCOM during Enduring Freedom; Major General David MacGhee, USAF, Commander, Air Force Doctrine Center (AFDC), Colonel Gary Cox, USAF, and Lieutenant Colonel John Hunerwadel and staff at AFDC; Major General Robert Elder, USAF, former Deputy CFACC and Commander, CENTAF (Forward); Major General Michael Hamel, USAF, Commander, 14th Air Force; Major Generals Deptula and Wood; Brigadier General Charles Dunlap, Jr., USAF, Staff Judge Advocate, Air Combat Command; Christopher Bowie, Deputy Director of Strategic Planning, Headquarters United States Air Force; Brigadier General Allen Peck, USAF, Deputy Commander, 9th Air Force; Captain Robert Harward, USN, Commander, Task Force K-Bar during Enduring Freedom; Colonel Michael Longoria, USAF, Commander, 18th Air Support Operations Group and senior air liaison officer to the land component commander during Enduring Freedom; Colonel Matt Neuenswander, Commander, USAF Air-Ground Operations School; Colonel Allen Wickman, USAF, Commander, 98th Range Wing; Lieutenant Colonel Robert Charette,

USMC, Commander, Marine Fighter/Attack Squadron (VMFA) 323; Lieutenant Colonels Cline and Gersten; Pat Pentland of Science Applications International Corporation (SAIC); Colonel Igor Gardner, Lieutenant Colonel Brett Plentl, and Major Jefferson Reynolds, former Air Force Fellows at RAND; Major Charles Hogan, USAF, Air Command and Staff College; Majors Mark Davis, USA, and Craig Wills, USAF, School of Advanced Air and Space Studies; Major Mark Main, USAF, Headquarters 14th Air Force; and my RAND colleagues James Dobbins, Edward Harshberger, David Ochmanek, Bruce Pirnie, Carl Rhodes, and Alan Vick. Finally, I offer special thanks to my RAND colleague Karl Mueller and to Kenneth Pollack of the Brookings Institution for their helpful technical reviews of an earlier draft and to my editor, Patricia Bedrosian, for keeping me honest in matters of punctuation and word choice. As always, it goes without saying that any errors of fact or interpretation that may remain in the pages that follow are mine alone.

I wish to dedicate this work to the memory of General Bill Creech, USAF (Ret.), Commander of Tactical Air Command from 1978 to 1984. General Creech is widely remembered by both his surviving peers and the many proteges he groomed to lead today's Air Force as having been the most influential person responsible for the markedly improved combat edge that the Air Force acquired during its renaissance era after Vietnam. I had the privilege of knowing General Creech well only during his later retirement years. Throughout those years, during which time we spoke as often as twice daily, he was a constant source of good counsel, an insistent stickler for the highest standards, an inspiring fellow student of the warrior arts, and an always helping friend.

Abbreviations

AAA	Antiaircraft Artillery
AB	Air Base
ABCCC	Airborne Battlefield Command and Control Center
ACC	Air Combat Command
ACTD	Advanced Concept Technology Demonstrator
AEF	Air Expeditionary Force
AFB	Air Force Base
AFFOR	Air Forces Forward
AFSB	Afloat Forward Staging Base
AFSOC	Air Force Special Operations Command
AGM	Air-to-Ground Missile
ALCM	Air-Launched Cruise Missile
ALO	Air Liaison Officer
AMC	Air Mobility Command
AMOCC	Air Mobility Operations Control Center
ANG	Air National Guard
AOC	Air Operations Center
AOR	Area of Responsibility

ARCENT	U.S. Central Command Army Forces
ASOC	Air Support Operations Center
ASOG	Air Support Operations Group
ASOS	Air Support Operations Squadron
ASW	Antisubmarine Warfare
ATO	Air Tasking Order
AWACS	Airborne Warning and Control System
BCD	Battlefield Coordination Detachment
BDA	Battle Damage Assessment
BLU	Bomb Live Unit
BRITE	Broadcast Request Imagery Technology
C2	Command and Control
C3	Command, Control, and Communications
C4	Command, Control, Communications, and Computers
CAG	Carrier Air Group
CALCM	Conventional Air-Launched Cruise Missile
CAOC	Combined Air Operations Center
CAP	Combat Air Patrol
CAS	Close Air Support
CBU	Cluster Bomb Unit
CDE	Collateral Damage Expectancy
CEM	Combined-Effects Munition
CEP	Circular Error Probable
CDS	Containerized Delivery System

CENTAF   U.S. Central Command Air Forces

CENTCOM   U.S. Central Command

CFACC   Combined Force Air Component Commander

CFLCC   Combined Force Land Component Commander

CIA   Central Intelligence Agency

CINC   Commander in Chief

CJCS   Chairman of the Joint Chiefs of Staff

CJTF   Combined Joint Task Force

CNN   Cable News Network

COMAFFOR   Commander of Air Force Forces

CONOPS   Concept of Operations

CONUS   Continental United States

CRG   Contingency Response Group

CSAR   Combat Search and Rescue

CVW   Carrier Air Wing

DEFCON   Defense Condition

DIRMOBFOR   Director of Mobility Forces

DMPI   Desired Mean Point of Impact

DPPDB   Digital Point Precision Data Base

DSP   Defense Support Program

DZ   Drop Zone

EBO   Effects-Based Operations

EFS   Expeditionary Fighter Squadron

ELINT   Electronic Intelligence

ER   Enhanced Range

ETAC	Enlisted Tactical Air Controller
EU	European Union
EUCOM	U.S. European Command
FAA	Federal Aviation Administration
FAC	Forward Air Controller
FAC-A	Airborne Forward Air Controller
FARRP	Forward-Area Rearming and Refueling Point
FLIR	Forward-Looking Infrared
FOB	Forward Operating Base
FRAGO	Fragmentary Order
FTI	Fast Tactical Imagery
GAT	Guidance, Apportionment, and Targeting
GBU	Guided Bomb Unit
GFAC	Ground Forward Air Controller
GPS	Global Positioning System
HDR	Humanitarian Daily Ration
IADS	Integrated Air Defense System
ICRC	International Committee of the Red Cross
ID	Identification
IFF	Identification Friend or Foe
IR	Infrared
ISI	Pakistan Inter-Services Intelligence Agency
ISR	Intelligence, Surveillance, and Reconnaissance
JAG	Judge Advocate General
JCS	Joint Chiefs of Staff

JDAM   Joint Direct Attack Munition

JFACC   Joint Force Air Component Commander

JIPTL   Joint Integrated and Prioritized Target List

JMEM   Joint Munitions Effectiveness Manual

JSOC   Joint Special Operations Command

JSOTF   Joint Special Operations Task Force

JSOW   Joint Standoff Weapon

JSTARS   Joint Surveillance Target Attack Radar System

JTF   Joint Task Force

JTIDS   Joint Tactical Information Distribution System

JTL   Joint Target List

KLA   Kosovo Liberation Army

LANTIRN   Low-Altitude Navigation and Targeting Infrared for Night

LD/HD   Low-Density/High-Demand

LGB   Laser-Guided Bomb

LZ   Landing Zone

MAAP   Master Air Attack Plan

MARLO   Marine Aviation Liaison Officer

MASINT   Measurement and Signature Intelligence

Mbps   Megabits per Second

MCAS   Marine Corps Air Station

MEU   Marine Expeditionary Unit

MLU   Mid-Life Update

MRE   Meal Ready to Eat

MTI	Moving Target Indicator
MTW	Major Theater War
NAC	North Atlantic Council
NALT	Northern Afghanistan Liaison Team
NAS	Naval Air Station
NASA	National Aeronautics and Space Administration
NATO	North Atlantic Treaty Organization
NAVCENT	U.S. Central Command Naval Forces
NFA	No-Fire Area
NIFO	Nose In, Fingers Out
NIMA	National Imagery and Mapping Agency
NMC	Not Mission-Capable
NMCC	National Military Command Center
NOAA	National Oceanic and Atmospheric Administration
NORAD	North American Air Defense Command
NRO	National Reconnaissance Office
NSC	National Security Council
NSL	No-Strike List
NVG	Night-Vision Goggles
OAF	Operation Allied Force
OEF	Operation Enduring Freedom
OG	Opposition Group
OGA	Other Government Agency
OODA	Observe, Orient, Decide, and Act
OPLAN	Operations Plan

OSW	Operation Southern Watch
PGM	Precision-Guided Munition
PSAB	Prince Sultan Air Base
QDR	Quadrennial Defense Review
Quikscat	Quick Scatterometer
R&D	Research and Development
RAF	Royal Air Force
RAAF	Royal Australian Air Force
RIO	Radar Intercept Officer
ROE	Rules of Engagement
RPG	Rocket-Propelled Grenade
RTL	Restricted Target List
SACEUR	Supreme Allied Commander Europe
SADL	Situation Awareness Data Link
SAM	Surface-to-Air Missile
SAR	Synthetic Aperture Radar
SAS	Special Air Service [Britain]
SEAD	Suppression of Enemy Air Defenses
SEAL	Sea–Air–Land
SIGINT	Signals Intelligence
SIPRNET	Secure Internet Protocol Router Network
SLAM	Standoff Land-Attack Missile
SLAM-ER	Standoff Land-Attack Missile—Extended Range
SOCEUR	Special Operations Command Europe
SOCOM	Special Operations Command

SOF	Special Operations Forces
SOLE	Special Operations Liaison Element
SPACECOM	U.S. Space Command
SPINS	Special Instructions
STO	Space Tasking Order
SWA	Southwest Asia
SWC	Space Warfare Center
SWF	Sensor-Fused Weapon
TACP	Tactical Air Control Party
TARPS	Tactical Aerial Reconnaissance Pod System
TF	Task Force
TLAM	Tomahawk Land-Attack Missile
TRANSCOM	U.S. Transportation Command
TRAP	Tactical Recovery of Aircraft and Personnel
TRIAD	Tri-Wall Aerial Delivery
TSC	Theater Support Command
TST	Time-Sensitive Targeting
TTP	Tactics, Techniques, and Procedures
UAE	United Arab Emirates
UAV	Unmanned Aerial Vehicle
UHF	Ultra-High-Frequency
UN	United Nations
USAF	United States Air Force
USAFE	United States Air Forces in Europe
USEUCOM	United States European Command

USAREUR	United States Army in Europe
USS	United States Ship
VTC	Video Teleconference
WCMD	Wind-Corrected Munitions Dispenser
WRM	War Reserve Materiel
WTC	World Trade Center

CHAPTER ONE

Introduction

On September 11, 2001, on a clear morning that will be forever remembered in American history, four jetliners—two Boeing 757s and two Boeing 767s, all on scheduled transcontinental flights from the East Coast and each fully laden with fuel for its coast-to-coast trip—were commandeered by radical Islamist terrorists almost simultaneously after their near-concurrent departures from Boston, Newark, and Washington, D.C., at approximately 8 a.m. Eastern Daylight Time. Upon being seized by the terrorists, the four aircraft were promptly turned into what would soon become de facto weapons of mass destruction against the United States and its citizens.

The basic facts of the terrorist attacks that fateful morning are now well enough known that they need no detailed elaboration here. Foremost among them, the first two hijacked aircraft (American Airlines Flight 11 and United Airlines Flight 175, both Boeing 767s) were flown within 18 minutes of each other into the twin towers of the World Trade Center (WTC) in New York City, ultimately reducing those long-familiar landmarks of the Manhattan skyline to 450,000 tons of rubble. The third aircraft (American Airlines Flight 77, a Boeing 757) was flown 40 minutes later into the southwest side of the Pentagon in Arlington, Virginia. The fourth aircraft (United Airlines Flight 93, also a Boeing 757), its planned target still unknown but thought to have been the White House or the U.S. Capitol building in Washington, D.C., fortunately had its mission thwarted before it could be accomplished by some brave and determined passengers who turned on their captors once they learned from frantic cell-phone conversations with friends and relatives on the ground what the other three airliners had just done. After an intense but failed struggle between the terrorists and their resisters, that aircraft was eventually brought to earth in a ball of fire in an empty field in western Pennsylvania. All of the terrorists (five on three aircraft and four on the fourth) and all passengers and crewmembers (250 in all) were killed in the four crashes. It remains unknown to this day whether and, if so, how many more potentially catastrophic hijackings had been planned for that morning and were at the brink of being carried out, only to have been averted at the last minute by timely federal action in canceling all further nonmilitary flights nationwide once the enormity and full implications of the morning's events had become clear. (As strong indications that additional hijackings had been planned, box-cutters—which were discovered to have been the weapons of choice in the four aircraft seizures—were found left behind by some passengers who were removed from grounded airliners that had returned to their gates only moments before takeoff.)[1]

The attacks caught the nation and its leaders completely off guard. They also instantly defined the face of early 21st-century conflict. What for nearly a decade had come to be loosely called the "post–Cold War era," for lack of a better phrase to describe the still-unshaped period that followed the collapse of Soviet Communism, was transformed in the short span of one morning into the era of fanatical transnational terrorism. Harvard University professor Samuel Huntington may have come closest to having captured the essence of this newly emergent era in his notion, first propounded amid great controversy in the early 1990s, of a growing worldwide "clash of civilizations."[2] The attacks, planned and executed by a determined band of murderous Islamist zealots, made for the boldest hostile act to have been committed on U.S. soil since Pearl Harbor. They also repre-

---

[1] Norman Friedman, *Terrorism, Afghanistan, and America's New Way of War*, Annapolis, Md.: Naval Institute Press, 2003, p. 3.

[2] See Samuel P. Huntington, *The Clash of Civilizations and the Remaking of World Order*, New York: Simon and Schuster, 1996.

sented the single most destructive instance of terrorist aggression to have taken place anywhere in the world. The loss of life caused by the attacks exceeded that from Japan's attack on Pearl Harbor in 1941. The main target of the attacks, the twin WTC towers, contained office space for more than 60,000 workers, and 40,000 to 50,000 people routinely worked there during normal business hours—a testament to the extent of fatalities that could have been occasioned in the worst case. In the final tally, nearly 3,000 innocent civilians died as a result of the attacks.[3] It did not take long for thoughtful people to begin wondering what the terrorists might have done to New York and Washington had they instead possessed a nuclear weapon or two.

President George W. Bush, who was visiting an elementary school in Sarasota, Florida, at the time of the initial attack into the WTC north tower, was first informed of the event at 9:07 a.m. Eastern Daylight Time, a scant five minutes after the second tower was hit. He was rushed thereafter to Air Force One, the presidential Boeing 747, whereupon the White House set in motion the government's emergency response plan and suggested that the president proceed without delay to Barksdale AFB, Louisiana, the headquarters of 8th Air Force and the site of the nearest available military command post. (The government's response was largely coordinated by the Federal Emergency Management Agency, which promptly activated its 10 regional emergency response centers nationwide.)[4]

Shortly after the second hijacked aircraft struck the WTC south tower, Vice President Dick Cheney was escorted by his Secret Service detail to the president's emergency operations center, an underground facility beneath the White House that had been hardened to offer at least some resistance to the effects of a nuclear detonation. First Lady Laura Bush was simultaneously moved to an undisclosed location,

---

[3] Early estimates were that as many as 6,800 had been killed. Fortunately, thousands of occupants of the two towers escaped the buildings just in time, between the moment of impact of the two aircraft and the eventual collapse of the buildings—caused by the melting of their upper steel girders as a result of the intense heat generated by the burning jet fuel—an hour or so later.

[4] Edward Walsh, "National Response to Terror," *Washington Post*, September 12, 2001.

and selected congressional leaders were temporarily dispatched to a secure facility 75 miles west of Washington. Vice President Cheney had earlier been advised that yet a third hijacked aircraft was headed toward the White House.[5] He accordingly urged the president to delay his return to Washington, saying: "We don't know what's going on here, but it looks like . . . we've been targeted."[6]

Immediately on the heels of the attacks, the Federal Aviation Administration (FAA) ordered all airborne domestic flights to land at the nearest suitable airport. The FAA also banned any further non-military takeoffs nationwide and, for the first time ever, halted all civil air traffic in the United States. As a result, some 33,000 airborne airline passengers were taken in by Canada as U.S. airspace was closed and incoming international flights were diverted and rerouted. At the same time, at the president's direction, a continuity-of-government plan that was rooted in the early days of the Cold War going back to the 1950s was set into motion. It was as a part of that plan that President Bush was kept airborne and moving aboard Air Force One until the apparent threat had subsided; that Vice President Cheney was briskly delivered to a White House bunker; and that House of Representatives Speaker Dennis Hastert (R-Illinois), second in the constitutional line of presidential succession, was flown by helicopter to a hardened facility away from Washington.[7] On Cheney's counsel and escorted by armed Air Force fighters, Air Force One shortly thereafter took the president from Barksdale to U.S. Strategic Command's headquarters at Offutt AFB, Nebraska, where he conducted, for the first time since the attacks, a secure video teleconference (VTC) with the National Security Council (NSC) to review the situation and de-

[5] William Safire, "Inside the Bunker," *New York Times*, September 13, 2001.

[6] James Gerstenzang and Paul Richter, "Jets Had OK to Down Airliners," *Los Angeles Times*, September 17, 2001. Cheney later added that although some White House advisers were arguing for the symbolic value of an early return to Washington by the president, "we'd have been absolute fools not to go into a button-down mode, make sure we had successors evacuated, make sure the President was safe and secure." (Mike Allen, "Quietly, Cheney Again Takes a Prominent Role," *Washington Post*, September 17, 2001.)

[7] James R. Asker, "Washington Outlook," *Aviation Week and Space Technology*, September 7, 2001, p. 33.

termine next steps. Only at 7:00 p.m. Eastern Daylight Time on September 11 did the president finally return to Washington to address the nation from the Oval Office. In that address, he affirmed that in responding to the attacks, as the nation surely would, the United States would "make no distinction between the terrorists who committed these acts and those who harbor them."[8]

Earlier that day, even as the attacks were still under way, the alert status of U.S. forces around the world was raised to Defense Condition (DEFCON) 3, their highest alert level since the Yom Kippur War of 1973. Air National Guard (ANG) F-16 fighters were launched from nearby Andrews AFB, Maryland, to provide a continuous combat air patrol (CAP) over the nation's capital. At the same time, Virginia ANG F-16s in nearby Richmond were put on the highest alert. E-3C airborne warning and control system (AWACS) aircraft were also placed on airborne orbits to monitor the airspace over New York City and Washington as tight restrictions were imposed on access to U.S. military installations worldwide.[9] Many of those installations went to Force Protection Condition Delta, their most secure lockdown status. Private offices were also shut down nationwide, and the most frantic stock selloff since the 1987 crash ensued on the heels of the attacks.

Throughout it all, the National Military Command Center (NMCC) in the Pentagon remained up and running. To help protect the air approaches to the Washington, D.C., and New York metropolitan areas, the Navy's Atlantic Fleet immediately put to sea two aircraft carriers, USS *George Washington* and USS *John F. Kennedy*, as well as five cruisers and two destroyers mounting Aegis radar systems. Moves also were implemented immediately after the attacks to update contingency plans for military operations in the most likely areas of possible U.S. combat involvement worldwide. The aircraft carrier

---

[8] Michael Grunwald, "Terrorists Hijack Four Airliners, Destroy World Trade Center, Hit Pentagon; Hundreds Dead," *Washington Post*, September 12, 2001.

[9] The fullest available details on these and other immediate U.S. military responses may be found in *The 9/11 Commission Report: Final Report of the National Commission on Terrorist Attacks Upon the United States*, New York: W. W. Norton & Company, 2004, pp. 20–46.

USS *Enterprise*, just exiting the Persian Gulf region en route home from a six-month deployment there, was turned around on the personal initiative of its commanding officer and was subsequently ordered to remain in the region for an indefinite period of time.[10] At the same time, USS *Carl Vinson* was about to enter the Persian Gulf to join *Enterprise* and thereby double the normal number of carrier air wings in that part of the area of responsibility of U.S. Central Command (CENTCOM). As the day drew to a close, Secretary of Defense Donald Rumsfeld declared that until better information could be made available, "all one can offer by way of assurance is a seriousness of purpose."[11] Rumsfeld added that "there is no question but that [what the nation had experienced that day] was a vicious, well-coordinated, massive attack."[12]

Although no one immediately claimed responsibility for the attacks, it did not take long for U.S. government officials to find strong evidence that the wealthy Saudi Arabian exile, Osama bin Laden, and his Islamist al Qaeda terrorist network had been behind them.[13] Senator Orrin Hatch (R-Utah) said that during a briefing earlier that day, the Senate Intelligence Committee had been told of electronic intercepts showing that "representatives affiliated with Osama bin Laden over the airwaves [were] reporting that they had hit two targets."[14]

---

[10] Greg Jaffe, "U.S. Armed Forces Are Put on the Highest State of Alert," *Wall Street Journal,* September 12, 2001.

[11] Rowan Scarborough, "Military Officers Seek Swift, Deadly Response," *Washington Times,* September 12, 2001.

[12] Dana Priest and Bradley Graham, "U.S. Deploys Air Defenses on Coasts," *Washington Post*, September 12, 2001.

[13] In one such reported indication, al Qaeda members in Afghanistan had been overheard to say shortly after the Pentagon was hit that the attackers were following through with "the doctor's program," in apparent reference to bin Laden's principal deputy, Ayman Zawahiri, an Egyptian physician who was commonly referred to informally as "the doctor." (Bob Woodward, *Bush at War*, New York: Simon and Schuster, 2002, p. 40.)

[14] Dan Eggen and Vernon Loeb, "U.S. Intelligence Points to Bin Laden Network," *Washington Post*, September 12, 2001. See also Jerry Seper and Bill Gertz, "Bin Laden, Cohorts Are Top Suspects," *Washington Times*, September 12, 2001. Al Qaeda, Arabic for "the base," was established by bin Laden in Peshawar, Pakistan, in the late 1980s as a welfare organization to pay pensions to the widows and orphans of Arab combatants who had died while

Lending strength to these suspicions, in a videotaped message at his son's wedding the previous May, bin Laden had called for such attacks against the "infidel West." Three weeks before the events of September 11, he told a London-based Arabic magazine of a pending "unprecedented attack, a very big one" against U.S. interests.[15] The attacks that finally occurred were soon assessed to have been an expansion and refinement of the failed 1993 plan to bomb the WTC that had been devised by terrorist leader Ramzi Yousef and financed by bin Laden.[16]

The day after the attacks, a *Washington Post*–ABC News poll reported that 94 percent of all Americans supported taking military action against the perpetrators, with more than 80 percent favoring a military response even if such strikes led to war.[17] A *USA Today*/Gallup/CNN poll showed that 86 percent of its respondents saw the attacks as an act of war against the United States.[18] Columnist

---

fighting Soviet troops alongside the Afghan mujaheddin. It later expanded, with bin Laden establishing businesses, training camps, and money-laundering rings in Afghanistan, Pakistan, Sudan, and throughout the Middle East, supported by his estimated wealth of some $250 million. It is an umbrella organization that embraces dozens of militant Muslim groups worldwide, with bin Laden providing the funds, training facilities in Afghanistan, and overall guidance but not necessarily daily control over those groups' activities. (Ahmed Rashid, "Al Qaeda Has Network of Sleepers Across North America," *London Daily Telegraph*, September 15, 2001.) Bin Laden's organization was responsible for the attacks on the U.S. embassies in Kenya and Tanzania in August 1998 and on the destroyer USS *Cole* at pierside in Yemen in October 2001.

[15] Seper and Gertz.

[16] In what later was widely presumed to have been a related action, the Afghan opposition leader Ahmed Shah Massoud was killed in northern Afghanistan just the day before the airliner attacks against the United States by a bomb detonated by two men posing as Arab journalists, with Massoud's associates immediately blaming bin Laden.

[17] Richard Morin and Claudia Deane, "Poll: Americans Willing to Go to War," *Washington Post*, September 12, 2001.

[18] Mark Memmott, "Poll: Americans Believe Attacks 'Acts of War,'" *USA Today*, September 12, 2001. That same day, an explosion in Kabul, first thought to have been U.S.-initiated, was later attributed by the Pentagon to the Northern Alliance opposition group as a presumed retaliation against the attack on Massoud. (John Ward Anderson, "Pentagon Denies Role in Explosions in Afghan Capital," *Washington Post*, September 12, 2001.) It is plausible that Massoud was killed to deny the United States a capable Afghan ally in any attempted U.S. retaliation for the imminent terrorist attacks, although that connection to September 11 has not yet been proven. Some powerful anecdotal evidence in support of that interpretation

Charles Krauthammer captured a growing sense among many Americans when he noted that the attacks had constituted not just a crime but an act of war and that suggestions being aired by some officials that the appropriate response should be to bring those responsible "to justice" were fundamentally wrong-headed. One might bring criminals to justice, Krauthammer remarked, but "you rain destruction on combatants." The perpetrators, he added, were "deadly, vicious warriors and need to be treated as such." He identified the enemy, "whose name many have feared to speak," as radical Islam.[19]

Russia's President Vladimir Putin was on chorus with most of the immediate worldwide reaction when he commented: "What happened today underlines the relevance of the offer of Russia to unite the powers of the international community in the fight against terrorism," a problem he portrayed as "the plague of the 21st century."[20] Within hours of the attacks, Putin spoke over the telephone with the president's national security adviser, Condoleezza Rice, and shortly thereafter sent President Bush a cable declaring that "barbarous terrorist acts aimed against wholly innocent people cause us anger and indignation."[21] Similarly, Britain's Prime Minister Tony Blair said that the perpetrators "have no value for the sanctity of human life." He vowed that Britain would stand "shoulder to shoulder" with the United States.[22] The respected British news weekly *The Economist* later characterized the events of September 11 as "acts that must be seen as a declaration of war not just on America but on all civilized people."[23]

---

is offered in John Lee Anderson, *The Lion's Grave: Dispatches from Afghanistan*, New York: Grove Press, 2002, pp. 183–219.

[19] Charles Krauthammer, "To War, Not to Court," *Washington Post*, September 12, 2001.

[20] David R. Sands and Tom Carter, "Attacks Change U.S. Foreign Policy," *Washington Times*, September 12, 2001.

[21] "Angered Putin Calls for Coordinated Response," *Moscow Times*, September 12, 2001.

[22] George Jones, "We Will Help Hunt Down Evil Culprits, Says Blair," *London Daily Telegraph*, September 12, 2001.

[23] "The Day the World Changed," *The Economist*, September 15, 2001, p. 13. Less than a month later, the magazine would further characterize those events as "one of the biggest

The attacks of September 11 represented something fundamentally new with respect to international terrorism, at least as far as the United States was concerned. They amounted to a wholesale redefinition of the phenomenon, elevating it from being essentially an occasionally lethal nuisance to having become a core strategic threat to U.S. security. Indeed, the conventional image of "terrorism" as it was most commonly understood before September 11 failed utterly to capture the full magnitude of what occurred that grim morning. At bottom, the attacks constituted the first truly unrestrained manifestation of an orchestrated and open-ended campaign of stateless asymmetrical warfare against the United States. Worse yet, they showed a willingness on the part of the perpetrators to cause indiscriminate killing of innocent civilians, to the point of using, without compunction, any and all varieties of weapons that might be available.[24]

Although what eventually became Operation Enduring Freedom, the initial military component of the ensuing U.S. global war on terror, did not begin until October 7, nearly a month later, it was clear from the very first days after the attacks that the Bush administration and the nation would take forceful action in response to the outrage of September 11. Indeed, immediately after President Bush was informed that the second WTC tower had been hit, he recalled that his precise thought at that moment had been: "They have declared war on us, and I made up my mind at that moment that we were going to war."[25] He so informed Vice President Cheney when he finally succeeded in contacting him five minutes after the third hijacked airliner was flown into the Pentagon. It soon became clear that the American response would be multifaceted and would consist not just of military operations but also of focused diplomacy, coalition-building and sustaining, heightened intelligence operations,

---

intelligence failures the world has ever seen." "Testing Intelligence," *The Economist*, October 6, 2001, p. 31.

[24] As a result of the attacks, fuel-laden jetliners now meet the federal criteria for weapons of mass destruction, weapons hitherto associated solely with nuclear, chemical, or biological threats.

[25] Woodward, p. 15.

efforts to track down and freeze or disrupt the financing of al Qaeda's activities, immigration control, enhanced homeland defense, and extensive police work. Yet there was little doubt that the leading edge of this response would be an air-dominated campaign to extirpate bin Laden's al Qaeda network in Afghanistan and that country's ruling Taliban theocracy, which had provided the terrorists safe haven and a base of operations.[26]

If raw news reporting may be said to represent the first draft of history, then this study seeks to offer a contribution to the second draft, namely, a more comprehensive, systematic, and analytical effort to integrate such reporting on the Afghan war into a coherent pattern that makes sense. Based on a comprehensive marshaling of the publicly available evidence, the study assesses the conduct of Operation Enduring Freedom from October 7, 2001, through late March 2002 against Afghanistan's Taliban rulers and bin Laden's al Qaeda infrastructure in that country. It focuses on joint and combined military activities at all levels, including special operations, space support, and all other combat and combat-support contributions to the precision air war that constituted the campaign's centerpiece. Its goal is to provide a well-buttressed account of the U.S. military response to September 11 aimed at helping to inform the U.S. policy community and U.S. public opinion, as well as to provide an analytic foundation for future such assessments once a more detailed record of that response becomes available.[27] The study first describes how senior officials in Washington and at CENTCOM developed the initial plans preparatory to the start of Operation Enduring Freedom, including the crafting of an appropriate force employment strategy, the deter-

---

[26] Evidently anticipating a U.S. retaliation, bin Laden had recently moved his headquarters to a new base in the Hindu Kush mountains in northeastern Afghanistan, where hundreds of al Qaeda combatants were fighting alongside the Taliban. Most of the foreign al Qaeda Arabs were said to live in restricted military compounds in Kabul and Kandahar. "Taliban" is the Afghan Dari variant of a Persian plural word for self-styled students of the Koranic text.

[27] For an earlier effort along similar lines to assess Operation Allied Force against Serbia's President Slobodan Milosevic in 1999, see Benjamin S. Lambeth, *NATO's Air War for Kosovo: A Strategic and Operational Assessment*, Santa Monica, Calif.: RAND Corporation, MR-1365-AF, 2001.

mination of needed U.S. and allied air and other assets in theater and elsewhere, and the securing of regional basing support and other bed-down needs. It then reviews combat operations from opening night through the achievement of the war's initial declared goals, from the early establishment of air control over Afghanistan to the rout of the Taliban in December 2001 and the subsequent Operation Anaconda, a U.S. Army-led effort two months later to root out the last remaining enemy holdouts in Afghanistan's Shah-i-Kot valley. With that as background, the remainder of the study considers what worked well during those operations, where unanticipated problems arose, and revealed deficiencies in the American military repertoire that might be correctable by improvements in training, tactics, techniques, procedures, and, in some cases, equipment and concepts of operations.[28]

---

[28] Although Operation Enduring Freedom persists to this day at a lower level of intensity, with U.S. and allied forces waging a continuing counterinsurgency effort against residual Taliban holdouts, this study focuses solely on the major joint and combined operations to break up al Qaeda's terrorist infrastructure and end the Taliban rule that constituted the first six months of U.S. combat involvement in Afghanistan.

CHAPTER TWO

A Nation Girds for War

As the initial shock and outrage triggered by the attacks of September 11 gave way to a more focused determination on the part of the nation and its leaders, the first inklings of the administration's eventual counteroffensive strategy began to emerge. The Bush administration's first task was to comprehend more fully what, in fact, had happened that day and to characterize it convincingly to the American people and to the world to lay the groundwork for an effective response. The tone of the administration's unfolding approach was set by President Bush himself the first day after the attacks. The president stated that bin Laden's al Qaeda was "an enemy who preys on innocent and unsuspecting people, then runs for cover, but it won't be able to run for cover forever. This is an enemy that tries to hide, but it won't be able to hide forever. This is an enemy that thinks its harbors are safe, but they won't be safe forever. . . . The United States will use all our resources to conquer this enemy. . . . We will be patient. We'll be focused, and we will be steadfast in our determination. This battle will take time and resolve, but make no mistake about it, we will win."[1]

Within minutes of having learned of the terrorist attacks, U.S. military commands throughout Europe, Asia, and the Middle East set up crisis action teams to implement heightened force-protection measures and to assess the status of the forces in their respective areas of responsibility (AORs) that might be committed to action in any

---

[1] "Text of Bush Statement," *Washington Post*, September 13, 2001.

short-notice military response. As Force Protection Condition Delta remained in effect for a second day at many U.S. military installations worldwide, the nation began preparing for what the president had described as "the first war of the 21st century."[2] The day after the attacks, Secretary of State Colin Powell expanded on an earlier statement made by the president in stressing that the United States "will hold accountable those countries that provide . . . support and facilities to these kinds of terrorist groups. We will be directing our efforts not only against terrorists, but against those who harbor and . . . provide haven and . . . support for terrorism."[3] Another early glimpse at the emerging U.S. strategy was provided the following day by Deputy Secretary of Defense Paul Wolfowitz when he commented: "It's not just simply a matter of capturing people and holding them accountable, but removing the sanctuaries, removing the support systems, ending states who sponsor terrorism." Wolfowitz promised that the United States and its allies would wage "a campaign, not a single action," adding that "you don't do it with just a single military strike, no matter how dramatic. You don't do it with just military forces alone, you do it with the full resources of the U.S. government."[4]

On September 15, following a weekend meeting with his inner circle of senior advisers at Camp David, the president left no room for doubt that his administration had assumed a combat footing when he declared to reporters that "we're at war. There's been an act of war declared upon America by terrorists, and we will respond accordingly." Shortly thereafter, Bush added in a radio broadcast that "those who make war on the United States have chosen their own destruction." He cautioned Americans to brace themselves for "a conflict without battlefields or beaches" and one in which victory "will not take place in a single battle, but in a series of decisive actions against terrorist organizations and those who harbor and support

[2] David Von Drehle, "Bush Pledges Victory," *Washington Post*, September 14, 2001.

[3] Joseph Curl, "U.S. Can Go to War with Any Enemies," *Washington Times*, September 13, 2001.

[4] Elisabeth Bumiller and Jane Perlez, "A Vow to Erase Terrorist Networks—bin Laden Is Singled Out," *New York Times*, September 14, 2001.

them." The president identified bin Laden as "a prime suspect" in the attacks.[5]

In a major address to a special joint session of Congress convened on the evening of September 20, the president also sharpened his emerging message, promising the legislators and the American people that "whether we bring our enemies to justice or bring justice to our enemies, justice will be done." Bush added: "It will not look like the air war over Kosovo two years ago, where no ground troops were used and not a single American was lost in combat. Our response involves far more than instant retaliation and isolated strikes. Americans should not expect one battle but a lengthy campaign unlike any we have ever seen. . . . We will direct every resource at our command—every means of diplomacy, every tool of intelligence, every instrument of law enforcement, every financial influence, and every necessary weapon of war—to the disruption and defeat of the global terror network."[6] The president further made it clear that the Taliban must hand over al Qaeda's leaders immediately or that the former would "share in their fate" and that this demand was not open to negotiation. He added that any nation that henceforth continued to harbor or support terrorism would be regarded by the United States as a hostile regime. At a nationally televised memorial service for the victims of the attacks held in Washington's National Cathedral the morning after his statement before Congress, the president punctuated those remarks with a solemn warning to al Qaeda that this war, "begun on the timing and terms of others . . . will end in a way, and at an hour, of our choosing."[7]

---

[5] Elaine Sciolino, "Bush Tells the Military to 'Get Ready'; Broader Spy Powers Gaining Support," *New York Times*, September 16, 2001. Those words were evidently persuasive enough to prompt Afghan citizens to begin stockpiling what little food they could gather and to flee their country in droves as neighboring Iran began sealing its borders against a wave of expected refugees.

[6] John F. Harris and Mike Allen, "President Outlines War on Terrorism, Demands bin Laden Be Turned Over," *Washington Post*, September 21, 2001.

[7] David Von Drehle, "Senate Approves Use of Force; Military Patrols Cities and Ports," *Washington Post*, September 15, 2001. See also "Allies in Search of a Strategy," *The Economist*, September 22, 2001, p. 13.

Unlike the initial statements made by the president on September 11 immediately after the attacks, simply expressing his sorrow and outrage at what had occurred, his words during the days that followed were considerably more focused and goal-oriented. Indeed, they went far toward helping to produce a sense of national unity in the United States that was perhaps unmatched since the nation's entry into World War II half a century earlier. Reflecting that spirit, Congress promptly granted the administration a $40 billion emergency funding package for conducting counterterrorist operations, with a provision for an immediate release of $10 billion for the White House to use at its discretion, including for a potential early military response should a suitable occasion for one present itself.[8] Congress also moved with dispatch to devise an empowerment instrument for President Bush, ultimately issuing a joint resolution that released the White House from any obligation to seek a formal declaration of war in the course of pursuing its military options.[9]

As yet a further sign of the strong groundswell of popular support enjoyed by the president in the immediate wake of the attacks, less than a week later, a *USA Today*/CNN/Gallup poll found that 88 percent of Americans favored military action in reprisal, with 65 percent prepared to back such action even if it meant reinstating the draft, a loss of 1,000 U.S. troops, and a high economic toll.[10] Furthermore, the president's approval rating soared to 84 percent during

---

[8] In a nine-category request for supplemental funding, the Department of Defense asked for roughly $4.6 billion to buy more kits for converting unguided bombs into satellite-aided Joint Direct Attack Munitions (JDAMs) and for another $1 billion to purchase satellite imagery from private companies. (Tony Capaccio, "U.S. Pentagon Asks $19 Billion for Weapons, Intelligence," Bloomberg.com, September 19, 2001.) Earlier in April, Boeing had won a $235 million contract for the production of 11,054 JDAMs, the vast majority (10,382) intended for the Air Force and the remainder for the Navy. (Hunter Keeter, "PGM Funding May Top List for Short-Term Military Spending Increase," *Defense Daily*, September 20, 2001, p. 5.)

[9] Alison Mitchell and Philip Shenon, "Work on $40 Billion Aid and a Military Response," *New York Times*, September 14, 2001. The United States had not formally declared war since the beginning of World War II, and there was widespread reluctance on all sides to do so in this case.

[10] Jim Drinkard, "America Ready to Sacrifice," *USA Today*, September 17, 2001.

that same week, as contrasted to its level of 50 percent only a month before.[11] That new high was about where President Franklin Roosevelt's rating had stood immediately after the Japanese attack on Pearl Harbor, and it exceeded the highest rating ever received by any other modern president, including the president's father in the early aftermath of the allied coalition's resounding victory in the 1991 Gulf War. By the end of the second week following the attacks, Bush's approval rating increased even more, to almost 90 percent.[12]

As the need for a forceful U.S. response was quickly becoming clear to nearly all, it was well understood by both senior administration officials and by the American public that marshaling the political and military wherewithal for an effective U.S. campaign in Afghanistan would draw American diplomacy and fighting forces into what one editorial rightly called "one of the world's most volatile and tangled regions."[13] As the details of the administration's unfolding response plan began to emerge, a multifaceted strategic approach appeared in the offing. The first challenge facing the nation was to build a worldwide coalition to lend needed material support and moral legitimacy to the impending war on terrorism. That challenge prompted the administration, predominantly in the person of Secretary of State Powell, to move briskly toward laying the initial diplomatic groundwork for further action.[14] The second challenge entailed developing a concrete military plan of action that specified the impending campaign's operational priorities and goals. The third was to craft a detailed force-employment plan for meeting those priorities and achieving the administration's declared objectives. Finally, there was the associated need to begin fielding and prepositioning the required U.S. combat and combat-support assets of all services for any such action. All of that occurred within the scant 26 days that sepa-

---

[11] Richard L. Berke, "Poll Finds a Majority Back Use of Military," *New York Times,* September 16, 2001.

[12] "A Leader Is Born," *The Economist,* September 22, 2001, p. 33.

[13] "Rendezvous with Afghanistan," *New York Times,* September 14, 2001.

[14] Alan Sipress and Steven Mufson, "U.S. Lines Up Support for Strike," *Washington Post,* September 13, 2001.

rated the attacks of September 11 and the onset of Operation Enduring Freedom the following October 7. Before any of those overlapping initiatives could be put into motion, however, the administration first had to establish an unprecedented air defense umbrella over the United States to ensure against any further terrorist use of aircraft as weapons—however remote such a possibility may have seemed now that all civil air traffic in U.S. airspace had been indefinitely grounded.

Ensuring Homeland Air Defense

In a telling testament to the Cold War's end, the United States maintained only a token air defense posture before the terrorist attacks of September 11. Since 1997, that posture had been provided entirely by the Air National Guard, which kept fighters poised on round-the-clock 15-minute alert status at bases on the East, South, and West Coasts of the country, primarily to maintain the sovereignty of American airspace against unauthorized intruders. Accordingly, what little the nation enjoyed by way of a quick-response armed fighter posture was hopelessly unsuited to the challenge of responding to what was, in effect, a surprise attack from within.[15]

As an illustration in point, a response timeline for September 11 maintained by the North American Aerospace Defense Command (NORAD) later indicated that two alert-postured Air National Guard F-15s from Otis AFB on Cape Cod, Massachusetts, had been scrambled six minutes after FAA officials notified NORAD's Northeast Air Defense Sector that American Airlines Flight 11 had departed from its approved course from Boston to Los Angeles. By that time,

---

[15] Even as early as the 1960s, thanks to a decision made by Secretary of Defense Robert McNamara, the nation's air defense alert posture was radically pared back from its much higher level of the previous decade, on the premise that since a ballistic missile barrage could not be successfully defended against, it made no sense to waste money defending against the far less imposing Soviet bomber and cruise missile threat when the smarter approach was simply to rely on the deterrent effect of the nation's assured-destruction nuclear retaliatory capability.

however, the first WTC tower had already been hit at 8:46 a.m., and the fighters were still some 70 miles (eight minutes flying time) away from New York City when the second WTC tower was struck at 9:02 a.m.[16]

Shortly thereafter, in response to an FAA alarm about American Airlines Flight 77, two ANG F-16s sitting alert at Langley AFB, Virginia, were subsequently scrambled at 9:35 a.m., a scant seven minutes before that hijacked airliner flew into the Pentagon. While Flight 77 was still under the control of the hijackers, senior duty officers in the National Military Command Center in the Pentagon conferred with law enforcement and air traffic control personnel about feasible response options. The alert-scrambled F-16s from Langley, however, did not arrive to establish a protective CAP over Washington until 15 minutes after the 757 struck the Pentagon roughly 40 minutes after the second WTC tower had been hit.[17] An additional 27 minutes passed after that event before the fourth and, as it turned out, final aircraft went down in a remote Pennsylvania field, thanks to the courageous actions of the passengers.

In a later statement, Under Secretary of Defense Wolfowitz remarked that although it had been the heroism of the passengers aboard United Airlines Flight 93 that ultimately had brought the last aircraft down outside Shanksville, Pennsylvania, the Air Force had been "in a position to do so if we had to."[18] Indeed, President Bush himself later indicated that on the immediate heels of the attacks, he had personally authorized the military to down any additional

---

[16] William B. Scott, "NORAD, Fighters on High Domestic Alert," *Aviation Week and Space Technology*, October 1, 2002, p. 37. See also Bradley Graham, "Military Alerted Before Attacks," *Washington Post,* September 15, 2001.

[17] Matthew Wald, "Pentagon Tracked Deadly Jet But Found No Way to Stop It," *New York Times*, September 15, 2001.

[18] Esther Schrader and Paul Richter, "Fighter Jets Assume New Protective Role," *Los Angeles Times*, September 15, 2001. It remains unclear, however, whether the intercepting pilots would have been able to receive approval to fire in sufficient time, since there were no standing rules of engagement for such an unanticipated situation. Hitherto, NORAD had not been in the business of monitoring aircraft movements over the United States unless they had originated from abroad.

hijacked airliners should such action be deemed essential to protect the nation's capital. Vice President Cheney added that he had "wholeheartedly concurred" with the president's decision, noting that for a moment it was feared that as many as six airliners may have been hijacked. As Cheney put it, "if the plane would not divert, or if they wouldn't pay any attention to instructions to move away from the city, as a last resort our pilots were authorized to take them out."[19] As it later turned out, however, the three District of Columbia ANG F-16s that were launched in response to an urgent plea from the White House to "get in the air now" in an effort to do something about the fourth aircraft had not been alert-postured and accordingly were not carrying air-to-air missiles. Two of the three, purely by happenstance, were armed solely with 20mm inert cannon training rounds. The pilots later indicated that they had contemplated ramming the hijacked aircraft as a last resort had matters come to that.[20]

None of this should have been in any way surprising. Nor did it reflect badly on the Air Force's preparedness, since what occurred on the morning of September 11 was literally a bolt from the blue that had never been taken into account in U.S. air defense contingency planning. The vice chairman of the Joint Chiefs of Staff (JCS), Air Force General Richard Myers, who was due imminently to become the next chairman, later told members of the Senate Armed Services Committee that he had personally phoned CINCNORAD immediately after the attacks in New York to apprise him of the situation. However, Myers added, only a "handful" of U.S. fighters fielded within reasonable range of the city were on alert that morning. As he freely admitted: "We're pretty good if the threat is coming from outside. We're not so good if it's coming from inside."[21]

By day's end on September 12, however, the air defense picture had changed dramatically, with dozens of Air Force F-15s and F-16s

---

[19] Gerstenzang and Richter, "Jets Had OK to Down Airliners."

[20] William B. Scott, "F-16 Pilots Considered Ramming Flight 93," *Aviation Week and Space Technology,* September 9, 2002, pp. 71–73.

[21] Bradley Graham, "Fighter Response After Attacks Questioned," *Washington Post,* September 14, 2001.

and Canadian CF-18s (under a binational agreement with the United States) maintaining round-the-clock CAPs over more than 30 American cities, including Los Angeles, San Francisco, and San Diego in addition to New York and Washington. These CAPs were flown under the operational aegis of NORAD, which directed and managed them through its three subordinate regional operations centers at Elmendorf AFB, Alaska (for the Alaska NORAD Region), Canadian Forces Base Winnipeg (for the Canadian NORAD Region), and Tyndall AFB, Florida (for the Continental U.S. NORAD Region). The fighter CAPs, unprecedented in American history, enforced a blanket ban on nonmilitary air traffic nationwide. A spokesman for NORAD declared that if any unauthorized aircraft appeared determined to pose a threat to the civilian population or to national assets, the downing of such an aircraft by missile or cannon fire was "not out of the question."[22]

In addition to these round-the-clock airborne CAPs, the greatly enhanced nationwide air defense posture, which eventually came to be code-named Operation Noble Eagle, maintained an undisclosed number of armed U.S. and Canadian fighters on alert at 26 bases throughout the United States. Moreover, for good measure, the federal government's little-known continuity-of-government plan, activated during the first hours after the attacks on September 11, was kept in effect and continued to move high-ranking civilian officials in and out of one of two secure facilities on the East Coast.[23] Finally, in just the first three days after the attacks, some 9,000 members of the

---

[22] "U.S. Air Force Flies Combat Patrols Over Dozens of American Cities," *Inside the Pentagon*, September 13, 2001, p. 1.

[23] The plan entailed some 100 officials at a time selected for so-called "bunker duty," living and working underground 24 hours a day away from their families on 90-day rotations, out of concern that al Qaeda might somehow obtain a portable nuclear weapon. The civilian cadre, numbering between 70 and 150 officials depending on the most recent threat intelligence, drew from every cabinet department and some independent agencies to hedge against a complete collapse of essential government functions. Few cabinet-rank principals or their immediate deputies left Washington on September 11. Those on rotation as a backup government came from the senior career ranks. A senior presence from the White House staff was also routinely included. (Barton Gellman and Susan Schmidt, "Shadow Government Is at Work in Secret," *Washington Post*, March 1, 2002.)

Air National Guard were activated to help support the enhanced air defense posture aimed at securing American skies from any further events like those of September 11. Even with that, Secretary of Defense Rumsfeld recommended calling up as many as 50,000 members of the reserves in all services—a move that would make for the largest number of reservists activated since the Persian Gulf War of 1991.[24]

On September 14, Rumsfeld announced that the overall alert status of U.S. forces worldwide had been reduced a notch to DEFCON 4, which put the alert level back to its normal peacetime status. Immediately after the attacks three days earlier, the Pentagon had ramped the alert level up to DEFCON 3. (The highest status, DEFCON 1, is reserved for actual war.)[25] By the end of the first week after September 11, the number of round-the-clock airborne CAPs over U.S. cities was reduced substantially and supplanted by increased reliance on ground-based fighter alerts at 26 bases, from any of which base or bases armed fighters could be airborne within several minutes of being scrambled.

Concurrently, a minor controversy began to unfold over which U.S. military entity should be in charge of homeland defense, as NORAD maintained its leading role on the air defense front while others were suggesting that U.S. Joint Forces Command, with responsibility for 80 percent of all Army, Navy, Air Force, and Marine Corps forces stationed within the continental United States (CONUS), should have been assigned that role instead.[26] That controversy later led to a more serious interagency discussion over the question of homeland defense, which in turn ultimately led to the creation of U.S. Northern Command.[27]

---

[24] Thom Shanker and Eric Schmitt, "Rumsfeld Asks Call-Up of Reserves, as Many as 50,000," *New York Times*, September 14, 2001.

[25] Dan Balz and Bob Woodward, "A Day to Speak of Anger and Grief," *Washington Post*, January 30, 2002.

[26] Elaine M. Grossman, "Military Is Embroiled in Debate Over Who Should Guard the United States," *Inside the Pentagon*, September 20, 2001, p. 1.

[27] In the early aftermath of the terrorist attacks, President Bush formally authorized two Air Force generals to approve the downing of a commercial airliner in domestic U.S. airspace

As September drew to a close, the greatly heightened operational tempo of the expanded domestic CAP effort was plainly being felt by the involved fighter units. Some ANG units that normally flew as little as 15-20 hours a day five days a week were now averaging 45-60 flying hours a day seven days a week. That increase in the aircraft utilization rate, coupled with expanding overseas commitments occasioned by the beginnings of serious preparations for war against al Qaeda and the Taliban in Afghanistan, also levied a heavy toll on Air Force tanker and AWACS support, to a point where the North Atlantic Treaty Organization (NATO) provided at first five and later seven of its own AWACS aircraft for nearly seven months to ease the burden imposed on the Air Force's AWACS fleet by Noble Eagle.[28] In the end, in response to these increasingly onerous pressures, NORAD by the beginning of 2002 still maintained continuous fighter CAPs over New York City and Washington but had begun to move toward unpredictable random CAPs elsewhere because of the toll the high sortie rate of Operation Noble Eagle had come to impose.[29]

Forming a Coalition

Within a day of the attacks, President Bush took an aggressive lead in personally striving to build a broad-based international coalition be-

---

without first consulting with him. His standing order was that those generals had such authority only in a last-minute situation with an impending attack only minutes away and with insufficient time for them to consult with CINCNORAD. Authority for CONUS went to the commander of 1st Air Force headquartered at Tyndall AFB, Florida. For Alaska, it went to the commander of 11th Air Force at Elmendorf AFB. The downing of an aircraft to head off a threat to Hawaii would be authorized by CINCPAC based in Honolulu. (Eric Schmitt, "Generals Given Power to Order Downing of Jets," *New York Times*, September 27, 2001; and Vernon Loeb, "Rules Governing Downing Airliners," *Washington Post*, September 28, 2001.)

[28] William B. Scott, "Domestic Air Patrols Tax Tankers, AWACS," *Aviation Week and Space Technology*, October 8, 2001, p. 68.

[29] William B. Scott, "U.S. Reassesses Protective Flights," *Aviation Week and Space Technology*, January 21, 2002, p. 32.

fore committing to any military response against the terrorists and their benefactors. On September 12, he spoke by telephone not only with Britain's Prime Minister Tony Blair but also with France's President Jacques Chirac, with China's President Jiang Zemin, and, on two occasions, with Russia's President Vladimir Putin. That early canvass embraced the leaders of all permanent members of the United Nations (UN) Security Council. The next day, Secretary of State Powell stepped to the fore in spearheading the administration's effort to build a broad coalition, in the process setting the tone for the U.S. initiatives that were to follow. As this effort unfolded, the president explained that the coalition he intended to build would probably have less multinational representation than the one that had been assembled for the 1991 Gulf War and that the United States reserved the right to act alone in self-defense if need be: "We fully understand that some nations will feel comfortable supporting overt activities. Some nations will feel comfortable supporting covert activities; some nations will only be comfortable in providing information; others will . . . only feel helpful on financial matters. I understand that."[30]

For a time, with a view toward bolstering the U.S. case against al Qaeda in pursuit of allied support, Powell promised that "in the near future, we'll be able to put out a paper, a document, that will describe quite clearly the evidence we have linking [bin Laden] to the attack."[31] In the end, however, that promise was never fulfilled, since the president ultimately determined that the supporting evidence was too sensitive to be released for fear of disclosing U.S. intelligence sources and methods.[32] Powell conceded that no imminent U.S. mili-

---

[30] David E. Sanger, "Bush Is Deploying Jet Bombers Toward Afghanistan," *New York Times*, September 20, 2001.

[31] David Milbank and Vernon Loeb, "'U.S. Employing Calm, Multifaceted Response," *Washington Post*, September 24, 2001.

[32] Jim Vandehei, "Reluctant to Share Terrorist Evidence, Bush Retreats from bin Laden Pledge," *Wall Street Journal*, September 25, 2001. Later, as the start of the campaign neared, a senior foreign official who insisted on anonymity reported that bin Laden had telephoned his mother in Syria the day before the terrorist attacks informing her that he could not meet her there because "something big" was about to happen that would end their communications for a long time. That account was said to have come from an interrogation of bin

tary response would be forthcoming in any event, since it would naturally take time to refine any suitable plans and deploy the needed forces. He added, however, that the United States would not wait until the perpetrators of the attacks had been identified and tracked down if it saw an opportunity to take other warranted action, such as striking against terrorist training camps. He further noted that the United States was building a coalition to go not only after the perpetrators of the September 11 attacks, but "more broadly after terrorism wherever we find it in the world."[33]

The first concrete step taken by Powell toward that end was to engage NATO as a committed player in the emerging war against terrorism. Early on September 12, he spoke with NATO's Secretary General George Robertson and elicited from him a declaration preparing for an unprecedented invocation of the alliance charter's mutual defense clause. For its part, the North Atlantic Council (NAC), made up of NATO's 19 ambassadors, held three successive emergency sessions at NATO headquarters in Brussels within 36 hours of the attacks, including a rare joint meeting convened by Secretary General Robertson with the NAC and the European Union's foreign ministers.[34] Before the day ended, the NAC invoked the mutual defense clause of NATO's charter for the first time in the alliance's 52-year history, declaring that "if it is determined that [the attacks of September 11 were] directed from abroad against the United States, it shall be regarded as an action covered by Article 5 of the Washington Treaty."[35] That declaration did not portend any immediate NATO action but rather was portrayed by Secretary General Robertson as "an act of solidarity." The unanimous resolution declared that

---

Laden's family members in Saudi Arabia following the attacks. (Philip Shenon and David Johnston, "U.S. Backs Away from Talk of More Attacks," *New York Times*, October 2, 2001.)

[33] Shenon and Johnston.

[34] "Old Friends, Best Friends," *The Economist*, September 15, 2001, pp. 20–21.

[35] Article 5 of the NATO charter stipulates that an armed attack against any ally shall be deemed an attack against all. It commits NATO to take all necessary measures, including the use of force, to restore security.

"the United States' NATO allies stand ready to provide the assistance that may be required as a consequence of these acts of barbarism."[36]

Some nations could not sign up for the impending war effort quickly enough. The same day that NATO invoked its charter's Article 5, Britain's Prime Minister Blair took a proactive stance in supporting the coalition's goals, stating that the leaders of France, Germany, other European Union countries, and Russia "all agreed that this attack is an attack not only on America but on the world, which demands our complete and united condemnation . . . and our support for the American people."[37] The British government offered a team of military planners to assist the United States, and British Army Lieutenant General Anthony Pigott, the assistant chief of the Defense Staff for operations, flew to Washington to coordinate planning with the Department of Defense for any military next steps.[38] In a similar spirit, France's President Chirac shortly thereafter declared that "when it comes to punishing this murderous folly, France will be at the side of the United States."[39] (True to that promise, France, in the end, was the only country other than the United States to commit aircraft to a shooting role in Operation Enduring Freedom.)[40]

Even Russia, for all the on-and-off prickliness of its relationship with the United States since NATO's air war against Serbia two years before, hastened to associate itself unambiguously with the Bush administration's effort, at least in principle. Russia's President Putin

---

[36] Suzanne Daley, "For First Time, NATO Invokes Pact With U.S.," *New York Times*, September 13, 2001.

[37] Philip Webster, "Blair Seeks United Democratic Response," *London Times*, September 13, 2001.

[38] Michael Evans, "Britain Offers Military Planning Team," *London Times*, September 14, 2001, and Michael Evans, "Britain May Send Forces to Central Asia This Week," *London Times*, September 24, 2001.

[39] Ambrose Evans-Pritchard, "EU Calls for 'Intelligent and Targeted' Response," *London Daily Telegraph*, September 15, 2001.

[40] It should be noted here, however, that the British Royal Air Force (RAF) provided Nimrod and Canberra surveillance and reconnaissance aircraft, as well as extensive tanker support, and the Royal Australian Air Force (RAAF) provided F/A-18s for air defense of the British island base of Diego Garcia. (See Chapter 3 for more on these contributions.)

declared that he had seen all the proof he needed with respect to al Qaeda's alleged complicity in the attacks. On September 12, he offered the United States two planeloads of medicine and 70 rescue workers and promised to share any pertinent intelligence Russia could muster on the origins of the airliner hijackings. That same day, Foreign Minister Igor Ivanov, noting that both Russia and America had been victims of terror, stressed that "what we need is closer ties and efforts in fighting terrorism."[41] Immediately thereafter, Deputy Secretary of State Richard Armitage made a special trip to Moscow with the goal of asking the Russians for their detailed knowledge of Afghanistan, as well as for the Russian Federation's blessing for the United States to seek access to air base facilities in the former Soviet republics of Tajikistan and Uzbekistan.

To be sure, Russia ruled out any participation by its own forces in actual combat, with the chief of the General Staff, General Anatoly Kvashnin, remarking that "the U.S. armed forces are powerful enough to deal with this task alone." Short of direct combat involvement, however, Putin seemed eager for Russia to become a part of the U.S. coalition. For openers, he agreed to work with NATO in seeking to "unite the entire international community in the struggle against terrorism."[42] That raised the intriguing possibility of an opening for Russia to redefine fundamentally its strategic relationship with the United States. As one harbinger of such a possibility, the Russian government in the immediate wake of the terrorist attacks promptly canceled an ongoing military exercise that was simulating a war with the United States. Russia also sent a team of regional experts to the Central Intelligence Agency (CIA) shortly after the attacks to provide intelligence about the topography and caves in Afghanistan drawn from their intimate knowledge acquired during the Soviet Union's nine-year war there.[43] With respect to the appealing pros-

---

[41] Susan B. Glasser and Peter Baker, "Bush and Putin Discuss Response to Terrorism," *Washington Post*, September 13, 2002.

[42] Joseph Fitchett, "NATO Unity, But What Next?" *International Herald Tribune*, September 14, 2001.

[43] Woodward, p. 103.

pect of a major improvement in Russian-American relations, Major General Aleksandr Vladimirov, the vice president of Russia's Collegium of Military Experts, commented that the attacks had offered "a unique chance to develop a real and close military cooperation with the United States and NATO. Now, it is finally clear to all that the West and Russia have a common enemy—Islamic fundamentalist terrorist organizations. If we are not complete idiots, we must not let this opportunity slip away."[44]

On one important count, the Russians did need some gentle coaxing by the United States. With respect to the U.S. need for regional basing access within easy reach of Afghanistan, Defense Minister Sergei Ivanov at first ruled out categorically any involvement of the former Soviet Central Asian states as staging areas for U.S. attacks, stating that he saw "absolutely no basis for even hypothetical suppositions about the possibility of NATO military operations on the territory of Central Asian nations."[45] Great sensitivities abounded on this issue on both sides. President Putin's dilemma entailed projecting a credible image as a seriously committed coalition partner while, at the same time, demonstrating his ability to maintain Russia's dominant sphere of influence in Central Asia at a time when the United States was seeking local permission to operate militarily from the latter's bases. For the United States, the challenge entailed secur-

---

[44] Maura Reynolds, "Russia Seeks to Unite Against a 'Common Enemy,'" *Los Angeles Times*, September 15, 2001. In a similar vein, Sergei Rogov, director of Moscow's USA and Canada Institute, remarked that "one thing is clear: For the first time since the end of World War II, for the first time in more than half a century, Russia and the United States have clearly got a common enemy. Having a common enemy is the main prerequisite for becoming allies. Russia and the United States have this chance, and it is totally up to them how to use it. Theoretically, the foundation for an alliance is there." (Reynolds, "Russia Seeks to Unite Against a 'Common Enemy.'")

[45] Susan B. Glasser, "Russia Rejects Joint Military Action with United States," *Washington Post*, September 15, 2001. The day after the attacks, Russia put its troops on the Afghan-Tajik border on alert in anticipation of a possible imminent U.S. strike into Afghanistan. These troops included two regiments of the 210th Division stationed in the Tajik capital of Dushanbe and another two regiments some 60 miles from the border, totaling around 10,000 troops. (Ben Aris, "Russian Troops Are Put on Alert," *London Daily Telegraph*, September 17, 2001.)

ing access to needed basing facilities in Central Asia without antagonizing the Russians and undermining their support for the coalition.

In the end, Russia's initially hard-over position began to give way as Putin held telephone conversations several days later with the concerned Central Asian leaders and, shortly thereafter, dispatched his top security aide, Vladimir Rushailo, to the region to discuss the issue face-to-face with those leaders.[46] The following day, Foreign Minister Ivanov informed Secretary Powell that Moscow would not object if the United States sought to enlist the support of the former Soviet republics for the impending campaign against bin Laden, declaring that "each [Central Asian] country will decide on its own to what extent and how it will cooperate with the U.S. in these matters."[47] Two days later, during a 42-minute conversation with President Bush, Putin reaffirmed that no Russian troops would be put on the ground in Afghanistan, but that the United States would be granted the use of Russian airspace for humanitarian flights and that Russia would provide on-call combat search and rescue (CSAR) support as might be needed to help extract any U.S. aircrews who might be downed in northern Afghanistan. As for U.S. basing in the former Soviet republics, Putin said, in a major concession: "I am prepared to tell the heads of governments of the Central Asian states . . . that we have no objection to a U.S. role in Central Asia as long as it has the object of fighting the war on terror and is temporary and is not permanent."[48] President Bush readily gave him that assurance.

In ratifying this, the Russian president avowed that Russia was ready to cooperate with the United States "in the widest sense of the word" short of playing a direct military role, since it was already overburdened by its own terrorist predicament in Chechnya and

---

[46] Maura Reynolds, "Russia Mulls Options to Help U.S.," *Los Angeles Times*, September 18, 2001.

[47] Steven Mufson and Alan Sipress, "Bush to Seek Nation's Support," *Washington Post*, September 20, 2001. See also Michael Wines, "Russia Faces Fateful Choice on Cooperation with U.S.," *New York Times*, September 21, 2001.

[48] Woodward, p. 118.

could scarcely afford to open a second front.[49] On September 24, in the most decisive alignment of Russian military and intelligence resources with a U.S.-led campaign since the Soviet Union's collapse, Putin rallied the Central Asian countries to the U.S. side in approving the use of their air bases for conducting U.S. and allied military strikes.[50] No doubt at least one proximate goal underlying this major shift in policy was to seize the opportunity to help defeat Islamic fundamentalism along Russia's southern flank in Central Asia—and, at the same time, to get the United States to ease off from its constant criticism of Russian military activities in Chechnya.

By far the most daunting, yet also most critical, challenge with respect to eliciting allied support was presented by Pakistan, whose base access and political support were deemed essential for any future campaign's success. When Secretary Powell declared to the nations of the world that "you're either with us or against us," he clearly had Pakistan first and foremost in mind, since the intelligence service and senior leadership of that next-door Islamic neighbor of Afghanistan had not only sponsored the rise of the Taliban but also was widely thought to have provided support to bin Laden and given al Qaeda freedom to operate.[51]

Almost immediately after the September 11 attacks, the Department of State began pressuring Pakistan for intelligence and logistical support, with a view toward paving the way for tracking down the perpetrators and retaliating against any countries that may have supported them. The use of Pakistan's airspace would also be necessary for any serious U.S. campaign against al Qaeda in Afghanistan. Before September 11, Pakistan had paid lip service to U.S. efforts to find bin Laden but had offered little by way of tangible help beyond

---

[49] Susan B. Glasser, "Putin Confers with Bush, Central Asian Presidents," *Washington Post*, September 24, 2001.

[50] Michael Wines, "Putin Offers Support to U.S. for Its Antiterrorist Efforts," *New York Times*, September 25, 2001.

[51] Jane Perlez, "Powell Says It Clearly: No Middle Ground on Terrorism," *New York Times*, September 13, 2001.

that. In light of that, a senior administration official said that "the time has come to choose sides."[52]

First out of the blocks in this effort was Secretary of State Powell, who spoke with Pakistan's President Pervez Musharraf the day after the attacks and read to him an action list of measures the administration wished for him to undertake.[53] Concurrently, Deputy Secretary of State Armitage met with the head of Pakistan's Inter-Services Intelligence (ISI) Department, Lieutenant General Mahmoud Ahmed, who happened to have been in Washington the day of the attacks on a previously scheduled visit. Of that meeting, a senior administration official said that there had been "an extremely candid exchange from our side, one that left little room for misunderstanding. It is safe to say the rules have changed. They changed yesterday."[54]

The administration's demands included sharing intelligence on bin Laden and his whereabouts, sealing Pakistan's 1,500-mile border with Afghanistan, cutting off energy shipments to Afghanistan, allowing U.S. forces to use Pakistani airspace (including air transit rights for U.S. carrier-based strike aircraft), and providing a springboard from which U.S. ground forces might conduct counterterrorist operations in Afghanistan. Armitage reportedly told Ahmad that "you're either 100 percent with us or 100 percent against us."[55] This de facto ultimatum forced Pakistan once again to confront a recurring dilemma it had faced ever since its creation in 1947 over whether to side decisively with the United States and its allies or instead to strad-

---

[52] Jane Perlez, "U.S. Demands Arab Countries 'Choose Sides,'" *New York Times,* September 15, 2001.

[53] R. W. Apple, Jr., "No Middle Ground," *New York Times*, September 14, 2001.

[54] Apple, "No Middle Ground." According to one account, Mahmoud Ahmed at first demurred by saying that "much history" affected any Pakistani decision to go after bin Laden, to which Armitage snapped back: "History starts today." (Carla Anne Robbins and Jeanne Cummings, "Powell's Cautious Views on Quick Strikes and Faith in Coalitions Shape Bush Plan," *Wall Street Journal,* September 21, 2001.)

[55] Michael Elliott, "'We're at War,'" *Time,* September 24, 2001.

dle the divide between pro-Western and conservative Islamic groups, the latter typically driven by extremist agendas.

The pressure tactic worked. On September 14, after a four-hour meeting chaired by Musharraf, Pakistan's military leadership consented to open its airspace for the transit of any U.S. air and cruise missile attacks against the Taliban and al Qaeda. It further agreed to share intelligence with the United States and to stem the flow of fuel and supplies from Pakistan to Afghanistan, while ruling out any participation by its own forces in any attacks on Afghanistan.[56] Washington's requests were not deemed inappropriate or overly difficult to support, and Pakistan's response set an encouraging tone of cooperativeness for further negotiations as U.S. war plans evolved.[57] Pakistan's generals were instructed by Musharraf to make available as necessary the nation's airspace and airfields for use in supporting U.S. operations in Afghanistan. They also were put on notice to cut off all fuel supplies to the Taliban and to deny the Taliban and al Qaeda the use of Pakistani banks.[58] In return for this courageous support on Musharraf's part, considering the deep-seated anti-Americanism and widespread pro-Taliban sentiment that pervaded Pakistan, the United States pledged to offer, among other things, assistance in reducing the country's $6 billion foreign debt and $800 million in direct aid.[59]

---

[56] There were reports that India also shared sensitive intelligence information with the United States on militant extremists in Afghanistan and Pakistan, including photographs and maps, videotapes of training camp activities, transcripts of conversations, and reports on how bin Laden was financing terrorist groups and running terrorist training facilities in Afghanistan and Pakistan. ("India Says It Gave U.S. Secret Data," *Washington Times*, September 17, 2001.)

[57] Kamran Khan and Molly Moore, "Pakistani Leaders Agree on Measures to Assist U.S.," *Washington Post*, September 15, 2001. Musharraf wasted little time in promising that the Taliban's days were numbered. ("A Battle on Many Fronts," *The Economist*, October 6, 2001, p. 15.)

[58] John F. Burns, "U.S. Demands Air and Land Access to Pakistan," *New York Times*, September 15, 2001.

[59] Judy Keen, "Bush Lauds New Partnership with Pakistan," *Washington Post*, February 14, 2002. Thousands of demonstrators took to the streets in Pakistan to protest Musharraf's decision to support the United States in Afghanistan.

In yet another gesture of unity with the United States, Pakistan on September 16 sent a senior delegation to Afghanistan to warn the Taliban rulers that they faced massive U.S. attacks if they did not assist in the capture of bin Laden and hand him over to the Americans. The high-level group, led by Major General Faiz Gilani, one of the ISI's top officers, announced that the Taliban had "only a few days" to comply with that demand or face an eventual American-led attack that would target not only bin Laden and his associates but also the Taliban themselves.[60] In response, the Taliban ordered all foreigners out of Afghanistan, on the pretext that their safety could no longer be guaranteed. Shortly thereafter, they rebuffed the American demand for bin Laden, insisting first on "convincing evidence" that the Saudi exile was responsible for the attacks and that the Organization of the Islamic Conference, a collection of more than 50 Muslim countries, formally request bin Laden's handover, a position the United States was bound to reject.[61]

Among the Gulf states, Saudi Arabia and Kuwait reportedly told U.S. officials in private within the first week after the attacks that their territory could be used in support of military action in the impending war against terrorism. They also promised to sustain a sufficient flow of petroleum products to help provide fuel for the coalition's war machine.[62] Secretary Powell and the president's national security adviser, Condoleezza Rice, consulted continually with the Saudi ambassador to Washington, Prince Bandar bin Sultan, in the early days following the attacks to secure Saudi support. For its part, Oman was slower to grant basing access. It was not clear at first whether it would approve strike operations from its base on the island of Masirah in the Arabian Sea. Neighboring Bahrain, however, which hosts the U.S. Navy's Fifth Fleet, quickly announced that it was

---

[60] John F. Burns, "Pakistani Team Giving Afghans an Ultimatum," *New York Times*, September 17, 2001.

[61] John F. Burns, "Taliban Reject Pakistan's Call for bin Laden," *New York Times*, September 18, 2001.

[62] David Graves, "Allies in the Gulf Guarantee Supplies of Fuel," *London Daily Telegraph*, September 18, 2001.

"prepared to cooperate with the United States as required at the present stage."[63]

Despite Saudi Arabia's declaration of support in principle, however, there were gathering hints that the royal family had begun to balk at allowing the United States to use its brand-new Combined Air Operations Center (CAOC) at Prince Sultan Air Base near al Kharj, as Secretary Powell continued to work hard to persuade the Saudi government to reverse a decade-old policy that had precluded any U.S. conduct or even command of offensive air operations from Saudi bases.[64] Powell himself denied a report that he had been seeking to convince the Saudi government to reverse its position on these two sticking points, avowing that the Saudis "have been providing everything we have asked them for so far" and neither confirming nor denying that they had approved the use of the CAOC. Yet it was common knowledge that ever since the allied victory in the 1991 Persian Gulf War, the Saudis had allowed tanker, reconnaissance, and support aircraft to operate from Saudi bases, as well as combat aircraft involved in enforcing the no-fly zone over southern Iraq as a part of Operation Southern Watch, but had repeatedly refused to countenance any other U.S. offensive operations.[65]

In a tacit confirmation of that persistent roadblock, Pentagon officials revealed on September 22 that negotiations were continuing with the Saudi leadership on the use of military facilities there, including the CAOC, adding that the U.S. government was confident that the Saudis would eventually grant the United States the access and operating latitude it needed.[66] As one might have surmised, that

---

[63] Ben Barber, "Taliban Threatens to Invade Pakistan," *Washington Times,* September 16, 2001.

[64] The CAOC enables commanders to monitor and track the movements of all aircraft operating in CENTCOM's AOR over thousands of miles, as well as to gather all pertinent information in one central place, including weather, satellite imagery, and real-time information provided by airborne intelligence, surveillance, and reconnaissance (ISR) platforms.

[65] The Saudis also allowed a presence of some 5,000 U.S. military personnel in Saudi Arabia, while severely restricting any open reporting on that presence.

[66] John H. Cushman, Jr., "More Reserves Called Up," *New York Times,* September 23, 2001.

statement discomfited the Saudis considerably and, for a time at least, seemed to have made matters worse rather than better. One U.S. general rightly commented that public discussion of plans to use the CAOC to direct air operations against the Taliban had "put [the Saudis] in a really tough position. We should have known better."[67]

As the onset of Enduring Freedom neared, some U.S. officials suggested that the Saudis were being "very difficult" and that the United States was having "real problems with access" that were impeding preparations for the impending campaign.[68] Yet just days before the bombing started, Secretary Rumsfeld declared in Riyadh, after a meeting with senior members of the royal family, that he was not concerned about getting Saudi approval to use military facilities, especially the CAOC, adding that "those kinds of things get worked out." Rumsfeld further noted that there was no doubt "in anyone's mind" that military action would soon commence.[69]

Additional basing options for getting at landlocked Afghanistan were sought from nearby Uzbekistan, Tajikistan, and Turkmenistan, all of which were largely hostile to the Taliban. As noted above, it was understood from the outset by the Bush administration that the United States would need full Russian support in securing basing rights in those former republics of the Soviet Union. During the Soviet era, the Uzbek capital of Tashkent had been the headquarters for all Soviet military forces in Central Asia. It offered a major air base option, with another at Termez directly adjacent to the Afghan border. Uzbek Foreign Minister Abdulaziz Kamilov said that his country was "prepared to discuss all the possible forms of cooperation in this respect. . . . We're prepared to discuss any issue that would be

---

[67] Vernon Loeb and Dana Priest, "Saudis Balk at Use of Key Facility," *Washington Post*, September 22, 2001. As a hedge against an ultimate Saudi denial of the CAOC's use, the Defense Department was considering instead using an alternate CAOC being built at al Udeid Air Base in Qatar.

[68] Michael R. Gordon, "Rumsfeld Meets Saudis and Says He's Satisfied with Level of Support," *New York Times*, October 4, 2001.

[69] Thomas E. Ricks, "Rumsfeld Confident of Use of Saudi Bases," *Washington Post*, October 4, 2001.

conducive to eliminating terrorism in our region and strengthening stability."[70]

By a stroke of serendipitous good luck toward that end, the United States had recently helped the Uzbek government resist the Islamic Movement of Uzbekistan, which was bent on creating an Islamic state in the Ferghana valley spanning portions of three former Soviet Central Asian republics. Uzbekistan's president, Islam Karimov, was clearly appreciative of that help and seemed dismissive of Russian Defense Minister Ivanov's early proscription of any consideration of U.S. use of Central Asian bases when he declared: "We didn't assume any responsibility that we would always coordinate our foreign policy with anybody."[71] In the end, with Russia's concurrence, the Uzbek leader consented to allow U.S. forces to use Uzbek airspace for any attack that might take place across the country's 80-mile border with Afghanistan.[72] During his visit to Central Asia to meet with officials in Almaty, Putin's security adviser Rushailo announced that hotlines would be set up connecting Central Asian leaders with Moscow to help facilitate such operations.

For their part, Tajikistan's leaders likewise did not immediately rule out such U.S. access, saying only that they would "definitely" consult with Russia before approving any such operations. The Tajik parliamentary leader, however, hinted strongly that Tajikistan would ultimately find a way to help the United States, commenting that "for the sake of the goal, I think everything might be done, including providing a corridor."[73] Clearly, Tajikistan and Uzbekistan both had ample reason to be concerned about appearances in a region that was still dominated by Russia, regarded by Russia as its sphere of influence, and populated by Muslims disinclined to support attacks on other Islamic believers. Once it became clear that the Tajik govern-

---

[70] Peter Baker, "Uzbeks Eager to Join U.S. Alliance," *Washington Post*, September 17, 2001.

[71] Baker, "Uzbeks Eager to Join U.S. Alliance."

[72] John F. Harris, "Bush Gets More International Support," *Washington Post*, September 17, 2001.

[73] Peter Baker, "Tense Tajikistan Braces for Instability," *Washington Post*, September 19, 2001.

ment would also be cooperative, however, a Pentagon official suggested that the United States would seek to keep any air operations originating from Tajikistan secret by stationing U.S. aircraft at remote airfields to enable the Tajik government to deny their presence in the country.[74]

President Bush spent much of his time and energy during the initial days after the attacks on the telephone with foreign leaders, working to build a coalition by lending his personal authority to the effort. In all, he called the leaders of more than 80 countries in pursuit of their support, extracting dozens of early pledges of assistance by persuading those leaders to take a public stance before worldwide sympathy for the United States began to wane.[75] On the eve of the campaign, the president said that 27 countries had granted overflight and landing rights.[76] That was a remarkable achievement for less than a month's worth of diplomatic effort.

The uniquely appalling character and magnitude of the September 11 attacks, coupled with the determined yet measured character of the administration's gathering response, naturally helped to bring together many coalition players who otherwise would have been more hesitant. As the campaign neared, the question was not whether an adequate coalition would be organized and ready so much as whether that steadily expanding coalition would remain cohesive a year later, after the most searing memories of September 11 had begun to fade. For the moment, however, the effort to build a coalition had produced impressive results by any measure, in considerable part thanks

---

[74] Rajiv Chandrasekaran, "Afghan Clerics Suggest That bin Laden Leave," *Washington Post*, September 21, 2001.

[75] The United Arab Emirates broke diplomatic relations with the Taliban, leaving Pakistan and Saudi Arabia as the sole countries with formal ties to the Afghan rulers. Not long thereafter, Saudi Arabia also broke ties with the Taliban, leaving only Pakistan with a diplomatic link to Kabul and rendering the Afghan rulers almost completely isolated. Later, Musharraf declared that Pakistan would continue to maintain its diplomatic contact, on the avowed premise that "at least there should be one country who ought to be able to have access to them." (George Jones and Anton La Guardia, "War Will Begin Within Days," *London Daily Telegraph*, September 26, 2001.)

[76] Mike Allen and Bill Miller, "President Releases Tally of Progress Against Terrorism," *Washington Post*, October 2, 2001.

to U.S. sensitivity to the special concerns of those countries whose leaders had signed on only reluctantly. As a testament to that sensitivity, four days before Operation Enduring Freedom began, as Rumsfeld left Washington on a last-minute three-day visit to Saudi Arabia, Oman, Egypt, and Uzbekistan in search of additional arrangements, Pentagon officials noted a desire to minimize any use of bases in Pakistan to avoid destabilizing a critical supporter and to help ensure that shaky country's continued cooperation. Asked about U.S. plans to use Pakistan, a senior administration official said "we are working very hard not to. And if we do, we want to be very discreet."[77]

Shaping a Strategy

The Bush administration also lost no time laying out the beginnings of a plan for responding to the attacks militarily. Concurrently with its move to build a viable international coalition, it also began the task of devising a course of action and setting operational priorities. Toward that end, the president met twice with his senior national security principals in Washington on September 12, during which he authorized them to go public immediately with the broad outlines of what was being contemplated. Clearly the first requirement toward enlisting broad-based popular support was to bound the emerging strategy so as to quell any tendency for expectations to exceed what was likely to prove manageable in the near term.

To help nip in the bud any such nascent hopes for instant gratification, Secretary of Defense Rumsfeld cautioned that any effective counteroffensive would require "a sustained and broadly based effort. And I don't think that people ought to judge outcomes until a sufficient time has passed to address what is clearly a very serious problem for the world. And it's not restricted to a single . . . state or nonstate

---

[77] Michael R. Gordon and Eric Schmitt, "Pentagon Tries to Avoid Using Pakistan Bases," *New York Times*, October 3, 2001.

entity."[78] Leaving no room for doubt that a serious counteroffensive was in the works, however, Rumsfeld added, in a videotaped address to U.S. military personnel worldwide: "It is my duty as head of this department to tell you that more, much more will be asked of you in the weeks and months ahead. This is especially true of those of you who are in the field. We face powerful and terrible enemies, enemies we intend to vanquish, so that moments of horror like yesterday will be stopped."[79] As borne out by the tone of that pronouncement, the Bush team was plainly not thinking of any replay of the largely symbolic cruise missile attacks against vacated or otherwise insignificant targets that had been a frequent response technique of the previous administration.[80]

Secretary of State Powell similarly warned against thinking "that one single counterattack will rid the world of terrorism of the kind we saw yesterday. This is going to take a multifaceted attack along many dimensions."[81] In a preview of the broad-based counterterrorism strategy that would eventually emerge, Powell observed that unlike the long years of the Cold War, when the opponent was clearly defined in time, space, and other dimensions, "this is different. The enemy is in many places. The enemy is not looking to be found. The enemy is hidden. The enemy is, very often, right here within our own country. And so you have to design a campaign plan that goes after that kind of enemy, and it isn't always blunt-force military, although that is certainly an option. It may well be that the diplomatic efforts,

---

[78] Eric Schmitt and Thom Shanker, "Administration Considers Broader, More Powerful Options for Potential Retaliation," *New York Times*, September 13, 2001.

[79] Vernon Loeb and Dana Priest, "Retaliatory Options Are Under Study," *Washington Post*, September 13, 2001.

[80] After the terrorist attacks on the American embassies in East Africa in 1998, the Clinton Pentagon launched nearly 80 cruise missiles, at a cost of over $1 million apiece, against a suspected chemical weapons facility in Sudan and at terrorist training camps in Afghanistan. That expensive but half-hearted retaliatory gesture caused little discernible damage to al Qaeda's organization or its behavior.

[81] Rowan Scarborough, "Officials Talk of Military Response," *Washington Times*, September 13, 2001.

political efforts, legal, financial, other efforts may be just as effective against that kind of enemy as would military force be."[82]

The following weekend, the president met at Camp David with his war council, whose members engaged in what several participants later called an "intense debate" over how best to characterize and focus the coming war. The president was said to have mostly just listened to this debate. The following day, he summoned his national security adviser, Condoleezza Rice, and directed her to coordinate a comprehensive strategy that would implement his decision to proceed with a phased response, beginning with a highly focused attack on al Qaeda and the Taliban in Afghanistan, but eventually reaching beyond Afghanistan to any terrorist operations with the global reach to harm the United States, to include any states known to sponsor such operations. In a real sense, the ultimate goal of this activity could be said to terrorize the terrorists, in effect, by turning the tables and putting *them*, for a change, in a defensive and reactive mode. On this point, Rumsfeld announced that the United States was preparing "a very broadly based campaign to go after the terrorist problem wherever it exists" and that the nation would "use the full spectrum of [its] capabilities. . . . We intend to put them on the defensive, to disrupt terrorist networks and remove their sanctuaries and their support systems. This will take a long, sustained effort."[83]

The emerging strategy comprised four main components. The first envisaged a sustained military effort against the perpetrators of the September 11 attacks, starting with bin Laden and his multinational network. The second entailed a heightened campaign against states known to harbor or support terrorists.[84] The third, as already

---

[82] Todd Purdum, "Leaders Face Challenges Far Different from Those of Last Conflict," *New York Times*, September 15, 2001.

[83] Thomas E. Ricks, Kamran Khan, and Molly Moore, "Taliban Refuses to Surrender bin Laden; U.S. Develops Options for Military Action," *Washington Post*, September 19, 2001.

[84] The administration's declaration that state sponsors would be included in the campaign prompted both Iraq and Iran to begin dispersing their military forces, primarily ground-force units, from known bases to remote locations in apparent anticipation of possible U.S. attacks. (Bill Gertz, "Fearful, Iran and Iraq Hunker Down," *Washington Times*, September 17, 2001.)

discussed above, looked to the formation of a worldwide counterterrorism coalition. The fourth and final one involved developing and implementing new homeland security measures to fight terrorism on the domestic front.[85]

This phased strategy grew out of a recognition that it would take several weeks even to marshal the forces that would be needed to handle the Afghan portion properly, let alone deal with other countries known to have lent support to al Qaeda. At the same time, it had the virtue of deferring any immediate need to accommodate and resolve some persistent differences of view that had arisen within the administration's most senior leadership. Indeed, as Week Two after September 11 began to unfold, the first signs of a widening fault line in the administration emerged as one faction, prominently including Wolfowitz and the chief of staff to Vice President Cheney, Lewis Libby, pressed for a broad-based military response not only against bin Laden in Afghanistan but also against suspected terrorist bases in Iraq and in Lebanon's Beka'a valley. More specifically, they were advocating expressly including Iraq on the target list, with the goal of bringing down Saddam Hussein. As Wolfowitz expressed it to reporters at the Pentagon: "I think the President made it very clear . . . that this is about more than just one organization, its about more than just one event." Wolfowitz added that "anybody who houses a terrorist, encourages terrorism, will be held accountable."[86]

In opposition to this faction, a more moderate group led by Secretary of State Powell argued for attending to first things first and for holding any anti-Iraq decision in abeyance until those prior concerns were satisfactorily addressed. Those who had worked the hardest to create a large multinational coalition, notably Powell and Armitage, insisted that any initial military moves be focused solely on responding to the September 11 attacks, namely, against the Taliban and al Qaeda in Afghanistan and nothing beyond that, at least for the time

---

[85] Doyle McManus and Robin Wright, "Broad New U.S. Strategy to Fight Terror Emerging," *Los Angeles Times*, September 16, 2001.

[86] Thomas E. Ricks, "Warplanes Begin Deploying to Gulf, Central Asia," *Washington Post*, September 20, 2001.

being. The sometimes strained character of the confrontation between the opposed administration factions was especially dramatized
when Powell, at a meeting of senior advisers chaired by Bush, countered Wolfowitz's earlier call for "ending states" that sponsor terrorism by warning that any attack on Iraq would "wreck" the gathering
coalition.[87] An underlying issue here concerned the inherent tension
between the natural desire to do something quickly and the felt need
to hold out for more deliberate and successful action once the time
was right.[88] For the moment, at least, Rumsfeld sided with the
growing inclination within the president's war council to leave Iraq
and other potential targets beyond Afghanistan out of the initial
planning. He was later to insist, however, that "this is not [just] an
Afghan problem. It is a worldwide problem of terrorist networks."[89]

One professed appeal of the hard-line school's proposed conduct
of concurrent or closely sequential operations against other states
known to have sponsored terrorism was that the threat of such action
offered an escape clause, in effect, to any state leadership that, in the
formulation of a Rumsfeld aide, might decide that "it should do
something else [other than supporting international terrorism] for a
living."[90] Rumsfeld's Defense Policy Board, chaired by Richard Perle
and including Henry Kissinger, James Schlesinger, former Vice President Dan Quayle, and former Congressman Newt Gingrich, among
others, likewise urged attacking Iraq as soon as possible after the Af-

---

[87] Patrick E. Tyler, "Bush Advisers Split on Scope of Retaliation," *New York Times*, September 20, 2001. On Wolfowitz's call for "ending states," Powell countered later: "We're after
ending terrorism. And if there are states and regimes, nations, that support terrorism, we
hope to persuade them that it is in their interest to stop doing that. But I think 'ending terrorism' is where I would leave it and let Mr. Wolfowitz speak for himself." (Tyler, "Bush
Advisers Split on Scope of Retaliation.")

[88] A senior White House aide later said that Wolfowitz was in complete agreement with
Bush's strategy for going after al Qaeda first, adding that charges that he was pushing a separate agenda were simply "not true, not helpful, and grossly unfair to Paul." (Elaine Sciolino,
"U.S. Prepares to Brief NATO on Strategy to Fight bin Laden," *New York Times*, September
25, 2001.)

[89] Tony Harnden, "Rumsfeld Spells Out What U.S. Victory Will Mean," *London Daily
Telegraph*, September 24, 2001.

[90] Harnden.

ghan portion was completed. Even Great Britain, the nation's staunchest ally, however, was hinting that it was not quite ready to go that far, at least yet.[91] In the end, the president's war council arrived at a consensus view that since the United States could not reasonably expect to take on every conceivable terrorist adversary at once, it would focus, in the first instance, on al Qaeda and those countries believed to support it and then consider engaging in broader counterterrorist operations only later.[92] A senior administration official confirmed that the initial phase would be against bin Laden and his al Qaeda infrastructure in Afghanistan, citing "broad agreement" within the administration that this was the appropriate focus for the moment and that next steps remained under continuing review.[93]

On this one point, the service chiefs were said to have diverged sharply, if discreetly, from the administration's more outspoken hardliners out of their shared concern that using force against a government that could not be convincingly shown to have been complicit in the September 11 attacks would risk losing the support of precisely those states on whose airspace and logistical support the nation would have to rely to prosecute the impending war against the Taliban and al Qaeda in Afghanistan.[94] In particular, the chairman of the JCS, Army General Hugh Shelton, strongly opposed including Iraq in the attack plan at such an early stage, arguing that the only justification for that would be incontrovertible evidence that Saddam Hussein had been directly involved in the September 11 attacks.[95] Participants in these deliberations later remarked, however, that Bush

---

[91] Michael Hirsh and Roy Gutman, "Powell in the Middle," *Newsweek*, October 1, 2001.

[92] Doyle McManus and James Gerstenzang, "Bush Takes CEO Role in Waging War," *Los Angeles Times*, September 23, 2001.

[93] David E. Sanger and Eric Schmitt, "U.S. Puts Afghan Strike Ahead of Full Plan," *New York Times*, September 22, 2001. Rumsfeld also indicated that he was invoking a rarely used law from the Civil War era, the Feed and Forage Act, that authorized the military to spend more than Congress had appropriated for clothing, fuel, and medical supplies.

[94] Barton Gellman and Mike Allen, "The Week That Redefined the Bush Presidency," *Washington Post*, September 23, 2001.

[95] Woodward, p. 61.

by that time had persuaded himself that a robust coalition of governments could be formed at least to deal with the opening round of the impending campaign, given his belief that an important segment of world leadership opinion had genuinely rallied to the U.S. cause.

A question also arose early on during these deliberations as to whether the emerging U.S. strategy should make ousting the Taliban an explicit objective. Powell and others at the State Department urged caution about broadening the impending war's strategy aims that far. Their underlying concern was that making regime change an express war goal could risk entangling the United States in Afghan civil strife, with no assurance that a stable post-Taliban government would emerge. (On this point, retired Marine General Anthony Zinni, who had most recently served as the commander of CENTCOM, cautioned against any resort to military action with no prior thought and planning devoted to anticipating and dealing with its likely consequences politically. "You can't just go in and devastate a country," he said. "A military [operation] that strikes and leaves will only perpetuate the problem" unless it is accompanied by a broad economic and diplomatic strategy for ensuing postwar stability.)[96] For their part, senior Pentagon officials urged taking the war straight to the heart of the Taliban's rule and instruments of control to deny bin Laden safe haven while sending a clear message to other state sponsors of terrorism.[97] In the end, the Taliban rulers decided this question for themselves when they truculently refused to hand over bin Laden and chose instead to defy the United States overtly.

On September 15, after a lengthy debate at Camp David over whether Iraq should be included or kept out of the initial strategy, Cheney finally joined Powell, Tenet, and White House chief of staff Andrew Card in opposing any immediate action against Iraq. Rums-

---

[96] Dana Priest, "Zinni Urges Economic, Diplomatic Moves," *Washington Post*, September 14, 2001. Zinni and the former JCS vice chairman and later Supreme Allied Commander in Europe, General Joseph Ralston, had sustained U.S. military ties with Pakistan after the 1998 military coup, even though there were calls from the State Department and Congress for those ties to be ended.

[97] Alan Sipress, "U.S. Debates Whether to Overthrow Taliban," *Washington Post*, September 24, 2001.

feld reportedly did not commit one way or the other, with the end result being four to zero against attacking Iraq, with Rumsfeld abstaining.[98] The argument for a broader campaign from the very start, mainly advanced by Rumsfeld and Wolfowitz, was not rejected outright. However, it was deferred by the president, whose decision on that score a senior adviser later said had "settled" the issue, at least for the time being.[99] To be sure, it was understood by everyone all along that the problem was not simply Afghanistan. However, when informed by the CIA's director, George Tenet, that the United States had a 60-country challenge in running down al Qaeda worldwide, the president responded: "Let's pick them off one at a time."[100] The core message in the president's subsequent special address to the joint session of Congress the evening of September 20 was a direct result of seven straight days of such debate within his innermost war cabinet.

During the course of these marathon sessions, Tenet made an early hard push to deploy CIA paramilitary operatives and uniformed special operations forces (SOF) to aid Afghan opposition groups while Taliban and al Qaeda targets were being bombed and to conduct any such bombing without any Vietnam-like incrementalism. At first, the Pentagon was skeptical of the CIA's proposal, out of a belief that the opposition groups possessed little proven skill at fighting the Taliban. Indeed, even the CIA itself had judged that the most well-organized group, the Northern Alliance, was outnumbered two to one by the Taliban, with around 20,000 fighters to the Taliban's estimated 45,000. A CIA program was already under way to fund, to the tune of several million dollars a year, those remnants of the mujaheddin who had long fought the Soviets and who had been funded earlier by the CIA during a long portion of the Soviet Afghan war. Before September 11, however, there had been little CIA confidence that it was really an "alliance," since the group's various warlords

---

[98] Bob Woodward and Dan Balz, "At Camp David, Advise and Dissent," *Washington Post*, January 31, 2002.

[99] Jane Perlez, David E. Sanger, and Thom Shanker, "From Many Voices, One Battle Strategy," *New York Times*, September 23, 2001.

[100] Woodward, p. 33.

typically sided with the highest bidder and could easily be bought off by the Taliban, with al Qaeda's financial help.[101]

Yet as the Taliban began hunkering down in anticipation of a U.S. retaliation in the wake of the September 11 attacks, the Northern Alliance came forward on its own and offered the support of its combatants to help capture or kill bin Laden, with its Washington representative, Haron Amin, announcing that "the international community has no chance of hunting down Osama bin Laden without us."[102] In short order, Tenet's proposal resonated favorably with President Bush, who had already begun gravitating toward the introduction of American ground troops as a symbol of U.S. determination. On that point, deputy national security adviser Stephen Hadley later commented that "for the first time, America is getting serious [about terrorism], because it is going to put its people at risk."[103]

By way of background to the president's eventual backing of Tenet's proposal, to provide the CIA the fullest possible freedom to forestall further al Qaeda attacks, intelligence directives known as "presidential findings" had been issued after al Qaeda terrorists bombed the American embassies in Nairobi, Kenya, and Dar es Salaam, Tanzania, in 1998. These highly classified directives retained the legal ban on assassination of national leaders, but they authorized the use of lethal force as needed for U.S. self-defense—including, presumably, preemptive self-defense.[104] After having been briefed on a detailed CIA plan for Afghanistan by Tenet, Bush signed a Memorandum of Notification on September 17 that approved all of what Tenet had proposed and that empowered the CIA to use lethal

---

[101] Woodward, p. 35.

[102] Tom Carter, "Rival Alliance Offers Help to Hunt Down bin Laden," *Washington Times*, September 20, 2001. Led by Ahmed Shah Massoud, widely known as "the Lion of Panjshir," the Northern Alliance seized nominal control of Afghanistan several years after the Soviet withdrawal, until Pakistan changed its allegiance and armed the Taliban militia, which put Massoud and his men on the run to the Panjshir valley, where they had held out ever since.

[103] James Carney and John F. Dickerson, "Inside the War Room," *Time*, December 31, 2001–January 7, 2002.

[104] Bob Woodward and Vernon Loeb, "CIA's Covert War on bin Laden," *Washington Post*, September 14, 2001.

covert action to disrupt the al Qaeda and other terrorist networks worldwide. It also gave the CIA free rein to operate inside Afghanistan with its paramilitary teams (see Chapter Three for more on this subject).[105]

As for the style of the administration's approach, President Bush made a determination as early as September 12 that he would personally chair and direct the meetings of his inner war council, since he considered that to be a commander-in-chief function that could not be delegated and wanted it to be clear to all, both within and beyond his administration, that he was personally setting the direction and tone of the nation's strategic planning.[106] Yet at the same time, throughout the daily high-level strategy deliberations that ensued during the weeks that followed, Bush made a studied point to remain above the more minor details. One aide commented that when less momentous issues were presented to him, the president would reply: "Don't bring this to me. I've given you a task, and I have full confidence in you to carry it out."[107] That style represented a perceptible departure from the more intensely hands-on approach taken by the Clinton administration and by many of its NATO counterparts during portions of the earlier Operation Allied Force in 1999 when it came to day-to-day high-level involvement with the minutiae of options planning and execution. Also, the president made a special point to keep his closest political advisers, Karl Rove and Karen Hughes, out of the war deliberations to avoid radiating any appearance of infusing domestic political considerations into the proceedings.

Bush's preferred approach was to set the overall direction and tone and then to leave it to his often divided senior security principals to work out the details. Before September 11, the Bush NSC principals, namely, the Secretaries of State and Defense, the director of Central Intelligence, and the chairman of the JCS, along with others

---

[105] Woodward, p. 101.

[106] Woodward, p. 38.

[107] Carney and Dickerson.

depending on the subject matter, convened roughly twice a month under the chairmanship of the president's national security adviser. Now its members found themselves meeting twice daily during the initial weeks after the attacks, once at 9:30 a.m. with the president and later in the evening without the president, to review the day's events and plan for the next 24 hours.[108] Among the main players in this process, Vice President Cheney was portrayed by insiders as the cool and mature policy hand. For his part, Secretary of State Powell, just as he did 10 years earlier during the months leading up to the Gulf War when he was the JCS chairman, epitomized the voice of caution and moderation. Secretary Rumsfeld, operating from a different vantage point, cited the attacks as grim proof of what he had repeatedly warned of throughout the preceding year, namely, an "asymmetrical threat." He advocated a forceful strategy that would come to effective terms not only with bin Laden but also with any proven state sponsors of international terrorism.[109]

Fortunately, despite all its understandable and appropriate here-and-now fixation on the immediate challenge of responding on multiple fronts to the terrorist attacks and the implications of those responses, the Bush administration did not lose sight of the larger picture of U.S. defense strategy and force modernization needs. Under Secretary of Defense Wolfowitz rightly noted that although the attacks and the need to respond to them with dispatch had changed some of the defense and security policy landscape, the just-completed Quadrennial Defense Review (QDR) should not and would not be set aside altogether: "I wouldn't agree that it changes everything. It changes a great deal. . . . But I don't think that means that the requirements that we contemplated for 10 and 15 years from now are necessarily all that different."[110] Numerous defense officials similarly emphasized that although the number-one priority in the wake of

---

[108] McManus and Gerstenzang.

[109] This characterization was advanced in Perlez, Sanger, and Shanker.

[110] Christian Lowe, "Relevance of QDR in Question," *Defense Week*, September 24, 2001, p. 1.

September 11 had become the war on terror, that necessary priority would not be allowed to divert attention away from transforming the military for future threats and needs more broadly defined.

It was in this spirit that the QDR, which had been largely completed before September 11, was finally submitted to Congress by Secretary Rumsfeld on October 1. Not surprisingly, as a direct result of the terrorist attacks, the report elevated homeland security to the status of first among four core U.S. military missions. The QDR also deferred any imminent decisions on major program cuts, and it amended the Defense Department's long-standing two-war strategy for hedging against major regional contingencies.[111] All in all, however, the most senior Pentagon leaders successfully avoided allowing themselves to succumb to the natural urge that was widely felt during the first days after the September 11 attacks to drop everything in a knee-jerk response aimed at focusing narrowly on the war against terror to the exclusion of all else.

Crafting a Plan

As early as September 12, Pentagon and CENTCOM officials began closely reviewing the existing military response options, including six alternatives for striking at bin Laden's resources in Afghanistan. These options had been developed three years earlier in the wake of the bombing of two U.S. embassies in East Africa by bin Laden's agents in August 1998. They were said to include small-scale covert operations by the Army's counterterrorist Delta Force, a major aerial bombing campaign, and a land invasion by U.S. Army troops.[112]

Yet CENTCOM had no contingency plan for dealing specifically with the Taliban and al Qaeda's terrorist organization in Afghanistan. According to one authoritative account, "there was nothing on the shelf that could be pulled down to provide at least an

---

[111] Thom Shanker, "New Blueprint for Military Shifts Priority to U.S. Soil, Revising Two-War Strategy," *New York Times*, October 2, 2001.

[112] Woodward and Loeb.

outline," a fact that caused Secretary Rumsfeld to inform General Myers that he was not pleased with what he had seen, that what he had seen was neither imaginative nor creative, and, in effect, that he felt "we've [still] got a long way to go. You need to know that."[113] As just noted, Pentagon spokesmen did confirm that CENTCOM had drafted preliminary plans for possible operations in Afghanistan in the wake of the embassy bombings out of growing concern over the future threat posed by bin Laden, who had been detected by U.S. intelligence in the Afghan mountains several times in 2001. They added, however, that those efforts had been hindered by a shortage of available airfields in the region and by poor roads, poor communications, and poor electrical power and water supplies inside Afghanistan.[114]

During the initial war cabinet sessions at Camp David that immediately followed the terrorist attacks, General Shelton, the outgoing JCS chairman, had proposed three military response options. The first envisaged an immediate cruise missile attack against al Qaeda training camps, which were known to be empty. That alternative, derisively labeled the "pound sand" option by White House chief of staff Andrew Card, was quickly ruled out as ineffectual. The second entailed a combination of cruise missile and bomber attacks over a period of time ranging from two to 10 days. The third involved the same air attack plan, buttressed by an insertion of U.S. ground forces.[115] The latter two options would require prior diplomatic effort to arrange for foreign airspace transit approvals, as well as a forward deployment of appropriate equipment and personnel to temporary bases near Afghanistan to ensure that adequate CSAR assets were in place to ensure a safe aircrew recovery in case a U.S. aircraft went down over hostile terrain.

---

[113] Woodward, p. 25.

[114] Paul Richter, "Experts Weigh Risks of Air, Ground Campaigns in Afghanistan," *Los Angeles Times*, September 14, 2001.

[115] Woodward, p. 80.

During these deliberations, the president emphasized to his war council that he did not want a mere "photo-op war" but instead a "realistic scorecard" and "a list of thugs" who could be tracked down and captured or killed by U.S. direction. Above all, he cautioned, "the American people want a big bang. I have to convince them that this is a war that will be fought with many steps."[116] To make good on this, he directed the Department of Defense to draw up a menu of military response options to deal with what he called the attackers' "acts of war." In turn, Rumsfeld, JCS Chairman Shelton, and JCS Vice Chairman Myers led the planning effort for a response that would draw on forces from U.S. European Command (EUCOM) and CENTCOM. That impending response would range from small-scale covert operations to a broad air and land campaign against the Taliban regime in Afghanistan that harbored Osama bin Laden and the heart of his al Qaeda organization.[117]

When the commander of CENTCOM, Army General Tommy Franks, was first approached with this need by Secretary Rumsfeld, Franks responded that it would take months to position the required number of forces in the AOR and to develop adequate plans for a major operation in Afghanistan. To that, Rumsfeld countered that "you don't have months" and that CENTCOM planners needed to think instead in terms of days or weeks. According to numerous informed reports, Franks was sent back to the drawing board after he presented his initial thoughts on a campaign option to Rumsfeld, whose response was said to have been: "Try again."[118] Recalled one insider: "[Franks] was told, 'Go off, be more creative, we don't want to put huge forces on the ground, and your time lines are too

---

[116] Woodward, p. 49.

[117] The Taliban had come into power in 1996 with considerable support from Pakistan's ISI agency and was providing safe haven for al Qaeda terrorists, who had relocated to Afghanistan from Sudan in May 1996, in return for substantial cash provisions and military help by bin Laden.

[118] Woodward, pp. 43–44.

long.'"[119] Six days after the terrorist attacks, Rumsfeld was still concerned, in the words of one of his aides, that CENTCOM was not "looking aggressively enough at aggressive options."[120] The initial options briefing prepared for the president by CENTCOM also ran acropper of General Shelton, who "wasn't comfortable with the targets," according to one informed source. It was finally cleared, however, to be shown to the president.[121]

Close on the heels of this push to generate a more realistic and usable war option, a tight lid was clamped on any public discussion of the process as Rumsfeld sternly cautioned all government employees in the know against revealing "information that could cost the lives of men and women in uniform."[122] In the first sign of what was to become his signature position on operational security, he laid down the law against leaks of sensitive planning details, commenting that the nation was witnessing the definition of a new 21st-century battlefield and that as an "old-fashioned" type, he was "inclined to think that if you're going to cock it, you throw it, and you don't talk about it a lot."[123] This mounting emphasis on operational security was also evident as CENTCOM took down its Internet Web site, with other U.S. military organizations planning to do likewise.

Initially, Pentagon officials labeled the impending campaign Operation Infinite Justice. Later, Rumsfeld abandoned that code name after Islamic scholars objected on the asserted ground that only God can impose "infinite justice." Only on September 25 did he rename the looming war against al Qaeda Operation Enduring Freedom. As Rumsfeld explained it, "'enduring' suggests that this is not a

---

[119] Thomas E. Ricks, "War Plan for Iraq Is Ready, Say Officials," *Washington Post*, November 10, 2002.

[120] Ricks, "War Plan for Iraq Is Ready, Say Officials," p. 99.

[121] Michael Elliott, "'We Will Not Fail,'" *Time*, October 1, 2001.

[122] Alison Mitchell and Richard L. Berke, "Differences Are Put Aside as Lawmakers Reconvene," *New York Times*, September 12, 2001.

[123] "Rumsfeld Warns Against Leaks," *Washington Times*, September 13, 2001.

quick fix. . . . It will take years, I suspect."[124] It also bears noting that at the outset of the administration's public positioning on what was to come, President Bush referred several times to the emerging war against terrorism as a "crusade." He later retracted that usage because of its inadvertent and potentially damaging connotation of the Christians' medieval wars against Muslims in the Holy Land, stressing that war against terrorism did not mean war against Islam.

It soon became clear that another goal of the impending campaign would be a full and complete takedown of the Taliban regime in addition to the destruction of al Qaeda's terrorist infrastructure in Afghanistan. As early as September 18, Secretary Rumsfeld had declared that a central objective of the coming effort would be to affect the Taliban's behavior.[125] Yet for a time, although the president was insistent that he wanted bin Laden "dead or alive," the administration did not commit itself to treating al Qaeda and the Taliban as inseparable. On September 21, however, the Taliban rulers pointedly refused to hand over bin Laden and vowed instead to square off in a "showdown of might" with the United States.[126] Indeed, as the onset of combat neared, they claimed that they were hiding bin Laden "for his safety and security."[127] They also threatened to execute any Afghan UN workers who sought to communicate with anyone outside Afghanistan. Once the Taliban leadership rebuffed Washington's demand for bin Laden, the Bush administration lifted all limitations

---

[124] Rowan Scarborough, "Rumsfeld Cautions Against Mass Strike," *Washington Times*, September 26, 2001. Earlier, the budding campaign was also called, for a brief period, Infinite Reach and then Noble Eagle—the latter of which eventually became the code name for the homeland air defense effort.

[125] Rowan Scarborough, "Bombing Plan Spares Civilian Structures," *Washington Times*, October 4, 2001.

[126] Rajiv Chandrasekaran, "Taliban Rejects U.S. Demand, Vows a 'Showdown of Might,'" *Washington Post*, September 22, 2001.

[127] Brian Knowlton, "Taliban Say They Are Hiding bin Laden; Saudi Must Be 'Purged,' U.S. Warns," *International Herald Tribune*, October 1, 2001. Rumsfeld later commented that the U.S. government had no reason to believe that statement.

in its preparations for the impending war.[128] When the Taliban announced that they were prepared to wage a "holy war" against the United States were they to be attacked, Cheney threatened in response the "full wrath" of the world's sole surviving superpower.[129] By then, more and more residents had begun to be observed fleeing Kabul, with looting widespread and Taliban agents rounding up young men at gunpoint to defend the country's capital.

There was no doubt about congressional support for the coming effort. Within days of the terrorist attacks, the Senate passed a 98–0 resolution authorizing "all necessary and appropriate force," without a single dissenting vote or even debate.[130] Shortly thereafter, the House of Representatives passed a similar resolution by a vote of 420–1, the lone dissenter being Congresswoman Barbara Lee, a Democrat from Berkeley, California. Within the executive branch, defense officials both in and out of uniform who had become habituated to eight years of recurrent gradualism on the part of the previous administration were plainly abandoning their reactive mindset regarding the use of force and starting to think more aggressively. Rumsfeld remarked that "several countries have exhausted themselves pounding that country [Afghanistan]" and that the United States did not intend to repeat their mistakes. He added that the fight would require a broad effort and that "a lot of it will be special operations," with the ultimate goal being "to drain the swamp [the terrorists] live in."[131] The principal U.S. coalition partner, Great Britain, lost no

---

[128] David E. Sanger, "Bin Laden Is Wanted in Attacks, 'Dead or Alive,' President Says," *New York Times*, September 18, 2001.

[129] Jeanne Cummings, "Bush Recruits International Leaders in Effort to Build Antiterror Alliance," *Wall Street Journal*, September 19, 2001.

[130] The resolution in full stated "that the President is authorized to use all necessary and appropriate force against those nations, organizations, or persons he determines planned, authorized, committed, or aided the terrorist attacks that occurred on September 11, 2002, or harbored such organizations or persons, in order to prevent any future acts of international terrorism against the United States by such nations, organizations or persons." ("Text of Joint Resolution," *Washington Post*, September 15, 2001.)

[131] Michael R. Gordon, "Scarcity of Afghan Targets Leads U.S. to Revise Strategy," *New York Times*, September 19, 2001.

time cementing its role in the coming action. As early as September 21, Prime Minister Blair returned to London from Washington carrying with him the American war plan as it stood at the time so that it could be coordinated with the unfolding British contribution, called Operation Veritas, which envisaged the use of British Army special forces, the Parachute Regiment, the Royal Marines, and the RAF's four C-17 transports, among other aircraft.[132]

Beyond the many declaratory indicators noted above, the emerging U.S. response was further telegraphed by the first signs of serious planning activity under way both in Washington and at CENTCOM. Ever since the bombing of the American embassies in East Africa by bin Laden's agents in 1998, CENTCOM's headquarters staff had been refining options for running bin Laden to ground, featuring both small- and larger-unit land-force operations (with more than 2,000 Rangers) and selective air attacks.[133] These constituted the baseline for planning a course of action against al Qaeda in Afghanistan. Administration officials said that the prospective target list for the impending campaign could include, among other things, bunkers and caves in eastern Afghanistan housing Taliban soldiers and bin Laden recruits; the airports at Kabul, Jalalabad, and Kandahar; and homes and government buildings in Kabul and Kandahar used by top Taliban rulers.[134] Yet another target identified early during this planning was the so-called Arab Brigade in the north, also referred to as Brigade 055, which was the Taliban's top fighting force composed of some 1,000 graduates of bin Laden's training camps, who were so loyal that any member who retreated under fire would be shot. The target approval process was said by one insider to have been "a bit constipated" at first, with persistent uncertainty over who

---

[132] Michael Evans, "Coalition Troops Set for Covert Action," *London Times*, September 22, 2001.

[133] Carla Anne Robbins, Greg Jaffe, and Robert S. Greenberger, "Small-Scale Steps Could Be Key in Military's Reaction to Attacks," *Wall Street Journal*, September 17, 2001.

[134] Jack Kelly, "U.S. IDs Possible Sites for Retaliation," *USA Today*, September 17, 2001.

had authority to issue a clearance for engaging various target types.[135] Nevertheless, as the onset of combat operations neared, an administration official noted that most target nominations had already been submitted by CENTCOM to the Joint Chiefs of Staff. That official described the enemy center of gravity as the Taliban themselves and indicated an intent to spare civilian infrastructure such as bridges, electrical power, and water supply.[136]

Indeed, underlying and pervading this planning was a determination to bend every effort to avoid causing collateral damage to Afghan noncombatants to avoid further inflaming anti-American attitudes throughout the Islamic world. Moreover, most American military officers readily accepted the importance of taking special care to avoid any such unintended damage. As one later commented after the war was under way, "our mores in America are, we don't kill innocent people [if] that could be prevented. We have extreme sensitivity to that. For people to say we missed opportunities, that to me oversimplifies the situation."[137] According to the procedures that were finally established, General Franks would have to ask Washington for permission to attack any target that entailed a likelihood of moderate or high collateral damage. The one exception, by an authoritative account, was if the CIA had bin Laden or other top al Qaeda leaders in the sight of its armed MQ-1 Predator drone.[138] Fortunately, the unprecedentedly high accuracy of today's air-delivered weapons is such that many target types no longer require 2,000-lb or 1,000-lb bombs, whose destructive radius can cause far more unintended collateral damage than the equally accurate but considerably smaller 500-lb guided Mk 82 general-purpose munition.

---

[135] John G. Roos, "Turning Up the Heat: Taliban Became Firm Believers in Effects-Based Operations," *Armed Forces Journal International*, February 2002, p. 37.

[136] Scarborough, "Bombing Plan Spares Civilian Structures."

[137] Quoted in Christopher J. Bowie, Robert P. Haffa, Jr., and Robert E. Mullins, *Future War: What Trends in America's Post-Cold War Military Conflicts Tell Us About Early 21st Century Warfare*, Arlington, Va.: Northrop Grumman Analysis Center, January 2003, p. 24.

[138] Woodward, p. 166.

The emerging strategy accordingly sought to rely on precision standoff weapons to the fullest extent possible, with any commitment of ground troops in strength to be undertaken only if deemed absolutely essential. At the same time, indicating that there would almost surely be at least some ground component to the emerging plan, Secretary Rumsfeld cautioned that "cruise missiles do not get people who are operating in the shadows. And the era of antiseptic warfare—planes dropping bombs from 20,000 feet, cruise missiles flying off into the night, no one getting hurt on the coalition side—that will not work with this enemy, let there be no doubt."[139] Also, with a view toward indicating clearly that Washington's bone of contention was with the Taliban and al Qaeda and not with the Afghan people as a whole, President Bush on September 30 approved a $100 million humanitarian relief plan for air-dropping food into Afghanistan, partly aimed at minimizing resentment in Pakistan over the continuing flow of refugees from Afghanistan. (A serious side concern associated with this effort entailed ensuring that the food did not fall into Taliban hands.)

There were also accelerated contacts between CIA elements in the forward area and various Afghan opposition groups, notably the Northern Alliance, a loose aggregate of anti-Taliban resistance fighters funded mainly by Russia, India, and Iran and composed mostly of representatives from the minority Uzbek, Tajik, and Hazara communities. That group controlled a small portion of northern Afghanistan that lay beyond the effective reach of the Taliban. For years, the CIA had been running paramilitary teams into Afghanistan and had also cultivated working ties with southern Pashtun opposition elements. These accelerated contacts represented a major expansion of the U.S. government's effort to engage and empower the most promising elements of the Afghan resistance. Also involved as a potential player in the impending Taliban takedown was Abdul Haq, a former mujaheddin leader who had fought the Soviets and had recently returned to the region after years of living in the West.

---

[139] Bill Nichols and Dave Moniz, "Experts Predict U.S. Will Fight First Extended Commando War," *USA Today*, September 17, 2001.

This U.S. effort to enlist the support of Afghan opposition groups was complicated by the persistence of major ethnic rivalries between the northern and southern factions, notably the southern Pashtun tribes of which the Taliban themselves were radical offshoots.[140] Nevertheless, CIA operatives moved aggressively to establish contact with both northern and southern opposition groups, both out of a perceived need for allies on the ground who could help track down bin Laden and also to dispel any impression among the Afghan rank and file—as well as elsewhere throughout the Muslim world—that the United States was at war with Afghanistan, as opposed to bin Laden and the Taliban. Yet another motivation was a desire to encourage early Taliban defections and to offer the opposition groups a role in solidifying a stable postwar Afghanistan.

Beyond the various declarations of intent and mounting signs of ongoing planning activity outlined above, a series of tangible events also began to accumulate, all of which pointed to imminent U.S. military action in Afghanistan. The president's address to the joint session of Congress on September 20 came as the U.S. military was engaged in the beginnings of a broad-based deployment effort in support of combat operations that could last for months or more. That same day, Lieutenant General Charles Wald, the commander of U.S. Central Command Air Forces (CENTAF), departed his headquarters at Shaw AFB, South Carolina, for Saudi Arabia with several of his key deputies to lay the foundation for conducting an air war from the just-opened CAOC at Prince Sultan Air Base, a facility that had been completed only six weeks before the September 11 terrorist attacks.

With time rapidly running out for the Taliban and al Qaeda, Under Secretary of Defense Wolfowitz may have meant to help lay a basis for tactical surprise when he declared on September 25, after

---

[140] Alan Sipress and Marc Kaufman, "Taliban Opponents Increase U.S. Contacts," *Washington Post*, September 22, 2001. The most important ethnic cleavage was between the Pashto speakers in the south, who were mostly Sunni Muslims who had looked to Pakistan for support, and the Persian speakers of the north, who were Shiites looking to Iran for backing.

briefing NATO's ambassadors in Brussels, that "it cannot be stressed enough that everybody who is waiting for military action . . . needs to rethink this thing. . . . In this campaign, it's worth emphasizing [that] one of the most important things is to acquire more information about an enemy. . . . That is one of the reasons why it is not so easy to lay out a specific campaign plan and lots of specific actions. . . ."[141] Whatever the case, concern had begun to mount in U.S. military circles by late September that time was quickly becoming of the essence, considering that winter was approaching and that snow had already begun falling on the Khyber Pass, which threatened to make any planned ground operations ever more difficult. Concern also was voiced for an expeditious implementation of the emerging campaign plan before opposition in the Islamic world grew to a point where it would be hard to sustain even minimal support from key Muslim countries.

In short, at the time of the September 11 attacks, there was no plan in existence for U.S. military action in Afghanistan. Yet in the space of just a little over three weeks, the U.S. government pulled together an effective international coalition, crafted the beginnings of a serviceable war strategy, moved needed forces and materiel to the region, developed alliances with indigenous anti-Taliban elements in Afghanistan, arranged for regional basing and overflight permission, laid the groundwork for an acceptable target approval process, and prepared to conduct concurrent humanitarian relief operations. The strategy ultimately settled on by the Bush administration and by CENTCOM was focused exclusively on Afghanistan, with any consideration of possible military measures against Iraq or other rogue regimes to be deferred until the proximate goals in Afghanistan were achieved. Those proximate goals were to bring down the Taliban regime, destroy al Qaeda's base of operations, and hunt down bin Laden and his principal deputies while concurrently eliminating as many other al Qaeda terrorists as possible. The course of action

---

[141] Alan Sipress and Thomas E. Ricks, "Military Strike Not Imminent, Officials Say," *Washington Post*, September 27, 2001.

agreed upon to accomplish these three goals envisaged a heavy use of precision air-delivered munitions, enabled and aided by U.S. SOF teams to identify, designate, and validate targets; conduct direct-action operations against Taliban and al Qaeda leaders; and work with indigenous Afghan opposition groups, the latter of whom would bear the brunt of the campaign's effort on the ground against Taliban forces. The plan further envisaged an aggressive use of CIA paramilitary operatives in working with friendly Afghan resistance forces, as well as the employment of the CIA's armed MQ-1 Predator unmanned aerial vehicles (UAVs) in tracking down and eliminating Taliban and al Qaeda leaders.

This strategy was built from the ground up and was expressly tailored to the tasks at hand, since none of the preexisting contingency plans on file at CENTCOM was even remotely appropriate to the special needs of Enduring Freedom. Among the strategy's many premises and unifying themes, the most crucial was the abiding importance of avoiding noncombatant fatalities and collateral damage to nonmilitary infrastructure to signal both to the Afghan rank and file and to the Muslim world at large that the war was against the Taliban and al Qaeda, not against Afghanistan or Islam as a whole. That meant an unwavering focus on Taliban and al Qaeda military equities and a scrupulous avoidance of such civilian infrastructure targets as electrical power, bridges, and roads that would be needed to support humanitarian aid delivery and postwar reconstruction once the Taliban were defeated and replaced by an interim successor government. It further meant the smallest possible U.S. military presence on the ground in Afghanistan, a concern that necessarily ruled out any heavy U.S. conventional ground-force involvement.

As for the instruments for carrying out the strategy, CENTCOM would rely unusually heavily on Navy and Marine Corps carrier-based strike fighters, supported by Air Force and RAF tankers, owing to the limited availability of accessible bases in the region within easy reach of Afghanistan by land-based fighters. It also would draw on a highly redundant network of space-based and air-breathing ISR platforms to provide CENTCOM and those prosecuting the war at the tactical level with continuous situation awareness of the highest possible fidelity. The campaign would open with measured and precise attacks by a combination of Navy cruise missiles, Navy carrier-based strike fighters, and Air Force heavy bombers against fixed Taliban air defense, command-and-control, and leadership targets, with the goal of establishing complete control of the air as soon as possible and causing as much early disorientation and disarray among the Taliban and al Qaeda leadership as could be achieved within the campaign's rules of engagement and operational limitations. Once those near-term goals were achieved, combat operations would then shift to enemy caves and bunkers, logistical nodes, troop concentrations, and training facilities, with the primary emphasis on engaging emerging targets of interest as they presented themselves and dismantling the Taliban and al Qaeda establishments in detail on the installment plan.

The administration's coalition partners would be relied on to provide needed basing support and airspace transit approvals. The actual air campaign, however, would be conducted only by U.S. forces and those of the nation's most trusted allies, out of concern on the administration's part to avoid the sort of friction and delays that were encountered during Operation Allied Force two years earlier, which had been conducted by 19 separate and often highly independent-minded NATO allies, each with its own narrow interests and agenda. If there was any agreed timetable by which the campaign was to be conducted, the administration never brought it to public light. On the contrary, its most senior leaders gave every indication going in that they had no clear idea of what the endgame would look like, that their expectations of success in the short run were modest at best, and that the preferred watchwords for the American people should be patience and forbearance. Secretary Rumsfeld would later freely admit that the war was initiated with no clear road map and that he and General Franks found themselves constantly adapting to changing events as they occurred.

By September 29, Secretary of State Powell reported that the Uzbek government had finally approved an American CSAR presence in Uzbekistan, which was deemed essential for any U.S. bombing effort in the northernmost reaches of Afghanistan. As the start of Operation Enduring Freedom neared, there was still only a single team of seven CIA paramilitary operatives on the ground in enemy territory and no apparent likelihood of getting any U.S. SOF teams inserted any time soon thanks to continued inclement weather.[142] Nevertheless, President Bush in the end settled on the most extensive of the retaliatory options that had been presented to him earlier by General Shelton. He reportedly said at the time: "Let's hit them hard. We want to signal this is a change from the past. We want to cause other countries like Syria and Iraq to change their views. . . . We are going to rain holy hell on them."[143]

The Buildup of Forces

Finally, initial troop mobilizations and deployments forward to CENTCOM's AOR (see Figure 2.1) began even as the Bush administration was only beginning to crystallize its war strategy and develop a concrete plan for carrying it out. To begin with, as noted above, the president on September 14 signed an order authorizing the Department of Defense to call up 35,000 reservists, mostly to help with the stepped-up air defense of the United States and with other homeland defense functions, such as checking commercial ships in ports, and to assist in various military intelligence-related activities.[144] The president further granted Secretary Rumsfeld a handshake agreement to begin coordinating any future call-up need that would exceed 50,000 Guard and Reserve personnel. That same day, two tanker ships were

---

[142] For a spellbinding after-action account of this team's experience in Afghanistan by its leader, see Gary C. Schroen, *First In: An Insider's Account of How the CIA Spearheaded the War on Terror in Afghanistan,* New York: Ballantine Books, 2005.

[143] Bob Woodward and Dan Balz, "Combating Terrorism: 'It Starts Today,'" *Washington Post,* February 1, 2002.

[144] Neely Tucker and Vernon Loeb, "District, Nation Move to High Alert," *Washington Post,* September 15, 2001.

Figure 2.1
CENTCOM's Area of Responsibility

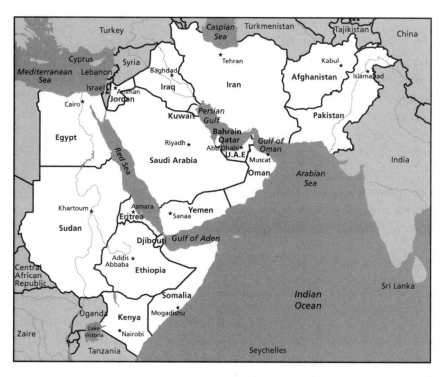

ordered to transport 235,000 barrels of marine diesel fuel to Diego Garcia in the Indian Ocean, with another 28,000 tons of jet fuel dispatched from Greece to southern Spain, presumably for Moron Air Base, a major staging base for U.S. Air Force (USAF) tankers.[145] Further indicators of what was to come included a repositioning of the Air Force's C-17 airlifters, a standing down of Air Force heavy bombers to complete needed repairs and modifications, a recall of tanker aircraft from test programs, and marshaling key personnel, all of

---

[145] Michael Smith, "Attack 'Could Come This Weekend,'" *London Daily Telegraph*, September 15, 2001.

which took place within the first week after the attacks.[146] Also within a week of the attacks, the Department of Defense quietly asked a number of contractors to help quickly replenish depleted war reserves by accelerating their production of vital war materiel, notably the GBU-31 JDAM, advising them not to worry about contractual and other details, which would be properly attended to in due course.[147] Another need identified early entailed acquiring an enhanced surge capability for prolonged combat operations, as well as improving mission-capable rates in some flying units, which had been as low as 50 percent, to nearly 90 percent through an increased provision of spare parts and an accelerated maintenance schedule unhindered by training or exercise pressures.[148] Alongside these developments, an unprecedented clampdown was imposed on all reporting of U.S. military activity. When media representatives complained at a Pentagon press conference about the scarcity of information about that activity, Secretary Rumsfeld replied almost gleefully: "Good!"[149]

U.S. and British combat aircraft were already deployed in substantial numbers in Saudi Arabia and Kuwait and at Incirlik Air Base, Turkey, in support of Operations Northern and Southern Watch over Iraq. The United States also maintained prepositioned equipment in Qatar, Bahrain, and Oman. On September 19, President Bush ordered two dozen heavy bombers and tankers moved forward to the Indian Ocean island of Diego Garcia, which had been made available by Great Britain, to put the aircraft within easier operating reach of Afghanistan. The deployment order included B-52s from the 5th Bomb Wing at Minot AFB, North Dakota, and the 917th Bomb Wing of the Air Force Reserve Command at Barksdale AFB, Louisi-

---

[146] David A. Fulghum and Robert Wall, "Military Aids Inquiry, Plans for Retribution," *Aviation Week and Space Technology*, September 17, 2001, p. 57.

[147] Vago Muradian, "DoD Asks Industry to Prepare for Surge; Focus on Precision Munitions, Spares," *Defense Daily*, September 17, 2001.

[148] David A. Fulghum, "Pentagon Anticipates No Shopping Spree," *Aviation Week and Space Technology*, September 24, 2001, p. 45.

[149] Dave Moniz, "In New Type of War, Public Will Receive Little News," *USA Today*, September 19, 2001.

ana, and B-1B bombers from the 28th Bomb Wing at Ellsworth AFB, South Dakota, and the 366th Wing at Mountain Home AFB, Idaho.[150] That initial order issued to the Air Force and Navy reportedly included a goal of having those aircraft ready for combat employment by September 24.[151] On September 21, Rumsfeld signed a second deployment order dispatching an additional 100 U.S. combat and combat-support aircraft to the region, adding to the 175 that were already in place there. That second order included U-2 and RC-135 Rivet Joint ISR aircraft.

As for naval assets, two aircraft carriers, USS *Carl Vinson* and USS *Enterprise*, were already operating on station in the AOR with their embarked air wings ready for action, with a third carrier battle group led by USS *Theodore Roosevelt* ordered to deploy from its home port of Norfolk, Virginia, to the AOR on September 18. The latter group included USS *Bataan*, an amphibious assault ship carrying the 26th Marine Expeditionary Unit consisting of 2,100 marines with organic AH-1 Cobra attack helicopters and AV-8B Harrier strike fighters, amphibious assault vehicles, and artillery. It also included two cruisers, a destroyer, a frigate, and two attack submarines, making in all a 14-ship package with more than 15,000 sailors and marines, more or less representative of the composition of the other carrier battle groups.[152] At the same time, the carrier USS *Kitty Hawk* departed for the AOR from her home port of Yokosuka, Japan, without her full air wing complement to provide what came to be referred to as a sea-based "lily pad" from which U.S. SOF teams would be staged into Afghanistan. To free up her flight and hangar decks to make room for a variety of SOF helicopters, *Kitty Hawk* carried only eight strike fighters from her air wing of more than 50.[153] She would

---

[150] Eric Schmitt and Michael R. Gordon, "U.S. Dispatches Ground Troops and Top Officer," *New York Times*, September 21, 2001.

[151] Elliott, "'We Will Not Fail.'"

[152] Craig Timberg, "Anxiety, Uncertainty at Norfolk Station," *Washington Post*, September 19, 2001.

[153] Rebecca Grant, "An Air War Like No Other," *Air Force Magazine*, November 2002, p. 33.

not arrive on station until October 13. By October 1, however, *Carl Vinson* and *Enterprise* were in position to begin strike operations, and USS *Theodore Roosevelt* was expected to join them within a week.

With respect to ground-force movements, within the first week after the attacks, the Department of Defense issued a warning order signed by Secretary Rumsfeld to the XVIII Airborne Corps, which consisted of the 82nd Airborne Division, the 101st Airborne Division, the 3rd Infantry Division, and the 10th Mountain Division.[154] That order represented the leading edge of what was soon to become the largest American ground-force mobilization since the 1991 Persian Gulf War. Concurrently, CENTCOM's ongoing Bright Star joint training exercise with Egypt, previously slated for September, was used to move additional U.S. ground forces into Egypt. These would remain in the region long after the exercise was completed, the reported goal being to pre-position more supplies, aircraft, and troops in Saudi Arabia, Bahrain, Kuwait, and Diego Garcia. Army Special Forces Command at Fort Bragg, North Carolina, also received a deployment order, and planning was afoot to send CSAR teams to several former Soviet republics in Central Asia. Not surprisingly, there was no reporting whatever up to that point about Navy SEAL (sea–air–land) special warfare activity. The most capable U.S. special operations team for going after top al Qaeda leaders, however, was presumed by many to be the Navy's Special Warfare Development Group, formerly known as SEAL Team Six.[155]

President Bush's coalition-building efforts paid clear dividends, albeit some on the installment plan, as Great Britain provided basing support at Diego Garcia, France granted the United States the use of its large base at Djibouti, and Oman was finally expected to offer up its air base on Masirah island. As for the more delicate case of Saudi Arabia, CENTCOM remained intent on conducting the impending air war from its new CAOC at Prince Sultan Air Base, and Saudi offi-

---

154 Thomas E. Ricks, "Pentagon Issues Order to Elite Units in Infantry," *Washington Post*, September 17, 2001.

155 Reported in Michael Smith, "U.S. Aims to Take Vital Afghan Air Base," *London Daily Telegraph*, September 25, 2001.

cials were said finally to have approved that use and also to have consented to look the other way if some Enduring Freedom missions were flown from Saudi runways, so long as Washington did not formally request permission to operate from Saudi bases or announce its use of those bases.[156]

With respect to the equally delicate case of Pakistan, President Musharraf had agreed early on to allow U.S. transit of Pakistani airspace. He also approved a limited U.S. ground presence in Pakistan to support special operations forays into Afghanistan and offered to upgrade Pakistani medical facilities to help handle any friendly casualties, with the planned deployment to be kept as austere as possible to maintain a low profile and footprint. Yet as the planning for Operation Enduring Freedom unfolded, bargaining continued with Pakistan over the issue of base access. It was clear from the outset at CENTCOM that Pakistani basing support would be critical for providing a staging point for fuel resupply into Afghanistan, first by air and eventually by overland shipment once a substantial part of the country was secured by U.S. and friendly indigenous Afghan ground forces. It also was hoped that Pakistan would host Air Force tanker and transport aircraft on an as-needed basis.[157] The breakthrough finally came on September 18, when the airport at the Pakistani capital of Islamabad was closed for two hours to allow the initial wave of U.S. military transport aircraft to land.[158] After that, the quiet flow of U.S. assets into Pakistan by military airlift became a routine activity.

In addition, it soon became clear that any sustained operations over Afghanistan would require airspace transit approval and basing support not only from Pakistan, but also from the former Soviet Central Asian republics along Afghanistan's northern frontier. From the

[156] Greg Jaffe, "As More Forces Head to Region, U.S. Seeks Greater Access to Bases Ringing Afghanistan," *Wall Street Journal*, September 24, 2001.

[157] David A. Fulghum and Robert Wall, "U.S. To Move First, Plan Details Later," *Aviation Week and Space Technology*," September 24, 2001, p. 40.

[158] Tim Butcher, "British Muscle and U.S. Jets Arrive in Jittery Islamabad," *London Daily Telegraph*, September 19, 2001.

very start of their planning, administration officials had been busily investigating the possible availability of more than 30 bases in the region, including some in Uzbekistan, Tajikistan, Turkmenistan, Kazakhstan, and Kyrgyzstan.[159] The CIA had already been operating its Predator UAVs over Afghanistan from a site in Uzbekistan for more than a year, and there were reports that the Air Force as well had been flying Predators from the region in search of bin Laden's hideouts. Those, however, were covert activities conducted beneath public scrutiny.[160] What was needed was an arrangement that would permit more overt, if still low-profile, operations.

There had been early speculation that the United States would seek to operate Air Force F-15Es from Uzbekistan and to put CSAR teams into Tajikistan, with F-16s also operating occasionally out of Tajik airfields, but only from remote locations and for short periods, thus allowing Tajik authorities to deny their presence. The Air Force also wanted access to Tajik airfields to provide readily available landing options in case of inflight emergencies or situations involving aircraft battle damage that might require a prompt precautionary landing.[161] Yet as September moved toward its third week, not a single Central Asian state had yet agreed even to approve a U.S. CSAR presence to support a bombing effort in the north, let alone grant its permission for the coalition to conduct offensive strike operations from its territory. (It was long-standing U.S. practice that no aerial attacks would be approved without an adequate CSAR capability in place and ready to act on immediate notice if necessary.)

At long last, an agreement in principle was reached with Uzbekistan and Tajikistan on September 21 that would permit American SOF units to operate from their territory. The next day, Pentagon officials disclosed that U.S. CSAR aircraft would "probably" operate out of Uzbekistan, but that no combat aircraft had yet been deployed

---

[159] Michael Evans, "U.S. Plans for Battle on Multiple Fronts," *London Times*, October 1, 2001.

[160] Woodward, p. 77.

[161] Rowan Scarborough, "Intercepts Foretold of 'Big Attack,'" *Washington Times*, September 22, 2001.

there.[162] The first U.S. aircraft arrived in Uzbekistan that night. Earlier that same day, President Imamali Rakhmonov of Tajikistan said that his government had affirmed its "willingness to cooperate with the international community, including the U.S. government, in the fight against international terrorism." The Russian news agency Interfax concurrently reported that two U.S. C-130s had arrived at a former Soviet air base near the Uzbek capital of Tashkent and unloaded equipment and approximately 100 U.S. military personnel, as Pentagon officials confirmed that the United States had begun deploying assets to Tajikistan and Uzbekistan.[163]

Less than a week before Operation Enduring Freedom commenced, more than 1,000 troops of the U.S. Army's 10th Mountain Division departed for Uzbekistan and Tajikistan, bringing the total U.S. fielded force in the region to more than 30,000 personnel.[164] It also was also reported that six EC-130E Commando Solo aircraft of the Air National Guard's 193rd Special Operations Wing based in Harrisburg, Pennsylvania, had deployed to one of the former Soviet republics to broadcast messages into Afghanistan as a part of a growing psychological operations effort against the Taliban and al Qaeda.[165] At roughly the same time, a small contingent of Air Force Special Operations Command (AFSOC) MH-53 Pave Low helicopters intended for CSAR support made their long-awaited arrival in Uzbekistan and Pakistan. One of the many welcome features of these moves for U.S. planners was the operational security that came from placing U.S. aircraft "where CNN can't film them taking off."[166]

Much of this basing access represented a windfall by-product of the close military-to-military ties that had been cultivated by the United States with the former Soviet Central Asian republics during

---

[162] Cushman.

[163] Susan B. Glasser, "First U.S. Planes Land at Uzbek Air Base," *Washington Post,* September 23, 2001.

[164] Vernon Loeb and Thomas E. Ricks, "U.S. Sends Troops to Ex-Soviet Republics," *Washington Post,* October 3, 2001.

[165] Andrea Stone, "'Soldiers Deploy on Mental Terrain," *USA Today,* October 3, 2001.

[166] Elliott, "'We Will Not Fail.'"

the 1990s, such as a joint American and Central Asian exercise that CENTCOM had organized in the town of Osh in southern Kyrgyzstan.[167] In an important precursor development that helped facilitate this much-needed access, Uzbekistan had signed an agreement in 1995 with the United States to conduct joint military training exercises, including an invitational hosting of U.S. Army Rangers to advise the 80,000-strong Uzbek military and the reciprocal dispatching of 16 Uzbek army officers to Fort Campbell, Kentucky, and Fort Bragg, North Carolina. It became increasingly apparent in hindsight that that earlier investment of effort had played a significant role in providing the United States a new strategic foothold in a part of the world that, just a few short years earlier, would not even have been deemed friendly.

The first hint of initial clandestine operations in Afghanistan was a news report on September 23 that British Special Air Service (SAS) troops had been fired upon indiscriminately by Taliban soldiers who had been spooked by their activities near Kabul. This report portrayed the SAS forces working in concert with MI6 (British foreign intelligence) and CIA units in search of bin Laden in conjunction with Northern Alliance opposition fighters. There was a further hint of SAS troops on the ground in Afghanistan communicating with an RAF Nimrod aircraft, using state-of-the-art radios for communicating in burst transmissions lasting only seconds or less to avoid enemy interception or position location.[168] This may have represented intentional British government disinformation. It also could have been nothing more than baseless rumor-mongering, although there was indeed significant British SOF involvement in Enduring Freedom in the end.

A more authoritative report put the first insertion of a CIA paramilitary team into Afghanistan to begin coordinating with the Northern Alliance on September 26. (Northern Alliance forces were

---

[167] Thomas E. Ricks, "Former Soviet Republics Are Key to U.S. Effort," *Washington Post*, September 22, 2001.

[168] James Clark, Tony Allen-Mills, and Stephen Grey, "SAS Troops Clash with Taliban Unit Deep Inside Afghanistan," *London Sunday Times*, September 23, 2001.

said to have been already benefiting from air resupply routes from Dushanbe, Tajikistan, to a bare-base airstrip in Afghanistan north of Kabul.) That team departed Pakistan in a CIA-owned Russian Mi-17 helicopter, which crossed a 15,000-foot ridgeline at the Anjoman Pass to enter the Panjshir valley of northeastern Afghanistan. It consisted of a senior CIA officer and a group of covert operatives carrying communications gear and $3 million in $100 bills to be dispensed to opposition-group leaders. Its personnel were attached to the highly compartmented Special Activities Division of the CIA's Directorate of Operations. The team's mission was to lay the groundwork for a subsequent insertion of U.S. SOF cells to provide target location and designation for U.S. combat aircraft. Formally designated the Northern Afghanistan Liaison Team (NALT), the unit was assigned the code-name Jawbreaker. It entered Afghanistan with minimal backup by way of provisions for being safely extracted if anything were to go wrong.[169]

In the first reported major opposition-group move against the Taliban, General Abdul Rashid Dostum claimed that his United Front had captured the strategic town of Zari on September 24 after a four-day offensive.[170] With its large Soviet-built airport, that town's seizure by the resistance could help accelerate the subsequent capture of Mazar-i-Sharif 80 miles to the north and, in the process, cut off thousands of Taliban fighters from their bases in the south. Also on the eve of Enduring Freedom's start, the Pentagon confirmed a Taliban claim that a Predator drone had gone down in Afghanistan. Secretary Rumsfeld conceded that contact with the drone had been lost, possibly as a result of a systems failure. He said that there was no reason to believe that it had been downed by hostile fire.[171]

---

[169] For the fullest available treatment of this team and its many activities during the initial months of Enduring Freedom, see Schroen.

[170] Ahmed Rashid, "Taliban in Key Defeat as Rebels Turn to Ex-King," *London Daily Telegraph*, September 25, 2001.

[171] The first U.S. drone lost was a General Atomics-built I-Gnat UAV operated by the CIA from a base in one of the Central Asian republics, also before the formal start of Operation Enduring Freedom. It went down near the Tashkurghan Pass in northern Afghanistan's

By this time, the number of U.S. aircraft in the region had grown to between 400 and 500, including 75 on each of the Navy's three aircraft carriers on station. That number included such support aircraft as tankers and electronic warfare and ISR platforms. Many dozens of Air Force combat aircraft were deployed to the Persian Gulf states of Kuwait, Saudi Arabia, and Oman; to Diego Garcia; and—in an unprecedented post–Cold War move—to the two former Soviet republics of Uzbekistan and Tajikistan where Russia still maintained thousands of troops. These included B-52s, B-1Bs, F-15Es, and F-16s, as well as E-3s and tanker and other support aircraft.[172] Concurrently, detachments from the 82nd Airborne and 101st Air Assault Divisions were reported arriving at bases in Pakistan near the border towns of Quetta and Peshawar, with U.S. fixed-wing resupply aircraft landing at a base near Tashkent, Uzbekistan, and with Northern Alliance forces moving toward Mazar-i-Sharif to open a bridgehead for American forces to follow.

As combat operations neared, the Afghan city of Kandahar, the breeding ground and capital of the ruling Taliban, fell into panic and feverish preparations for an anticipated attack, with parts of the city all but emptied as occupants fled to Pakistan or other parts of Afghanistan. Taliban forces began fortifying lines around Kabul in preparation for attack after an initial period of disarray, digging trenches and rounding up any able-bodied men. Northern Alliance spokesmen estimated that the Taliban had some 4,000 to 5,000 men, including many Pakistanis and Arabs, defending Kabul.[173] Through all of this and more, the stage was finally set for a sweeping allied combat operation to commence imminently that would eliminate al Qaeda's foothold in Afghanistan and drive the Taliban from power.

Samangan province near the Uzbek border. (David A. Fulghum, "Afghanistan Crash Reveals U.S. Intel Operation," *Aviation Week and Space Technology*, October 1, 2001, p. 28.)

[172] Ricks, "Warplanes Begin Deploying to Gulf, Central Asia."

[173] Peter Baker, "Taliban Preparing Capital for War," *Washington Post*, October 4, 2001.

CHAPTER THREE

The United States Strikes Back

When the planning for Operation Enduring Freedom first began even before the smoke from September 11 had fully cleared, CENTCOM, by the admission of its own leaders, knew little of a military nature about Afghanistan. Before that time, its attention had been focused elsewhere in Southwest Asia, most notably toward Operation Southern Watch (OSW) and associated Iraq-related concerns. As then–Lieutenant General Charles Wald, the first Combined Force Air Component Commander (CFACC) for Enduring Freedom, later recalled, "we didn't know much" about the enemy going into the planning process.[1] Once tasked to come up with a plan against the Taliban and al Qaeda, however, those on the CENTCOM and U.S. Central Command Air Forces (CENTAF) staffs who bore the main force mobilization, target development, and weaponeering responsibilities did the needed homework in the shortest possible time. As a result, within just eight days after the CAOC was put on a war footing at Prince Sultan Air Base in Saudi Arabia on September 18, General Wald had a more than sufficiently accurate picture of Afghanistan for confident air operations planning. As a result, early predictions that it would take 60 to 90 days, at a minimum, to preposition the needed equipment and plan and train for any joint-force

---

[1] "Notes from NDIA's 2002 Space Policy and Architecture Symposium, February 26–27, Falls Church, Virginia," *Inside the Air Force*, March 1, 2002.

campaign were belied by the start of combat operations on October 7, less than a month after the terrorist attacks occurred.[2]

In an important sense, the first round in the war against the Taliban was diplomatic rather than military. It came in the form of Pakistan's agreement shortly after the September 11 attacks, in response to strong pressure from the United States, to sever its ties with the Afghan regime. That event deprived the Taliban of much-needed access to airlift and ground transportation, as well as to intelligence and other means of support. It also caused a serious, albeit not crippling, blow to Taliban morale. As a result, by the time the shooting started, the Taliban were already more isolated than ever from the rest of the world and were notably weakened by their loss of a major source of resupply.[3]

Three days before the onset of hostilities, Secretary of Defense Rumsfeld remarked that the war against terror would have more in common with the Cold War than with a set-piece conventional conflict like Desert Storm. He said: "If you think about it, in the Cold War it took 50 years, plus or minus. It did not involve major battles. It involved continuous pressure. It involved cooperation by a host of nations. It involved the willingness of populations in many countries to invest in it and to sustain it. It took leadership at the top in a number of countries that were willing to be principled and to be courageous and to put things at risk; and when it ended, it ended not with a bang, but through internal collapse."[4] Some of that may have been intentional disinformation aimed at misleading the enemy as to what was about to take place and about U.S. expectations with respect to Enduring Freedom. Consistent with it, other officials likewise urged people not to expect a massive bombing effort, with one Air Force general declaring: "The number of militarily significant tar-

---

[2] On those estimates, see David A. Fulghum, "War Plans, Defense Buildup Take Shape," *Aviation Week and Space Technology*, September 17, 2001, p. 36.

[3] This point is developed in Kenneth M. Pollack, *The Threatening Storm: The Case for Invading Iraq*, New York: Random House, 2002, pp. 299–300.

[4] Michael Duffy, "War on All Fronts," *Time*, October 15, 2001.

gets [in Afghanistan] you can count on your fingers and toes."[5] That statement was later belied by what actually occurred as the bombing effort unfolded.

The Operational Setting

Afghanistan, roughly the size of Texas, is an ethnically diverse country with a primitive infrastructure that has been ravaged by more than two decades of fighting. It was described by one observer as "a poverty-stricken charnel house that is ruled by illiterate gunmen, brutish warlords, and superstitious mullahs."[6] The country's population consists of around 25 million people, of whom perhaps 20 percent, or five million, in September 2002 were refugees in Pakistan, Iran, and other countries. Pashtuns represent a plurality of the population, with some claiming a majority. Tajiks, at 25 percent, are the next largest ethnic group, with Hazaras at perhaps 9 percent, Uzbeks at perhaps 6 percent, and smaller numbers of Aimaks, Turkmen, and Baloch making up the rest. Most of these inhabitants speak either Pashto or an Afghan variant of Farsi called Dari, with the remainder speaking one of more than 30 additional splinter languages. In many respects, the Afghan scene today still resembles the setting into which imperial British forces sought, unsuccessfully, to invade and colonize two centuries ago. Many of the country's residents continue to subsist in near-15th-century conditions.

Afghanistan also features some of the most rugged and forbidding terrain anywhere in the world, dominated by deep valleys surrounded by high mountain ranges and beset by hard winters with blowing snow that makes helicopter operations all but impossible. Landlocked and situated almost 400 miles from the nearest sea at its southernmost border, the country has no electrical power grid to speak of; no major bridges, military bases, or highways; and few

---

[5] Fulghum, "Afghanistan Crash Reveals U.S. Intel Operation," p. 28.

[6] Jon Lee Anderson, p. 56.

command-and-control links of any note. Its 12,000 miles of road are mostly unpaved. Thanks to the nine-year Soviet occupation during the 1980s, Afghanistan also is one of the most heavily mined places anywhere in the world, with an estimated 10 million land mines still planted all over the country, making a serious hazard both to friendly land forces and to the indigenous population.[7]

The Taliban regime assumed power in 1996 after the resistance forces to the Soviet occupation collapsed into internecine fighting in the years that followed the Soviet withdrawal in 1989. When Operation Enduring Freedom began on October 7, 2001, that regime controlled more than 90 percent of the country. The Taliban army, such as it was, comprised an estimated 45,000 troops, including some 12,000 foreigners consisting of Pakistanis, Uzbeks, Arabs, and others.[8] Its equipment inventory was a hodge-podge of around 100 obsolete T-55 and T-62 tanks and other vehicles inherited from the failed Soviet occupation. This ragtag arsenal also included Soviet-made Katyusha rockets and some 80 armed helicopters. It was supplemented by newer weapons, mostly automatic rifles, machine guns, and mortars that had been supplied by Osama bin Laden and other wealthy Saudi supporters, along with a few Scud short-range conventional ballistic missiles.

The Taliban's air and air defense forces were no less rudimentary. The former consisted of fewer than 50 MiG-21 and Su-22 fighter aircraft, many out of service, that had been captured from defeated post–Soviet Afghan factions in 1996. As for the latter, the Taliban's would-be integrated air defense system (IADS) was neither integrated nor a "system" worthy of the name. Some reports said that it included three SA-3 surface-to-air missile (SAM) sites but that their

---

[7] In 2001, 16 UN employees were killed and 20 more injured while participating in tightly disciplined mine-clearing operations. The year before, a total of 13,542 antipersonnel mines and 636 antitank mines had been removed by such operations. Roughly one-third of the 68,000 Soviet combat casualties in Afghanistan were caused by land mines. (Thomas E. Ricks, "Land Mines, Aging Missiles Pose Threat," *Washington Post*, September 25, 2001.)

[8] Molly Moore and Kamran Khan, "Afghanistan: A Nightmare Battlefield," *Washington Post*, September 17, 2001, and Paul Watson and Norman Kempster, "Taliban Will Unravel If Key Players Gone, Experts Say," *Los Angeles Times*, September 20, 2001.

crews lacked the needed technical competence to keep them in operationally usable condition.[9] The Taliban's surface-to-air weapons inventory was also known to include man-portable SA-7 infrared SAMs, 300 to 550 antiaircraft artillery (AAA) guns of calibers up to 100mm, and an undetermined number of U.S.-made Stinger shoulder-fired infrared SAMs left over from the original stock of around 1,000 that had been provided to the mujaheddin by the United States during the last years of the Soviet occupation. An estimated 100 to 200 of these weapons were thought to remain unused and in Taliban hands.[10]

This air defense threat, although modest in the extreme, was not entirely inconsequential from a combat mission planner's perspective. Earlier in 2000, a number of Uzbek MiG-29s, Su-17s, and Su-24s had conducted bombing forays into Afghanistan in support of the Northern Alliance, with one Su-24 having reportedly been downed by Taliban fire.[11] Even in the worst case, however, the Taliban's air defense posture presented a far less imposing threat than what U.S. and allied fighter aircrews had routinely faced for years over Iraq in connection with their enforcement of the northern and southern no-fly zones. As for the Taliban's fighter force, as many as 40 Taliban pilots were believed capable of getting MiG-21s and Su-22s into the air.[12] However, CENTCOM's main concern over those aircraft was not the traditional challenge they represented, which was miniscule, but rather the possibility that they might be loaded with explosives and flown on suicide missions into eventual U.S. ground encampments.

---

[9] Fulghum, "Afghanistan Crash Reveals U.S. Intel Operation."

[10] This weapon is effective out to a slant range of around 10,000 feet, but it is aimed easily only during daylight, since visual target acquisition is required to get a quick infrared seeker lock. Of those presumed to remain in the Taliban's possession, most at the start of Enduring Freedom were 13 or more years old and may have been inoperable, since their battery packs have fairly short life spans.

[11] Paul Lewis, "Russia Opens Way for U.S. Attack," *Flight International*, October 2–8, 2001, p. 11.

[12] Conversation with Lieutenant General Charles F. Wald, USAF, Headquarters United States Air Force, Washington, D.C., May 15, 2002.

Although CENTCOM may have sought to retain an element of tactical surprise with respect to the exact timing of the campaign's start, ample preattack warning was provided by the Bush administration, with one senior official declaring three days before the initial strikes that the campaign would involve "a very precise effort over several days to take out the elements of Taliban control." Putative targets to be struck in that endeavor were said to include enemy airfields, training camps, headquarters facilities, and materiel, with a view toward achieving "a nearly instantaneous shift in the balance of power" as key Taliban elements either deserted or changed sides and joined up with indigenous Afghan opposition groups.[13] Moreover, shortly before the bombing began, Vice President Dick Cheney phoned numerous world leaders, including Russia's Vladimir Putin, Israel's Ariel Sharon, Egypt's Hosni Mubarak, and Uzbekistan's Islam Karimov, to inform them that operations against the Taliban and al Qaeda would be commencing very shortly. Administration sources conceded up front that the initial attacks might not succeed in eliminating bin Laden or the Taliban leader, Mullah Mohammed Omar.

Opening Moves

Operation Enduring Freedom began under clear skies on the night of October 7 against preplanned targets in and around Herat, Shindand, Shibarghan, Mazar-i-Sharif, and the southern Taliban stronghold area of Kandahar (see Figure 3.1). As the air war against the Taliban and al Qaeda got under way, President Bush declared that "today we focus on Afghanistan, but the battle is broader. Every nation has a choice to make. In this conflict, there is no neutral ground."[14] The attacks were carried out by five Air Force B-1B and 10 B-52 heavy

---

[13] Neil King, Jr., and Greg Jaffe, "U.S. Plans to Use a Bombing Campaign to End Taliban Protection of bin Laden," *Wall Street Journal,* October 5, 2001.

[14] Jeanne Cummings and Neil King, Jr., "Military Response by U.S. Is Broader Than Plan Initially Proposed to Bush," *Wall Street Journal,* October 8, 2001.

Figure 3.1
Afghan Operating Area

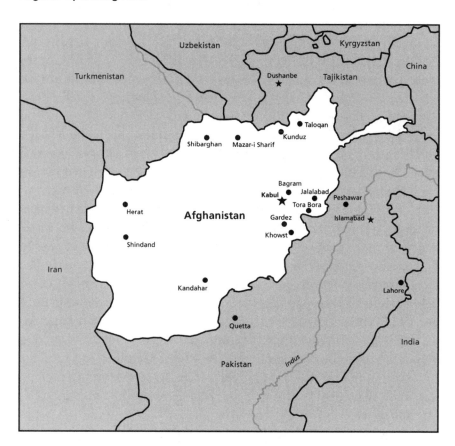

bombers operating out of Diego Garcia in the Indian Ocean and by 25 Navy F-14 and F/A-18 fighters launched from USS *Enterprise* and USS *Carl Vinson* in the North Arabian Sea. Two Air Force B-2 stealth bombers from Whiteman AFB, Missouri, also participated in the opening-night attacks, each carrying 16 2,000-lb satellite-aided GBU-31 Joint Direct Attack Munitions (JDAMs) directed against Taliban early warning radars and military headquarters buildings.[15]

---

[15] The JDAM's fuse can be selected for either an air burst or a penetrating mode.

The attack aircraft were supported by accompanying F-14 and F/A-18 fighter sweeps and by electronic jamming of enemy radar and communications transmissions by Navy EA-6Bs.[16] In addition, a total of 50 Tomahawk land-attack missiles (TLAMs) were fired in the first wave against fixed high-priority targets by two Aegis destroyers, USS *McFaul* and USS *John Paul Jones*; a Spruance-class destroyer, USS *O'Brien*; and an Aegis cruiser, USS *Philippine Sea*; as well as two U.S. and British nuclear attack submarines.

H-hour for those attacks was 9:00 p.m. local time. The heaviest bombing that night by far was conducted by Air Force B-52s, which rained both JDAMs and hundreds of 500-lb Mk 82 unguided bombs on al Qaeda terrorist training camps in the valleys of eastern Afghanistan. For their part, strikes from the Navy's carriers involved distances to target of more than 600 nautical miles, with an average sortie length of more than four and a half hours and a minimum of two in-flight refuelings per fighter each way to complete the mission. The first wave was launched at 6:30 p.m. local time, two and a half hours before the initial weapon impacts. Navy fighters carried laser-guided bombs (LGBs), JDAMs, the AGM-84 SLAM-ER (Standoff Land Attack Missile—Extended Range), and the AGM-154 JSOW (Joint Standoff Weapon), the last of which had been used in combat for the first time only recently before in Iraq in early 2001 during an OSW mission.[17] Britain's Royal Air Force (RAF) provided Tristar and VC-10 tankers to help supplement Air Force KC-135s and KC-10s in providing inflight refueling for the Navy fighters.[18]

Thanks to the prior hard work done by the U.S. diplomatic and political-military communities in securing the needed approval, the attacking aircraft were able to transit Pakistani airspace en route to their targets. In announcing the campaign's start, President Bush said: "On my orders, the United States military has begun strikes.

---

[16] Thomas E. Ricks and Vernon Loeb, "Initial Aim Is Hitting Taliban Defenses," *Washington Post*, October 8, 2001.

[17] Steve Vogel, "'They Said No. This Is Our Answer,'" *Washington Post*, October 8, 2001.

[18] Michael Evans, "U.S. Troops and Helicopters Set for Ground War," *London Times*, October 11, 2001.

These carefully targeted actions are designed to disrupt the use of Afghanistan as a terrorist base of operations and to attack the military capability of the Taliban regime."[19] To head off any false hopes of instant gratification, the president further cautioned that victory would not come immediately or easily but rather would accrue through "the patient accumulation of successes."[20]

Within hours of the initial air strikes, bin Laden appeared in a videotaped worldwide broadcast via the Arab al-Jazeera television station praising the September 11 attacks and taunting the United States, which bin Laden said had been "struck by Almighty God in one of its vital organs."[21] All signs indicated that the videotape had been prepared in advance, with bin Laden anticipating the allied attacks and aiming to extract the maximum propaganda value from them. As part of a calculated effort to help offset that anticipated propaganda offensive, two C-17s flying from Ramstein Air Base, Germany, dropped 34,400 packets of food and medical supplies within 45 minutes after the first bombs hit their targets to provide interim sustenance for the thousands of refugees who were expected to flee Afghan cities during the bombing. Leaflets and transistor radios preset to a station explaining the intent of the air attacks were later similarly air-dropped by C-17s.

Some of the attacks on opening night were aimed at targets in and around Kandahar, including the Taliban's national headquarters and the local airport's radar facilities.[22] Others engaged a Taliban tank concentration and the headquarters of two Taliban divisions near the northern city of Mazar-i-Sharif, where General Dostum and a number of his fighters were doing battle against Taliban forces. Having been given advance notice of the campaign's impending start,

---

[19] Patrick E. Tyler, "U.S. and Britain Strike Afghanistan, Aiming at Bases and Terrorist Camps; Bush Warns 'Taliban Will Pay a Price,'" *New York Times*, October 8, 2001.

[20] "The Next Phase," *The Economist*, October 13, 2001, p. 13.

[21] John F. Burns, "Bin Laden Taunts U.S. and Praises Hijackers," *New York Times*, October 8, 2001.

[22] Peter Baker, "Kabul and Kandahar Hit in Attacks Through the Night," *Washington Post*, October 8, 2001.

opposition-group elements commenced artillery fire concurrently with the first air attacks on Taliban positions around the Bagram Air Base located 35 miles north of Kabul. (Bagram had not been used for conducting flight operations since 1999, and it would remain unusable by allied forces as long as the Taliban occupied the high ground overlooking it.) The Taliban made themselves easy targets by returning to Bagram in trucks at night to stay close to the Northern Alliance front line. Northern Alliance fighters soon took control of Bagram. Five days earlier, they had already begun installing a landing strip in Golbahar not far from Bagram, with an estimated completion of the job within just a day or two.

Although it was reported at first that electrical power had been cut off in Kabul for several hours during the first night, it later turned out that CENTCOM had *not* attacked the electrical power grid in Afghanistan's capital.[23] Other targets struck the first night included Taliban Scud missile launchers, which the Bush administration feared might be used against Pakistan.[24] Bomb detonations were also reported near Jalalabad close to Afghanistan's eastern border with Pakistan, the site of a bin Laden training camp located 12 miles south of the city. Although the latter attacks served to eliminate some important enemy infrastructure, they otherwise had no immediate operational effect, since it was known that al Qaeda's training bases had been empty for several weeks and since the Taliban had vacated their arms depots and government headquarters and dispersed their military hardware in the immediate wake of the September 11 attacks. Pakistani intelligence reported that bin Laden and his family members had moved to deeper hiding inside Afghanistan.

The goal of the initial attacks was to establish uncontested control of the air over Afghanistan by neutralizing the Taliban's air defenses, which were alerted and ready, to the limited extent of their

---

[23] Rowan Scarborough, "U.S. Gunship Attacks Taliban Troops," *Washington Times*, October 16, 2001.

[24] Michael Hirsh and John Barry, "Behind America's Attack on Afghanistan," *Newsweek*, October 7, 2001.

capabilities, on October 7.[25] Beyond that, the declared intent of CENTCOM's air component commander, General Wald, was to disrupt and destroy terrorist activities and to establish the needed conditions for any desired future allied military action.[26] In that respect, General Wald's mission statement was to the point and read as follows: "On order, CFACC provides air support for friendly forces working with the Northern Alliance and other opposition forces in order to defeat hostile Taliban and al Qaeda forces and set the conditions for regime removal and long-term regional stability."[27]

An administration spokesman later remarked that the first night's bombing had not been expressly intended to kill bin Laden. "The only objectives," the spokesman said, "were to kill obvious things out in the open [so as] to allow us to fly with impunity day and night, when we'll work on harder targets."[28] The morning after the initial attacks, Secretary Rumsfeld said that bin Laden had not been a specific target but that the bombing had been meant "to create conditions for sustained operations" against his organization.[29] Rumsfeld further said that an associated goal of the attacks was to "create conditions for sustained antiterrorist and humanitarian relief operations in Afghanistan," which "requires that, among other things, we first remove the threat from air defenses and from Taliban aircraft."[30]

Other administration officials, however, suggested later that one of the campaign's early goals had indeed been to scare bin Laden and his aides out of hiding, as well as to gather as much intelligence as

---

[25] Conversation with Lieutenant General Charles F. Wald, USAF, Headquarters United States Air Force, Washington, D.C., May 15, 2002.

[26] Conversation with Major General David A. Deptula, USAF, Director of Plans and Programs, Air Combat Command, Langley AFB, Virginia, June 28, 2002.

[27] Lieutenant General Charles F. Wald, USAF, "Operation Enduring Freedom: The CFACC Viewpoint," briefing to the Air Combat Command (ACC) Commanders' Conference, 2002.

[28] Rowan Scarborough, "Pentagon Will Not Rush Manhunt," *Washington Times*, October 9, 2001.

[29] Peter Baker, "Kabul and Kandahar Hit in Attacks Through the Night."

[30] Bill Gertz, "Precision Bombing Is the Weapon of Choice," *Washington Times*, October 8, 2001.

possible regarding their whereabouts, to insert SOF into Afghanistan poised to move in on bin Laden quickly if he could be located, and to reassure Muslim leaders worldwide that American war aims were limited.[31] With respect to enemy leadership as an intended target, it was not by happenstance that the Taliban ruler, Mullah Omar, was believed to have only narrowly escaped being killed in the first night's bombing. Omar reportedly vacated his compound in Kandahar and sought shelter in a nearby irrigation tunnel just minutes before his house was attacked.[32] Reports from Kandahar later indicated that his residence at the edge of town had been destroyed, even though he and bin Laden remained alive.

Some of the aircrews participating on the first night reported encountering sporadic AAA and man-portable infrared SAM fire. However, no Taliban aircraft took to the air to oppose the U.S. attacks. In fact, no enemy fighters ever got airborne at any time during the entire war. To all intents and purposes, the United States achieved uncontested control of the air over Afghanistan above 20,000 feet almost immediately during the war's earliest days. Several aircrews reported that they had been fired on in the Kandahar region by ZSU-23/4, 57mm, and 100mm AAA.[33] (The 57mm rounds would all fizzle out well below the normal operating altitude of the fighters, although on occasion a single 100mm shell would be seen to detonate overhead if a jet momentarily dipped below 20,000 feet.) Despite that, however, the absence of a significant enemy IADS enabled the use of smaller strike packages than those employed during

---

[31] Duffy.

[32] Douglas Frantz, "Murky Picture Emerges of Life Under Bombardment," *New York Times,* October 11, 2001.

[33] Also, on an least one occasion, an F-15E crew on a night mission over Kabul sometime after October 17 (the first day that F-15Es took part in the war) had to dodge a SAM that had been fired into the air, probably without radar guidance, in its direction. The launch of the missile revealed the SAM site's position, and the F-15E crew rolled in on it and destroyed the site with a 500-lb GBU-12 LGB. (Mark Bowden, "The Kabul-Ki Dance," *The Atlantic Monthly,* November 2002, p. 76.)

previous conflicts because fewer support aircraft were needed for defense suppression.[34]

After all aircraft had recovered safely, General Myers announced that the initial attacks had hit 31 targets inside Afghanistan, including early warning radars, ground forces, command-and-control facilities, al Qaeda infrastructure, and Taliban airfields and aircraft. Most of the 31 targets struck during the first night, which featured around 275 individual weapon aim points, were in the categories of air defense assets and leadership facilities. The British chief of the Defense Staff, Admiral Sir Michael Boyce, added that of those 31 targets, all were military installations, 23 of which had been located in remote areas.[35] General Myers suggested that the relatively small number of targets attacked the first night should not be taken one way or another as a reflection on the operation's success. "Don't assume," he said, "that fewer numbers means less effort or effectiveness."[36]

Concurrently during the night of October 7, several Air Force C-17s arrived at Khanabad Air Base outside Karshi in Uzbekistan, some 100 miles north of the Afghan border. Those aircraft delivered several Air Force HH-60 Blackhawk helicopters for possible use in CSAR missions. AFSOC MH-60G Pave Hawk helicopters capable of carrying up to 10 troops were also flown into Uzbekistan to support possible CSAR and other SOF operations. Before Secretary Rumsfeld's visit to Central Asia several days previously, a U.S. Special Operations Command (SOCOM) contingent from MacDill AFB, Florida, had arrived in two C-130s at Tuzel Air Base outside Tashkent, the Uzbek capital, and later had flown on to Khanabad after con-

---

[34] The EA-6B used its USQ-113 jammer to disrupt Taliban communications. VAQ-137, the EA-6B squadron embarked in USS *Theodore Roosevelt*, was the first such squadron to deploy and operate in combat with night-vision goggles (NVGs).

[35] Bill Gertz, "Afghanistan Hits Will Continue Until Taliban Is Ousted," *Washington Times*, October 9, 2001.

[36] Dan Balz, "U.S. Strikes Again at Afghan Targets; Americans Told to Be Alert to Attacks," *Washington Post*, October 9, 2001. Myers said that al Qaeda camps were hit because they have an "inherent great training capability." He also said that they were not "totally empty."

sulting with Uzbek officials.[37] Efforts were immediately undertaken to improve the Khanabad airport, including the installation of runway lights, to prepare it for more intensive operations yet to come. Earlier, SOCOM planners had considered operating out of the more modern airfield at Samarkand, but they finally settled on Karshi-Khanabad to keep any U.S. operations deconflicted from civilian traffic, since Samarkand was a busy tourist and cultural attraction and since the United States had promised the Uzbek government that it would maintain the smallest possible profile and footprint.

The second day of combat over Afghanistan saw only about half the number of aircraft that had been committed to bombing missions the first night. B-2s again flew straight to Afghanistan nonstop from the United States. Attacks again began at night but this time continued on into daylight hours, indicating increased confidence at CENTCOM that the Taliban's minimal air defenses had been largely neutralized. Secretary Rumsfeld reported continued progress toward disabling Taliban airfields and "eliminating the air defense sites."[38] In fact, they had been negated, to all intents and purposes, "within the first fifteen minutes or so," according to General Wald.[39] Because of the exacting battle-damage assessment (BDA) reporting rules that had been insisted upon by CENTCOM's director of intelligence, however, it took the Defense Department several days to declare with full confidence that the high-altitude threat had been neutralized. At least three SAM sites accordingly were reattacked on the third day to provide the needed BDA confirmation that they had indeed been destroyed.[40] In a tacit confirmation of the effects of the BDA rules, Secretary Rumsfeld said: "I'm confident they [the Taliban] have both

---

[37] C. J. Chivers, "Second Wave of Troops Arrives in Uzbekistan," *New York Times*, October 8, 2001.

[38] Patrick E. Tyler, "After a Lull, Dawn Bombing Caps Night of Heavy Strikes," *New York Times*, October 9, 2001.

[39] Conversation with Lieutenant General Charles F. Wald, USAF, Headquarters United States Air Force, Washington, D.C., May 15, 2002.

[40] Robert Wall, "Taliban Air Defenses Target U.S. Weakness," *Aviation Week and Space Technology*, October 15, 2001, p. 36.

aircraft and helicopters that we've not found, that we don't know exist. We also know there are some ... that we have not gotten yet."[41]

Also because of the strict BDA rules, General Myers reported to the president's war council that 16 of the 35 targets attacked on the second day needed to be evaluated and possibly revisited. Most of the airfields had been neutralized by that time. One SA-3 site was believed to be still intact but not threatening.[42] All the same, Rumsfeld told a press conference that "we're finding that some of the targets we hit need to be rehit."[43] Indeed, it was not until October 25 that Pentagon officials finally declared that the campaign had effectively taken out the Taliban's air defenses and severed most of their communications. General Myers stated that "success is yet to be determined," but that the campaign was "proceeding according to . . . plan."[44]

From the first night of the war, the CAOC's plan had been to make Afghanistan's airfields unusable but, in the interest of preserving core infrastructure for future use once the Taliban were defeated, not to render them completely irreparable. However, because of the attrition-based perspective of CENTCOM's intelligence directorate and associated BDA rules that could only be satisfied by satellite photography regardless of other sources of confirmation, seven days of "aircraft plinking" ensued whereby CENTCOM directed the CAOC to destroy every military aircraft and helicopter in Afghanistan, even though the coalition had achieved the desired effect of uncontested air control almost from the first minutes of the campaign onward.[45] In fact, the prompt establishment of allied air dominance above 20,000 feet had allowed the early use of many other friendly aircraft over Afghanistan, including tankers, ISR platforms, airlifters, and

---

[41] Robert Wall, "Targeting, Weapon Supply Encumber Air Campaign," *Aviation Week and Space Technology*, October 22, 2001, p. 26.

[42] Woodward, p. 216.

[43] Woodward, p. 220.

[44] Eric Schmitt and Steven Lee Myers, "U.S. Steps Up Air Attack, While Defending Results of Campaign," *New York Times*, October 26, 2002.

[45] Comments on an earlier draft by Major General David A. Deptula, USAF, Director of Operations, Pacific Air Forces, Hickam AFB, Hawaii, January 24, 2004.

SOF assets, all of which enabled the overall tempo of operations to be increased. It remains unknown how many strike and strike-support sorties were wasted and how many aircrews were put at needless risk to satisfy those reporting rules.

In any event, within just a few days, General Myers reported that allied air supremacy over Afghanistan had been established. He said that the 31 targets hit the first night and the 13 struck on the second day included the destruction of a terrorist training camp called Garmabak Ghar, a SAM battery near Kandahar, an airfield in Shindand where Taliban MiG-21s and Su-22s were based, and an airfield at Mukurin in western Afghanistan. Officials said that the strikes had included the first use of a 5,000-lb bomb designed to penetrate hardened bunkers, as well as the use of cluster bombs intended to kill enemy military personnel in the open. Initial BDA suggested that 85 percent of the 31 targets attacked the first night had been damaged or destroyed. The enemy troop concentrations that also had been attacked were relatively small, numbering in the hundreds rather than thousands of Taliban soldiers.[46]

The largest attacks up to that point occurred on the campaign's third day and commenced during daylight hours for the first time. Those attacks focused on Kabul, Kandahar, and Herat. They targeted, among other things, a military academy, artillery units, and training camps. Pentagon officials reported that at least seven of bin Laden's largest and most well-equipped training camps had been destroyed as a result. Some, built by Soviet forces during the occupation, contained classrooms, prayer halls, bunkers, testing grounds, and firing ranges, as well as underground tunnels and concrete storage spaces for weapons and chemicals. It also was reported that two male relatives of Mullah Omar had been killed during these attacks. During the course of these expanded attacks, B-2s dropped satellite-aided GBU-37 5,000-lb earth penetrator weapons for the first time in combat on deeply buried leadership targets and then flew on to Diego Garcia, where their engines were kept running and their engine oil

---

[46] Bradley Graham and Dan Balz, "U.S. Controls Skies, Hunts New Targets and Encourages Anti-Taliban Forces," *Washington Post*, October 10, 2001.

was topped off, after which fresh aircrews returned the aircraft to Whiteman AFB. The jets received six inflight refuelings altogether between their takeoff at Whiteman and their initial landing at Diego Garcia.[47]

During the fifth consecutive day of bombing, mountain cave complexes harboring al Qaeda combatants and equipment were attacked for the first time with GBU-28 5,000-lb laser-guided bunker busters.[48] Imagery analysis suggested that Mullah Omar's Chevrolet Suburban may have been hit, although it was never established for sure who was in it.[49] Over the course of the first five days, B-52s and B-1Bs dropped some 500 JDAMs, 1,000 Mk 82 unguided bombs, and 50 CBU-87 cluster bombs. During the same period, 15 F-14s and F/A-18s dropped 240 JDAMs, 1,000-lb and 2,000-lb LGBs, and one BLU-109 hard-target munition.[50] Enemy AAA fire continued to be sporadic at best. There were no confirmed reports of any Stinger infrared SAMs having been fired, but concern was expressed that these weapons were being husbanded by the enemy for possible later use against U.S. helicopters.

There had been early speculation that the bombing effort would be fairly brief and would begin winding down by the end of the first week, after which it would be supplanted by a new phase of combat involving a significant ground offensive.[51] That speculation turned out to have been premature by a wide margin. On the contrary, the bombing was ramped up and remained intense for many weeks. In response to media questions as to why what was generally expected to have been an air campaign lasting only a few days was continuing for

---

[47] Alan Sipress and Molly Moore, "Pakistan Grants Airfield Use; U.S. Pounds Taliban Bunkers," *Washington Post*, October 11, 2001. One B-2 sortie, lasting 44.3 hours from takeoff to initial landing, set a new record as the longest combat mission ever flown.

[48] Bradley Graham and Vernon Loeb, "Cave Complexes Smashed by Bombs," *Washington Post*, October 12, 2001.

[49] Bradley and Loeb, "Cave Complexes Smashed by Bombs."

[50] William M. Arkin, "A Week of Air War," *Washington Post*, October 14, 2001.

[51] Thomas E. Ricks, "Next Phase to Include More Troops," *Washington Post*, October 9, 2001.

so long, a senior administration official attributed that seeming discrepancy to purposeful prior disinformation: "People may have said that, but you should put stock in what the secretary said, that we're not going to telegraph what we're doing. Those who were saying it would only go for two or three days were only focused on particular aspects of it. Rumsfeld has always said this was going to go on for a long time."[52] A week into the campaign, a *Newsweek* poll showed that public support for President Bush's handling of the war was holding steady at 88 percent.[53]

As the second week of Enduring Freedom got under way, two AC-130 gunships were committed for the first time as a part of a strike package that flew on October 15, evidently reflecting a CENTCOM belief that the AC-130's crew members could identify targets better than the faster-moving fighters. FAC-As (airborne forward air controllers) in F-14s also loitered overhead and identified targets for attack, with the AC-130 crews functioning as their own combat controllers. (No ground controllers were yet being used because, owing to continued adverse weather, CENTCOM had not yet been able to insert a SOF presence into Afghanistan.) The introduction of the AC-130, equipped with computer-aimed 105mm and 40mm cannons and a 25mm Gatling gun, reflected growing confidence at CENTCOM that the Taliban surface-to-air threat had been largely eliminated—at least at night, when the AC-130 was normally employed in combat. That aircraft was assigned targets near the Taliban stronghold of Kandahar. The same day, large secondary explosions were touched off by bombing attacks against the enemy's cave hideouts, one of which started a raging underground fire that lasted for nearly four hours.[54]

That same day, U.S. aircraft attacked 12 target complexes around Kandahar and Kabul. The attacks included five TLAMs, 10

---

[52] Vernon Loeb and Thomas E. Ricks, "Pentagon: Taliban 'Eviscerated,'" *Washington Post,* October 17, 2001.

[53] Howard Fineman, "Bush's 'Phase One,'" *Newsweek*, October 15, 2001.

[54] Thom Shanker and Steven Lee Myers, "U.S. Sends in Special Plane with Heavy Guns," *New York Times*, October 16, 2001.

Air Force bombers, and 90 Navy and Marine Corps fighters operating from all four aircraft carriers now on station in CENTCOM's AOR—USS *Enterprise, Carl Vinson, Theodore Roosevelt,* and *Kitty Hawk.*[55] The next day, a similar series of attacks was performed by 85 carrier-based fighters, five Air Force heavy bombers, and several AC-130s.[56] The combined weight of effort that was reflected in these attacks led Marine Corps Lieutenant General Gregory Newbold, the director of operations on the Joint Staff, to suggest—prematurely, as it turned out—that the Taliban's combat power had been "eviscerated."

As Operation Enduring Freedom entered its tenth day, the Taliban's foreign minister, Mullah Abdul Wakil Muttawakil, issued an appeal to senior Pakistani officials for the latter to ask for an American bombing pause while would-be Taliban "moderates" sought to persuade Omar to agree on a formula for turning over bin Laden. That appeal suggested a split in the Taliban leadership. Muttawakil's presence in Pakistan while Secretary of State Powell was paying a one-day visit there may have been a tacit sign of the bombing's growing effectiveness on the Taliban. His appeal was apparently not authorized by Omar, and Muttawakil was not thought to be in Omar's innermost circle of a half-dozen clerics.[57] A Pentagon official later commented perfunctorily that there was no U.S. interest whatever in considering a bombing pause.

Earlier, General Franks had requested that a dozen Air Force F-15E Strike Eagles be deployed to the AOR to take part in the campaign.[58] On October 17, F-15Es from the 366th Wing at Mountain

---

[55] Although *Kitty Hawk,* as noted above, served primarily as an afloat staging platform for SOF helicopter operations, her detachment of eight F/A-18s deployed primarily for carrier strike group defense also took part in overland strike operations into Afghanistan as required by the CAOC.

[56] Wall, "Targeting, Weapon Supply Encumber Air Campaign," p. 28.

[57] John F. Burns, "Taliban Figure Asks Bombing Halt to Make Deal on bin Laden," *New York Times,* October 16, 2001.

[58] Steven Lee Myers and Thom Shanker, "Pilots Told to Fire at Will in Some Zones," *New York Times,* October 17, 2001.

Home AFB, Idaho, began operating out of al Jaber Air Base in Kuwait against Taliban troop positions, in the first use of land-based fighters in Enduring Freedom.[59] Because of the great distances involved, the two aircraft carriers deployed in the North Arabian Sea to conduct day and night strike missions into Afghanistan could each cover only around 10 hours in country using a 14-hour first-launch to last-recovery operating window, making for only 20 hours of carrier coverage a day altogether. F-15Es out of al Jaber, along with Air Force Reserve Command F-16s equipped with Litening II infrared targeting pods, were accordingly used to fill the gaps in carrier coverage. The F-15Es were especially effective because of their extensive loiter time and their ability to carry up to nine GBU-12 500-lb LGBs, which entailed the least danger of causing collateral damage other than the even smaller Maverick and Hellfire air-to-ground missiles. (They flew from Kuwait into Afghanistan by circumnavigating Iran.) The F-16s were similarly valuable because they performed the FAC-A role and offered a laser target marker with their Litening pods, producing a beam visible in night-vision goggles that dramatically reduced the need for radio voice communications.[60] Low-flying SOF helicopters equipped with thermal cameras were used to designate occupied and active caves for F-15E and F-16 attacks as the Pentagon announced that the campaign was now systematically seeking to barrage enemy mountain redoubts in eastern and southern Afghanistan with precision munitions. During those attacks, two F-15Es also destroyed the Ministry for the Prevention of Vice and Propagation of Virtue, the hated enforcement arm of the Taliban's totalitarian theocracy.[61]

Carrier-based F-14s and F/A-18s used AGM-65 laser-guided Mavericks and BLU-109 earth-penetrator versions of the 2,000-lb

---

[59] Karen DeYoung and Vernon Loeb, "Land-Based Fighters Join Airstrikes in Afghanistan," *Washington Post*, October 18, 2001.

[60] Comments on an earlier draft by Lieutenant Colonel Mark Cline, USAF, CENTAF A-3/DOXP, Shaw AFB, South Carolina, August 13, 2003.

[61] Bowden, "The Kabul-Ki Dance," p. 78. See also "Afghan War Continues for Second Month," *Air International*, December 2001, p. 323.

JDAM against enemy-occupied caves. As in the case of the F-15Es, their attack tactics were hindered by the fact that the cave entrances were typically situated on steeply sloping terrain. Many passageways in the mountain cave complexes lay deep under rock and stretched for miles. Some were ancient underground aqueducts used by al Qaeda to hide and store ammunition and supplies. Others were natural limestone caverns and tunnels.

After the campaign's tenth day, the target list was greatly expanded and engagement zones were established throughout the country to facilitate attacks against Taliban and al Qaeda forces. Although these engagement zones were similar to the kill boxes that had been set up during Operation Desert Storm a decade before, they did not allow U.S. aircrews to attack at will anything that moved within them without prior CENTCOM approval, owing to persistent uncertainties about the location of friendly Afghan opposition forces and U.S. and allied SOF units in proximity to known or suspected enemy positions. Nevertheless, their establishment did indicate an impending shift in emphasis from preplanned targets toward pop-up targets of opportunity. In connection with that expanded license, two AC-130 gunships attacked Taliban garrisons in a built-up area near Kandahar.[62]

The next phase would seek to take down the Taliban's military establishment piece by piece, enabling Afghan opposition groups to capture Kabul and eventually install a new government. Attention was now turned to what were called "emerging targets," including Taliban vehicles that had been moved after the initial attacks, as well as other enemy troops and weapons as they were detected and identified. General Myers reported that the bombing attacks to date had merely been "stage-setters" for the next phase, which would entail the insertion of SOF teams on the ground to track down Taliban leaders and al Qaeda terrorists.[63] By the tenth day, during which 100 aircraft

---

[62] Michael R. Gordon, "U.S. Hopes to Break the Taliban with Pounding from the Air," *New York Times*, October 17, 2001.

[63] Mark Mazetti and Richard J. Newman, "Fight to the Finish," *U.S. News and World Report*, October 22, 2001.

participated in strike operations (in contrast to only 40 the first night), more than 2,000 bombs and missiles had been expended, mostly against fixed targets. For the impending next phase to follow shortly, Air Force General Charles Holland, the commander of SOCOM, was designated the senior operational commander for very narrow, surgical portions of the action, with Holland reporting not to General Franks but instead directly to Secretary Rumsfeld and President Bush.[64]

From Fixed to Fleeting Targets

At the 11-day point, the Department of Defense formally announced that the war effort had shifted from mainly attacking fixed targets to seeking out targets of opportunity, notably enemy troop concentrations and vehicles, in designated engagement zones. In light of the substantially reduced AAA threat, U.S. aircraft were now cleared to descend to lower altitudes as necessary to attack, around the clock, any emerging targets that were observed to be on the move. As the deputy director of operations for the Joint Chiefs of Staff, Rear Admiral John Stufflebeam, put it, "we now have the access to be able to do engagement zones that we might not have had with an air defense capability that we've recently taken out."[65] In three consecutive days of the war's heaviest bombing, 95 aircraft (mostly Navy fighters, along with some Air Force heavy bombers) attacked a dozen designated target areas, including Taliban airfields, AAA positions, armored vehicles, ammunition dumps, and training camps.

In this new phase of operations, FAC-As would positively identify targets and then clear other aircraft to attack them. Admiral Stufflebeam explained that the engagement-zone arrangement did not precisely equate to a "free-fire, free-target environment" but rather to one in which aircraft would be directed to targets once the latter were

---

[64] Mazetti and Newman, "Fight to the Finish."

[65] Rowan Scarborough, "U.S. Splits Afghanistan into 'Engagement Zones,'" *Washington Times,* October 18, 2001.

confirmed to be valid. He declined to indicate how many such zones had been designated and attacked, since that would telegraph U.S. capability. However, he said, "there isn't any part of the country that couldn't be put under an engagement zone." To cite a case in point of how this process worked in practice, two Taliban armored vehicles and a multiple rocket launcher were detected by coalition ISR assets northeast of Kandahar during the Northern Alliance's advance on that city. The CAOC first presented these targets to CENTCOM headquarters, whose intelligence staff validated and approved the targets, and then checked with the CIA, with its own special operations liaison element, and with other SOF entities to ensure that they had no personnel in the area. Having met those two requirements, the CAOC team then created a one-mile box, activated an engagement zone over it for a few hours, and sent fighter aircraft in to destroy the targets. As one participant described it, creating engagement zones in that manner "became a very difficult management process and not one that we would want to repeat, with verifying, opening, closing, and deactivating. It slowed things down but ensured that fratricide would not occur."[66]

The successful insertion of a small number of SOF personnel into southern Afghanistan after 11 days of nonstop bombing signaled the beginning of a new use of air power in modern war. As Secretary Rumsfeld commented, aircraft "can't crawl around on the ground and find people."[67] The commander of the USS *Theodore Roosevelt* carrier battle group, Rear Admiral Mark Fitzgerald, pointed out that the strategy had shifted from attacking prebriefed targets such as airfields, air defenses, and communication nodes to engaging pop-up targets like tanks and troops in the field.[68] Harking back to the "tank-plinking" effort of Operation Desert Storm, the emerging strategy

---

[66] Comments on an earlier draft by Major Charles Hogan, USAF, Air Command and Staff College, Maxwell AFB, Alabama, December 22, 2003. "Most of this," he added, "was done on the [CAOC] floor in the ill-named TST [time sensitive targeting] cell."

[67] Thomas E. Ricks and Vernon Loeb, "Special Forces Open Ground Campaign," *Washington Post*, October 19, 2001.

[68] Jim Drinkard, "U.S. Hits Troops Near Kabul," *USA Today*, October 22, 2001.

came to be called "Taliban-plinking" by some, with the intended goal of picking off Taliban and al Qaeda leaders and other targets of value one at a time. Ground FACs were able to laser-designate a fighter's bombs onto the intended target after the aircrew had dropped the bombs on geographic coordinates through cloud cover. It was reported on October 19 that Ab Baseer al-Masri, a leader of al-Gama'a al-Islammiya, an Egyptian terrorist group believed funded by bin Laden, had been killed near Jalalabad. If that report was correct, he would have been the first terrorist leader to die in the campaign.[69]

During the night of October 21, around 100 U.S. Army Rangers parachuted onto a Taliban airfield near Kandahar, while a smaller contingent believed to be an Army Delta Force unit raided a command site known to have been used by Mullah Omar. A videotape of the operation subsequently released by the Department of Defense showed the drops being conducted from three C-130s. General Myers described the operation's purpose as intelligence-gathering and said that the Army troops had encountered "light resistance."[70] The operation was widely assessed later to have been mainly a show-of-force event that produced little of intelligence value and proved to be of no strategic consequence. The entire mission lasted five to six hours, with little time actually spent by the troops on the ground. A major target during this second phase of the war was the barracks of the Taliban's 55th Brigade at Mazar-i-Sharif. The commanders of that special unit were mostly "Afghan Arabs" from Egypt and Saudi Arabia who had previously graduated from bin Laden's terrorist training camps. They were portrayed as the Taliban's most case-

---

[69] Sandra Laville and Michael Smith, "Bin Laden's Henchman 'Killed in Bomb Raid,'" *London Daily Telegraph*, October 19, 2001. A core problem with bin Laden and al Qaeda as adversaries was and remains that they are unwaveringly undeterrable by traditional means. In a clear testament to this, a Pakistani news editor, Hamid Mir, was said to have been taken blindfolded to a mud hut in the Afghan mountains on November 7 to interview bin Laden, who told him calmly: "This place may be bombed. And we will be killed. We love death. The U.S. loves life. That is the big difference between us." (Evan Thomas, "Gunning for bin Laden," *Newsweek*, November 26, 2001.)

[70] Greg Jaffe, "U.S. Offensive in Afghanistan Enters Riskier Phase of Commando Raids," *Wall Street Journal*, October 22, 2001.

hardened ideological shock troops and the nexus where the Taliban and al Qaeda most closely intersected.[71]

In contrast to the earlier Desert Storm experience, detailed information from CENTCOM about the war's progress remained sketchy at best, making it hard for outside observers to judge how well the campaign was proceeding. By his own admission, General Franks was anything but forthcoming in this regard. A year before the war started, he had candidly characterized his job as CENTCOM's commander by telling a reporter: "My business is a secret business. . . . My job is not to educate the ignorant."[72] So motivated, and with a deep disinclination to engage with the press, Franks routinely declined all requests for interviews and press conferences during the early part of Enduring Freedom until he was finally persuaded by Rumsfeld's public affairs staff to be more accessible.

As the rate of visible progress slowed down, General Myers said that "this is going to be a very, very long campaign. It may take until next spring. It may take until next summer. It may take longer in Afghanistan."[73] Frustration among some Air Force leaders with the effort's direction gradually became apparent, with one Air Force general saying that he was "extremely pessimistic with the lack of imagination" shown during the first week of bombing. "Are we ever going to get it," this general asked? The same general complained that although Air Force and Navy aircrews were performing superbly at the tactical level, they seemed to be attacking targets simply as an end in itself, with no clear connection between the targets attacked and overall desired goals.[74] For a time, there was such a shortage of approved targets that some scheduled carrier-based fighter missions were cancelled outright.

---

[71] Romesh Ratnesar, "The Ground War: Into the Fray," *Time*, October 29, 2001.

[72] Quoted in Dana Priest, *The Mission: Waging War and Keeping Peace with America's Military*, New York: W. W. Norton & Company, 2003, p. 144.

[73] Peter Pae, "U.S. Predicting Fight Will Last Until Well into Spring," *Los Angeles Times*, October 22, 2001.

[74] Arkin, "A Week of Air War."

The decisionmaking approach for Enduring Freedom was very much the opposite of that of the Gulf War, in which General Norman Schwarzkopf largely ran the effort from his forward headquarters in Riyadh, Saudi Arabia, issuing broad guidance to his component commanders and expecting them to develop and execute specific operational-level plans. Instead, decisionmaking for Afghanistan was closer in character to that of Operation Allied Force, in which top civilians and the JCS chairman in Washington kept General Wesley Clark on a short leash. In the case of Enduring Freedom, Rumsfeld and Myers developed a routine of having twice-daily VTCs with General Franks. Franks would present his ideas and indicate his assessment of the campaign's progress and what he needed, and Rumsfeld and Myers would then provide overall direction and guidance. For example, after the first week of bombing, when Franks asked to be provided with AC-130 gunships, Rumsfeld and Myers queried him about the benefits and risks of using that platform and finally approved his request. Franks had some leeway to pursue his preferences at the operational and tactical levels but little when it came to the administration's strong determination to avoid causing any collateral damage to Afghan civilians and infrastructure.[75]

As in previous wars, there were bound to be collateral damage incidents, as well as a resultant collateral damage management problem as both the enemy and critics of the war both at home and abroad took advantage of them. Taking the offensive early on in the propaganda war to milk the most out of this Western sensitivity, the Taliban's ambassador to Pakistan, Abdul Salam Zayeef, promptly charged that the opening-night attacks had killed up to 20 Afghan civilians. That was the first volley in what was to become a relentless Taliban effort to exploit the collateral damage issue to the hilt. Secretary Rumsfeld dismissed Zayeef's charge as "probably false," declaring that all targets that first night had been carefully selected with the ex-

---

[75] Eric Schmitt, "Seeking a Blend of Military and Civilian Decisionmaking," *New York Times,* October 24, 2001.

press intent to avoid causing civilian casualties.[76] Indifferent to that irksome fact and with the war still less than a week old, Zayeef next charged that 140 Afghan civilians had been killed in subsequent U.S. bombing attacks, including 15 in a mosque in Jalalabad that he alleged had been destroyed. U.S. officials countered that they had received no such collateral damage reports.[77] Zayeef later accused the United States of "genocide," in an absurd claim that more than 1,000 civilian fatalities had been incurred during the first 16 days of bombing.[78] By the start of November, Zayeef had charged that 1,500 Afghan civilians had been killed in the 25 days of U.S. bombing to date.[79]

The Taliban also quickly learned to exploit the collateral damage issue to their military advantage. They soon discovered what the United States would not bomb and made a beeline for such locations in quest of sanctuary. Once they recovered from their initial disorientation during the campaign's first few days, Taliban units moved with almost practiced regularity out of their barracks and into residential areas, religious buildings and mosques, and cultural centers and relief organization facilities, openly flouting the international laws of armed conflict by operating out of those facilities in complete disregard for civilian safety. In one example of such conduct, a Taliban truck said to have been on a humanitarian mission to deliver food accidentally tipped over, spilling crates of tank and mortar shells that had been concealed under a thin layer of flour.[80]

Secretary Rumsfeld reported that Taliban units were also positioning tanks, artillery, and armored vehicles in close proximity to residential areas and were using mosques, schools, and hospitals as

---

[76] Balz, "U.S. Strikes Again at Afghan Targets; Americans Told to Be Alert to Attacks."

[77] Graham and Loeb, "Cave Complexes Smashed by Bombs."

[78] Jonathan Weisman, "Pentagon Denies Taliban Casualty Claim," *USA Today,* October 23, 2001.

[79] William Branigin and Doug Struck, "U.S. Intensifies Bombing," *Washington Post,* November 1, 2001.

[80] Bradley Graham and Vernon Loeb, "Taliban Dispersal Slows U.S.," *Washington Post,* November 6, 2001.

command centers and ammunition storage depots.[81] He also cited the Taliban's use of mosques as meeting places to complicate U.S. targeting.[82] In an effort to counter these tactics, U.S. aircraft dropped hundreds of thousands of leaflets explaining that the United States was not at war with Islam or Afghanistan but rather was seeking to liberate the Afghan people from the al Qaeda invaders. The leaflets also warned, in both Dari and English: "The Taliban are using civilian areas to hide their equipment, endangering everyone in the area. Flee any area where military equipment or personnel are located."[83] Despite this effort, Pakistan's President Musharraf advised General Franks at the end of the third week of bombing that the United States needed to "rethink" its campaign, in considerable part because of allegedly mounting civilian casualties.

By the end of October, the Department of Defense had confirmed the following collateral damage incidents:

On October 8, an errant TLAM struck a UN facility in Kabul, inadvertently killing four UN employees. The building those workers occupied was situated near a Taliban communications tower that may have been the intended target.[84]

On October 13, as a result of incorrect target coordinates, an F/A-18 inadvertently dropped a 2,000-lb JDAM on a residential neighborhood in Kabul, a mile from its intended target, which was a Taliban helicopter at a nearby airfield. Four civilians were killed and eight injured in the incident.[85]

On October 16, an F/A-18 dropped a JDAM on a warehouse that was thought to house Taliban troops. It turned out that the

---

[81] Steve Vogel, "Over Afghanistan, Gantlets in the Sky," *Washington Post*, October 29, 2001.

[82] Thom Shanker and Steven Lee Myers, "U.S. Set to Aid Afghan Rebels, Rumsfeld Says," *New York Times*, October 19, 2001.

[83] Woodward, pp. 202–203.

[84] David A. Fulghum and Robert Wall, "U.S. Stalks Taliban with New Air Scheme," *Aviation Week and Space Technology*, October 15, 2001.

[85] Thomas E. Ricks, "U.S. to Target Elite Taliban Assault Force in Next Phase," *Washington Post*, October 14, 2001.

warehouse, one of several in a targeted complex of buildings that were being used for military storage by the Taliban, had been made available to the International Committee of the Red Cross (ICRC) to store emergency food and shelter materials for Afghan refugees. An Afghan guard inside the warehouse was wounded. A Pentagon statement later insisted that "U.S. forces did not know that the ICRC was using one or more of the warehouses." Secretary Rumsfeld branded as "ridiculous" a concurrent Taliban charge of massive civilian casualties, including at least 200 alleged killed as a result of an attack at Karam near Jalalabad.[86]

On October 20, two 500-lb bombs dropped by an F-14 missed targeted Taliban vehicles and landed in a residential area northwest of Kabul, with no information provided on possible injuries.

On October 21, a JDAM dropped by an F/A-18 missed a targeted vehicle storage building outside Herat and landed 300 feet away from a senior citizen residence. No information was provided on possible injuries caused by the errant weapon.

On October 26, two F/A-18s and two B-52s again bombed the ICRC warehouse complex in Kabul, after it was not removed from the CENTCOM target list. The complex was said by the ICRC to have been marked with a large red cross. The Pentagon attributed the mistaken warehouse bombing to "human error in the targeting process."[87]

Despite these errors, CENTCOM made conscientious and determined efforts to avoid causing such collateral damage incidents. Attacking aircrews were obliged to honor a strict visual target identification requirement before releasing their munitions, and CENTCOM enforced that requirement to the letter. At the campaign's 17-day point, Secretary Rumsfeld and General Myers were said to have overruled a target selection by General Franks only once, in an instance that involved a military complex located in a residential

---

[86] Karen DeYoung and Marc Kaufman, "Bombs, Lawlessness Threaten Aid Efforts," *Washington Post*, October 17, 2001.

[87] Andrea Stone, "Pentagon Confirms Errant Bomb Strikes," *USA Today*, October 29, 2001.

area that was believed to have presented too high a risk of civilian casualties.[88]

With respect to complaints voiced by some alleging an indiscriminate use of cluster bomb units (CBUs), General Myers countered that CBUs had been employed only when they were deemed to have been the most effective munition for a given target.[89] His response pointed up the important fact that notwithstanding the heinousness of al Qaeda's attacks against the United States on September 11, 2001, CENTCOM did not conduct Operation Enduring Freedom with any greater disregard for civilian life than did NATO against Serbia in Operation Allied Force two years earlier. On the contrary, it was even more fastidious in that regard, despite pressures from many quarters for the United States not to let its hands be tied by excess efforts to avoid civilian casualties on the premise that "this time we had finally been pushed too far." In fact, *no* number of civilian casualties sustained as a result of the September 11 attacks would have justified the United States' willfully ignoring the laws of armed conflict in Afghanistan. That the nation made every effort to honor those laws to a fault notwithstanding the terrorist outrage that drove it to go after the Taliban and al Qaeda in the first place constitutes powerful testimony to the fact that American warfighters do not follow the rules just because some higher authority makes them do it. That said, President Bush was well within the bounds of reason when he reminded critics of Enduring Freedom: "We also need to highlight the fact that the Taliban are killing people and conducting their own

---

[88] Schmitt, "Seeking a Blend of Military and Civilian Decisionmaking."

[89] As an aside on this point, one early mistake made was that the humanitarian daily ration (HDR) food packs that were being air-dropped to Afghan refugees were the same yellow color as undetonated CBU submunition canisters. This prompted understandable concern that Afghan civilians would confuse the two, even though the HDR packs were rectangular and the CBU submunitions were cylindrical. The error was eventually corrected by changing the color of the HDR packages to blue, but not before the Afghan countryside had been littered with numerous unexploded CBU canisters that could be lethal if picked up by unwitting civilians.

terror operations, so [let's] get a little more balance here about what the situation is."[90]

Closing Ranks with the Opposition Groups

It was clear from the earliest planning stages of Enduring Freedom that the United States would need to forge an effective working relationship with Afghan opposition groups if a stable post-Taliban political regime was ever to be arrived at. Before the start of the campaign, the best-organized of these groups, the Northern Alliance, had been a fractious amalgam of ethnic, tribal, and religious subgroupings cemented together mainly by a common desire to see the Taliban gone. Also called the United Front and recognized by the UN as the rightful government of Afghanistan, it was made up of four factions whose commanders had led the mujaheddin against the invading Soviets from 1979 to 1989. Those commanders subsequently turned on each other during the early 1990s after the Soviet occupiers were driven out. Once the Taliban took control of Afghanistan in 1996, these resistance factions were driven into the mountains and valleys of the far northeast, where they joined ranks to a degree. Their most prominent military leader was Ahmed Shah Massoud, a charismatic ethnic Tajik guerrilla fighter who had figured prominently in the defeat of the Soviets and who was minister of defense and senior military leader of the Northern Alliance.

After Massoud's assassination on September 10, almost surely by al Qaeda agents, his deputy, General Mohammed Fahim, took over the reins of alliance military leadership. Fahim claimed, rather extravagantly, that he could field 115,000 fighters against the Taliban's 45,000. In fact, the Northern Alliance had hitherto shown scant evidence of being able to dislodge the Taliban on its own.[91] On the

---

[90] Woodward, pp. 272–273.

[91] Indeed, another Northern Alliance faction leader, Abdullah (like many Afghans, he uses only one name) commented that although Massoud had been determined to capture Kabul,

contrary, Taliban forces outnumbered it by at least three to two. Moreover, the combat capability of the Northern Alliance was extremely limited. Like the Taliban, it was essentially a light-infantry and guerrilla force, with very limited armor and artillery assets.

The Northern Alliance factions were quite willing, at least in principle, to support the United States in its plan to evict the Taliban and destroy al Qaeda's power base. As one leader volunteered, "we don't see any objections. It's not like inviting an army to Afghanistan to do the job for us. Rather, we're in a situation where part of Afghanistan is being occupied by terrorists."[92] Another faction leader, General Dostum, an ethnic Uzbek warlord who had fought on both sides of nearly every conflict in Afghanistan since the Soviet defeat, actually called for U.S. assistance by satellite telephone as soon as it became clear that Washington would be going to war against the Taliban.

Not only that, the Northern Alliance was already at work on its own. As early as October 9, with the help of CIA money, 35 to 40 Taliban commanders and some 1,200 Taliban fighters were persuaded to defect, in the process giving the alliance control of a major Taliban resupply route northwest of Kabul.[93] In a telling testament to the power of money as an effective lubricant in eliciting cooperative Afghan behavior, one Taliban commander later on, as the war progressed, was offered $50,000 to defect. "Let me think about it," the commander replied. A Special Forces A-Team attached to a Northern Alliance unit promptly directed a JDAM attack right outside the commander's headquarters. The next day they called the commander back. "How about $40,000?" The commander accepted.[94]

Some resistance leaders redefined the meaning of fickle. General Dostum, to cite a notable case in point, was portrayed by one account

---

that goal had since ceased being a Northern Alliance priority, perhaps suggesting that the alliance lacked sufficient strength to take the capital without outside assistance at that point.

[92] Peter Baker and Molly Moore, "Anti-Taliban Rebels Eager to Join U.S. Retaliation," *Washington Post*, September 24, 2001.

[93] Woodward, p. 214.

[94] Woodward, p. 299.

as a "vain and sadistic monster out of a novel by Graham Greene or Joseph Conrad," who had run the secret police for the pro-Soviet government in Kabul during the 1980s and then switched sides to become a predator after the Soviets were defeated and driven out.[95] Asked about the extent to which he believed the Northern Alliance could be trusted, General Franks replied candidly: "Well, we're not sure." Franks added that the United States was "establishing contact with these opposition groups so we can determine where we have common goals, where we have common interests, where we can see a way ahead that will be satisfying to both of us."[96] As all of this was being sorted out, Ambassador James Dobbins was assigned by the State Department to work with the resistance groups and coordinate an effort on their part to create an interim post-Taliban coalition government that would be at least minimally acceptable to all. A key part of his daunting mission was to identify credible leaders from among the southern Pashtun tribes who might be ready to collaborate against the Taliban and to bring them together with opposition-group leaders in the north.[97]

The Campaign Hits a Slump

By late October, a sense of frustration had begun to set in both among outside observers of the war's progress and in some concerned segments of the U.S. military as well. The initial hope had been that the Taliban would collapse fairly quickly under the continuing weight of the nonstop air attacks. Indeed, their forces, having experienced nothing remotely like such an intensity of air-delivered firepower from the less capable Soviet Air Force more than a decade earlier, at first seemed petrified in the face of American air power and did not

---

[95] Evan Thomas and Melinda Liu, "Warlords: For Sale or Rent," *Newsweek*, November 5, 2001.

[96] Molly Moore and Kamran Khan, "Big Ground Force Seen As Necessary to Defeat Taliban," *Washington Post*, November 2, 2001.

[97] Patrick E. Tyler, "U.S. Names Envoy to Rebels," *New York Times*, November 6, 2001.

disperse in a tactically sensible way. Those forces later showed themselves, however, to be somewhat more resilient than initially expected.

The first air attacks against the Taliban front line did not occur until October 16, almost two weeks into the war. At that point, Secretary Rumsfeld for the first time openly acknowledged U.S. air power's cooperation with Northern Alliance combatants.[98] Yet even with that shift in emphasis, attacks during the war's first three and a half weeks, averaging only around 63 combat sorties a day, continued to be directed mainly against fixed Taliban assets, with relatively little concentration on the Taliban's fielded troop strength. That continuing pattern finally prompted the first signs of opposition-group criticism of U.S. strategy as a close associate of the late Massoud and the Northern Alliance's minister of the interior, Yonus Qanoni, urged the United States to go after Taliban front-line positions more aggressively instead of "always bombing airports" that presumably had already been destroyed.[99] Part of the reason for the continued focus on Taliban airfields even well into the campaign's third week, however, had to do with CENTCOM's BDA rule that required national satellite-imagery confirmation for all target destruction claims; that only rarely accepted air-breathing UAV imagery or any other source of BDA information, such as weapon-system video; and that accordingly resulted in a needlessly high target revisit rate. Qanoni would have had no awareness of that fact.

In light of the seeming lack of demonstrable progress in the campaign, a growing number of skeptics both in and out of government began to predict either a quagmire or an outright U.S. failure. Barely six days after the bombing began, National Public Radio's Daniel Schorr opined darkly that "this war is in trouble." Less than two weeks into the campaign, an academic air power theorist simi-

---

[98] Joseph Fitchett, "AC-130 Use Signals Start of Attack on Troops," *International Herald Tribune*, October 17, 2001.

[99] William Branigin, "U.S. Team Visits Rebel Commanders," *Washington Post*, October 22, 2001. On the frustrations over these desultory early air attacks aainst Taliban forces felt by the CIA's Jawbreaker team and the Northern Alliance leaders it was assisting, see Schroen, pp. 233–313.

larly concluded that "the initial air strategy against Afghanistan is not working."[100] Soon thereafter, a prominent reporter for the *New York Times* intoned, with like-minded pessimism, that "signs of progress [in the campaign] are sparse."[101]

Alongside these emanations from outside critics predisposed to assume the worst, one began to hear quiet complaining by more informed U.S. officers behind the scenes as well that needless mistakes were being made in the way the campaign was being conducted. Said one such military insider, "we should have been working with the Northern Alliance on the 12th of September."[102] Still other failings cited in media interviews with concerned officials, both civilian and uniformed, included CENTCOM's alleged error in initially going after empty al Qaeda training camps rather than attacking, early on and hard, those front-line Taliban forces that were defending Mazar-i-Sharif and Kabul.[103]

Concerns began to be voiced as well in some congressional quarters that the administration's strategy was too timid, with too few U.S. forces so far on the ground, an overdependence by administration planners on the Northern Alliance, and steadily accumulating incidents of accidental collateral damage. With respect to the last point, the Northern Alliance's foreign minister, Abdullah Abdullah, toward the end of October insisted on closer U.S. coordination with the Northern Alliance to deal with the mounting problem of Afghan civilians becoming inadvertent casualties of U.S. air attacks on Alliance-held territory.[104] These expressions of concern from such widely dissimilar circles naturally put the Bush administration on the

---

[100] Robert A. Pape, "The Wrong Battle Plan," *Washington Post*, October 19, 2001.

[101] Matthew Rose, "News Media Showed Tendency to Misfire During Early Phase of War in Afghanistan," *Wall Street Journal*, December 24, 2001.

[102] Rowan Scarborough, "Pentagon Insiders Criticize Tactics, Missed Opportunity," *Washington Times*, November 1, 2002.

[103] For more on this, see Schroen, pp. 233–313.

[104] Keith B. Richburg and William Branigin, "U.S. Jets Expand Afghan Strikes," *Washington Post*, October 29, 2001.

defensive in its effort to refute allegations that the war effort had become ineffectual.

With respect to mounting complaints about the campaign's alleged failure to go after fielded Taliban forces more aggressively, CENTCOM countered by citing a persistent absence of much actionable intelligence on elusive Taliban troops, as well as the close proximity of Taliban and opposition-group forces and the resultant danger of friendly forces being killed or injured by U.S. near-misses. Moreover, although the opportunity for joint U.S. work with the Northern Alliance had been available and waiting to be exploited almost from the very beginning of the campaign, CENTCOM's slowness in inserting SOF teams into Afghanistan to empower the opposition groups was not a result of any particular risk aversion or lack of nerve but simply because of some hard realities presented by the situation. During a mid-October meeting of the administration's senior security advisers, President Bush pressed General Franks for an update on CENTCOM's earlier promise to get SOF personnel promptly established on the ground in Afghanistan to provide targeting information that would enable U.S. aircraft to attack Taliban front-line positions. Yet even after the war's tenth day, the most recent of several tries by CENTCOM to insert the first SOF unit into position still had to be aborted at the last minute because of bad weather, which prohibited safe helicopter operations.

Furthermore, CENTCOM's effort to insert a SOF presence into Afghanistan as soon as possible remained stalled not only because of a prolonged spate of uncooperative weather but also because of continuing difficulties the State Department was experiencing in securing Uzbek government approval for the use of Uzbekistan as a staging point for such operations. On top of that, the few CIA paramilitary operatives who were already in position in Afghanistan were expressing concern that any U.S. SOF units that might successfully link up with Northern Alliance units could not be sufficiently protected and assured of safe extraction were a situation involving sudden combat to turn quickly sour. For his part, General Franks remained deeply skeptical of forming close ties with the Northern Alliance, as a result of which the campaign was "not giving the Northern Alliance a hole to go through."[105]

The war's progress was further impeded as the United States and the Northern Alliance leaders struggled to reconcile their conflicting agendas. At one point, CIA director Tenet candidly admitted that the Bush administration had put its fate in Afghanistan into the hands of the opposition groups, who, in the words of one reporter, "were going to act at a time, place, and pace of their own choosing. . . . It was a mercenary force—not under U.S. command. That was the price of admission when it was decided at the front end that the tribals were going to do the bulk of the ground fighting and not the U.S. military."[106] In an effort to break the logjam with respect to closing ranks with the opposition groups, President Bush finally indicated to General Franks that the SOF contingent that was awaiting action in Afghanistan needed to get moving. Within days of that presidential prod, the State Department persuaded Uzbekistan's President Karimov to yield at long last in allowing his country to be used as a debarkation point, and the CIA finally worked out its continuing differences with Fahim. Of this trying experience, Secretary Powell later recalled: "We were marrying a First World force with a Fourth World army."[107]

Finally, on October 19, two AFSOC MH-53J Pave Low helicopters successfully delivered Army Special Forces A-Team 555 to a landing zone in Afghanistan's Shamali plains, which had been marked by a CIA team that was already in place and awaiting its military compatriots. These Army troops, with their attached Air Force combat controllers, would provide the first eyes on target for enabling what eventually became a remarkably successful U.S. exercise in SOF-centric air operations. For nearly a week, A-Team 555 was one of only two U.S. SOF teams in the country. It had the full range of available allied strike assets on constant call. Each team member was

---

[105] Scarborough, "Pentagon Insiders Criticize Tactics, Missed Opportunity."

[106] Woodward, p. 230.

[107] Carney and Dickerson.

responsible for approximately 300 lb of equipment, which included laser range-finders and target designators.

Four days after its successful insertion into Afghanistan, A-Team 555 had advanced to within 500 meters of the Taliban front line. By the end of the first week, it had registered some notable successes in calling in air strikes. That experience set the pattern for three more A-teams that were inserted later in October, making four teams in all, plus two 15-man battalion-level units. Their combined composition of only 78 soldiers in all constituted the entire SOF presence in Afghanistan during the war's early period. They were ferried into position in a dilapidated Soviet-made Mi-8 helicopter and went for weeks without seeing other Americans. Once in Afghanistan, they moved on horseback, even though virtually none of the team members had ever ridden a horse. To support them, targets were frequently assigned as necessary well inside the normal 72-hour air-tasking cycle.

Shortly after the initial A-Teams were in place, the CAOC divided Afghanistan into 30 engagement zones to facilitate the prompt vectoring of strike aircraft toward emerging TSTs. Each SOF team commander was provided with an Inmarsat satellite phone. Said one team leader: "We saturated the battlefield with small close-support cells and we hit the Taliban if they were engaging us. . . . We engaged them while they were moving and if they tried to retreat. They simply could not move."[108] On more than a few occasions, however, a team would detect a convoy of Taliban or al Qaeda trucks, in one case as many as 20 vehicles, and be unable to call in an aircraft to attack it, for reasons that may have had to do with communications problems or rules-of-engagement constraints. Whatever the explanation, the Taliban had ample reason to be unimpressed by this seemingly lackluster performance and to believe that they could easily weather such modest air attacks.[109]

The Bush administration remained reluctant to back the Northern Alliance unconditionally because of Pakistan's opposition to an

---

[108] Dana Priest, "Team 555 Shaped a New Way of War," *Washington Post*, April 3, 2002.

[109] Woodward, p. 264.

advance on Kabul solely by northern Uzbeks and Tajiks, without any participation by the pivotal Pashtun elements from the south, where Hamid Karzai, with a mere 400 to 500 fighters, was the only resistance leader who was doing much of any note. The recently assassinated alliance military commander Massoud had sworn that he would never take Kabul without Pashtun involvement. It was not clear, however, whether Fahim would be as respectful of the important political sensitivities that attended such a major move. Moreover, because the situation with the Pashtun in the south remained so unsettled and because so many southern tribal leaders still maintained close ties to the Taliban, the CIA was not yet prepared to insert its paramilitary teams into that portion of Afghanistan.[110] A delicate balancing act accordingly ensued, dominated by U.S. efforts to convince the Pashtun that they badly needed to redirect their priorities from supporting the Taliban to joining forces with the Northern Alliance.

On top of all this, a number of bad-news events that occurred in close succession added to the mounting feeling of frustration in many quarters. On October 19, an HH-60 Blackhawk helicopter crashed in Afghanistan near the Pakistani border, killing two Army Rangers. The next morning, a CSAR effort by the 15th Marine Expeditionary Unit aboard USS *Peleliu* was aborted because of reported ground fire near the crash site. Several days later, a Marine TRAP (tactical recovery of aircraft and personnel) team with two CH-53 helicopters finally extracted the survivors, and an F-14 subsequently destroyed the wreckage to keep it out of Taliban hands.[111] In a subsequent CSAR event, one of two AFSOC MH-53 Pave Low helicopters that had been dispatched to rescue a seriously ill SOF soldier departed controlled flight in freezing rain and crash-landed in northern Afghanistan. The second MH-53 rescued the downed crew members and extracted them from Afghanistan, after which an F-14 from USS *Theodore Roosevelt* destroyed the highly classified equipment aboard

---

[110] Woodward, p. 226.

[111] Cesar G. Soriano, "Elite Marine Unit Makes First Strike on Taliban," *USA Today*, November 5, 2001.

the unrecoverable MH-53 that had crashed to prevent it from falling into enemy hands.[112]

Just days earlier, during a time when General Fahim was temporarily out of the country, the continuing absence of significant U.S. air strikes on Taliban positions had begun to demoralize Northern Alliance fighters. To make matters worse, after his return to Afghanistan, Fahim failed to advance his combatants into battle. At the same time, the Taliban's troop strength opposite Fahim's positions had grown by some 50 percent, now totaling 10,000 to 16,000 fighters.[113] Of this stalemated Northern Alliance offensive, it was reported that the bombing so far was not dividing the Taliban. Instead, wrote a well-placed CIA observer, the Taliban leadership "remains united and defiant around Mullah Omar, while tribal commanders sit firmly on the fence waiting to see who will prevail before committing themselves."[114]

In yet another setback for the campaign's progress, resistance leader Abdul Haq, who had slipped into Afghanistan on October 21 on his own initiative to help rally the opposition, was captured by the Taliban only five days later.[115] The CIA reportedly denied his urgent request for weapons, a field radio, and extraction by helicopter when he was first besieged. Former Reagan administration national security adviser Robert MacFarlane sought to persuade CENTCOM to dispatch some support aircraft to Haq's location instead. By the time any such help could have arrived, however, Haq had already been summarily tried, tortured, and executed. He was the second charismatic Afghan leader after Massoud to be killed by the controlling al Qaeda and Taliban. Unlike Massoud, however, Haq was a Pashtun from Afghanistan's ethnic majority. As such, he could have been a credible post-Taliban national leadership candidate. Later, Secretary

---

[112] James Dao and Thom Shanker, "Americans Rescue Soldier Who Fell Ill," *New York Times*, November 5, 2001.

[113] Woodward, p. 254.

[114] Woodward, p. 234.

[115] Jon Lee Anderson, p. 223.

Rumsfeld denied that the U.S. military had tried to assist Haq as he was being surrounded, indicating that the resistance leader had received help instead from "another element of government."[116] Administration officials eventually disclosed that the CIA had diverted an airborne Hellfire-armed MQ-1 Predator drone to the area in a last-minute attempt to protect Haq. The drone attacked a Taliban convoy in an effort to save Haq, but failed to prevent the Taliban from eventually capturing him.[117]

The Northern Alliance's first advance on Mazar-i-Sharif was stalled by a Taliban counterattack, the rapidity and boldness of which came as a surprise. Said one Pentagon source, "they fought like maniacs. We didn't expect that. Intelligence got it wrong."[118] That untoward setback led the JCS spokesman, Rear Admiral Stufflebeem, finally to admit that he had been "a bit surprised at how doggedly [the Taliban were] hanging on to their power" and that they had "proven to be tough warriors." That was a decidedly downbeat departure from previous assessments, notably the claim only a week earlier by General Newbold that the Taliban had been "eviscerated."[119] For his part, General Franks, speaking in Uzbekistan, commented that the situation was, in his view, "not at all a stalemate. My boss, the Secretary of Defense, and the President have not indicated to me any frustration with the [war's] pace."[120] Nevertheless, given the close succession of these seeming setbacks outlined above, it was all but predictable that hand-wringing on the part of some observers would occur sooner or

---

[116] Jonathan Weisman and Andrea Stone, "U.S. Expects Longer War," *USA Today*, October 29, 2001, and Vernon Loeb and Marc Kaufman, "CIA Sent Aircraft to Rescue Slain Leader," *Washington Post*, October 29, 2001.

[117] For more on this episode, described by the leader of the CIA's Jawbreaker team as "a prime example of what happens when amateurs involve themselves in intelligence activities," see Schroen, pp. 265–267.

[118] Michael Smith, "U.S. Special Forces Beat Retreat as Enemy 'Fought Back Like Maniacs,'" *London Daily Telegraph*, October 26, 2001.

[119] Paul Richter and Peter Pae, "U.S. Concedes Taliban Battle Will Be Tough," *Los Angeles Times*, October 25, 2001.

[120] Kendra Helmer, "General Franks, in Uzbekistan, Says Fight Against Terrorism Has Not Stalled," *European Stars and Stripes*, October 31, 2001.

later. As one reporter so inclined finally expressed this nagging pessimism, "like an unwelcome specter from an unhappy past, the ominous word 'quagmire' has begun to haunt conversations among government officials and students of foreign policy, both here and abroad."[121]

In time, the Bush administration was forced to concede that it had little choice but to bite the bullet with respect to unleashing the Northern Alliance, irrespective of the Pashtuns' continuing slowness to join the war effort in a significant way. Vice President Cheney all along had been unconvinced that holding the Northern Alliance back had made the most sense, given the urgency of bringing the war to as expeditious a conclusion as possible. At one point, he asked outright whether CENTCOM was working the sorts of targets that would provide that group with the greatest incentive to get moving.[122] After repeated frustrations in trying to forge a broad-based opposition-group coalition, the administration finally proceeded reluctantly to unshackle its combat operations from such political considerations and to accelerate the bombing of Taliban positions without concern for the limited Pashtun involvement. Secretary Rumsfeld insisted that the United States was now ready for Northern Alliance forces to move on Kabul as soon as the time was ripe.[123] Since there was little likelihood of a broader post-Taliban government being organized within the next few days, administration officials finally acknowledged that they had no choice but to stop impeding the Northern Alliance's determination to advance on Kabul at its earliest opportunity.[124] As a senior official put it, "it's become clearer in the past week

---

[121] R. W. Apple, Jr., "Quagmire Recalled: Afghanistan as Vietnam," *New York Times*, October 31, 2001. Of these complainers and worriers who seemed to be expecting instant gratification from the campaign, Secretary Rumsfeld said derisively: "They've got the attention span of gnats." (Woodward, p. 283.)

[122] Woodward, p. 215.

[123] Thomas E. Ricks and Alan Sipress, "Attacks Restrained by Political Goals," *Washington Post*, October 23, 2001.

[124] Carla Anne Robbins and Alan Cullison, "U.S. Is Prepared to Support an Assault on Kabul by Northern Alliance Forces," *Wall Street Journal*, October 23, 2001.

that we've stopped trying to calibrate the military and the political." This official characterized the new approach as "let's do what we need to do. Let's get on with it and get it over with."[125] As a White House aide put the same point somewhat differently, until now "the military track [had] been held up waiting for progress on the political track" until the administration realized that "we had to get rid of the idea—or rather the illusion—that we could micromanage [Afghanistan's] political future."[126]

Despite continuing complaints from some opposition-group leaders that the United States was not doing enough by way of bombing the right targets, a senior Pentagon official predicted that the Taliban would cease being an effective fighting force within just a few days.[127] The impending fall of Mazar-i-Sharif would make the nearby airport immediately available for U.S. use. Once that objective was secured, Taliban resistance in the north would then collapse. The capture of Mazar-i-Sharif would also enable the opening up of a supply line to Afghanistan from neighboring Uzbekistan.

At that point, Secretary Rumsfeld indicated that the United States was prepared to provide direct military assistance to the opposition groups, amid continuing concern among some diplomats at the State Department over the downside political risks of accepting the Tajik- and Uzbek-dominated Northern Alliance as the sole U.S. proxy when there were also southern Pashtun interests that demanded recognition and honoring. Rumsfeld later added that U.S. airlifters were dropping ammunition, food, and supplies to the Northern Alliance and that working with the opposition groups would help provide needed targeting information for allied air attacks.[128] At long

---

[125] Alan Sipress and Vernon Loeb, "U.S. Steps Up Strikes on Taliban Troops," *Washington Post*, November 1, 2001.

[126] Joseph Fitchett, "Major Drive Seen for Afghan Cities," *International Herald Tribune*, October 31, 2001. In fact, however, the administration continued to oppose the Northern Alliance's move into Kabul until it was a fait accompli.

[127] Mazetti and Newman, "Fight to the Finish."

[128] Thom Shanker and Steven Lee Myers, "U.S. Set to Aid Afghan Rebels, Rumsfeld Says," and Fitchett, "Major Drive Seen for Afghan Cities."

last, U.S. SOF forces, including Air Force combat controllers, melded seamlessly with Fahim's combatants—to the point of riding into battle alongside them on horseback, in the latter case armed with ultra-high-frequency (UHF) radios, laptop computers, and laser range-finders and target designators. That convergence finally spurred Fahim into action. His fighters went on the offensive in northern Afghanistan on October 21, with the goal of isolating the Taliban in the pivotal city of Mazar-i-Sharif. A White House official later commented: "We said, 'OK, if you won't move until we start hitting targets in front of you, we'll hit targets in front of you.' And we started bombing the valley."[129]

The Allied Contribution

America's allies continued to offer their support as the war unfolded. At the outset of Enduring Freedom, the Bush administration had made little effort to encourage such offers out of avowed concern that expanding the coalition beyond Great Britain (along with some very modest additional personnel and equipment support provided by Turkey, Canada, and Australia, the latter of which provided a small contingent of F/A-18s and Boeing 707 tankers for the defense of Diego Garcia) would introduce unwelcome political complications into the conduct of the campaign.[130] The administration was reluctant to submit the nation yet again to the frustrations of coalition decision-making in light of the previous administration's experience with the more meddlesome NATO allies during Operation Allied Force two years earlier. Instead, the administration's national security principals—Secretary of Defense Rumsfeld, in particular—insisted that this time around, the coalition would be determined by the needs of the situation rather than the other way around. As late as

---

[129] Carney and Dickerson, "Inside the War Room."

[130] For further details on the spectrum of allied contributions to Enduring Freedom, see Nora Bensahel, *The Counterterror Coalitions: Cooperation with Europe, NATO, and the European Union*, Santa Monica, Calif.: RAND Corporation, MR-1746-AF, 2003, pp. 55–63.

mid-November, Secretary of State Powell felt compelled to reassure a
Senate committee on this point that the limited coalition involvement the administration had ultimately accepted did not "in any way,
shape, fashion, or form constrain the President in the exercise of
his constitutional responsibilities to defend the United States of
America."[131]

After weeks of repeatedly deflecting such allied offers of assistance, however, the administration ultimately consented to take a
second look at them, no doubt motivated in part by mounting indications of gradually wavering international support for the campaign.
Great Britain, already a close partner of the United States in the war
effort, lobbied hard for the inclusion of additional European allies.
George Robertson, the secretary general of NATO, likewise strongly
advocated a greater involvement by willing NATO countries, a number of which had readily offered up aircraft to fly food and other
needed humanitarian relief supplies into neighboring Central Asian
countries for transshipment to Afghanistan. For their part, the Germans, French, Dutch, Spanish, and Italians were all champing at the
bit to participate. These NATO countries soon came to represent a
coalition in waiting whose members were increasingly frustrated by
Washington's reluctance to include them.

In particular, Germany on November 6 offered to contribute
3,900 military personnel in what would, if accepted by the Bush administration, constitute the first involvement of German ground
forces in a combat operation and their first deployment outside
Europe since the end of World War II. France sought to provide both
combat aircraft and SOF personnel, even though the Pentagon had
indicated that it had no requirement for the latter and had thus far
been unable to secure any suitable regional basing option for the former. Italy's Prime Minister Silvio Berlusconi offered the Italian
Navy's aircraft carrier *Garibaldi*, with its complement of Harrier
fighters and attack helicopters, as well as 10 Tornado deep-strike
fighters and 1,000 paratroopers. The Dutch government offered a

---

[131] Mark Mazetti, "Now, It's Eyeball to Eyeball," *U.S. News and World Report*, November 19, 2001, p. 17.

contingent of MLU (mid-life update) F-16s equipped with special photo reconnaissance pods, as well as two transport aircraft and two P-3C surveillance aircraft, and a number of allies provided naval vessels for operations in the Arabian Sea to interdict any al Qaeda terrorists who might attempt to flee Afghanistan by sea.[132] With these allies strongly insisting that they wished to be cooperative players, the Bush administration gradually backed away from its earlier position and indicated its willingness in principle to honor their desire.[133]

Hitherto, the only NATO member-states other than the United States that were materially involved in the campaign were Great Britain and Canada. The British contribution included several Royal Navy submarines armed with TLAMs and a total of 10 RAF tankers (both Tristars and VC-10s) and reconnaissance aircraft (Canberra PR9s and a Nimrod R1), with the Canberras and tankers reportedly operating out of Seeb and the Nimrod out of Thumrait, both in Oman.[134] Significantly, the RAF's tanker contribution provided 20 percent of the total inflight refueling capacity that was available for Enduring Freedom missions.

Canada's contribution, code-named Operation Apollo, included a detachment of two CP-140 Aurora long-range patrol aircraft for conducting surveillance operations in the Gulf region. It also included a strategic airlift detachment of CC-150 Airbus A-310s and a tactical airlift detachment of three CC-130 aircraft for transporting military personnel and materiel into the theater.[135] In the first of a number of subsequent moves to expand this allied involvement, France contributed two Mirage IVP strategic reconnaissance aircraft

---

[132] Ambrose Evans-Pritchard, "EU Leaders Demand a Place in the Front Line," *London Daily Telegraph*, November 7, 2001.

[133] David E. Sanger and Michael R. Gordon, "U.S. Takes Steps to Bolster Fighting Terror," *New York Times*, November 7, 2001.

[134] "Afghan Air War Continues for Second Month," p. 324. The Nimrod was used for signals intelligence (SIGINT) collection.

[135] The Canadian task force headquarters, along with that of the British, was collocated with CENTCOM headquarters at MacDill AFB, Florida. At its height, the Canadian involvement in Operation Enduring Freedom numbered more than 3,400 people.

that operated out of a forward base in the Persian Gulf region, and the Pentagon asked Germany to provide Fuchs armored vehicles equipped to check terrain for chemical, biological, and radiological contamination, as well as some SOF and other personnel. As the Germans eagerly complied with this request, Chancellor Gerhard Schroeder remarked that Germany's determination to be a part of Operation Enduring Freedom amounted to a decision that would "find its way into the history books."[136]

The Fall of Mazar-i-Sharif and Kabul

Situated on the storied 4,000-mile-long Silk Road that meanders through Central Asia, Mazar-i-Sharif was widely regarded as the pivot point where the battle for northern Afghanistan would be decided.[137] The city straddles a highway that touched many centers of anti-Taliban activity. It also controlled the highway from Kabul to Uzbekistan. Its capture by anti-Taliban forces would enable the opening of a bridgehead to Uzbekistan from which greatly increased U.S. assistance could then flow.

As early as October 21, Northern Alliance forces began marshalling for an attack on Mazar-i-Sharif, with a view toward eventually moving from there on to Kabul. The following day, Secretary Rumsfeld said: "Our efforts from the air clearly are to assist those forces on the ground in being able to occupy more ground."[138] That was the clearest indication to date that the campaign's emphasis had evolved from destroying fixed targets to assisting opposition-group efforts to dislodge and evict the Taliban.

---

[136] Steven Erlanger, "Germany Ready to Send Force of 3900," *New York Times*, November 7, 2001.

[137] The city was appropriately named. In Dari, Mazar-i-Sharif means "the graveyard of the righteous."

[138] Thom Shanker and Steven Lee Myers, "Rumsfeld Says Attacks Seek to Help Rebels Advance," *New York Times*, October 23, 2001.

The most intense ground fighting to date since the start of Enduring Freedom occurred on October 23 as Northern Alliance and Taliban forces exchanged heavy artillery fire. General Dostum indicated that he was getting U.S. bombing support for his operations, adding that he provided a daily target list and that American aircraft then attacked wherever requested.[139] Until that time, coalition bombing attacks had carefully avoided going after front-line Taliban positions to prevent Northern Alliance forces from taking the capital on their own prematurely, which Pakistan had strongly opposed. The ensuing stalemate was about to be broken decisively, however, with between 5,000 and 10,000 Taliban and Northern Alliance forces now massed opposite each other along a 20-mile line. Partly in support of the impending effort, Secretary Rumsfeld signed a deployment order on October 26 sending the RQ-4 Global Hawk high-altitude UAV to the war, with an expected arrival of the aircraft at a base in the United Arab Emirates (UAE) on November 13. Still not operational and of which the Air Force had but four prototypes in its test inventory, the RQ-4 had only recently shifted from ACTD (advanced concept technology demonstrator) to system design and demonstration status.[140]

The Northern Alliance was pursuing a calculated strategy aimed at hastening the Taliban's collapse by striking from all sides. The close involvement of U.S. SOF teams enabled the imposition of effective opposition-group pressure in the north, while CIA paramilitary operatives sought to organize the application of similar pressure in the south, especially against Kandahar. The southern Pashtun forces were not nearly as coherent as those in the north, and U.S. relations with those forces were far less cultivated. The shift in strategy that led to this heightened effort to work more closely with the opposition groups and, in effect, to clear the Northern Alliance to pursue its

---

[139] Doug Struck, "Rebel Leader Claims to Be Guiding Air Strikes," *Washington Post*, October 24, 2001.

[140] The RQ-4 mounts an integrated sensor suite with electro-optical and infrared sensors and a synthetic aperture radar (SAR), can fly as high as 65,000 feet, can remain airborne for up to 36 hours, and can identify some targets as far away as 30 miles. (Steven Mufson and William Branigin, "U.S. Sets Stage for Offensive," *Washington Post*, November 2, 2001.)

goals followed an NSC situation review two weeks before, which had called for accelerated efforts to bring down the Taliban.[141] In the end, as noted above, military needs were determined to outweigh diplomatic considerations, and the coalition pressed ahead despite continuing concerns over the possible political consequences of continuing the campaign into Ramadan and over Pakistan's sensibilities regarding the capture of Kabul by the Northern Alliance singlehandedly.

Toward that end, the Northern Alliance's full-up offensive finally began on October 28. Despite persistent bad weather, that day saw ramped-up U.S. air attacks against Taliban artillery positions that were threatening a Northern Alliance supply line. The coordination between U.S. air operations and Northern Alliance activities on the ground was said by Secretary Rumsfeld to be improving, as attested by those opposition-group leaders who agreed that U.S. aircraft were helping to ensure their survival by engaging Taliban targets near the Tajik border. In a concurrent but unrelated ground event, Taliban guards at an airfield and at Mullah Omar's compound were killed by long-range U.S. sniper fire. Such direct action was called "a warm-up for things to come."[142] Also relatedly, in a third attempt against Mullah Omar, a building in Kandahar thought to house him was struck by a precision air-delivered munition at 4:30 a.m., indicating a clear U.S. intent to kill anyone who may have been sleeping inside it.[143] A proximate goal of both day and night air attacks was to disable Taliban artillery fielded in a position to threaten a river crossing that was crucial to a Northern Alliance supply line.[144]

Initially, CENTCOM thought that the Northern Alliance leadership had given up on overrunning Kabul in 2001. In the end, how-

---

[141] Michael R. Gordon, "Alliance of Convenience," *New York Times*, October 23, 2001.

[142] Steven Lee Myers and Eric Schmitt, "Material Seized in U.S. Ground Raid Yields Few Gains," *New York Times,* October 30, 2001.

[143] Michael R. Gordon and Steven Lee Myers, "U.S. Will Increase Number of Advisers in Afghanistan," *New York Times,* November 1, 2001.

[144] Thom Shanker with Dexter Filkins, "U.S Planes Hit Taliban Positions Threatening Rebels," *New York Times,* October 29, 2001.

ever, the latter succeeded in amassing tens of thousands of fighters for an imminent assault on Mazar-i-Sharif that, if successful, would set the stage for a move against the capital city as the next step.[145] One reason for the increasingly urgent sense of a need to take Mazar-i-Sharif was that doing so would enable the opening of a land bridge to Uzbekistan, the border of which was only 40 miles away, in order to allow the transshipment of fuel and supplies into Afghanistan by land transport rather than by the far more costly air route. By the end of October, air strikes in support of the Northern Alliance were finally stepped up significantly. Secretary Rumsfeld said that 80 percent of all combat sorties were now dedicated to backing the opposition-group effort. Rumsfeld also admitted that U.S. military personnel were serving in a liaison role with the Northern Alliance and that a "very modest number" of U.S. troops—between a dozen and 100 Army Special Forces personnel, plus some AFSOC combat controllers—were operating in direct support of the air campaign.[146] This was the first official reference to U.S. forces being on the ground in Afghanistan.

There were still, however, no available bases in the nearby Central Asian republics to support U.S. strike operations. That meant that all U.S. land-based fighter sorties had to be flown from friendly states in the Gulf region.[147] Uzbekistan had offered the use of its airfield at Karshi-Khanabad, but mainly for CSAR and humanitarian operations. Pakistan confirmed that it was allowing a third airfield, Dalbandin, around 45 miles from the Afghan border, to be used by U.S. forces. In the end, CSAR units operated out of Jacobabad in southern Pakistan and Karshi-Khanabad in Uzbekistan. Bases like Jacobabad and Karshi-Khanabad also were available for allied aircraft to divert to in case they encountered battle damage or inflight emer-

---

[145] Julius Strauss and Dashti Qala, "Waves of Jets Herald the Start of Northern Alliance Offensive," *London Daily Telegraph*, October 29, 2001.

[146] Thomas E. Ricks and Doug Struck, "U.S. Troops Coordinating Airstrikes," *Washington Post*, October 31, 2001.

[147] Scarborough, "Pentagon Insiders Criticize Tactics, Missed Opportunity."

gencies. Both locations involved helicopter flight times of several hours to locations in central Afghanistan.[148]

Similarly, USS *Kitty Hawk* was dedicated to supporting SOF operations, but its ocean station was hours of flight time from Afghanistan by helicopter. Accordingly, SOF helicopters operating off the flight deck of *Kitty Hawk* that were not equipped for inflight refueling had to be refueled in Pakistan en route to their final destinations. The most immediate need was for a quick-response airfield within Afghanistan once one could be secured and made operational, in part because delivering humanitarian aid to Afghanistan by air was turning out, to no one's surprise, to be both inefficient and expensive.[149] Yet there was some continuing reservation in Washington at that still-early point in the campaign about establishing a higher-visibility U.S. presence in Afghanistan out of concern to avoid projecting any appearance of U.S. forces "holding ground" there.

The Pentagon was now also surveying options for basing F-15Es and A-10s in Tajikistan, Kyrgyzstan, and Kazakhstan. Tajikistan finally offered the use of three of its airfields for supporting allied strike operations, even though the air base infrastructure it had inherited from the Soviet Air Force was in exceedingly poor condition. It was doubtful that all three airfields would be deemed serviceable.[150] As CENTCOM and CENTAF debated what mix of aircraft to put in, one option envisaged a squadron each of F-16s and F-15Es, for a total of 48 combat aircraft. Another option envisaged fewer fighters and a small detachment of AC-130s.[151]

---

[148] Robert Wall, "USAF to Bolster Pilot Rescue Ability," *Aviation Week and Space Technology*, August 12, 2002, p. 30.

[149] Michael Evans, "Special Forces' Reach Curbed by Flight Time," *London Times*, November 8, 2001.

[150] Greg Jaffe and Alan Cullison, "Tajikistan Offers U.S. Military Three Airfields to Use in Intensifying Its Bombing Campaign," *Wall Street Journal*, November 8, 2001. The bases included Kulyab south of Dushanbe, Kurgan-Tyube in southern Tajikistan, and Khundjand to the north.

[151] Rowan Scarborough, "Air Force Gets Use of Airfield in Tajikistan," *Washington Times*, November 10, 2001.

Planning for possible Air Force strike sorties out of Tajikistan meant planning for bare-base operations in a major way. Transshipment of a Harvest Eagle war reserve materiel (WRM) kit to support a detachment of F-15Es and 550 attached personnel, including showers, rations, quarters, and communications, would require four C-5s. Delivery of a Harvest Falcon WRM kit to support a larger detachment of F-16s, providing for 1,100 personnel, would require 10 C-5 sorties. Also required was sufficient ground area for installing a munitions storage facility situated far enough away from quarters and flight operations so as not to present a safety hazard. Fuel bags associated with such bare-base contingency plans were sized to contain 50,000, 100,000, and 210,000 gallons.[152] (Neither of these options, in the end, was carried out.)

By November 1, small teams of U.S. SOF personnel were reported to be on the ground in Afghanistan, albeit hampered by fog and sandstorms, 100-knot winds, and subfreezing temperatures in the north, plus recurrent Taliban fire and coordination problems with the opposition groups. Those impediments slowed the teams' effort to identify Taliban positions for air strikes. They also hindered the use of helicopters for ferrying them from their jump-off points to landing zones inside Afghanistan. The number of U.S. SOF personnel reported in action at that point was still only around two dozen. The front lines remained fairly static, with the Taliban fighters more energetic than expected and with opposition-group leaders complaining about what they portrayed as persistently anemic U.S. air support. Describing one SOF team's aborted insertion under Taliban fire, Secretary Rumsfeld explained: "We have a number of teams cocked and ready to go; it's just a matter of having the right kind of equipment to get them there and the landing zones in places where it's possible to get in and get out. . . . The ground fire was simply too heavy [for us] to unload the folks."[153]

---

[152] Vernon Loeb, "Pentagon Eyes Use of Tajikistan Air Base," *Washington Post*, November 13, 2001.

[153] Eric Schmitt and Thom Shanker, "Trouble in Deploying Commandos Is Said to Hurt U.S. Air Campaign," *New York Times*, November 2, 2001.

On November 2, the Joint Staff followed through on Secretary Rumsfeld's earlier approval of a deployment order sending Global Hawk and an E-8C Joint Surveillance Target Attack Radar System (JSTARS) aircraft to the war zone. The latter move indicated that an accelerated ground phase of the unfolding campaign was imminent. Rumsfeld also indicated that he wanted the number of U.S. SOF personnel assisting the Northern Alliance to be increased by three to four times "as soon as humanly possible."[154] By that time, three Army Special Forces A-teams had already been inserted into Afghanistan, and 90 percent of the U.S. strike sorties were being conducted in direct support of the opposition groups.[155]

With the increased use of B-52s against the Taliban front lines, Northern Alliance leaders who once criticized the bombing now came to praise it and to draw increased hopes of achieving mission success from it.[156] The A-teams were now bringing in heavy air attacks against the Taliban's two circles of defensive trenches around Mazar-i-Sharif. Enemy supply lines and communications were cut, hundreds of enemy vehicles and bunkers were destroyed, and thousands of Taliban fighters were either killed or captured or managed to escape.[157] Until precise target designation could be provided by on-scene terminal attack controllers, CENTCOM had been forced to limit the use of B-52s against frontline Taliban troops, out of legitimate concern that unguided Mk 82 500-lb bombs could cause friendly casualties. Soon thereafter, the number of U.S. SOF personnel on the ground doubled to about 100. As a result, said Secretary

---

[154] Mufson and Branigin, "U.S. Sets Stage for Offensive."

[155] Woodward, p. 294.

[156] The odd camaraderie between Northern Alliance and Taliban fighters on occasion helped lead to the latters' undoing. One Northern Alliance fighter told of calling a known Taliban counterpart on a portable radio after an air strike, asking, "Hi. Are you still there?" The Taliban combatant replied boastfully, "Fine, they missed us—they were 200 meters south." The Northern Alliance fighter then radioed the Americans, "OK, 200 meters north," and the Taliban contingent was taken out by a JDAM strike. (Scott Peterson, "A View from Behind the Lines in the U.S. Air War," *Christian Science Monitor,* December 4, 2001.)

[157] Peterson, p. 301.

Rumsfeld, "the targeting is improving. When you're doing it without contact with forces on the ground, and you compare that with doing it with precision weapons and people on the ground who can give you precise coordinates, you just have an enormous advantage."[158]

On November 4, during a visit to Dushanbe, Tajikistan, Rumsfeld declared that the Taliban had ceased functioning as a government. General Myers concurrently reported that the bombing was now focusing on targets near Bagram, Taloqan, Kunduz, and Mazar-i-Sharif, four key locations situated close to Taliban lines.[159] This phase of the war saw the first use of the BLU-82/B 15,000-lb high-explosive bomb, two of which were dropped on Taliban positions from an MC-130 Combat Talon aircraft in an attempt to kill large numbers of enemy troops by the tremendous overpressure created by the weapon.[160] There also was the first reported use of Air Force RQ-1 Predator drones marking enemy targets with lasers for AC-130 gunships to attack. To complement the six AC-130s that were operating out of Oman, the Pentagon sent three more to Uzbekistan. That made a total of nine in theater, almost half of AFSOC's entire AC-130 inventory. U.S. attack helicopters were also employed in Enduring Freedom for the first time, against targets close to Kabul, and a few Marine Corps AV-8B Harriers operating from USS *Peleliu* saw limited action in the first week of November.

On November 6, Northern Alliance sources reported the capture of the districts of Zari, Aq Kupak, and Keshendeh on the approach to Mazar-i-Sharif during an overnight fight that followed a sustained U.S. bombing effort to clear the way. Some 200 Taliban fighters were reported killed and 300 taken prisoner. By this time, the total number of U.S. and allied aircraft directly committed to the war

---

[158] Eric Schmitt and Steven Lee Myers, "U.S. Escalating Efforts to Bomb Taliban Caves," *New York Times*, November 6, 2001.

[159] Edward Walsh, "U.S. Campaign on Schedule, Generals Say," *Washington Post*, November 5, 2001.

[160] David A. Fulghum, "Big Bomb Strikes Kandahar Defenses," *Aviation Week and Space Technology*, December 3, 2001, p. 23. For a time, this munition was confused in press reports with the BLU-72 fuel-air explosive weapon, which is no longer in use.

had risen to nearly 500. The average daily combat sortie rate during this ramped-up phase of the campaign was approximately 120 sorties a day, with most of those being Navy strike fighter missions. Most fighter operations continued to be conducted above 16,000 feet to remain above the lethal reach of any Taliban or al Qaeda infrared SAMs and AAA.

In an effort to increase the number of available carrier-based attack aircraft, the Navy for the first time began generating a small number of daily strike sorties from USS *Kitty Hawk*, which hitherto had been devoted almost entirely to supporting SOF helicopter operations. As many as a dozen tankers were airborne in the area at any moment to support these strike operations. General Franks asked for an additional carrier to be deployed to the region to relieve *Enterprise*, which finally left for home on October 23, thereby ending her cruise extension that began immediately after the terrorist attacks on September 11. The Navy found itself forced to juggle various deployment options to honor that request, with one sympathetic official commenting that "they're living with 12 carriers in a war where we need 15."[161] In the end, the USS *Theodore Roosevelt* carrier battle group arrived in the North Arabian Sea on October 17 to relieve the departing *Enterprise* battle group. The Pentagon also dispatched the carrier USS *John C. Stennis* to the theater from its home port in San Diego on November 12 to relieve USS *Carl Vinson*.[162] As this activity attested, the Bush administration was eager for Mazar-i-Sharif to fall before the onset of winter so that it could point to an indisputable benchmark of progress in the five-week-old effort.[163]

Air operations against Taliban front-line positions in northern Afghanistan were conducted for eight consecutive days in preparation for a Northern Alliance push on Mazar-i-Sharif and Kabul. The first

---

[161] Rowan Scarborough, "Air Force Slow to Transfer Special Bomb Kits to Navy," *Washington Times*, November 7, 2001.

[162] Bill Gertz and Rowan Scarborough, "Pentagon to Send Fourth Carrier to Afghanistan," *Washington Times*, November 8, 2001.

[163] Roland Watson and Michael Evans, "America Turns Up the Heat," *London Times*, November 7, 2001.

goal was to capture Shibarghan 50 miles to the west of Mazar, which was fortified by the Taliban as a main defensive bastion protecting Mazar. Toward that end, on November 7, Northern Alliance forces captured Shulgareh, a town 25 miles south of Mazar, with the expectation that Mazar itself would fall in turn within days. By this time, two air strikes on average against Taliban front-line positions were occurring for every one devoted to al Qaeda cave and tunnel complexes. In his first Pentagon briefing since the war began, General Franks said that the capture of Mazar would enable the opening of a land bridge from Uzbekistan, where CSAR helicopters, SOF reconnaissance teams, and elements of the Army's 10th Mountain Division had been prepositioned.[164] Franks insisted, in the face of hard media questioning, that his approach had not been excessively timid: "It is only those who believe this should be done in two weeks' time . . . who are disappointed in this."[165]

On November 9, Northern Alliance forces finally took Mazar-i-Sharif in the culmination of what one observer called "a slow-motion offensive paved with negotiated surrenders."[166] They attacked with T-55 tanks, armored vehicles, infantry, and even combatants charging on horseback, advancing northward into a city that had already been stunned by prior aerial bombardment. Thousands of Taliban fighters evacuated their bunkers and fled the city, leaving only their wounded behind in the city's hospitals. The local airport was also captured. USS *Theodore Roosevelt* launched scores of fighter sorties in direct support of the battle for Mazar-i-Sharif. The ensuing success made for the first tangible victory in Enduring Freedom, as well as a notable morale booster all around at a time when concerns about the campaign's halting progress had begun to mount across the board. As a CAOC staffer reflected on this experience in hindsight, "one of the best things about winning Mazar was the show of a success to

---

[164] Thom Shanker and Dexter Filkins, "U.S. Commander, Saying Rebels Need Help, Hints More Troops," *New York Times*, November 9, 2001.

[165] Bill Gertz, "General Happy with Campaign's Progress," *Washington Times*, November 9, 2001.

[166] Pollack, *The Threatening Storm*, p. 301.

our friends and enemies and the momentum it provided on the ground. . . . Morale in the CAOC went way high and stayed high after this victory and the quick move to Kabul. The feeling in the CAOC was that we had just crushed the adversary in the first half of the Superbowl and knew we would pile up the score in the second half. . . . Consequently, the most important thing to do now was to concentrate and not get a big head."[167]

Three Northern Alliance warlords—Generals Dostum, Attah Mohammed, and Mohammed Mohaqiq—were collectively able to achieve the fall of Mazar-i-Sharif only by setting aside their large differences and working together. After thousands of Taliban soldiers had fled the city, Secretary Rumsfeld reported that Northern Alliance forces had taken "effective control." Pakistan's President Musharraf said that Operation Enduring Freedom had, as a result, "now turned the corner."[168] The Bush administration continued, however, to insist that the Northern Alliance not capture Kabul on its own, without Pashtun involvement.

After Mazar-i-Sharif fell, U.S. strike aircrews found it increasingly hard to determine where enemy forces were hiding because of the fluid state of play on the ground. On more than one day, all airborne Navy fighters ended up returning to their carriers without dropping a single weapon because of a lack of any target assignments. As the commander of the air wing embarked in USS *Carl Vinson*, Captain T. C. Bennett, put it, "we simply are not sure who are the good guys and who are the bad guys."[169]

On November 11, A-Team 555 shifted its focus to Taliban positions at the Bagram Air Base near Kabul. In short order, the team called in 25 air attacks, which resulted in the destruction of 29 enemy tanks and six command posts and 2,200 enemy casualties. That, in turn, cleared the way for the Northern Alliance to advance on

---

[167] Comments on an earlier draft by Major Charles Hogan, USAF, December 22, 2003.

[168] Brian Knowlton, "Anti-Taliban Forces Continue Their March," *International Herald Tribune*, November 12, 2001.

[169] Robert Wall, "Navy Adapts Operations for Afghan Hurdle," *Aviation Week and Space Technology*, November 19, 2001, p. 35.

Kabul.[170] That same day, Northern Alliance forces surged on three sides against Taliban forces defending Kabul. President Bush encouraged them to move southward, but he asked them at the same time to stop short of entering the city until a political agreement with southern Pashtun elements could be reached. The Northern Alliance's foreign minister Abdullah replied that his resistance forces would abide by this request for a time, but that if no agreement with Pashtun leaders was reached, they would press ahead into Kabul on their own.[171]

U.S. air attacks now concentrated on Taliban forces deployed north of Kabul, with Air Force C-17s regularly air-dropping horse feed, along with ammunition, weapons, and water, to Northern Alliance fighting units.[172] Alliance forces had advanced to within 35 miles of Kabul, but the fortifications and defenses around the capital were assessed to be more formidable than those at Mazar. EC-130 Commando Solo aircraft transmitted radio broadcasts offering $25 million to anyone willing to betray bin Laden to a point that led to his capture. They also transmitted music and news 10 hours a day and warned the Afghan populace to keep clear of Taliban and al Qaeda military assets, stressing that the war was not against the Afghan people and that those assets could be attacked at any time. In the end, in just three days (from November 9 to November 12), the Northern Alliance went from controlling only 15 percent of Afghanistan to controlling nearly half of the country, as Kabul was abandoned and thousands of Taliban and al Qaeda combatants fled south to Pakistan and east to the mountains of Tora Bora.[173]

In Pakistan to meet with President Musharraf, Secretary Rumsfeld declared that the campaign's weight of effort thus far had still not succeeded in dislodging the Taliban and that the bombing would ac-

---

[170] Woodward, p. 309.

[171] William Branigin and Keith B. Richburg, "Alliance Surges Across North," *Washington Post*, November 12, 2001.

[172] Vernon Loeb and Thomas E. Ricks, "Pressure to Curtail War Grows," *Washington Post*, October 30, 2001.

[173] Loeb and Ricks, p. 314.

cordingly continue through Ramadan. Rumsfeld further noted that requests for a slowdown or halt of the bombing during the month-long Muslim fasting period, an appeal that had been made repeatedly by Musharraf, would not be honored, noting that Muslims them-selves had frequently ignored Ramadan during their intramural wars throughout the ages. "History is replete," Rumsfeld said, "with in-stances where Muslim nations have fought among themselves or with other countries during various important holy days for their religion, and it has not inhibited them historically."[174]

Thanks in large measure to the substantial allied progress that had been registered over the preceding three days, a long stalemate on the ground was followed by a remarkable series of allied gains in close succession. In short order, opposition forces captured Herat in west-ern Afghanistan 80 miles from the Iranian border, which earlier had been the locus of successful U.S. air attacks against Taliban defenders without the benefit of allied SOF teams on the ground designating targets. That victory came just days after the win at Mazar had cleared the way for the Northern Alliance to concentrate its energies on the taking of Kabul. The Taliban had badly underestimated both Ameri-can air power and the Northern Alliance's determination. The result was not just a tactical retreat on their part but a rout. Once American ground FACs had been inserted into Afghanistan and were in posi-tion to designate Taliban targets, allied progress on the ground began moving rapidly. As one observer later wrote, "the relentless pounding broke the spirits of the Taliban, whose forces began to defect in ever larger numbers."[175] The Taliban still, however, controlled southern and eastern Afghanistan and the long border with Pakistan.

On November 13, Northern Alliance forces captured Kabul. That event came as a major surprise to all. Taliban defenses simply imploded and their forces beat a precipitous retreat without even at-tempting to put up a fight as Northern Alliance formations poured in

---

[174] Tim Weiner, "Rumsfeld Says Ramadan Won't Halt U.S. Attacks," *New York Times*, November 5, 2001.

[175] Bowden, "The Kabul-Ki Dance," p. 86.

on Taliban positions to the north. The Taliban had all but completely evacuated the city by 5:30 a.m. on the morning after the attack began. More than 50 percent of the supporting U.S. air strikes involving some 60 aircraft were now committed to engaging emerging targets, which were loosely defined as "any movement of forces you could pick up and positively identify."[176]

The most consuming activity on Secretary Rumsfeld's part throughout this phase of the campaign was said to be getting allied SOF teams used properly. As one senior official recalled, "he just pushed and pushed on that." The consensus afterward was that the turning point in the campaign came when SOF target spotters went to work in earnest with the B-52s. After 10 successive days of that, Mazar-i-Sharif fell, followed in short order by Herat and Kabul. Rumsfeld later commented that "each place [where that] happened, the results got very good very fast."[177] (One of his personal guide rules from the very start of the campaign entailed managing public expectations wisely. Said one official: "He wants to underpromise and overproduce."[178])

The rapid collapse of enemy resistance was caused as much by Taliban defections as it was by any particular battlefield prowess on the part of the Northern Alliance. Some 5,000 Taliban defected altogether, which allowed Kabul to be taken without a fight. Another 3,000 Taliban and al Qaeda personnel were estimated to have escaped into Pakistan, with a senior Taliban official reporting through the Afghan Islamic Press agency in Pakistan that bin Laden and Omar remained "safe and well" in Afghanistan.[179]

---

[176] Keith B. Richburg and Molly Moore, "Taliban Flees Afghan Capital," *Washington Post,* November 13, 2001.

[177] Thomas E. Ricks, "Rumsfeld's Hands-On War," *Washington Post,* December 9, 2001.

[178] Mazetti and Newman, "Rumsfeld's Way."

[179] John Pomfret and Rajiv Chandrasekaran, "Taliban Faces Tribal Revolt," *Washington Post*, November 15, 2001. On the unwillingness of the Bush administration and CENTCOM to commit U.S. ground troops more directly in a manner that might have prevented this, one writer complained that the way Operation Enduring Freedom was being conducted, namely, almost exclusively by medium- and high-altitude bombing attacks, would "do nothing to dispel the widespread impression that Americans are fat, indolent, and

Taliban soldiers who had been captured by Northern Alliance units early after September 11 were said to have been sublimely over-confident that they could easily handle U.S. soldiers and technology, perhaps based in part on their dim recollections of having successfully fended off the far less capable Soviets. By and by, however, the fact that the Taliban were facing a new and more effective enemy was well borne out by a summary assessment of the highest-ranking Taliban defector to date. Haji Mullah Khaksar, the Taliban's deputy interior minister who defected to the Northern Alliance as Kabul was falling on November 13, said: "Kabul has seen many rockets, but this was a different thing. The American bombing of Taliban trenches, cars, and troops caused us to be defeated."[180] The bombing forced the Taliban leadership, in an emergency session convened the previous night, to abandon Kabul to prevent a bloodbath after, in the graphic words of one reporter, "two weeks of eating airstrikes and dying in the night clueless."[181] Yet despite that continuing air effort, the bombing was not nearly as intensive as it might have been. The CAOC had a very elaborate bombing plan all laid out and ready to go with the start of the Northern Alliance's final advance on the Afghan capital. In the end, however, that plan proved unnecessary. The CIA's liberal use of money also helped to buy off the enemy commanders who were arrayed along the route of advance between Bagram and the capital city. The Northern Alliance essentially walked into Kabul.[182]

Afterward, Northern Alliance leaders agreed to meet with other Afghan tribes and factions in the south on neutral ground in Europe

---

unwilling to fight the barbarians on their own terms," that is, face-to-face on the ground. This writer saw the Afghan war as just one more example of what he called the "body-bag syndrome" at work. He added, disparagingly, that "our bombing campaign reveals great technical and logistical prowess, but it does not show that we have the determination to stick a bayonet in the guts of the enemy." (Max Boot, "This Victory May Haunt Us," *Wall Street Journal*, November 14, 2001.)

[180] Peterson.

[181] Robin Moore, *The Hunt for bin Laden: Task Force Dagger*, New York, Random House, 2003, p. 122.

[182] Comments on an earlier draft by Major Charles Hogan, USAF, December 22, 2003.

to discuss power-sharing arrangements in a post-Taliban government. In so doing, they abandoned their earlier insistence that any such convocation must take place in Kabul. That concession opened the way for the beginning of an effort to organize a transition government. Northern Alliance representatives met with Ambassador Dobbins in Tashkent, Uzbekistan, and then at Bagram Air Base outside Kabul to confirm their willingness to participate in talks at a venue to be chosen by the United Nations.

With the fall of Mazar-i-Sharif and Kabul, the Taliban theocracy had been all but dismantled, and the foreign al Qaeda presence in Afghanistan was clearly on the run. As a Taliban representative observed many months later of the regime's increasingly felt vulnerability, "we couldn't gather in large groups because that made us a target. We were waiting for our comrades to tell us what to do, but there was nothing to do but hide."[183] Although a substantial number of al Qaeda and Taliban combatants, leaders and foot soldiers alike, succeeded in eluding the campaign's effects, the interim victories that culminated in the fall of Mazar-i-Sharif and Kabul nonetheless opened up new and expanded opportunities for CENTCOM to further prosecute the war. Those opportunities included a much-broadened latitude for conducting special operations against enemy holdouts now secluded in mountain caves and elsewhere and the ability to operate both combat and support aircraft at will out of Tajikistan and Afghanistan.

---

[183] Romesh Ratnesar, "Grading the Other War," *Time*, October 14, 2002.

CHAPTER FOUR

A Shift in Strategy

The capture of Mazar-i-Sharif and Kabul by Northern Alliance forces, aided decisively by American air power working in close harmony with allied SOF teams, was a major breakthrough.[1] Indeed, progress in the campaign had accelerated so far ahead of U.S. expectations that General Franks was moved to consider a substantial reshaping of CENTCOM's strategy. A senior Pentagon official remarked in this regard that "this has moved so fast, we have to step back and review where we go next." Another spokesman added, in a similar vein, that "given [recent] developments, it's time to take stock."[2]

Although the rout of the Taliban from Afghanistan's capital was an important interim victory, the first phase of Enduring Freedom was by no means over yet. Taliban forces continued to fight hard to retain control of Kunduz and Kandahar, the latter of which was the religious movement's primary and last remaining stronghold. Accordingly, CENTCOM's center of focus shifted to those two key areas, where the majority of U.S. air strikes were now being concentrated. Allied SOF teams were now engaged systematically in enabling the aerial plinking of enemy targets of opportunity by sealing

---

[1] Coalition countries that provided special operations forces for Enduring Freedom included Australia, Canada, Denmark, France, Germany, Norway, Poland, Turkey, and the United Kingdom. See Bensahel, pp. 55–63.

[2] Thom Shanker and Steven Lee Myers, "Rapid Changes on the Ground Lead the Pentagon to Focus on Counterguerrilla Tactics," *New York Times*, November 15, 2001.

off roads near Kandahar, selectively blowing up bridges, and calling in attacks on moving vehicles. All of this was enhanced by a multi-spectral ISR umbrella that stared relentlessly down on Afghanistan from a multiplicity of air and space assets operating constantly overhead. Most of the war's critics who had fretted earlier, sometimes outspokenly, about an impending "quagmire" fell quickly silent in the face of these successes. CENTCOM planners were now planning to make use of the airfields at Mazar-i-Sharif to the north and at Bagram, near Kabul, farther south. Toward that end, about 160 U.S. SOF troops and British Marines were delivered by eight C-130s to Bagram on November 15 immediately after the capture of Kabul.

As the siege of Kunduz unfolded, allied air strikes increased in number and grew more intense. The city still harbored an estimated 2,000 to 3,000 Taliban combatants, including special units made up of expatriate Arabs, Chechens, and Pakistanis. Because there was no organized resistance against the Taliban in the south of Afghanistan anything comparable to that which had been put up so effectively by the Northern Alliance in the preceding engagements, it was feared that introducing Northern Alliance forces into Pashtun territory to fill the resultant vacuum might have explosive consequences, making it necessary for U.S. ground troops to carry the combat burden there alone to prevent such an undesirable outcome. Fortunately, however, as the concurrent effort to forge an interim post-Taliban coalition government continued to show progress, the Northern Alliance consented to yield exclusive power in Kabul to a transitional leadership which, by UN Security Council injunction, would be "broad-based, multiethnic, and fully representative."[3] Ambassador Dobbins elicited this important concession from the Northern Alliance in a meeting with its principals at Bagram Air Base immediately after the fall of Kabul.

In yet another encouraging sign of progress, the first confirmed reports were cited, based on intercepted enemy radio traffic, that the bombing in the Kandahar area had finally succeeded in killing

---

[3] John F. Burns, "Alliance in Kabul Will Share Power, U.S. Envoy Reports," *New York Times*, November 20, 2001.

some senior al Qaeda leaders.[4] Principal among them was bin Laden's military chief, Mohammed Atef, who had intimate ties to the terrorist leader through his daughter's marriage to bin Laden's son.[5] Atef was reputed to have been closely involved in the planning of the ambush of the U.S. Army Rangers in Somalia in 1993, the subsequent American embassy bombings in Africa in 1998, and the September 11 airliner attacks against the U.S. homeland. He was killed while inside a targeted house by an LGB dropped by an Air Force F-15E, which, by happenstance, was in the process of conducting what turned out to have been the longest fighter combat mission in history (15.8 hours).[6]

At this point in the campaign, General Franks declared that the Taliban military had been "fractured" and that the next step was to find and capture bin Laden and his principal al Qaeda deputies.[7] After the fall of Mazar-i-Sharif and Kabul, most of the original 60,000-strong Taliban membership, many of whom were believed to be still armed, were simply absorbed back into the nearest towns and mountains and melted away into the broader Afghan population. Bin Laden himself, who had already gone into deep seclusion even before the terrorist attacks of September 11, had not been heard from since his presumably prerecorded videotape message right after the start of Enduring Freedom. He was evidently taking special care to avoid engaging in any satellite telephone or radio communication that might be intercepted by U.S. sensors and thereby reveal his location. Accordingly, greater emphasis was now placed by CENTCOM on intelligence-gathering and on finding and rooting out al Qaeda and

---

[4] James Dao, "More U.S. Troops in bin Laden Hunt; Hideouts Bombed," *New York Times,* November 19, 2001.

[5] Only three of al Qaeda's top 20 leaders believed to have been in Afghanistan at the start of the war were thought to have been killed by U.S. military action. In addition to Atef, Fahmi Nasr and Tariq Anwar, both senior leaders of the Egyptian Islamic Jihad movement, were later designated as killed in action.

[6] Comments on an earlier draft by then–Lieutenant General T. Michael Moseley, USAF, who was the CENTAF Commander and CFACC for Enduring Freedom at the time.

[7] Bill Gertz, "Forces Tighten the Noose on bin Laden," *Washington Times,* November 16, 2001.

Taliban leaders who had slipped into hiding. By mid-November, U.S. and British SOF units were said to have narrowed their search for bin Laden to a 30-square-mile area in southeastern Afghanistan.[8]

Hunting Down an Elusive Quarry

With the Taliban's remaining days in power clearly numbered, the Pentagon was now indicating that the campaign had entered a new phase, with less well-defined front lines and with the emphasis now placed on "Taliban-plinking" and on rooting out al Qaeda combatants wherever they might be found. Almost certainly in connection with this changed emphasis, Secretary Rumsfeld confirmed that Global Hawk UAV surveillance operations over Afghanistan had finally begun.[9] As for the campaign's level of effort to date, the Joint Staff's spokesman, Rear Admiral Stufflebeam, reported that around 10,000 munitions had been expended during the first 45 days of combat. That expenditure rate was roughly comparable to the weapons delivery rate of Operation Allied Force, which saw 23,614 munitions employed over its 78-day course. A major difference between the two campaigns, however, was the overall proportion of precision weapons employed (around 60 percent in Operation Enduring Freedom, as compared to only 35 percent in Allied Force).[10] The lower number of air-delivered munitions dropped in comparison to the far more intensive Desert Storm campaign a decade earlier reflected, among other things, a much lower number of high-value targets in Afghanistan, the proximity of many targets to concentrations of civilian population, and an overriding determination on the part of the

---

[8] Ellen Knickmeyer, "Taliban Offers to Surrender Kunduz," *Washington Times*, November 19, 2001.

[9] Thomas E. Ricks, "In the South, U.S. Faces a Guerrilla War," *Washington Post*, November 21, 2001, and Vernon Loeb and Bradley Graham, "Navy Ordered to Block Any Bid by bin Laden to Escape by Sea," *Washington Post*, November 22, 2001.

[10] Tony Capaccio, "Sixty Percent of Bombs Dropped on Afghanistan Precision-Guided," Bloomberg.com, November 20, 2001.

Bush administration to preserve Afghan infrastructure and minimize noncombatant casualties.

On November 22, Northern Alliance tanks and troops advanced in strength on Kunduz and promptly encountered a sustained Taliban artillery barrage. Opposition forces responded by laying down the heaviest counterfire barrage in the 11 days since they had seized Taloqan 30 miles east of Kunduz. Four days later, the alliance captured Kunduz, with around 400 remaining Taliban holdouts surrendering after an air strike put 15 JDAMs directly on their positions.

In the meantime, in a deployment code-named Operation Swift Freedom, approximately 1,200 U.S. Marines entered southern Afghanistan on November 25, heralding the first involvement of conventional U.S. ground troops on a significant scale in the seven-week campaign. The Marines were flown into an airstrip 80 miles southwest of Kandahar to reinforce a foothold that had initially been secured by an Army Special Forces A-Team and that soon came to be called Forward Operating Base (FOB) Rhino. Until that deployment, the only U.S. ground presence in Afghanistan had consisted of a few hundred SOF personnel working with a smaller number of CIA paramilitary operatives. The Marines arrived in a stream of CH-46 and CH-53 helicopters and were quickly followed by C-130s, which carried their supplies. They were components of two Marine Expeditionary Units (MEUs), the 15th MEU aboard USS *Peleliu* and the 26th MEU aboard USS *Bataan*, which had been combined into an ad hoc brigade designated Task Force (TF) 58 under the command of Brigadier General James Mattis.[11]

The site for FOB Rhino was selected because it was near the last remaining Taliban stronghold of Kandahar and also was collocated with a network of roads leading from Afghanistan to Pakistan and Iran. The establishment of the base signaled a clear shift away from the prior U.S. reliance on proxy Afghan opposition groups. Hitherto, the United States had pursued a low-risk strategy that enlisted indigenous Afghan resistance fighters in lieu of U.S. ground forces to

---

[11] Thomas E. Ricks and Bob Woodward, "Marines Enter South Afghanistan," *Washington Post*, November 26, 2001.

do the hard work on the ground to minimize the likelihood of U.S. combat casualties. One of several opportunity costs of that strategy was its inability to produce the desired outcome whenever U.S. and opposition-group interests diverged. The Marine Corps presence was not introduced as an intended occupying force but rather to establish an expanded capability on the ground to help contain any further Taliban and al Qaeda movement. In an early incident, Marine Corps AH-1W Super Cobra attack helicopters coordinated an attack by F-14s against a convoy of 15 Taliban vehicles that were detected on the move.

A major problem was created for U.S. in-country flight operations by often choking clouds of sand and dust, which would quickly clog any orifice on airframes or engines. Helicopters were especially adversely affected by the harsh desert conditions, which often forced "no-hover" landings in which the pilot would touch down while the aircraft was still moving forward so as to avoid being enveloped by the blinding dust wake. As a result, helicopter rotor-head bearings had to be greased after every flight, two or three times more often than was the normal practice. Dust also distorted the clarity of night-vision goggles during helicopter landings at night, especially by the big CH-53. In short order, Navy Seabees laid down a serviceable runway at FOB Rhino and installed electrical power and other needed service support. After that was done, Air Force C-17s began landing in Afghanistan for the first time, carrying both needed materiel and humanitarian relief supplies. [12] The buildup of Super Cobra, Huey, and troop transport helicopters also continued at FOB Rhino, doubling the overall number of aircraft now available to TF-58. The runway length also was extended to 6,800 feet, with Seabee graders working continually to keep it cleared of piling dust.

---

[12] Shortly before this long-awaited development began, paradrops of wheat, blankets, and other humanitarian relief for Afghan civilians had been suspended after a wooden container weighing 1,800 lb crashed through the roof of a house north of Mazar after its parachute had failed, killing an Afghan woman inside. Airdrops of smaller humanitarian daily ration (HDR) food packets from C-17s, however, continued.

The first conventional U.S. Army presence, consisting of fewer than 100 light infantry troops, concurrently entered Afghanistan in the form of a rapid reaction force comprising elements of the 10th Mountain Division. The Army contingent was sent to the Mazar-i-Sharif and Bagram airports to help provide force protection for U.S. SOF and other operations that were being conducted from those sites. It was drawn from the larger U.S. Army presence (numbering roughly a thousand personnel) that had been holding in place and awaiting further orders for weeks in a garrison at Karshi-Khanabad in Uzbekistan. Once that deployment was completed, between 1,500 and 2,000 U.S. military personnel had arrived in Afghanistan. The goal, however, continued to be to maintain as light a U.S. footprint as possible.[13]

As the endgame of the counter-Taliban portion of Enduring Freedom drew ever closer, a major revolt by some 700 captured Taliban and hard-core al Qaeda fighters occurred at the end of November in General Dostum's personal fortress six miles west of Mazar-i-Sharif, which had been converted by the Northern Alliance into a makeshift prison. The revolt triggered a major gun battle in which hundreds of the prisoners rushed their guards and seized their weapons, killing some in the process. The battle lasted six and a half hours and was not brought under control until U.S. SOF personnel and British SAS troops, aided by Navy fighter aircraft, were summoned to contain and terminate the uprising. During the course of that revolt, hundreds of enemy prisoners were killed. The uprising also resulted in the first U.S. combat fatality to occur in the campaign, a CIA officer, Johnny Spann, who had been participating in the interrogation of the enemy prisoners.[14] Of the joint-service cooperation that was reflected in this and other campaign events, the Air Force chief of staff, General Jumper, commented that "no one element can do the whole job, so we all work together. What we see in action over

---

[13] Steven Lee Myers, "Marines Build Firepower in the South, Bolstering Their Patrols and Readiness," *New York Times*, December 3, 2001.

[14] For more details on the prison uprising, see Moore, pp. 167–181.

Afghanistan today is a combination of air, land, and sea power cooperating and working together. The results speak for themselves."[15]

Secretary Rumsfeld further reported that U.S. SOF forces in and around Kandahar were not working any longer in liaison with indigenous opposition forces but instead were now operating independently as the cutting edge of an accelerated push against the Taliban and al Qaeda. In connection with that push, SOF units were now cleared to plan and execute direct-action attacks whenever deemed necessary, a long-awaited move that led to hundreds of reported enemy deaths. One U.S. official spoke of an "unrestricted hunting license" having been given to U.S. SOF forces for going after Taliban militia and al Qaeda personnel. General Franks was said to have granted the involved SOF units their greatest freedom of action since Vietnam. Those units worked in small teams, primarily at night, identifying Taliban and al Qaeda positions around Kandahar and engaging them without seeking prior CENTCOM approval. Much of this direct-action work came in the form of quick responses to tips.[16] Ultimately, Army Special Forces units married up with converging opposition-group forces, with the A-Team code-named Texas 12 accompanying Karzai and his fighters from the north and Texas 17 with Gul Agha Sharzai and his forces from the south. (Sharzai was later appointed governor of Kandahar.)

As the pressure on Kandahar mounted, General Myers said that the Taliban retreat from the city was "more disorganized than organized. . . . It's defections and it's withdrawal, and it's just trying to blend into the landscape."[17] The flight of the Taliban reduced the hoped-for number of targets of opportunity, since it was all but impossible to identify valid targets with Taliban personnel so commingled with fleeing Afghan civilians. However, a 15,000-lb BLU-82/B

[15] Comment by General John P. Jumper, USAF, November 13, 2001, quoted in "USAF Talking Points: The War on Terrorism," SAF/PA, November 28, 2001.

[16] Rowan Scarborough, "Special Forces Get Free Rein," *Washington Times*, November 23, 2001.

[17] Thomas E. Ricks and Bradley Graham, "U.S. Special Forces on the Trail of Taliban Leaders," *Washington Post*, November 14, 2001.

was dropped by an MC-130 on one dug-in Taliban position south of Kandahar to useful effect. Plainly beaten down by the continuing air strikes, the remaining Taliban holdouts at one point offered to surrender their last stronghold if those in the city who were still loyal to Mullah Omar could be spared. To that, Secretary Rumsfeld replied that the United States was adamantly opposed to any settlement arrangement that allowed Omar to escape.[18] Bombing attacks accordingly continued in the vicinity of Kandahar and near Jalalabad to the east, where bin Laden was thought to be hiding in a mountain cave complex near the village of Tora Bora. Shortly thereafter, on November 28, elements of both Northern Alliance and Pashtun opposition forces encircled Kandahar and prepared to move in on it, using on-call support by Marine Corps attack helicopters operating out of FOB Rhino.

On December 1, air attacks on Kandahar intensified as opposition forces moved to within 10 miles of that last remaining Taliban holdout and a loose encirclement of the city progressively became a siege. Concurrently, talks among the four Afghan opposition groups continued in Bonn as a draft agreement for a post-Taliban government gradually began to take shape, with now-exhausted Afghan delegates and UN mediators at long last down to the point of arguing over the allocation of 25 to 30 jobs needed to staff an interim Afghan government. Weeks later, Hamid Karzai, who eventually emerged as post-Taliban Afghanistan's interim leader, would characterize as the war's "decisive battle" a notable attack that occurred on November 18 by carrier-based strike fighters, aided by U.S. SOF teams and combat controllers on the ground, against a convoy of around 1,000 Taliban soldiers travelling in as many as 100 vehicles.[19]

In the meantime, the first case of a fratricidal bombing error occurred on December 5, 2001, when a JDAM was inadvertently called in on a combat controller's own position. The mistaken aim point

---

[18] Maura Reynolds and Paul Richter, "U.S. Opposes Any Deal with Taliban Forces," *Los Angeles Times,* November 20, 2001.

[19] "In a Desert Outpost, Afghan War Was Won: U.S. Firepower Decimated Taliban at Tarin Kot," *Washington Post,* December 31, 2001.

resulted in three U.S. and five Afghan soldiers killed and 20 American and 18 Afghan soldiers wounded. It occurred when a SOF team called for an air strike against Taliban units positioned five miles north of Kandahar. Karzai, who was nearby and who was being protected by the SOF forces, barely escaped being killed by the single 2,000-lb GBU-31 that had been dropped by a B-52. He was only slightly hurt. His survival averted a potential strategic disaster for the United States, since Karzai had emerged as the consensus candidate among all contending parties negotiating in Bonn to be Afghanistan's interim leader. The American soldiers were standing close to where the JDAM impacted, producing the first American military fatalities during the eight-week war.[20] (A week earlier, five Army Special Forces troops were similarly injured when a Marine Corps F/A-18 dropped a bomb too close to their position during the prison uprising in Mazar-i-Sharif.) In the case of the friendly fire incident north of Kandahar, it was initially thought that the wrong target coordinates had been provided to the B-52's crew. It was later determined that the GPS (global positioning system) receiver used by the combat controller to establish target coordinates had just been given a new battery pack and that the controller did not remember that the device was programmed to revert to its own coordinates whenever the battery was changed. Fortunately, the controller survived.[21]

Toward the Consolidation of Initial Gains

By early December 2001, the United States had accomplished much of what it had sought by way of initial military and political goals in Afghanistan. The Taliban were in flight; the cities of Mazar-i-Sharif, Herat, and Kabul were in the hands of opposition forces and calm;

---

[20] James Dao and Eric Schmitt, "Bin Laden Hunted in Caves; Errant U.S. Bomb Kills Three GIs," *New York Times*, December 6, 2001.

[21] Vernon Loeb, "'Friendly Fire' Deaths Traced to Dead Battery," *Washington Post*, March 24, 2002, and John Hendren and Maura Reynolds, "The U.S. Bomb That Nearly Killed Karzai," *Los Angeles Times*, March 27, 2002.

the al Qaeda terrorist infrastructure in Afghanistan had been demolished or dispersed; and a post-Taliban interim Afghan leadership had been successfully formed in Bonn. As the final battle for Kandahar continued, the main focus of CENTCOM's attention now shifted to the mountain cave complex at Tora Bora, which was cut into the 13,000-foot-high peaks of the Spin Ghar range 35 miles southwest of Jalalabad, to which large numbers of Taliban and al Qaeda combatants were believed to have fled.[22] The complex featured tunnels as much as eight feet wide and extending as far as a thousand feet into the mountain, with ventilated chambers that were heated and lighted by generators.[23] Al Qaeda fighters had accumulated ample weapon stores in the Tora Bora mountains and succeeded in pushing back the initial opposition-group forays with heavy mortar fire. The senior British military advisor to General Franks and the commander of the United Kingdom's national contingent to Operation Enduring Freedom, RAF Air Marshal Jock Stirrup, predicted that hunting through the caves for hard-core enemy holdouts would present the coalition with its biggest challenge to date.[24]

There were earlier reports that Russia had provided useful intelligence on the Afghan cave complex that derived from military maps developed during the decade-long Soviet occupation of Afghanistan.[25] Perhaps aided by that information, around 90 percent of U.S. bomber and fighter attack missions were now devoted to cave-related emerging targets, which included cave entrances. (Even though a cave entrance was fixed, it was considered to be functionally equivalent to a mobile target whenever real-time intelligence indicated activity in or near it.) Three SOF combatants and two CIA operatives infiltrated into the heart of Tora Bora and used laser designators for four

---

[22] Tora Bora in Pashto, the local language, means "black dust."

[23] Johanna McGeary, "Hunting Osama," *Time*, December 10, 2001.

[24] Michael Evans, "British Special Forces to Join Cave Assault," *London Times*, December 3, 2001.

[25] Thom Shanker and James Dao, "U.S. Ready to Send Additional Troops to Hunt bin Laden," *New York Times*, November 21, 2001.

straight days to mark targets and call in air attacks.[26] Approaching winter weather, however, had begun to affect the use of LGBs adversely as increasing cloud cover obscured targets and prevented LGB seeker heads from acquiring the laser spots provided by ground combat controllers.

One early indication that the Pentagon was now content with the self-sufficiency of U.S. SOF teams in Afghanistan was the departure of USS *Kitty Hawk*, which had been used as a staging base for SOF operations during the early phase of the war, for her home port in Japan the second week of December. There were no plans to commit the 1,500 Marines at FOB Rhino to an al Qaeda manhunt in the Tora Bora mountains. Marine Corps infantrymen did, however, join up with British and Australian SOF combatants in spreading out to block the main routes leading into and out of Kandahar in an attempt to prevent al Qaeda and Taliban escapees from slipping through the Safed mountain range into Pakistan.

Concurrently, in an initiative that led to a rude awakening for CENTCOM, as many as 1,500 southern Pashtun opposition-group fighters were mobilized to scour the Tora Bora complex for any secluded enemy combatants. The opposition-group fighters had been both eager and effective when it came to driving Taliban forces out of the cities and putting themselves in charge in the Taliban's place. Their interests clearly diverged from those of the United States in Tora Bora, however, when it came to hunting down al Qaeda holdouts who were dug in and determined to fight to the finish. Instead, many Afghan resistance fighters who were in a position to cut private deals accepted huge bribes from al Qaeda members to provide them safe passage to Pakistan.[27] As a result, a substantial number of enemy combatants were allowed to get away.

---

[26] Woodward, p. 315.

[27] By some reports, individual Afghan soldiers were paid as much as $5,000—a near-astronomical sum in Afghanistan—by escaping al Qaeda fighters to look the other way. (Norman Friedman, *Terrorism, Afghanistan, and America's New Way of War*, Annapolis, Md., Naval Institute Press, 2003, p. 200.)

Meanwhile, on December 4, the four Afghan opposition groups whose representatives had been negotiating in Bonn finally agreed to a UN-drafted text laying out the broad outlines and responsibilities of an interim post-Taliban government, as well as an implementation schedule and a recommended course toward a more permanent arrangement. Implementation of the agreement would supplant any remaining governing authority on the part of Burhanuddin Rabbani, who had been ousted by the Taliban in 1996 but continued to be recognized by the UN as Afghanistan's legitimate leader. An executive council of the interim government would serve for six months, during which time a separate commission would organize a grand national council (or "loya jirga") of ethnic and provincial leaders to agree on a new executive and legislature to serve for as long as two years while a constitution for Afghanistan was being written, after which yet another loya jirga would ratify the constitution and elections for national leadership would be held. Hamid Karzai, who remained in Afghanistan during the Bonn proceeding, was appointed head of the interim executive council that was scheduled to assume power in Kabul on December 22. Months later, in a concerned progress report on the effort, Ambassador Dobbins would rightly portray this collective achievement as "a minor miracle."[28]

The continuing battle for Kandahar was fought mainly from the air and entailed more than two months of strikes against the city's outskirts. Most of the bombs that were dropped hit their intended aim points, and relatively few civilian fatalities were incurred. By way of illustration of the discriminate force employment that was made possible by the precision weapons available to the United States, in one case an attack by F-15Es flattened three known al Qaeda houses that were lined up in a row. Yet two burlap tents directly adjacent to them that belonged to the UN Food and Agricultural Organization were left unharmed by the attacks. Similarly, a house across town that

---

[28] James Dobbins, "Afghanistan's Faltering Reconstruction," *New York Times*, September 12, 2002. On December 16, Rumsfeld flew to Bagram and met with Karzai and General Mohammed Fahim, the Northern Alliance commander who became Afghanistan's post-Taliban defense minister.

was partly occupied by Arab terrorists was attacked, killing 25 occupants. But only the targeted Arab foreigners were among the fatalities.[29] Thanks to such selective and discriminate bombing, Kandahar escaped significant war damage entirely, apart from the Taliban's headquarters buildings, some telecommunications facilities, Taliban military equipment, and known al Qaeda offices and barracks.

Earlier, on December 6, the Taliban had offered to surrender to Karzai in return for guarantees of personal safety for Mullah Omar and other top Taliban leaders. That offer presaged an imminent collapse of the Taliban. As noted previously, Rumsfeld replied that Omar would not be allowed to go free. For his part, Karzai found himself in the discomfiting position of being caught between Washington's demands for the arrests of Omar and other top Taliban leaders and the conflicting interests of many of his fellow Pashtun, who were angered by the American bombing and inclined to regard Karzai as overly submissive to the United States. Nevertheless, Karzai insisted that he would make no concessions to the Taliban. With respect to Omar, said Karzai, it "is a question for Afghans." As for the foreign al Qaeda fighters in Afghanistan, "they must be dealt with and brought to justice. They are guilty of ruining Afghanistan and causing terrorism."[30] The now-former Taliban ambassador to Pakistan, Abdul Zayeef, confessed after the attempted deal was rejected that the Taliban were now finished as a political force, adding: "I think we should go home."[31] On December 9, the five-year rule of the Taliban came to an end, and Karzai rode triumphantly into Kandahar in an unarmed convoy. The next day, only nine weeks after the onset of Enduring Freedom, Under Secretary of Defense Wolfowitz

---

[29] John Pomfret, "Kandahar Bombs Hit Their Marks," *Washington Post*, December 12, 2001.

[30] John Pomfret, "Taliban Accepts Surrender Deal," *Washington Post*, December 7, 2001.

[31] On January 3, Pakistani officials arrested Zayeef and turned him over to the United States, whereupon he was promptly incarcerated along with other Taliban detainees.

declared that the United States had "accomplished one major objective, which [was] the defeat of the Taliban government."[32]

The Battles of Tora Bora and Zhawar Kili

With the fall of Kandahar 63 days after the start of the campaign, Secretary Rumsfeld declared that the war effort had now entered a new phase, with a principal focus on finding bin Laden and his top lieutenants, stabilizing post-Taliban Afghanistan, and addressing humanitarian concerns in the war-ravaged country. Rumsfeld stressed the crucial importance of maintaining a tight lock on "why we went there," which meant not relenting for a moment in the continuing hunt for al Qaeda fugitives.[33] Hard-core al Qaeda combatants continued to hold out in the Tora Bora mountains, having found armed shelter in as many as 200 separate caves.[34] That made imminent what the JCS chairman, General Myers, called "a very tough battle" to root them out and capture or kill them.[35]

In connection with that effort, an Air Force B-52 delivered one AGM-142 Have Nap missile equipped with a rock-penetrating warhead against a cave entrance of special interest in Tora Bora that presented a demanding access challenge requiring that a precision munition be actually flown into it.[36] Also, another 15,000-lb BLU-82/B bomb was dropped on a portion of the Tora Bora cave complex believed to be housing al Qaeda leaders, such that no one could get

---

[32] Thom Shanker and Eric Schmitt, "Taliban Defeated, Pentagon Asserts, But War Goes On," *New York Times*, December 11, 2001.

[33] Bradley Graham and Thomas E. Ricks, "Rumsfeld Says War Far From Over," *Washington Post*, December 8, 2001.

[34] Anthony Cordesman, *The Lessons of Afghanistan: Warfighting, Intelligence, Force Transformation, Counter-Proliferation, and Arms Control*, Washington, D.C.: Center for Strategic and International Studies, June 28, 2002, p. 20.

[35] Susan B. Glasser, "U.S. Attacks on al Qaeda Intensify," *Washington Post*, December 10, 2001.

[36] Thom Shanker and Eric Schmitt, "Marines Advance Toward Kandahar to Prepare Siege," *New York Times*, December 5, 2001.

either into or out of it. JDAMs dropped by B-52s and F-16s caused massive rockslides in the Tora Bora mountain valley. One detonation set off secondary explosions that sent a plume of smoke more than a mile high into the sky. Some al Qaeda combatants on the receiving end of these attacks were heard to beg for mercy over their radios as dozens were confirmed killed. Six AC-130 gunships teamed up with Predator UAVs and joined the battle, raking the mountain ridgelines with highly accurate cannon fire.[37] At this point, General Myers called the Tora Bora battle a "pitched fight."[38]

There was an early report that bin Laden's principal deputy, Ayman Zawahiri, had been killed in Tora Bora.[39] A subsequent conflicting report indicated that Zawahiri himself remained unharmed, but that his wife and three daughters had been killed as a result of the air attacks. In all, according to the claim of a regional Afghan opposition leader, some 18 al Qaeda principals were killed in the heavily fortified Milawa cave complex, which was thought at the time to be the last remaining al Qaeda bastion. All of this, however, was and remains unconfirmed.

After the bombing of the Tora Bora mountains continued nonstop every day for three weeks, it was finally suspended for a brief period to allow opposition-group formations to advance on the caves in search of al Qaeda fugitives. Those formations advanced on Tora Bora on three sides, forcing the most hard-core remnants of al Qaeda to flee from their low-lying caves and seek refuge in the higher mountains of eastern Afghanistan. At the same time, U.S. SOF commanders inserted small and specialized "snatch and grab" teams empowered with prior approval to kill any al Qaeda leaders on sight. Earlier, British and U.S. SOF teams had begun checking some caves them-

---

[37] John Kifner, "Anti-Taliban Troops Take Up Positions on Mountainsides," *New York Times,* December 12, 2001.

[38] John Kifner and Eric Schmitt, "Fierce al Qaeda Defense Seen as a Sign of Terror Leader's Proximity," *New York Times,* December 14, 2001.

[39] Susan B. Glasser, "Al Qaeda Aides Killed in Raids," *Washington Post,* December 5, 2001.

selves after receiving a confirmed report that bin Laden had recently been spotted in the White Mountains.[40]

In light of the unusual fierceness of the al Qaeda resistance at Tora Bora, it was presumed at first that bin Laden had been surrounded and cornered. Later, however, administration spokesmen reluctantly conceded that there was only a 50–50 chance that he was still in hiding there. General Franks admitted that U.S. intelligence monitors "simply don't know" where he is.[41] Rumsfeld added: "It is a question mark as to his exact location. . . . My feeling is that until we catch him—which we will—we won't know precisely where he was."[42] U.S. intelligence thought it had a confirmed lead on him only 48 hours previously. Then the contact simply vanished.

Later, administration sources conceded that SIGINT indications and subsequent detainee interrogations had strongly suggested that bin Laden had been holed up in the area when the bombing began but that he had succeeded in getting away sometime during the first 10 days of December.[43] There was concern for a time thereafter that he and other al Qaeda principals might try to escape by sea, which led to a stepped-up surveillance effort in the Arabian Sea and Persian Gulf. As of late December 2001, as many as 100 vessels had been queried by allied warships in search of any such enemy fugitives. The only good news in all of this was that although the terrorist leader remained at large, he had at least been constrained in his freedom of movement by his need to remain unseen as well as denied the use of

[40] Stephen Farrell and Michael Evans, "SAS Searches 'bin Laden' Cave System," *London Times,* December 4, 2001.

[41] Molly Moore and Susan B. Glasser, "Remnants of al Qaeda Flee Toward Pakistan," *Washington Post,* December 17, 2001.

[42] Molly Moore and Susan B. Glasser, "Afghan Militias Claim Victory in Tora Bora," *Washington Post,* December 18, 2001.

[43] Barton Gellman and Thomas E. Ricks, "U.S. Concludes bin Laden Escaped at Tora Bora," *Washington Post,* April 17, 2002.

satellite phones and radio communication, thanks to the relentless U.S. monitoring of all frequencies.[44]

In the only U.S. loss associated with the Tora Bora fighting, a B-1B bomber en route to bomb targets in Tora Bora went down over the Indian Ocean on December 12 about 60 miles north of Diego Garcia after developing multiple malfunctions. The aircraft commander tried to return to base, but the aircraft became unflyable and the four crewmembers ejected and were safely recovered after floating in the ocean for two hours.[45] The incident was the first of only three fixed-wing aircraft losses in Enduring Freedom (the others were a Marine Corps KC-130 and an AFSOC MC-130). All were unconnected to any hostile action.

With the Tora Bora cave complex now all but obliterated, some of the al Qaeda survivors sought to regroup in caves in eastern Afghanistan at Zhawar Kili and nearby in the vicinity of Khost. That development prompted 118 consecutive attack sorties in the area over a four-day period, beginning on January 3, 2002, by B-52s, B-1Bs, F/A-18s, and an AC-130, including against the al Badr training camp, where some Taliban tanks and artillery tubes were destroyed. The cave complex at Zhawar Kili covered nine square miles and featured 70 interconnected caves and tunnels offering literally miles of sheltered space.[46] Some 250 bombs were dropped on caves at Zhawar Kili alone.[47] It took nearly two weeks of bombing to complete the destruction of the al Qaeda complex there, with Air Force combat controllers attached to U.S. SOF teams identifying and designating most

---

[44] In fact, bin Laden and his al Qaeda associates had become especially careful about using cell phones to communicate ever since the Chechen secessionist leader Dzhokar Dudayev was thought to have been killed on April 24, 1996, by a Russian Air Force antiradiation missile while talking on a satellite telephone. On this, see Benjamin S. Lambeth, *Russia's Air Power in Crisis*, Washington, D.C.: Smithsonian Institution Press, 1999, p. 144.

[45] David Stout, "U.S. Bomber Crashes at Sea; Crew Members Are Rescued," *New York Times*, December 13, 2001. A Navy P-3 aided in the rescue effort, as did an Air Force KC-10 tanker that monitored the aircraft's position.

[46] Steve Vogel, "Al Qaeda Tunnels, Arms Cache Totalled; Complex Believed Largest Found in War," *Washington Post*, February 16, 2002.

[47] Esther Schrader, "U.S. Keeps Pressure on al Qaeda," *Los Angeles Times*, January 8, 2002.

of the aim points. In the process, all visible structures were leveled, and caves were sealed off in an area covering approximately three square miles.[48]

The attacks against Zhawar Kili and Khost represented the heaviest U.S. bombing since Tora Bora. What was initially envisaged as a 12-hour in-and-out intelligence-gathering operation ended up entailing a nine-day marathon of cave searching, mapping, and bombing. Navy SEALs later discovered abandoned caves in the area stacked high with piles of small arms, mortar shells, and other ammunition. When they blew up the arms caches with demolition charges, secondary explosions rocked the valley for days. AFSOC combat controllers played a pivotal role in this process, enabling attacking aircraft to drop precision weapons within sometimes perilously close distances from U.S. ground forces.[49]

As in Operation Desert Storm, many weapons effects achieved in Enduring Freedom were primarily psychological in nature. Bombs dropped by aircraft that were too high to be seen or heard by the enemy exploded as though they had come out of nowhere. Northern Alliance fighters often overheard Taliban soldiers on the radio speaking frantically of running for cover any time jet noise was heard. In one instance at night early during the campaign, Taliban forces were preparing to cross a bridge in foggy weather. The bridge was taken out by three concurrent JDAM hits right before their very eyes.[50] Although intangible, unquantifiable, and unpredictable, such second-order effects almost surely played a signal role in the unexpectedly early defeat of the Taliban.

As the war gradually wound down from nonstop aerial bombing to more pronounced ground-force involvement, CENTCOM ordered the Third Army headquarters, the core of U.S. Central Com-

---

[48] Steve Vogel and Walter Pincus, "Al Qaeda Complex Destroyed; Search Widens," *Washington Post*, January 15, 2002.

[49] James W. Crawley, "Caves of Zhawar Kili Yield Arsenal for Terror," *San Diego Union-Tribune*," January 17, 2002.

[50] Keith Richburg and William Branigin, "Attacks Out of the Blue: U.S. Air Strikes on Taliban Hit Military Targets and Morale," *Washington Post*, November 18, 2001.

mand Army Forces (ARCENT), moved from Fort McPherson, Georgia, to Kuwait to take charge of ground combat and humanitarian operations in Afghanistan. The Third Army had previously overseen the Operation Bright Star training exercise involving some 20,000 multinational troops in Egypt from October 8 to November 1. The contingent sent to Kuwait was commanded by Army Lieutenant General Paul Mikolashek, who became CENTCOM's designated land component commander for what remained of the continuing Afghan war.[51]

The Final Rout of the Taliban

On December 18, for the first time since the war started on October 7, the bombing of Operation Enduring Freedom came to a halt. That day, the American flag was raised over the reopened U.S. embassy compound in Kabul, with Ambassador Dobbins officiating under the protection of U.S. Marine Corps embassy guards. The week that followed was the first since the war began in which no munitions were dropped, although numerous armed F-14s, F/A-18s, B-52s, and B-1Bs continued to orbit on call over Kandahar and Tora Bora to attack any possible residual al Qaeda targets that might emerge. Those aircraft were joined by Italian Navy Harriers operating off the carrier *Garibaldi* and by French Super Etendard strike fighters from the carrier *Charles de Gaulle*.[52] All held their fire as allied SOF teams and Afghan resistance forces continued to comb the mountains for enemy stragglers and holdouts.

Although capturing bin Laden and Mullah Omar remained a preeminent U.S. goal, it was finally dawning on U.S. officials at all levels that hundreds of Taliban and al Qaeda fugitives had slipped across the border into Pakistan and evaded the Pakistani army by disappearing into the frontier tribal areas. Indeed, virtually the entire

---

[51] Bryan Bender, U.S. Shifts Command to Kuwait," *Boston Globe*, December 10, 2001.

[52] Douglas Frantz, "Hundreds of al Qaeda Fighters Slip into Pakistan," *New York Times*, December 19, 2001.

top Taliban and al Qaeda leadership succeeded in eluding their U.S. pursuers and surviving the campaign. For their part, the Afghan resistance groups showed scant interest in searching the highly defensible mountain caves for any remaining enemy fugitives.

Out of frustration over the continued failure of allied forces to capture bin Laden, General Franks finally proposed that U.S. troops be sent in to scour the mountainous terrain themselves, since it had become increasingly evident that the indigenous Afghan anti-Taliban fighters lacked both the inclination and ability to do so effectively.[53] The Marines of TF-58, who, by their own admission, committed perhaps five times more personnel strength than was needed to accomplish their assigned mission, indicated that they were mainly seeking intelligence information, and they encountered no resistance.[54]

As the dust gradually settled, the Pentagon came under sharp criticism from many quarters for not having inserted U.S. ground forces in strength in a more timely way into the Tora Bora fighting to help prevent the enemy from escaping. After it was over, a British SAS officer who had participated in allied ground operations said of the failure to capture bin Laden: "We raided caves where al Qaeda fighters put up desperate holding actions in some places. But orders never came to move into the valleys where bin Laden and other leaders were escaping, despite suggestions from our part. The idea was for native troops to provide a blocking force who were simply not up to the task."[55]

In sum, the battle of Tora Bora ended inconclusively, as did the battle of Zhawar Kili that followed it. In both cases, that inconclusiveness was, to a considerable degree, a result of the Bush administration's having elected to depend on the cooperation of constantly feuding and self-interested indigenous Afghan surrogates for whom

---

[53] Michael R. Gordon with Eric Schmitt, "Troops May Scour Caves for Qaeda, U.S. General Says," *New York Times,* December 20, 2001.

[54] Karl Vick, "Marines Hunt for al Qaeda Materials," *Washington Post,* January 2, 2002.

[55] Martin Arostegui, "The Search for bin Laden," *Insight Magazine,* September 2, 2002.

risking their lives to capture or kill al Qaeda fugitives or to prevent them from leaving the country was not high on their agendas. Over the course of that less than satisfactory experience, the CIA paid co- pious amounts of hard cash to Afghan opposition fighters, who at first promised to betray al Qaeda combatants and enable their loca- tion and capture and then helped them escape, accepting sizable bribes as a payoff for their assistance.[56]

As the American combat involvement in Afghanistan continued to wind down, it was reported at one point that resumed bombing in the eastern part of the country during the last week of December had killed the Taliban's chief of intelligence, Qari Amadullah. If con- firmed, that would have made him the most senior Taliban figure to have been killed during the war. Also at the end of December, the first RQ-4 Global Hawk high-altitude UAV was lost during an opera- tional mission because of a flight-control malfunction that caused the aircraft to enter a flat spin and crash.[57] Up until that time, Global Hawks had flown between 15 and 20 ISR sorties and had collected some 7,000 images in support of Operation Enduring Freedom since their commitment to the campaign a month before.

Early on January 1, 2002, a convoy of 200 Marine infantrymen, backed by Marine Corps AV-8B Harriers and AH-1W Super Cobras, pressed out of Kandahar to secure an abandoned enemy compound amid persistent concern over the Stinger infrared SAM threat, which continued to inhibit daylight operations at the Kandahar airport.[58] Hamid Karzai requested that allied bombing be continued as deemed necessary until all terrorist activity in Afghanistan was brought to an end. At the same time, Karzai expressed mounting concern over the growing incidence of accidental civilian fatalities that was being

---

[56] Susan B. Glasser, "The Battle of Tora Bora: Secrets, Money, Mistrust," *Washington Post*, February 10, 2002.

[57] That particular aircraft had mounted the Global Hawk program's only remaining electro- optical and infrared camera. The three remaining Global Hawks were equipped with syn- thetic aperature radars (SARs) only. (Amy Butler, "Global Hawk UAV Crash Claims Pro- gram's Only Infrared Camera," *Inside the Air Force*, January 4, 2002, p. 1.)

[58] Karl Vick and Bradley Graham, "Raid Finds Untouched al Qaeda Compound," *Washing- ton Post*, January 3, 2002.

caused by errant U.S. bombs and by alleged U.S. failures to identify all targets fully before dropping. (Although earlier Taliban charges of collateral damage were almost comically overblown, more conservative early estimates suggested that the air campaign may have caused as many as twice the number of noncombatant deaths as the 500 or so that were assessed to have occurred in Serbia and Kosovo during Operation Allied Force.)[59]

By mid-January 2002, U.S. strike operations over Afghanistan had dwindled down to a trickle. Said an F-14 pilot assigned to the air wing embarked in USS *Theodore Roosevelt* in late January: "Here is a standard OEF flight: Launch, transit to the tanker, hold, hold, hold, hold, hold, top off at a tanker, hold, hold, hold, hold some more, hit a tanker again, come home for a night trap. Our mission now is equivalent to that of a relief pitcher hanging out in the bullpen, warming up, ready to go on a moment's notice. If he gets the call, his mission is singular—deliver the beanball. . . . [Our sorties now] are a far cry from all the action pre-Christmas."[60] In yet another sign of the campaign's growing transition from a largely air-centric operation to a more ground-dominated affair, the 101st Airborne Division arrived at Kandahar to relieve the 1,500 Marines who had initially established the first significant U.S. conventional ground presence at nearby FOB Rhino. That Army deployment showed a clear willingness on the part of the Bush administration to establish a longer-term U.S. military presence in Afghanistan.

There was one reported incident in February 2002 in which CIA and CENTAF watch officers in the CAOC were said to have observed live MQ-1 Predator video feed showing a tall man seemingly being greeted obsequiously by a small group of other individuals. Informed by a belief that the tall person just might have been bin Laden, the CAOC submitted a request up the chain of command for clearance for the Predator to fire a Hellfire missile at the group. By

---

[59] Michael Evans, "'Precision Weapons' Fail to Prevent Mass Civilian Casualties," *London Times*, January 2, 2002.

[60] Email to the author dated January 30, 2002, partly quoted in Sandra I. Erwin, "Naval Aviation: Lessons from the War," *National Defense*, June 2002, p. 16.

the time the target approval had been granted (reportedly within minutes), the men in question had dispersed. Later, what appeared to be the tall man and two others emerged from a wooded area, at which time the missile was finally fired, killing all three. It was never determined for sure whether they were al Qaeda or Taliban leaders.[61]

In the meantime, work proceeded apace on an air base for conducting allied combat operations from Kyrgyzstan as well as on improving airfield facilities in Uzbekistan and Pakistan. The United States had recently signed a one-year agreement with the government of Kyrgyzstan for the unrestricted use, including by strike aircraft and tankers, of the 13,000-foot runway at Manas International Airport outside Bishkek.[62] One function of these base improvements, according to Under Secretary of Defense Wolfowitz, was "more political than military," in that building them up and conducting operational exercises from them would "send a message to everybody, including [to] important countries like Uzbekistan, that we have a capacity to come back and will come back in—we're not just going to forget about them."[63]

By late February 2002, Operation Enduring Freedom had largely evolved from its initial character as a high-technology air war into a domestic policing action, in effect, as the United States now found itself striving to manage and pacify feuding warlords, protect the embryonic interim Afghan government, and ensure adequate force protection from sniper fire and other hostile action for the 4,000 U.S. ground troops who were now in the country. This new

---

[61] One account later claimed that journalists in Afghanistan had learned that the victims had been innocent Afghans who had been scavenging for scrap metal. Seymour M. Hersh, "Manhunt: The Bush Administration's New Strategy in the War Against Terrorism," *The New Yorker*, December 23/30, 2002, p. 72.

[62] The unusually long runway at Manas was built originally for Soviet long-range bombers. The airfield also features navigation aids that are up to Western commercial standards, as well as a large parking ramp and adequate fuel facilities. A similarly large former Soviet air base at Kulyab, Tajikistan, less than 100 miles from the Afghan border was rejected because of its poor condition. (Vernon Loeb, "Footprints in Steppes of Central Asia," *Washington Post*, February 9, 2002.)

[63] Eric Schmitt and James Dao, "U.S. Is Building Up Its Military Bases in Afghan Region," *New York Times*, January 9, 2002.

phase of American involvement was distinguished by sporadic bombing aimed less at defeating al Qaeda than at managing the clashing indigenous militia forces and defending the newly emergent government of Hamid Karzai, who freely admitted that he was ready to request U.S. air strikes as needed if that was what it took to end the continuing clashes between the armed factions that now controlled Afghanistan outside Kabul.[64]

In perhaps the single most serious errant attack of the entire war, U.S. air power was accidentally visited on an innocent Afghan wedding party on July 1, 2002, with survivors on the ground claiming 40 civilians killed and as many as 100 others wounded. The tragedy occurred well after the air war had, to all intents and purposes, ended. It was not clear at first whether the incident was caused by an errant bomb or by an AC-130 gunship that had been operating in the area. When some U.S. ground reconnaissance forces conducting an operation in a nearby area reported coming under enemy fire, they called in an AC-130, whose crew reported "deliberate and sustained antiaircraft fire." Concurrently, a B-52 had dropped seven JDAMs on an identified complex of caves in the same area, and one of those JDAMs was thought to have malfunctioned.[65]

It was later confirmed that the incident was indeed caused by the AC-130, which had mistakenly fired its cannons on a village in Uruzgan province where the wedding party was taking place, reportedly killing 48 Afghan civilians and wounding 117. The incident led the on-scene commander of coalition ground forces, Army Lieutenant General Dan McNeill, to order an inquiry after six Afghan provisional governors made the unprecedented demand that the United States henceforth seek the ruling council's approval before conducting any future such operations.[66] The Afghan villagers who sustained the inadvertent fire claimed that they had merely been shooting into the

[64] John F. Burns, "In a Shift, U.S. Uses Airstrikes to Help Kabul," *New York Times*, February 19, 2002.

[65] Thomas E. Ricks, "Errant U.S. Bomb Hits Civilians," *Washington Post*, July 2, 2002.

[66] Adam Brown, "Afghans Seek Curb on U.S. Operations," *Chicago Tribune*, July 13, 2002.

air, as is commonly done at festive events such as the wedding that was under way at the time. The incident was reminiscent of the Blackhawk downings over Turkey some years earlier, when firing first rather than checking further on the part of the two involved USAF F-15 pilots was, by every indication in hindsight, not warranted by the relatively low prevailing threat level. Both the wedding-party incident and the incident in which an Air National Guard F-16 pilot mistakenly dropped a 500-lb LGB on a group of Canadian troops conducting a live-fire training exercise, killing four, arguably entailed overreactions by aircrews to threats that were trivial even if they had been real. The latter mishap prompted the air component commander, Lieutenant General Moseley, to send a memorandum to all of his air commanders reminding them of "a well-defined mechanism to ensure you and I do not engage friendly forces. It is difficult to imagine a scenario, other than troops in contact, whereby we will not have time to egress the threat area, regroup, deconflict and then engage in a well thought-out and coordinated plan that ensures success. I need everyone's head in the game. We cannot afford another tragic incident."[67]

From the campaign's beginning, the U.S. goal had not been to conquer Afghanistan but rather to bring an end to Taliban rule and to destroy al Qaeda's network and support structure in that country. True to that goal, the Taliban regime was brought down only 102 days after the terrorist attacks of September 11. General Franks later remarked that his strategy had not envisaged a linear progression starting with air operations and then followed in sequence by the introduction of SOF and then conventional ground troops but rather a concurrent use of all available tools as needed. In the end, the U.S. commitment to overthrowing the Taliban and destroying al Qaeda's power base in Afghanistan turned out, in the words of one observer, to have been "about 110 CIA officers and 316 Special Forces person-

---

[67] Rowan Scarborough, "'Friendly Fire' Judge's Memo Assailed," *Washington Times*, July 30, 2002.

nel, plus massive air power."[68] The indigenous Afghan resistance to the Taliban was, needless to say, essential to the success of this strategy. During the course of the campaign and the planning effort that led up to it, Pakistan made a pivotal and courageous turn toward the United States, as did the former Soviet Central Asian republics and even Russia itself. Many European countries also proved themselves quick to lend a helping hand. Conventional U.S. ground forces, however, did not play a significant part in the campaign, and they would not until the start of Operation Anaconda two months later.

---

[68] Woodward, p. 314.

Operation Anaconda

After two months of relative quiescence following the fall of the Taliban and the installation of the interim Karzai government, U.S. ground forces met their fiercest test of the war in a bold attempt to encircle and capture or kill al Qaeda fugitives through an offensive that came to be called Operation Anaconda. This planned push into the high mountains of eastern Afghanistan was to be the first and only substantial combat involvement by conventional U.S. ground troops in Enduring Freedom. It began in a sparsely populated valley that lies between the lower Arma mountain range and the higher, snow-covered Shah-i-Kot peaks, the latter of which had long provided a natural redoubt for case-hardened fugitives of all types.[1] No outside force had ever before succeeded in subduing this forbidding part of Afghanistan, from Alexander the Great in 327 BC through the British colonialists of the 19th century to the failed Soviet invaders of more recent years. (The Soviet army lost 250 soldiers there in a single day in 1987, with about 200 of those having been stoned to death after being captured by Afghan mujaheddin resistance fighters.)[2]

The Shah-i-Kot valley area had been under close surveillance by CENTCOM ever since early January 2002, prompted by intelligence

---

[1] John F. Burns, "U.S. Planes Pound Enemy as Troops Face Tough Fight," *New York Times,* March 4, 2002.

[2] Richard T. Cooper, "Fierce Fight in Afghan Valley Tests U.S. Soldiers and Strategy," *Los Angeles Times,* March 24, 2002.

reports that Taliban and foreign al Qaeda combatants were regrouping there in an area near the town of Gardez. General Franks later noted that planning for Anaconda had begun weeks before the operation was finally launched, in response to indications of hundreds of al Qaeda combatants marshaling from Khandahar and from the collapsing northern Taliban lines to the age-old strongholds in Paktia province near the Pakistani border where the Shah-i-Kot valley lies.[3] This movement was initially detected and tracked by U.S. satellites and Predator UAVs, as well as by a number of U.S. SOF teams that were operating in the area. Over time, enemy forces continued to flow into the Shah-i-Kot area, to a point where it appeared that they might begin to pose a serious counteroffensive threat to the Karzai government. As Secretary of Defense Rumsfeld later reflected this concern, "their goal is to reconstitute, to try to throw out the new interim government of Afghanistan, to kill coalition forces, and to try to regain the ability to use Afghanistan as a base for terrorist operations. . . . We intend to prevent them from doing that."[4] General Myers likewise said later of this unfolding course of events, the al Qaeda fighters "started to get together in a place where they could have enough mass to be effective. And we've been following that, allowing it to develop until we thought it was the proper time to strike."[5]

Initial Planning

Two considerations underlay the steps that ultimately led to Operation Anaconda: (1) A desire on CENTCOM's part to preempt the growing concentration of al Qaeda fighters who were assembling and

---

[3] Vernon Loeb and Bradley Graham, "Seven U.S. Soldiers Die in Battle," *Washington Post*, March 5, 2002.

[4] John Hendren and John Daniszewski, "Seven U.S. Troops Are Killed in Assault on Enemy Fighters," *Los Angeles Times*, March 5, 2002.

[5] Eric Schmitt and Thom Shanker, "Afghans' Retreat Forced Americans to Lead a Battle," *New York Times*, March 10, 2002.

reequipping themselves in the Shah-i-Kot hinterland and (2) mounting intelligence, through communications intercepts, indicating a conviction by al Qaeda leaders that U.S. forces would not pursue them into the mountains and take them on in winter weather.[6] The first move to develop a concept of operations for Anaconda was prompted by CENTCOM on January 5, 2002, via a tasking in Fragmentary Order (FRAGO) 03-007 to the land component commander, Army Lieutenant General Paul Mikolashek, that identified Gardez and its immediate environs as the most dangerous remaining pocket of al Qaeda resistance and that assessed the number of enemy combatants concentrated there to be around 1,500 to 2,000.[7] General Mikolashek, however, had no forces in the area other than those overt SOF units that were under his command, plus a detachment of conventional Army troops from the 10th Mountain Division that had deployed to Karshi-Khanabad, Uzbekistan, mainly to provide force protection for the SOF contingent that operated from that site. Accordingly, the initial lead role for developing the concept of operations for Anaconda fell to Army Colonel John Mulholland, the commander of the 5th Special Forces Group. As the commander of Joint Special Operations Task Force (JSOTF) North and the associated TF Dagger based at Karshi-Khanabad, Mulholland was already at work, under CENTCOM direction, helping to consolidate the rout of the Taliban through unconventional warfare.[8]

The next day, on January 6, TFs Dagger and K-Bar (the latter operating out of Kandahar in Afghanistan under the command of JSOTF South) began planning a sensitive site exploitation of the Shah-i-Kot area in response to CENTCOM's tasker. (Sensitive site

---

[6] David A. Fulghum, "U.S. Troops Confront al Qaeda in Vicious Mountain Battle," *Aviation Week and Space Technology*, March 11, 2002, pp. 24–25.

[7] Major Mark G. Davis, USA, "Operation Anaconda: Command and Confusion in Joint Warfare," unpublished thesis presented to the faculty of the School of Advanced Air and Space Studies, Maxwell AFB, Alabama, June 2004, p. 70.

[8] Upon being designated the land component commander on November 26, 2001, Mikolashek assumed tactical control of all SOF in Enduring Freedom except for TF Sword (later TF-11), which performed missions that were so sensitive and compartmented that TFs Dagger and K-Bar, both overt SOF operations, were unaware of them. (Davis, pp. 21–23.)

exploitations entailed surveillance and intelligence collection from caves and bunkers as they were discovered throughout Afghanistan, with a view toward gathering information on the whereabouts of al Qaeda and Taliban leaders and ultimately capturing or killing them.)[9] With Mulholland taking the lead role in consultation with Army Major General Franklin Hagenbeck, the commander of the 10th Mountain Division collocated with him in Karshi-Khanabad, a draft plan was produced that envisaged a SOF-only push into the valley to force the Arab and Chechen al Qaeda fighters into the higher ridgelines that surrounded it, while the conventional troops of 10th Mountain and the 101st Airborne Division, along with allied and other SOF units and indigenous Afghan troops, would seek to seal off all known escape routes by establishing blocking positions astride them. These forces working in concert would employ an infantry procedure called "movement to contact," with the objective of locating and engaging an enemy force of unknown size and disposition through reconnaissance and maneuver.[10] The plan was briefed to Mikolashek, who approved the further refinement of it.

Even at this early stage, however, preparations for Anaconda were off to a bad start, with a bifurcated command arrangement and poorly defined command relationships that would soon lead to trouble as both became overwhelmed by the pace of unfolding events. Hagenbeck would later portray the disparate and often highly compartmented pockets of U.S. activity focused on the Shah-i-Kot valley as a collection, in effect, of individual component commanders reporting directly to General Franks. He would further suggest in hindsight that the organizational and command-and-control problems that ensued from this arrangement accounted for most of the confusion and poor communication that marred the planning and early execution of Anaconda.[11]

---

[9] Davis, p. 67.

[10] Moore, p. 275.

[11] Conversation with Lieutenant General Franklin L. Hagenbeck, USA, Headquarters United States Army, Washington, D.C., July 1, 2004.

For one thing, General Mikolashek, headquartered to the rear in Kuwait, and his designated forward surrogate, General Hagenbeck, did not have operational control of those SOF units that fell under the separate chain of command emanating from the Joint Special Operations Command (JSOC) headquartered at Fort Bragg, North Carolina, which oversaw all interservice SOF activities worldwide and which coordinated Special Forces, Defense Intelligence Agency, and CIA paramilitary forces in Afghanistan.[12] That divided command arrangement limited Hagenbeck's ability to control the full spectrum of operations that was about to unfold. Worse yet, it set up a situation in which the right hand would not know what the left was doing because of the tight compartmentation of the concurrent yet separate covert SOF operations in Anaconda's battlespace. For example, TF-11, a covert SOF unit under the control of JSOC, received direction straight from CENTCOM's director of operations that was unknown to General Mikolashek and to other SOF components.[13] As the discussion below will spell out in fuller detail, this highly stovepiped arrangement would occasion more than one untoward event with fateful consequences during the first three days of Anaconda.

A month later, as the concept of operations for Anaconda continued to grow in scope and scale, TF Dagger under Mulholland's command remained the designated mission planning agent. However, as General Mikolashek's forward representative, Hagenbeck now began to engage in closer cooperative planning with the SOF colonel. By February 13, as the planning for Anaconda had evolved further, Hagenbeck and Mulholland agreed that Hagenbeck should take over as the operation's lead planning agent, since the mission had broadened to a point where it had begun to exceed TF Dagger's ability to exercise adequate command and control of it. Accordingly, when the anticipated manning for the operation reached the point where it could no longer be effectively managed within narrow SOF channels, Anaconda—with the express backing of both General Mikolashek

---

[12] Moore, p. 52.

[13] Davis, p. 23.

and General Franks—became a conventional ground operation with SOF support, and Hagenbeck was formally designated the commander of Combined Joint Task Force (CJTF) Mountain, an amalgam of forces from the 10th Mountain and 101st Airborne Divisions, along with a small U.S. and allied overt SOF contingent and a larger number of indigenous Afghan fighters.[14] All of these forces would execute Anaconda at the appointed time. On the same day that General Hagenbeck assumed the role of lead planning agent for Operation Anaconda, CJTF Mountain commenced a forward deployment from Uzbekistan to Bagram Air Base in Afghanistan, the latter of which would become Anaconda's field headquarters. With respect to threat expectations, after nearly a month of all-source surveillance between early January and early February, CJTF Mountain reduced its assessment of enemy strength in the Shah-i-Kot valley to 150 to 200 from the much higher estimate of 1,500 to 2,000 initially conveyed in CENTCOM's FRAGO 03-007.[15]

Despite its nominal designation by General Hagenbeck as a "joint" combat entity, CJTF Mountain had no service representation other than from the Army in its organizational makeup. Moreover, beyond Hagenbeck himself, only two other personnel in CJTF Mountain (the chief of staff and director of operations) had had any previous experience at operating in a joint environment. In essence, Hagenbeck's forward command structure that was cobbled together in response to CENTCOM's tasking in FRAGO 03-007 was little more than a scaled-down Army division headquarters, albeit one with corps-level responsibilities, that included a division-level intelligence section without the resources to develop the high-fidelity intelligence that Operation Anaconda would require.[16] Not only that, the situation was further complicated when General Mikolashek assumed operational control of all ground operations in Afghanistan, at which

---

[14] The addition of the word "combined" to a multiservice Joint Task Force (JTF) designator indicates the inclusion of allied representation (in this case coalition SOF personnel) in the organization.

[15] Davis, p. 96.

[16] Davis, pp. 32–33.

time, as one assessment put it, those operations suddenly "shifted from a geographically dispersed SOF-centric force with decentralized planning to a large, concentrated conventional ground force with operations requiring detailed functional component planning."[17] Yet General Franks did not concurrently transfer control of all SOF operations to General Mikolashek, an omission that had the effect of restricting the ability of the latter to execute his newly assigned mission.

More important yet, neither General Hagenbeck nor General Mikolashek at any time in the planning for Anaconda up to this point had made any direct effort to enlist the air component's involvement in their planning, notwithstanding the fact that the mission had grown under Hagenbeck's direction into the largest pending commitment of U.S. ground troops (more than a thousand) to combat since Operation Desert Storm more than a decade before. By his own later admission, Hagenbeck assumed—incorrectly, as it turned out—that the Air Force air liaison officer attached to TF Dagger was routinely communicating CJTF Mountain's intentions and needs to the CAOC from the very start of Anaconda planning and that his own action officers and the CAOC staff were busy at work seeing to the necessary air support integration.[18] That unfounded assumption would prove to have serious consequences once it came time to execute Operation Anaconda.

True enough, as early as February 5, the air liaison officer attached to TF Dagger was fully aware that a significant ground push into the Shah-i-Kot area was in the works, and CENTAF was said to have been routinely provided with information copies of various messages from TF Dagger and CJTF Mountain regarding the operation almost from the start of planning for Anaconda.[19] However, no formal move was made by anyone at the land component's command

---

[17] Davis, p. 70.

[18] Conversation with Lieutenant General Franklin L. Hagenbeck, USA, Headquarters United States Army, Washington, D.C., July 1, 2004.

[19] Davis, p. 70.

level to seek the personal involvement of the air component commander, Air Force Lieutenant General T. Michael Moseley, and
his staff in the planning, even after the concept of operations
for Anaconda had grown from a low-profile SOF operation into
a major conventional ground advance into an ill-defined threat environment—and even though there was more than enough time to ex-
plore in full detail what the air component might contribute before
the operation's planned execution date of February 28.

For his part, with the major bombing portion of Enduring
Freedom having already concluded nearly two months before, General Moseley had his attention focused elsewhere on the planning
needs for a possible operation in Iraq to follow in 2003. As CJTF
Mountain's planning for Anaconda began to percolate, Moseley was
away from the CAOC touring the Gulf region with the commander
of Air Combat Command, General Hal Hornburg, conducting the
initial political-military coordination for any such operation. The
CAOC staff, moreover, had no reason to anticipate a major ground
effort that might require extensive close air support (CAS) in the absence of any direct tasking for such support from the land component. Even as the final planning for Anaconda was concluded on February 20, the special operations liaison element (SOLE) in the CAOC
was unaware of what was about to unfold within just a week. The
CAOC leadership remained similarly in the dark about a looming
operation that would soon demand the heaviest involvement by the
CAOC in joint air-ground operations at any time during the entire
course of the Afghan war.

With CENTCOM's air component, from General Moseley on
down, essentially unaware of the impending initiative, the details of
the Anaconda concept of operations were briefed to General Mikolashek on February 20 for his endorsement preparatory to being submitted to General Franks for the latter's ultimate approval. An information copy of the plan was subsequently sent that same day to the
Army's battlefield coordination detachment (BCD) in the CAOC in
the form of an advisory 28-page operations order and a 128-slide
PowerPoint briefing that outlined the planned operation. This
transmission, however, was accompanied by no covering explanation

or formal directive to the BCD to forward the package to General Moseley, let alone so much as a hint that support from the CAOC and from the air component more generally was desired, expected, and might prove to be necessary.[20] Moreover, the many needed preparations for possible air involvement that it assumed away suggested that Anaconda's planners had not accounted for such crucial considerations as aircraft transit times into and out of the combat zone, safe passage procedures and control systems, airspace deconfliction needs, and so on. Instead, perhaps guided by the earlier impression of seemingly constant aircraft availability throughout the SOF-directed air war that had done most of Enduring Freedom's heaviest lifting from mid-October to mid-December the previous year, CJTF Mountain's planners appeared to presume that any needed fixed-wing air support would naturally be available to them on call and with the right weapon loads were it to be needed in an emergency.[21]

This package was eventually brought by the BCD to the attention of the CAOC staff, to whom it came as a "total surprise," in the later recollection of the CAOC director at the time, Air Force Major General John Corley.[22] Once they became fully aware of the impending operation and its possible implications for the air component, the CAOC staff immediately briefed General Corley on the package that had been sent to the BCD and reported to him that the operations order for Anaconda had already been signed and disseminated with no preplanned air component involvement whatever. At that, in General Moseley's absence, General Corley tasked the CAOC

---

[20] In standard practice, the BCD, composed of some 40 ground-force personnel of varying specializations interspersed throughout the different divisions in the CAOC, is the Army's organizational representative to the air component, with the main function of aiding the air component in supporting the ground commander's scheme of maneuver. (Davis, p. 38.)

[21] As evidence of this, CJTF Mountain's initial Anaconda briefing on February 22 listed F-14s, F-15s, F-16s, F/A-18s, B-1Bs, B-52s, and AC-130s as presumed available and on call. In fact, the only air component attack platforms that would be nearby and immediately available over the Shah-i-Kot valley at H-Hour would be one B-52, one B-1B, and two F-15Es. (Davis, p. 107.)

[22] Conversation with Lieutenant General John D. W. Corley, USAF, Headquarters United States Air Force, Washington, D.C., May 13, 2003.

staff to start immediately compiling an inventory of all conceivable air-related aspects of Anaconda that might demand support from the air component on short notice should events call for it. He further established immediate contact with General Moseley, who was still on his Gulf region tour with General Hornburg, and filled Moseley in on what was known by the CAOC about Anaconda to date. General Moseley returned to the CAOC to get more fully briefed on February 23, just five days before Operation Anaconda was to commence. As General Corley later recalled, it was clear to all in the CAOC that "the complexity of the problem [of providing CJTF Mountain with adequate air support on such short notice] was enormous."[23] In a subsequent interview, Corley added that when he was first briefed on Anaconda by the BCD chief on February 21, "I was taken aback for a number of reasons. We were within days of executing a substantial operation . . . and, to my knowledge, the air component commander had not been informed. . . . I hoped that what it meant was that I was out of the loop. But given that I was the . . . CAOC director, I knew nothing about it, and I got blank stares from my A-Staff after I asked them."[24] Once it fully dawned on the CAOC staff what Operation Anaconda in fact envisaged, CAOC intelligence personnel discovered that the information that had been provided in CJTF Mountain's briefing slides forwarded to the BCD included planned helicopter landing zones (LZs) that the CAOC believed to be infested with as many as 10 times the number of enemy fighters as those presumed in Army planning.[25]

By February 24, General Moseley and the CAOC staff had become consumed in a near-frenetic pick-up game to marshal whatever needed air assets that could be mobilized on short notice. Up to that point, no one in the land component had declared any air support requirements for Anaconda, including such critical planning details as

---

[23] Conversation with General Corley, May 13, 2003.

[24] Quoted in Davis, p. 81.

[25] Elaine M. Grossman, "Left in the Dark for Most Anaconda Planning, Air Force Opens New Probe," *Inside the Pentagon*, October 3, 2002.

how much jet fuel might be needed.[26] More important yet, there was still no air support element attached to CJTF Mountain, and no request had been made by Hagenbeck's staff for Enlisted Tactical Air Controllers (ETACs). Normally, an air support operations center (ASOC) would be provided in any case only at the corps level, with only a smaller air support operations squadron (ASOS) assigned to each division and with the latter having the potential for being built up to a full ASOC if need be.[27] General Hagenbeck, however, did not take his assigned ASOS with him when he deployed from his U.S. headquarters to Karshi-Khanabad, since his request to do so had been disapproved on the grounds that CENTCOM wished to maintain the smallest possible personnel footprint in the region and that his force-protection mission did not require an ASOS. Accordingly, he did not have an ASOS available and on tap when he subsequently moved south to Bagram just before the start of Anaconda. Although he voiced concern at the time over having been ordered to deploy forward without the cover of an Air Liaison Officer (ALO) and a Tactical Air Control Party (TACP), he was under the assumption, as noted above, that both would naturally be available if and when his mission was changed to include offensive operations.[28] At the last minute, CJTF Mountain did ask the air component to provide it with a division-level air liaison officer, but its forward headquarters facility at Bagram had no UHF radio provisions, only limited communications to the CAOC, and no integrated picture of the operation that was about to unfold. The senior air liaison officer assigned to the land component commander, Air Force Colonel Michael Longoria, quickly realized that CJTF Mountain was severely lacking in what was needed by way of organic expertise to ensure adequate air

---

[26] As but one of many contingency measures, the CAOC provided 200,000 gallons of jet fuel to Bagram over the course of five days by means of Air Force C-17s and Marine Corps KC-130s. (Conversation with Lieutenant General John D. W. Corley, USAF, Headquarters United States Air Force, Washington, D.C., May 13, 2003.)

[27] The Air Force currently maintains five ASOCs worldwide: one in South Korea, one in Europe, and the remaining three supporting the Army's home-based corps at Forts Riley, Lewis, and Bragg.

[28] Cited in Davis, p. 53.

support for any possible contingency.[29] To redress that deficiency, in the words of another knowledgeable Air Force colonel, Longoria "immediately begged, borrowed, and stole every available air liaison officer and ETAC in theater and set up a small CAS cell at Bagram that later transitioned to a full-up ASOC. This foresight proved critical as the battle progressed."[30]

Remarkably, there had been no communication whatsoever between Generals Mikolashek and Moseley with respect to Anaconda at any time during this two-month planning effort, even though the two component commanders had routinely discussed other matters on a daily basis. The first time any such communication occurred was on February 26, after CJTF Mountain's plan was already a virtual fait accompli, in the scheduled VTC among all CENTCOM principals during which Anaconda was briefed to General Franks for his final approval. In the course of that session, General Moseley expressed unease over what he felt to be the inadequacy of air support provisions occasioned by the short notice the CAOC had been given. However, he did not voice any outright objection to the plan, possibly out of a guarded belief that he still had enough time to catch up before the operation began. Accordingly, Franks accepted the proposed command structure and command relationships for Anaconda, approved CJTF Mountain's plan, and authorized an execute date of February 28.

In his memoirs, Franks later recalled that the plan put forward for Anaconda by the land component was "very credible" yet "not completely coordinated" and that he was "looking at some uncomfortable general officers [most notably, in all likelihood, General Moseley] on those VTC screens." He further stated that he "had been pushing the importance of joint warfare on this team since a late Feb-

---

[29] The purpose of an ASOC is to advise and aid ground commanders on air power applications and to provide liaison between the Air Force and Army with regard to those applications. ASOCs are normally assigned to the Army's corps level, which partly explains why one was not assigned to CJTF Mountain at the start of planning for Anaconda.

[30] Colonel Matt Neuenswander, USAF, "JCAS in Operation Anaconda: It's Not All Bad News," *Field Artillery Journal*, May–June 2003.

ruary commanders' briefing [the February 26 VTC session noted above], just before Anaconda was scheduled to begin."[31] That, however, was quite late in the game to have begun emphasizing the importance of "jointness," considering that weeks of Anaconda planning had already gone by and that opening moves were scheduled to commence only 48 hours thereafter. For his part, General Moseley later recalled that at the time, both he and General Mikolashek "knew less of the [impending] operation than we would have liked."[32]

The declared mission of Anaconda was to capture or kill any al Qaeda and Taliban fighters who might be encountered by allied forces in the Shah-i-Kot area. In contrast to what most U.S. planners by that time had come to regard as the ill-advised approach of having relied principally on indigenous Afghan forces to do the hard fighting that had been followed at Tora Bora and that allowed too many al Qaeda combatants to escape to Pakistan, a senior administration official explained that "the thinking this time [was] that we needed more Americans to cut off escape routes and [to] keep the Afghans focused on the mission."[33] Toward that end, more than 1,400 conventional U.S. Army infantrymen and an additional 200 overt SOF troops were assigned to participate in the operation. These included TF Dagger, which consisted of Army and Air Force SOF personnel supporting three large indigenous Afghan forces, each with a separate commander; TF K-Bar, an amalgam of Navy, Air Force, and coalition SOF assets; TF Rakkasan, the largest involved unit consisting of three conventional infantry battalions (one from the 10th Mountain Division and two from the 101st Airborne Division), along with a supporting aviation element with 24 lift helicopters and eight AH-64 Apaches; and an additional contingent of overt SOF personnel not

---

[31] General Tommy Franks, *American Soldier*, New York, Regan Books, 2004, p. 378. Franks went on, however, to aver that what finally ensued was, in his judgment, a "truly joint operation" (p. 379).

[32] Comments on an earlier draft by Lieutenant General John D. W. Corley, USAF, December 19, 2003.

[33] Michael R. Gordon, "This Time, American Soldiers Join the Fray," *New York Times*, March 4, 2002.

only from the U.S. services, but also from Australia, Canada, Denmark, France, Germany, and Norway, in a unit called TF-64.[34] General Hagenbeck was determined to wait until enemy forces had consolidated south of Gardez before attacking. Once under way, the plan for Anaconda envisaged a three-day operation that would entail direct combat with, followed by the capture and detention of, any al Qaeda terrorists who might be encountered along the way.

About 1,000 Afghan fighters in all were involved in the planned blocking and trackdown effort. That effort would commence with an attack by TF Dagger and the three separate Afghan forces under the commands of Generals Zia Lodin, Zakim Khan, and Kamil Khan. The main advance under Zia Lodin would move from Gardez into the Shah-i-Kot valley both to clear a path for follow-on forces and to force enemy combatants up into the higher ground, cornering them there for a final assault. The other two Afghan forces would set up blocking positions at the northern and southern ends of the valley to contain the enemy, at which point TF Rakkasan would begin its air assault and establish blocking positions between the lower valley and the high ground to prevent al Qaeda fighters from escaping into nearby Pakistan to the east.[35]

In the earlier Tora Bora operation, as noted in the preceding chapter, indigenous Afghan anti-Taliban forces had been reluctant to comb the mountain cave complex for battle-hardened al Qaeda fugitives with whom they had no particular bone to pick. They seemed far more interested in looting caves that had already been abandoned by the enemy than in finding and capturing bin Laden and his associates. Unlike the case of Tora Bora, in which only a few dozen U.S. SOF personnel were involved, Anaconda featured a clear preponderance of American ground troops. This shift in approach indicated a CENTCOM belief that much of al Qaeda's fighting strength remained intact and represented more than just minor pockets of resistance. It also indicated an awareness by CENTCOM that it would

---

[34] Davis, p. 99.

[35] Davis, p. 102.

take more than just friendly Afghan forces to take them on and eliminate them.

Nevertheless, despite a clear desire to avoid repeating the mistakes of Tora Bora, General Hagenbeck planned to have most of the searching and sorting done by indigenous Afghan forces, with four companies of U.S. ground troops appropriately deployed in seven blocking positions to prevent any enemy forces from escaping (see Figure 5.1).[36] An important part of his mission entailed searching the three villages in the Shah-i-Kot valley (Serkhankel, Babukhel, and Marzak) house-to-house, and the indigenous Afghan forces were far more able than American and coalition forces to distinguish between al Qaeda combatants and the local population. Moreover, the use of indigenous Afghan fighters promised to avoid any appearance of American troops as an occupying force comparable to the Soviet army in the 1980s that might threaten to undermine the still-fragile Karzai government.[37]

In sum, CJTF Mountain's plan was to surround the Shah-i-Kot valley with overlapping rings of U.S. forces aimed at bottling up and then capturing or killing the several hundred al Qaeda fighters who were thought to be hiding in the area. In the end, however, Anaconda would instead prove to be a series of intense individual firefights in which al Qaeda holdouts, rather than retreating as before at Tora Bora, would stay on and fight to the death. It also would prove to be an experience in which fixed-wing air power, largely left out of the initial planning for Anaconda and summoned in full force only at the eleventh hour when events seemed headed for disaster, would be pivotal in producing what ultimately was a successful, if costly, outcome.

---

[36] For the most informed and detailed treatment of this and subsequent ground combat-actions throughout Anaconda, see Sean Naylor, *Not a Good Day to Die: The Untold Story of Operation Anaconda*, New York: Berkley Books, 2005.

[37] Davis, p. 104.

Figure 5.1
Operation Anaconda Planned Disposition of Forces

SOURCE: AF/XOL.

A Troubled Start

Although Anaconda was initially scheduled to commence on February 28, sandstorms and high winds grounded the Army's helicopters for several days, causing scheduled supply flights to be delayed or cancelled. After repeated weather postponements, the attack finally got under way on March 2, when hundreds of U.S. troops and indigenous Afghan fighters were inserted into blocking positions along the most likely escape routes from the area of main interest, a valley three miles wide and five miles long code-named Objective Remington that lies between a large north-south rise nicknamed the Whale (because of its distinctive shape) and the higher Shah-i-Kot mountains to the east. From that date until the operation ended nearly two weeks later, the weather in the area remained hazy but clear enough to enable needed air support, with the one exception of the night of

March 8, when a front drove through and limited CAS operations to satellite-aided JDAMs dropped from above the cloud cover.[38]

As the insertion began, General Zia Lodin, one of the three participating Afghan commanders, was advancing his forces toward the Whale in compliance with his assigned portion of the plan and accompanied by SOF troops from TF Dagger when he encountered not only enemy fire but also inadvertent friendly fire from an AC-130 gunship that was orbiting overhead and that had misidentified his convoy. That event undermined Zia's confidence in the operation, and he immediately began to balk at engaging in combat. Within hours, he withdrew all of his fighters under intense enemy fire and did not reengage until five days later, after the hardest part of the Anaconda fighting was over. During this initial encounter, a U.S. Army Special Forces soldier and three Afghan fighters lost their lives when cannon fire from the AC-130 struck the vehicle in which they were riding.[39] Three more U.S. troops and 14 friendly Afghan fighters were wounded by intense enemy mortar fire, which immediately put the attacking allied forces off balance and forced them to retreat six miles down the road. The enemy shelling further caused the attacking forces to break up and disperse widely, with the result that many of the 200 (out of an initially planned 400) allied ground troops who were inserted into the Shah-i-Kot valley on March 2 ended up having to defend themselves against enemy fire in platoon-sized or smaller groupings. A concurrent surprise occurred when a covert SOF team operating in the area without the knowledge either of CJTF Mountain or the CAOC called for a halt to the preplanned air strikes, with the result that TF Rakkasan commenced its air assault before the air component had completed its minimal preparation of the battlefield.[40]

---

[38] Comments on an earlier draft by Colonel Matt Neuenswander, USAF, Air Force Doctrine Center, Maxwell AFB, Alabama, June 28, 2004.

[39] Major Edgar Fleri, USAF, Colonel Ernest Howard, USAF, Jeffrey Hukill, and Thomas R. Searle, "Operation Anaconda Case Study," College of Aerospace Doctrine, Research, and Education, Maxwell AFB, Alabama, November 13, 2003, p. 27.

[40] Davis, p. 109.

Zia's sudden withdrawal and the ensuing temporary confusion in the attacking force that it created allowed hundreds of additional al Qaeda combatants, far more than had been anticipated by CJTF Mountain, to swarm into the valley from the east via the supply routes (referred to colloquially as "rat lines") that were used by enemy forces in the initial stages of the battle.[41] It also obliged U.S. forces to cope with an unplanned situation by having to abandon the originally briefed hammer-and-anvil approach that had been selected by CJTF Mountain, given the fact that the sudden withdrawal of Zia's combatants eliminated 50 percent of the combined force strength initially intended for the assault on Objective Remington. Thanks to that rude surprise, al Qaeda forces who otherwise would have had to contend with a flanking attack from the west were now able to concentrate fully on engaging those U.S. troops who were gradually flowing into the Shah-i-Kot valley. Once again, as before at Tora Bora, the reliability of the indigenous Afghan groups was overestimated by CENTCOM and by subordinate-level CJTF Mountain planners. Worse yet, uncooperative weather precluded the scheduled arrival of 50 percent of the U.S. conventional ground troops that had initially been slated to engage in combat operations on Day One. (They finally arrived a day later.)

A flight of AH-64 Apache attack helicopters preceded TF Rakkasan's move into the valley by reconnoitering the air assault's planned LZs in the vicinity of Objective Remington.[42] Because no al Qaeda presence in the area was detected from the air, the flight leader erroneously reported the LZs as cold. Almost immediately after being inserted, however, Rakkasan's troops found themselves beset by withering enemy mortar and heavy machine-gun fire from both the valley floor and the adjacent high ground. Equipped only with their per-

---

[41] Schmitt and Shanker, "Afghans' Retreat Forced Americans to Lead a Battle."

[42] Although the 101st Airborne Division routinely practiced using Apaches for close support (in what the Army calls close combat attack), CJTF Mountain's initial operations order for Anaconda had the eight available AH-64s designated for emergency CAS only, with the air component and SOF aviation expected to provide the bulk of any needed CAS throughout the operation. (Lieutenant General Franklin L. Hagenbeck, USA, interview on January 28, 2004, cited in Davis, p. 108.)

sonal weapons and with light machine guns and mortars, they lacked sufficient firepower of their own to negate the al Qaeda pressure. Accordingly, they called the Apaches back to perform a suppressive sweep of the suspected areas from which the hostile fire was emanating. On returning to the now-embattled valley, the Apache aircrews found themselves unable to provide the needed support because of the high density of enemy fire coming at them from multiple directions.[43] At times, the pressure from the al Qaeda defenders against the U.S. troops who were now pinned down in an open bowl came from all sides, with mortar rounds occasionally landing as close as 15 meters from those troops' positions.

In the end, all seven of the Apaches that had initially been committed to the fight were hit by al Qaeda fire, and five out of the seven were forced to return to their Forward-Area Rearming and Refueling Point (FARRP) to deal with the battle damage they had sustained. They eventually succeeded in flying the 100-mile distance back to Bagram but were inoperable on arrival and accordingly were forced to remain out of the fight until they underwent extensive field repairs and were recertified as being airworthy. One of the Apaches had taken a rocket-propelled grenade (RPG) hit in the engine, causing it to lose all of its oil. That aircraft barely made it back to Bagram, thanks to a "run-dry" feature that allows up to 30 minutes of flight time without engine oil.[44]

After the seven battle-damaged Apaches recovered successfully, 27 of the 28 main rotor blades among them were discovered to have sustained al Qaeda bullet penetrations. Five of the helicopters were repaired to a point where they were flying again within 24 hours. The remaining two, however, had to be airlifted out of the theater to a depot in the United States for major repairs, by which time an additional 24 Apaches that had been requested by General Hagenbeck as

---

[43] For an informed and vivid account of Army Apache operations on Day One of Anaconda, see Dodge Billingsley, "Choppers in the Coils: Operation Anaconda Was a 'Back to Basics' Campaign for U.S. Combat Helicopters," *Journal of Electronic Defense*, September 2002.

[44] Sean D. Naylor, "In Shah-i-Kot, Apaches Save the Day—and Their Reputation," *Army Times*, March 25, 2002, p. 15.

an emergency measure were en route to Bagram, via Air Force C-17s, from the United States.[45] General Myers later said that both the Apaches and the Army's CH-47 Chinooks had been "straining their capabilities" by operating at mountain elevations as high as 12,000 feet.[46] (The Chinook is typically used for moving troops, but only into areas that have already been secured.

Once the Apaches and General Lodin's indigenous force had withdrawn from the fight, and with only half of TF Rakkasan's forces having been inserted because of weather complications, the complexion of Anaconda changed significantly, in the words of one account, "from an operation focused primarily on land power to an operation increasingly dependent on Air Force, Navy, and later Marine air assets."[47] Because CJTF Mountain had not enlisted the involvement of the air component or laid the groundwork for an optimally effective joint air-ground operation until the last minute, however, this sudden dependence on fixed-wing air naturally encountered trouble when a need for emergency CAS arose. No CAS cell was manned in the CAOC at the time Anaconda commenced, and the two air liaison officers attached to CJTF Mountain quickly learned that their undermanned and poorly equipped air support cell that had been jury-rigged only the previous February 20, when the Anaconda operations order was first issued, was at the brink of being swamped by the need to prioritize multiple CAS requests and to deconflict the limited airspace over the valley as a profusion of calls for immediate fire support came pouring simultaneously into CJTF Mountain's command post from the 37 ETACs who were deployed throughout the area. At that point Colonel Longoria was released by General Mikolashek and flown to Bagram to establish a more fleshed-out and capable air support cell. In the process of doing that, Longoria also set in motion a plan to put fighter aircrews aboard the E-8 JSTARS to

[45] Erin Q. Winograd, "Additional Apaches Arrive in Afghanistan for Anti-Terror Campaign," *Inside the Army*, March 18, 2002, p. 1.

[46] Hendren and Daniszewski, "Seven U.S. Troops Are Killed in Assault on Enemy Fighters."

[47] Davis, p. 113.

serve as a de facto airborne battlefield command-and-control center (ABCCC), which helped immensely with airspace deconfliction and the prioritization of multiple concurrent CAS requests.

The Marine Corps' TF-58 also played an important stop-gap role in this unfolding battle. Once the Army's AH-64s were rendered combat-ineffective, TF-58's commander received an urgent request for support and promptly deployed five AH-1W Super Cobra attack helicopters and three CH-53 Super Stallion heavy lift helicopters to the combat zone. Less than 40 hours after receipt of their initial warning order, all five Super Cobras and two of the three CH-53s arrived at Bagram more than 700 miles away. By March 6, the Super Cobras and carrier-based Marine Corps AV-8B Harriers were flying continuous CAS missions in support of Anaconda.[48]

One participating Army unit leader later commented that the battle picture that had been painted by Anaconda's intelligence providers was "just a little bit different than the actual events" and that his men had, in fact, been inserted "at the base of an al Qaeda stronghold."[49] An informed senior officer in Washington subsequently confirmed that flawed intelligence had accounted in considerable part for the surprise that was encountered in the Shah-i-Kot valley: "[The inserted troops] were supposed to be the blocking force. And all of a sudden, they found themselves at the bottom of a valley with fire raining down on them from these guys in entrenched positions on a mountainside. They basically had them pinned down for 18 hours."[50] By this time, battlefield reports of enemy strength were stabilizing at more than 600 al Qaeda troops, a number considerably higher than CJTF Mountain's initial estimate of 150 to 200.[51]

An informative subsequent report on this grim experience was provided by an Air Force F-16 pilot who served as an air liaison offi-

---

[48] Neuenswander, "JCAS in Operation Anaconda."

[49] Esther Schrader, "Simple Mission Became 18-Hour Fight," *Los Angeles Times*, March 8, 2002.

[50] Schrader, "Simple Mission Became 18-Hour Fight."

[51] Moore, p. 281.

cer with the 3rd Brigade of the 101st Airborne Division, which had provided the bulk of the conventional ground forces and command-and-control support for Anaconda. This officer commanded the Tactical Air Control Party that had provided the Army contingent with all of its assigned Air Force ETACs.[52] In his words, "we jumped off the [helicopters] right into the middle of a hornet's nest." Almost immediately, all personnel involved in the insertion attempt came under heavy machine gun and mortar fire. One of the ETACs was pinned down for 15 hours within 500 meters of his original point of insertion. At the last minute, when it appeared that his position was about to be overrun, he made an urgent call for a JDAM attack against the hillside from which he was taking fire.[53] In a subsequent engagement, the same controller reported that his own position had begun taking mortar fire, whereupon he requested a LGB attack by an F-16 that was orbiting overhead. The ETAC talked the F-16 pilot's eyes onto the target, which was inside the danger-close criterion of 425 meters for the munitions the fighter was carrying. The F-16 scored a direct hit on the target.[54]

In a related episode, troops in one 10th Mountain Division company found themselves pinned down for six hours in the Shah-i-Kot valley by unrelenting enemy mortar fire. Finally, a B-52, one of several that had launched earlier from Diego Garcia without preas-

---

[52] This Air Force unit generally comprises a two-airman team assigned to work with an Army ground unit to direct CAS attacks against enemy targets on the ground. The responsibility of terminal attack controllers is to request and direct air strikes against enemy targets in close proximity to friendly forces and to control friendly attack platforms and ensure that they engage the right target.

[53] As the exchange reportedly went, the beleaguered ETAC called out on the radio: "B-52, I want you to put every f...ing bomb you have on that f...ing ridgeline, right f...ing now!" When the ETAC's commander reminded him that someone was probably taping the radio exchange, he replied: "Sir, if I survive this, they can court-martial me for poor radio discipline." "Roger that," his commander responded, "B-52, you heard the man, bomb the f...ing ridgeline with everything you've got right f...ing now!" That rare departure from the normally cool and professional radio voice discipline maintained even under duress by Air Force ETACs offered a telling reflection of the intensity of fire that the pinned-down Army troops were experiencing. (Email report forwarded to the author by Brigadier General R. Michael Worden, USAF, April 15, 2002.)

[54] Worden email.

signed targets, destroyed the offending al Qaeda position about a mile and a half away. "After that," said a U.S. combatant, "it was just sporadic. The threat was pretty much over by then."[55] Soldiers of the 10th Mountain Division described the fact that none of the 81 men in one company were killed, even though 27 had been wounded, as "the 18-hour miracle."[56] They had been under enemy fire from dawn until midnight, at which time they were finally extracted by helicopters. The onset of darkness aided CAS efforts by enabling AC-130 gunners to zero in on the source of enemy tracer rounds. By 1830, an AC-130 reentered the fight and cleaned out a nest of al Qaeda with 105mm cannon fire. Using thermal imaging, its gunners later detected 60 enemy already killed and then killed 28 more. It was subsequently estimated by on-scene commanders that 150 to 200 enemy fighters had been killed during the 18-hour battle. One Air Force controller detachment received more than 40 consecutive calls that first day from Army units reporting that they were under fire and in need of help. In all, some 800 bombs (around 500 of which were precision munitions) and thousands of rounds of AC-130 cannon fire were expended in support of the beleaguered friendly ground troops until they could finally be rescued.[57]

Fully half of the few previously planned air attacks on Anaconda's first day were aborted at the last minute by the excessively close proximity of U.S. troops to the intended al Qaeda targets. Even had that spur-of-the-moment complication not occurred, however, the air preparation for Anaconda was minimal at best. CJTF Mountain had planned for aerial munitions to be dropped on only 13 aim points out of a total of 22 known enemy firing positions and 40 cave entrances that had been identified by the CAOC's intelligence cell immediately before U.S. ground forces entered the Shah-i-Kot valley. It also had provided for no preparatory fire against suspected al

---

[55] John Daniszewski and Geoffrey Mohan, "Afghans Set Off to Root Out al Qaeda, Taliban Holdouts," *Los Angeles Times*, March 12, 2002.

[56] Dave Moniz, "Soldiers Describe '18-Hour Miracle,'" *USA Today*, March 7, 2002.

[57] Conversation with Lieutenant General John D. W. Corley, USAF, Headquarters United States Air Force, Washington, D.C., May 13, 2003.

Qaeda positions in the mountain caves. Moreover, the time allowed for the scheduled preparatory air attacks was cut back to only 20 minutes by General Hagenbeck, with the avowed goal of maintaining a hoped-for element of tactical surprise.[58] Once TF Rakkasan's urgent need for CAS became clearly evident, however, the air component responded in a timely manner to more than 150 immediate requests and dropped some 200 precision-guided munitions on al Qaeda positions in the first 24 hours of Operation Anaconda, with aircrews typically receiving refined target coordinates within 10 minutes or less of weapon release.[59]

The Showdown at Roberts Ridge

Less than 72 hours after Anaconda got under way, more unexpectedly fierce fighting broke out during an attempted predawn insertion of a SOF reconnaissance element into the high Shah-i-Kot mountains near Takur Ghar when the SOF troops encountered a sudden hail of large-caliber machine gun, RPG, and mortar fire from determined al Qaeda fighters who were holed up in the caves there. This was a covert operation planned and executed outside CJTF Mountain's chain of command. As such, it was not a part of General Hagenbeck's operation but rather a concurrent and loosely supporting SOF activity that overlapped with it and took place in the same battlespace. Nevertheless, it was part and parcel of the same divided command-and-control arrangement that got Anaconda off on the wrong foot in the first place by violating the cardinal rule of unity of command.

The first sign of trouble occurred at around 0300 on March 4, when two MH-47 helicopters from the 160th Special Operations

---

[58] The initial operations plan built by CJTF Mountain, however, included a written assumption that the enemy would become aware of the impending operation within 24 hours of its start because of leaks from the indigenous friendly forces involved. (Comments on an earlier draft by Major General David A. Deptula, USAF, Director of Operations, Pacific Air Forces, Hickam AFB, Hawaii, January 24, 2004.)

[59] Conversation with Lieutenant General John D. W. Corley, USAF, Headquarters United States Air Force, Washington, D.C., May 13, 2003.

Aviation Regiment (call signs Razor 3 and Razor 4) that were trans-porting two Navy SEAL teams and an Air Force combat controller attempted to set down in the predawn darkness on a high mountain ridgetop that had been designated Objective Ginger. The 10,200-foot-high LZ had been afforded some marginal bombing earlier and was thought to be undefended. As Razor 3 approached its assigned LZ in a small depression atop the ridgeline, the area turned out to be brimming with well-prepared al Qaeda combatants. The Chinook immediately encountered heavy machine-gun fire, at times from a range of only 50 yards, and took a direct RPG hit as it was preparing to land. As the pilot struggled to maintain control in the face of a sudden loss of oil pressure and hydraulic fluid occasioned by the en-emy fire, one of the SEALs fell out of the helicopter onto the ground not far below.[60]

The SEAL, Petty Officer First Class Neil Roberts, survived the fall, activated his infrared strobe light, and initially attempted to de-fend himself with his squad automatic weapon against the al Qaeda fighters who were rapidly advancing on him. He was quickly sur-rounded, however, hauled off to a sheltered location, and summarily executed.[61] While that was occurring, Razor 3's pilots were able to keep their badly damaged Chinook airborne long enough to perform a successful controlled crash-landing at a site some seven kilometers north of the position where Petty Officer Roberts had fallen out. A Hellfire-armed MQ-1 Predator UAV flying directly overhead ob-served the entire sequence, providing real-time video imagery to CJTF Mountain's command post at Bagram and to CENTCOM headquarters in Tampa, Florida. As General Hagenbeck later re-marked: "We saw him on the Predator being dragged off by three al Qaeda men."[62] No information derived from this imagery, however,

---

[60] Because the SEAL was expecting to be inserted at Objective Ginger, he was not tethered inside the Chinook's cabin as would have been the case otherwise.

[61] Bradley Graham, "Bravery and Breakdowns in a Ridgetop Battle," *Washington Post*, May 24, 2002.

[62] Thom Shanker, "U.S. Tells How Rescue Turned into Fatal Firefight," *New York Times*, March 6, 2002.

was available to the troops who were directly engaged on the ground with the enemy. The beleaguered SOF combatants were completely unaware that the Predator was overhead and was monitoring the proceedings.[63]

Once it became apparent to the crew of Razor 3 that Roberts had fallen out of the helicopter, what had begun as a simple reconnaissance foray that was expected to occur without incident became instantly transformed into an urgent rescue mission prompting an associated chain of events that was later described by a Pentagon after-action report as "one of the most intense small-unit firefights of the war against terrorism."[64] Shortly thereafter, having previously inserted its SOF team, Razor 4 arrived at the crash site of Razor 3, recovered the downed SEALS and helicopter crew members, and returned them to Gardez. While en route, the SEALs and pilots of Razor 4 formulated a plan to rescue Roberts or to recover his body. After delivering the recovered crew of Razor 3 to safety, they returned with five SEALs and the combat controller to Roberts's last known location on the mountaintop. At approximately 0500, Razor 4 successfully discharged its six-member element at Objective Ginger (now renamed Roberts Ridge for the fallen SEAL) and, although damaged by enemy fire, returned to its base. As the SEALs and combat controller worked their way to the high ground, they immediately began taking heavy enemy fire from above. In the process, the combat controller was mortally wounded and the SEALs, two of whom were also wounded, decided to disengage from their badly outnumbered situation. As they moved back down the mountain in search of protection, they contacted and received fire support from an AC-130 that was orbiting overhead and that covered their withdrawal.

In the meantime, back at the helicopter staging base, an Army Ranger quick-reaction force that had been sitting alert for just such a

---

[63] Robert Wall, "MH-47 Crews Detail Conflict's Exploits, Woes," *Aviation Week and Space Technology*, April 15, 2002, p. 23. One MH-47 that was badly damaged and had to be abandoned was recovered later by a Soviet-built Mi-26 heavy-lift helicopter.

[64] "Executive Summary of the Battle of Takur Ghar," Department of Defense, Washington, D.C., May 24, 2002, p. 1.

situation prepared to move forward with a 23-man contingent consisting of 10 Rangers and an Air Force combat controller, ETAC, and pararescueman aboard one MH-47 (call sign Razor 1) and 10 more Rangers aboard another (call sign Razor 2). At around 0615, the two Chinooks reached Objective Ginger and prepared to land, their crews unaware, because of poor communications, that the SEALs who had previously disembarked from Razor 4 were no longer atop the ridge-line—and also unaware that a group of armed al Qaeda fighters was in place and expecting their arrival. As Razor 1 approached from the south, it took an RPG hit in its engine compartment and was so riddled with heavy machine-gun fire that it could no longer be flown. It crash-landed hard in deep snow at the LZ. Four men aboard the helicopter were killed by enemy fire during the course of their insertion attempt. The surviving Rangers poured out of the downed aircraft into a withering barrage of al Qaeda fire and quickly scattered for shelter. However, there was scant protection to be found in the area. Some of the besieged soldiers were forced to dig foxholes on the spot with their bare hands. They made frantic radio calls for immediate fire support. Unfortunately, the AC-130 gunship that had provided covering fire earlier for the embattled troops aboard Razor 4 had to withdraw at sunrise just as Razors 1 and 2 began arriving at the LZ, due to an operating restriction that ruled out the aircraft's combat employment in daylight conditions because of its vulnerability to infrared SAMs and AAA if visually acquired. Had the gunship been able to remain on station, it very likely would have made short work of the enemy forces on Roberts Ridge. It was later estimated that well over 100 black-clothed al Qaeda fighters had been lying in wait for the attempted insertions.

As attested by the foregoing, the plan created for the attempted insertion of U.S. troops into Takur Ghar fell apart from its opening moments, thanks to the unexpectedly heavy enemy fire that was encountered at Objective Ginger and to the SOF contingent's lack of immediate fire support to negate it.[65] As happened two days earlier in

---

[65] Fulghum, "U.S. Troops Confront al Qaeda in Vicious Mountain Battle," pp. 24–25.

the case of CJTF Mountain's surprise encounter with unexpectedly heavy resistance during Anaconda's initial insertion attempt, fixed-wing air power had to be summoned as an emergency measure of last resort. The accompanying Air Force terminal attack controllers began calling in fighters to provide urgent CAS after the AC-130 was forced to depart the area at dawn.[66] Several hundred miles away, two airborne F-15E Strike Eagles (call signs Twister 51 and Twister 52) responded to the request, which stipulated strafe only. Upon their arrival at Roberts Ridge, it took the two aircrews three passes in dangerously close conditions to get a proper lineup of their aircraft on the designated enemy position. After satisfying the immediate CAS request, the aircraft pulled off, headed for the nearest tanker to refuel, and returned 20 minutes later to orbit the area while providing in-flight situation briefings to other fighters and bombers that had since arrived and were now operating in the vicinity of Roberts Ridge. Shortly thereafter, two F-16s (Clash 71 and Clash 72) arrived on scene and, for the next three hours, took turns with Twister in supporting the embattled SOF team. With Clash 72 remaining above the fight and monitoring its progress through his infrared targeting pod, the pilot of Clash 71 shot his gun empty in multiple strafe passes against the dug-in al Qaeda positions and then dropped three 500-lb LGBs on their emplacements in succession, walking the precision-guided bombs up the back side of the ridge to minimize the possibility of causing accidental fratricide. A B-52 armed with JDAMs also entered the fray to support the aircrews and SOF troops aboard Razor 1.[67]

Before the fighting on Roberts Ridge ended, the estimated enemy force had grown to 700 combatants, far more than the 150 to 200 that had originally been anticipated by CJTF Mountain.[68] To-

---

[66] Jonathan Weisman, "War's Deadliest Day," USA Today, March 6, 2002.

[67] Moore, pp. 286–287. For their bravery in providing this persistent support to the downed U.S. SOF personnel, notwithstanding their own repeated exposure to enemy fire, Clash 71 and all four aircrew members of Twister flight were awarded the Silver Star.

[68] Ann Scott Tyson, "Al Qaeda: Resistant and Organized," Christian Science Monitor, March 7, 2002.

ward the end of the day, a badly wounded Air Force pararescueman who had performed heroically in treating other wounded U.S. troops under enemy fire bled to death after the persistent intensity of fire ruled out any further daylight helicopter rescue attempts. Clearly, the operation's planners had overlooked the finite possibility that al Qaeda fighters might be in the area before the initial insertion attempt began. Viewed in hindsight, it should have been obvious that the dispersed caves in the Shah-i-Kot high ground had been created to provide shelter for exactly the kind of enemy attack that was mounted against the SEAL team during its initial insertion into Objective Ginger. Yet multiple known and preselected threat sites were not attacked as a precursor to the insertion, as a result of which the land component took huge and avoidable risks at the LZs.

In the end, the attempted insertion onto Roberts Ridge on March 4 featured the most intense combat faced by U.S. troops since the renowned October 1993 "Blackhawk Down" shootout in Mogadishu, Somalia, in which 18 U.S. Army Rangers were killed.[69] Although CJTF Mountain itself sustained no losses to enemy fire at any time during Anaconda, eight American covert SOF personnel were killed during the first three days in concurrent operations that General Hagenbeck did not control. They included one Navy SEAL, one Army aviator, one Army Special Forces soldier, an Air Force combat controller, an Air Force pararescueman, and three Army Rangers. Hagenbeck later indicated that 48 additional U.S. combatants were wounded during Anaconda's first three days.[70]

---

[69] Shanker, "U.S. Tells How Rescue Turned into Fatal Firefight." The now-classic account of the Mogadishu shootout is Mark Bowden, *Black Hawk Down: A Story of Modern War*, New York: Penguin Books, 1999.

[70] Thomas E. Ricks and Vernon Loeb, "U.S. Claims Advantage in Battle," *Washington Post*, March 7, 2002. In addition to Naylor, another detailed and credible replay of the engagements in the Shah-i-Kot valley and on Roberts Ridge on March 2 and March 4 by a writer who had intimate access to many of the participants may be found in Moore, pp. 271–295.

Recovering from the Initial Setbacks

Immediately after the Roberts Ridge encounter, General Franks said: "At the end of the day . . . the sure way to do work against the enemy is to put people on the ground, and that's what we've done in this case."[71] Yet there was no denying that the inauspicious start of Anaconda was anything but encouraging. General Hagenbeck frankly described the experience of March 4 as "a meat grinder." He also later acknowledged the role of faulty intelligence as at least one major culprit, noting that the initial threat assessment had anticipated only some 150 to 200 al Qaeda combatants in the area, a number that soared to between 600 and 700 after the first two days of combat.[72]

As the progress of Anaconda grew more favorable once General Moseley pulled out all the stops in pushing air power to the fight, the air component quickly increased the flow of assets in a maximum effort to support the still-embattled U.S. ground forces, with the number of fighter sorties out of al Jaber Air Base in Kuwait tripling between March 2 and March 4 and with the concurrent decision to move A-10s forward from al Jaber on March 3 and getting those aircraft engaged in time to cover the extraction of the survivors from Roberts Ridge on the evening of March 4. Air support was provided by AC-130 gunships and by B-52s, B-1s, F-14s, F-15Es, F-16s, and F/A-18s—and also by A-10s once the latter arrived in theater and began operating. In addition, 22 French strike fighters (16 Super Etendards from the aircraft carrier *Charles de Gaulle* and six Mirage 2000Ds operating out of the Manas airport in Kyrgyzstan) participated in the Anaconda fighting. (The Mirage 2000D pilots had previously sharpened their skills during a Red Flag training exercise at Nellis AFB, Nevada, and were familiar with operating in a moun-

---

[71] Thomas E. Ricks, "Battle Sends Broader Message of U.S. Resolve," *Washington Post*, March 5, 2002.

[72] Bill Gertz, "Nine U.S. Soldiers Killed in Afghanistan," *Washington Times*, March 5, 2002, and Thomas E. Ricks and Bradley Graham, "Surprises, Adjustments and Milestones for U.S. Military," *Washington Post*, March 10, 2002.

tainous environment.)[73] By the end of the first week, as allied air attacks became more consistent and sustained, al Qaeda resistance began tapering off and friendly forces seized control of ever more terrain.

Carrier Air Wing (CVW) 9 in USS *John C. Stennis*, which had taken up station in mid-December 2001, played a key part in Operation Anaconda, as did CVW 7 aboard USS *John F. Kennedy*. The embarked air wings each flew an average of 100 to 110 sorties a day, with distances of 800 miles and more to the target area and back, operating in what were typically 14-hour flying days. These sorties included some unique operations, such as F-14s carrying mixed weapon loads of GBU-12 LGBs and GBU-31 JDAMs. Navy E-2Cs provided airborne command-and-control support inside Afghanistan, and EA-6Bs provided 24-hour alert communications jamming as required.[74] On March 11, to help provide ISR support for these operations, CENTCOM flew its first RQ-4 Global Hawk mission since a December crash had grounded the tiny fleet.[75]

As the air contribution to Anaconda steadily improved in effectiveness, Air Force combat controllers and ETACs controlled hundreds of munitions deliveries from every type of attack platform in every U.S. and allied service involved in Enduring Freedom, with no further fratricide and no friendly losses to enemy fire. On occasion, Army mortar fire would keep al Qaeda troops pinned down at their mountain positions to prevent them from fleeing as air assets entered the fight to attack them with LGBs or JDAMs, in what General

---

[73] From March 4 to March 22, French fighters attacked 31 enemy positions in connection with Anaconda. For further details on the French and other allied operational contributions to Enduring Freedom, see Marie Lesure, "The 'Market Price' of Terrorism: U.S. Allies Add to Toll Paid by Taliban and al Qaeda," *Armed Forces Journal International,* June 2002, pp. 22–24.

[74] Comments during a panel presentation by Enduring Freedom carrier air wing commanders at the Tailhook Association's 2002 annual reunion and symposium, Reno, Nevada, September 6, 2002.

[75] "Global Hawk Back in the Fight After Post-Crash Stand-Down," *Inside the Air Force,* March 15, 2002, p. 9. The cause of the December crash was finally assessed as having been a failure of the UAV's rudder actuator.

Hagenbeck agreed was a role reversal from the traditional air-ground relationship, with air power in this case being the supported force element.[76] In one case, 100 to 200 al Qaeda fighters were observed running out of their caves, evidently fearing an imminent bombing attack. They were then engaged in the open and killed by a flight of two A-10s. F-15Es also strafed enemy positions on more than one occasion, including some in dangerously close proximity to friendly forces, in a mode of operation that was not, at least at the time, on the list of mission applications for which F-15E aircrews routinely trained.[77] Phase Two of Operation Anaconda from March 5 to March 12 saw a heightened intensity of CAS operations that ultimately rendered the surviving al Qaeda forces unable to sustain their resistance. Phase Three carried the fight to the Whale and Objective Ginger and finally laid waste to al Qaeda positions in the valley as dozens of aircraft operated continuously without incident in the cramped airspace above it. In a situation in which five times the expected enemy strength was taken on by CJTF Mountain, air support to Anaconda saw the greatest number of precision munitions dropped into the smallest geographic space in the history of air warfare.[78]

From an air perspective, the biggest problem presented by the initial planning of Anaconda entailed coordinating the many concurrent strike operations with too few prior preparations. That problem occasioned serious concerns both in the CAOC and aboard the participating aircraft carriers, since the congested traffic operating within the tightly confined airspace over the battlefield and the ever-present danger of a midair collision or other fratricide incident meant that there was no margin for error in managing the flow of aircraft through that airspace. Despite those concerns, however, neither the carrier air wings nor any other units engaged in the operation ever

---

[76] Conversation with Lieutenant General Franklin L. Hagenbeck, USA, Headquarters United States Army, Washington, D.C., July 1, 2004.

[77] Major Charles D. Dusch, Jr., USAF, "Anaconda Offers Lessons in Close Air Support," *Proceedings*, March 2003, p. 79.

[78] Conversation with Lieutenant General John D. W. Corley, USAF, Headquarters United States Air Force, Washington, D.C., May 13, 2003.

declined a sortie request from General Moseley. In the end, the application of allied air power in Anaconda was more responsive than in earlier portions of Enduring Freedom, and its concentration of fire was unprecedented in the Afghan campaign. Ten heavy bombers, more than 30 fighters, and two AC-130s continuously operated within a 70-square-mile battle area. That amounted to more than half the typical commitment of aircraft used over all of Afghanistan during the first weeks of Enduring Freedom.

The commander of CVW 9 later recalled that Anaconda had been inadequately planned from his perspective as a Navy CAS provider. The operation's leaders had counted on extensive rotary-wing support and had failed to give due consideration to the possibility of weather complications. The battle of Roberts Ridge ended up involving a heavy CSAR effort with numerous ETACs working a very small area. The sudden and unexpected demand for air support that was occasioned by it led to an airspace congestion problem of formidable proportions, with allied aircraft frequently stacked eight miles high over the combat zone. B-52s at the highest altitude of 39,000 feet dropped JDAMs through the flight paths of B-1 bombers and formations of fighters orbiting at 22,000–25,000 feet, EP-3s at lower altitudes, and AC-130s lower still at night, all followed by Predator UAVs, A-10s, and attack helicopters at the lowest altitudes.[79] Further complicating matters, three civil air routes ran through the airspace over the Shah-i-Kot valley beneath the operating altitudes of the B-52s, which created yet another deconfliction challenge for the CAOC (see Figure 5.2).[80] The overriding concern was not running out of aircraft but rather out of usable airspace. Often lower-priority requests would be denied because of a lack of sufficient airspace. With multiple JDAMs repeatedly falling through this densely occupied

---

[79] Comments during a panel presentation by Enduring Freedom carrier air wing commanders at the Tailhook Association's 2002 annual reunion and symposium, Reno, Nevada, September 6, 2002.

[80] Conversation with General T. Michael Moseley, USAF, Headquarters United States Air Force, Washington, D.C., February 12, 2004.

Figure 5.2
Operation Anaconda Aircraft Stack

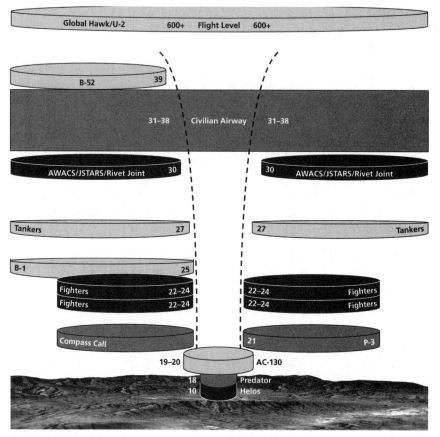

SOURCE: AF/XOL.
NOTE: Altitudes are in thousands of feet.

airspace, only the most exacting air discipline, combined with a significant measure of good luck, prevented a major inflight disaster.

Air Force terminal attack controllers later reported that coordinating and deconflicting all of those aircraft to allow them to drop bombs on multiple targets within such a confined battle area created a thoroughgoing nightmare. These experts had been in contact with CJTF Mountain's limited CAS cell at Bagram for days before Anaconda began. Yet because of inadequate prior planning, efforts to employ dedicated air support proved chaotic at first, especially during the first 12 to 24 hours of the operation. As but one testament to the magnitude of the problem, an F/A-18 came close to having a midair collision with a pair of A-10s operating over the valley during the night of March 5.[81] Ultimately, the only way the large number of aircraft operating simultaneously over the battlefield could be safely deconflicted was through the use of airborne forward air controllers, or FAC-As, mainly in A-10s and, to a lesser degree, F-16s.

Eventually, a pattern began to emerge. Said one ETAC, "it would be quiet, then a bunch of requests would come in at once. It really was feast or famine."[82] Since there were often multiple instances of friendly troops in simultaneous direct contact with the enemy, the demand for air support was so high that fighter pilots on occasion would break their two most cardinal rules by operating alone without a wingman when circumstances demanded it and by remaining on station below their "bingo" fuel limit—the amount of fuel needed to get safely home without an inflight refueling—against the guarded hope that there might be an available tanker in the vicinity with fuel to spare once they had delivered their requested fire support.

After the bulk of the effort to clear out the remaining al Qaeda fighters who had sought to hide in caves or withdraw from the valley drew to a close at Anaconda's 11-day point, Secretary of Defense Rumsfeld reported that the operation had entered what he called a "mopping up process."[83] Unlike the earlier case of Tora Bora, there was no easy way out for the trapped al Qaeda fighters this time. Coalition air and ground forces were still seeking to secure the eastern ridge of the Shah-i-Kot mountains, which contained dispersed pockets of some 100 to 200 enemy combatants who were thought to be still hiding there as U.S. forces hunted cave by cave for al Qaeda fugi-

---

[81] Neuenswander, "JCAS in Operation Anaconda."

[82] Lance M. Bacon, "Secret Weapons: The Airmen Who Are Winning the Ground War," *Air Force Times*, April 8, 2002, p. 14.

[83] Rowan Scarborough, "Afghan Operation Termed a Success," *Washington Times*, March 12, 2002.

tives at elevations of up to 10,000 feet. All the same, Rumsfeld seemed comfortable enough with the results that had been achieved to declare that "the people have been liberated. The al Qaeda in that country are no longer using the country as a haven or a sanctuary for terrorists [or] to conduct terrorist attacks against the rest of the world. We have the al Qaeda in Afghanistan on the run."[84]

The surviving al Qaeda forces appeared to have preserved their ability to communicate by means of runners, as well as possibly also by means of satellite telephones and short-range radios. General Hagenbeck later indicated that what he termed a "very smart, aggressive, sophisticated enemy" had used Internet connections through satellite phones to call in reinforcements and supplies in anticipation of Operation Anaconda as U.S. forces were pouring into the Shah-i-Kot valley, tacitly confirming that any hoped-for element of surprise—even tactical surprise—had been largely in vain from the very start.[85] Subsequent U.S. inspection of destroyed or abandoned al Qaeda cave emplacements showed that the enemy fighters possessed night-vision goggles identical to those used by U.S. forces, as well as sheaves of RPGs, long belts of machine-gun ammunition, and 75mm recoilless rifles suitable for attacking light armored vehicles and hovering helicopters. At one site, a trench was found connecting several enemy firing positions, one of which mounted a Soviet heavy machine gun apparently intended for antiaircraft use. Also discovered in one cave were Global Positioning System (GPS) receivers and a unidirectional radio transmitter that was difficult for U.S. equipment to detect and monitor.[86]

As Anaconda gradually wound down after nine days of the war's heaviest fighting, CENTCOM finally withdrew 400 U.S. troops from the combat zone, characterizing the withdrawal as merely a troop rotation and declaring that the operation had not yet ended.

---

[84] Scarborough, "Afghan Operation Termed a Success."

[85] Nathan Hodge, "Predator Helps Coalition Estimate Body Count," *Defense Week Daily Update*, March 19, 2002.

[86] Thomas E. Ricks, "In Mop Up, U.S. Finds 'Impressive' Remnants of Fallen Foe," *Washington Post*, March 20, 2002.

Soon thereafter, CENTCOM spokesmen said that the hardest part of the fighting was over. By that time, more than 2,500 bombs had fallen on enemy positions since the battle began on March 2.[87] At the end of the 17-day operation, Afghan and U.S. troops moved in at daybreak from three directions to take control of the high ground at long last.

The Pentagon later reported the confirmed number of Arab, Chechen, and other foreign al Qaeda fighters killed as 517, with another 250 believed killed but unconfirmed.[88] As General Hagenbeck noted, most of the enemy fatalities were caused by precision air-delivered munitions.[89] Step by step, the bombing destroyed the last known fortified stronghold of al Qaeda and the Taliban in Afghanistan and forced the surviving al Qaeda fighters to withdraw, thereby enabling the forces of CJTF Mountain finally to secure the Shah-i-Kot valley by March 16. Scores of Taliban and al Qaeda prisoners held at a detention facility in Guantanamo Bay, Cuba, later reported that they had surrendered during Anaconda after hearing psychological-warfare radio transmissions from EC-130 Commando Solo aircraft.[90] In all, fixed-wing aircraft flew an average of 65 CAS sorties a day during Anaconda and dropped nearly 3,500 bombs in support of friendly ground troops in the Shah-i-Kot region.

In sum, an operation that was initially expected to last only 72 hours went on for two weeks. The confrontation between U.S. troops and hard-core al Qaeda fighters in the Shah-i-Kot area was the largest U.S. ground engagement of the war to date. Conducted at times above 10,000 feet, it also was the highest-elevation land battle ever fought in U.S. history. After it was over, the commander of the participating 101st Airborne Division characterized it as "the largest,

---

[87] John Daniszewski, "Afghans Advance Toward al Qaeda, Taliban Holdouts," *Los Angeles Times*, March 13, 2002.

[88] Eric Schmitt and Thom Shanker, "Taliban and al Qaeda Death Toll in Mountain Battle Is a Mystery," *New York Times*, March 14, 2002.

[89] Conversation with Lieutenant General Franklin L. Hagenbeck, USA, Headquarters United States Army, Washington, D.C., July 1, 2004.

[90] Bob Arnott, "Electronic War in the Afghan Skies," MSNBC.com, March 11, 2002.

most intense direct combat engagement with an enemy force the 101st Airborne Division has been involved in since Vietnam."[91] In the end, however, it took the eleventh-hour intervention of CENTCOM's air component to compensate for the many planning oversights of CJTF Mountain and the covert SOF community once the going got rough.

The Endgame of Enduring Freedom

With Operation Anaconda successfully completed, what remained of the major air operations phase of Enduring Freedom proved largely uneventful. By late March 2002, the once-dilapidated Bagram Air Base that had been built and then abandoned by the Soviet occupiers during the 1980s was rapidly becoming a substantial U.S. military garrison, dominated by earth-filled security barriers, steel frames for new accommodations under construction, and heavy transport aircraft arriving almost hourly to offload needed materiel, consumables, and additional personnel. As many as 50 helicopters representing all services could be seen on the parking ramp at Bagram at times. Despite an early desire on the part of the Bush administration to maintain as small a footprint as possible, some 5,300 American troops were now on the ground in Afghanistan.[92] As that number gradually grew to 7,000 (and later to 18,000), the day of big battles and repeated bombing missions was over, and Operation Enduring Freedom segued into a lower-intensity counterinsurgency effort relying less on air strikes and indigenous Afghan involvement and more on allied forces, with operations featuring American, British, Canadian, and other coalition SOF personnel seeking to hunt down and capture or dispatch residual Taliban and al Qaeda holdouts. (Of the 7,000 U.S. troops who were in Afghanistan by late April 2002, 5,000 were concentrated at Bagram.)

---

[91] Bill Gertz, "Rumsfeld Says Afghan Battle's End Near," *Washington Times*, March 8, 2002.

[92] John F. Burns, "U.S. Planning New Operations to Root Out Scattered Afghan Holdouts," *New York Times*, March 18, 2002.

Later mop-up operations included a modest British Army push called Operation Ptarmigan into the southeastern Afghan mountains in mid-April on a search-and-destroy mission for any remaining Taliban and al Qaeda fugitives. In this first significant ground activity since Anaconda ended four weeks before, British troops were joined by indigenous Afghan fighters and were supported by allied air power.[93] Marine Corps F/A-18D Hornets from Marine Corps Air Station (MCAS) Miramar, California, which had deployed to Manas airport in Kyrgyzstan only days earlier, joined in support of this effort, as did the dozen French Mirage 2000Ds still stationed at Manas, the first of which had arrived the previous February 27 and which had already seen combat action in Anaconda.[94]

In early May 2002, the commander of British forces at Bagram said that in his personal view, the war in Afghanistan was "all but won. . . . In substantial parts of the country, the need for offensive operations is beginning to dwindle, and they will be completed in a matter of weeks rather than months."[95] For his part, General Franks countered shortly thereafter: "Is it about over? I wouldn't think so. I'm not convinced the network is totally done. As long as it's not done, we're going to be here working."[96] By the end of May, however, Under Secretary of Defense Wolfowitz stated emphatically: "Just in Afghanistan alone, I think the results have been impressive. . . . We've basically made Afghanistan impossible for terrorists to organize and work out of. We've captured and killed large numbers, and the ones that are left are on the run."[97]

Among the many signs that the large-scale portion of the air war was now winding down, eight B-1B bombers based in Oman began

---

[93] Peter Baker, "British Forces Lead New Afghan Mission," *Washington Post*, April 17, 2002.

[94] Once approval for its use was obtained, it took four months to prepare Manas to support operations by the U.S. 376th Air Expeditionary Wing.

[95] Cesar Soriano, "Allied Operations Said to Be Dwindling in Afghanistan," *USA Today*, May 9, 2002.

[96] Carol J. Williams, "Afghan Force Maintains High Profile Despite Risks," *Los Angeles Times*, May 16, 2002.

[97] Mimi Hall, "Poll: USA Less Optimistic on War," *USA Today*, May 31, 2002.

returning home to Dyess AFB, Texas, in early May 2002. (The B-1Bs had redeployed from Diego Garcia to Oman the previous December to reduce the burden of transporting munitions to the considerably more distant Indian Ocean island base, as well as to shorten the duration of B-1 combat sorties. The distance from Oman to southeastern Afghanistan was only 600 miles, compared to 2,000 miles from Diego Garcia.) [98] Once the Air Force bomber contingent on Diego Garcia had shrunk to a mere token number, the Australian F/A-18s that had deployed there at the beginning of Enduring Freedom to provide local air defense returned home on May 20. At the same time, the U.S. naval presence in the region was cut by half, to one carrier battle group and only 200 Marines afloat. [99] By early August 2002, the coalition presence on the ground in Afghanistan had declined to 11,000 troops, down from an earlier high of about 13,000. [100]

After Anaconda was successfully concluded, some of the now-intermittent U.S. strike sorties were flown as policing actions in support of the fledgling interim Karzai government. In one such operation in early May 2002, the CIA launched a Hellfire missile from one of its MQ-1 Predator drones in an unsuccessful attempt to kill Gulbuddin Hekmatyar, the leader of a militant Pashtun group who had vowed to topple the new Afghan provisional government. [101] In July, an A-10 operating out of Bagram dropped a 500-lb Mk 82 bomb in a peacekeeping action on an uninhabited area near a firefight between two opposed Afghan factions that had left one warlord's brother

[98] David A. Fulghum, "Aircraft Close on Battlefield," *Aviation Week and Space Technology*, December 10, 2001, p. 40. Once the B-1s redeployed to Oman, the plan was to maintain a 24-hour bomber CAP over Afghanistan, with each B-1 loaded with 2,000-lb JDAMs, cluster bombs, and unguided Mk 82 500-lb bombs and placed on a 12-hour patrol to provide on-call support against emerging targets as needed.

[99] Eric Schmitt, "U.S. Raids Along Afghan Border Seen as Lasting Past Summer," *New York Times*, May 6, 2002. The other carrier was able to go home partly because of the establishment of a forward presence of A-10s at Bagram with a 30-minute response time by the second week of Anaconda.

[100] Susan B. Glasser, "U.S. Challenged to Define Role in Afghanistan," *Washington Post*, August 3, 2002.

[101] Thom Shanker with Carlotta Gall, "U.S. Attack on Warlord Aims to Help Interim Leader," *New York Times*, May 9, 2002.

dead. The intent of that gesture was to make what a U.S. spokesman called "a show of force."[102] Unfortunately, the United States lost some of the goodwill with the Afghan rank and file it had gained earlier by freeing their country from the grip of the Taliban when some local warriors in eastern Afghanistan persuaded CENTCOM to approve air attacks against their enemies, falsely claiming that those they had targeted were al Qaeda forces on the run. Such misdirected attacks caused civilian fatalities once at the wedding noted above and twice to gatherings of Afghans loyal to Karzai.

As it turned out, the major air portion of Operation Enduring Freedom was conducted in two stages, the first of which brought down the Taliban regime and the second of which concentrated on seeking out and engaging any remaining Taliban and al Qaeda hold-outs. For a time, Taliban commanders seemed to believe genuinely, if also benightedly, that they had a fighting chance to defeat the United States just as they had defeated the Soviets. In the end, however, U.S. forces and friendly Afghan fighters were assessed to have killed at least 5,000 Taliban and al Qaeda combatants, wounded twice that many, and taken 7,000 more prisoner, even though only four of the top 50 Taliban leaders surrendered or were captured. For its part, the United States lost 39 soldiers during the first year of Enduring Freedom, including 16 who were killed in what the Pentagon called "combat or hostile situations."[103] In all, 13 coalition partners contributed military personnel, either directly to the campaign or to the International Security Assistance Force that was later established in Kabul. The reported cost of the war by the end of its first year was $10 billion.[104]

On the first anniversary of the commencement of Enduring Freedom, by which time there were 10,000 American military personnel in Afghanistan, Secretary Rumsfeld said that American troops would remain there for "as long as it takes." After Rumsfeld spoke,

---

[102] "U.S. Drops Bomb as Two Afghan Factions Clash," *Los Angeles Times*, July 19, 2002.

[103] Margaret Cox, "U.S. Role Is Far from Over," *Atlanta Journal and Constitution*, October 6, 2002.

[104] Cox.

the U.S. ambassador to Kabul likewise declared that "military operations are continuing, especially in the eastern part of the country, and they will continue until we win."[105] To this day, despite its signal achievements between early October 2001 and late March 2002, Operation Enduring Freedom has not yet been declared over by CENTCOM. Hard-core Taliban holdouts in the Afghan hinterland continue to wage a rearguard effort to undermine the still-shaky Karzai government, and a secure Afghanistan under a stable, democratically elected leadership remains nowhere near at hand. On the contrary, a record high of more than 18,000 U.S. troops in the country continue to conduct peacemaking and counterinsurgency operations that, by all indications, appear to be open-ended.

Anaconda Issues

As might have been expected, the eight American combat fatalities that were incurred during the first three days of Operation Anaconda prompted a sharply critical response from some quarters in Washington and elsewhere. Some air power partisans suggested that a desire for an impressive showing by the land component before the end of hostilities, after allied air power had done so much of the heavy lifting during the preceding five months, lay at the center of the land component's decisionmaking. Others less inclined to be so harshly judgmental assessed the underresourced plan instead as a result simply of CJTF Mountain's inexperience at joint planning and operations, faulty assessments of the likely al Qaeda threat, ill-informed assumptions about the extent of air support that would be needed to make the plan work, and general overconfidence. Whatever the explanation, because so little prior air support had been requested by CJTF Mountain and by those in the separate covert SOF chain of command who planned the Roberts Ridge insertion, coalition troops entered the fight virtually unprotected by any preparatory and suppres-

---

[105] David Blair and Toby Harnden, "U.S. Troops Will Stay in Afghanistan 'Until We Win,'" *London Daily Telegraph*, October 8, 2002.

sive fire other than from the seven Apache attack helicopters that were quickly driven off the first day by unexpectedly fierce enemy resistance.

Immediately after the Roberts Ridge encounter (an operation, to be sure, conducted by JSOC and CENTCOM rather than CJTF Mountain), some in the Air Force faulted those who had allowed it to happen for not having made better use of CENTCOM's air component before commencing their insertion, with one general reportedly saying that "the way we lost those seven guys was a repeat of Somalia."[106] Secretary of Defense Rumsfeld rejected that comparison. But more than a few Air Force officers persisted in maintaining that SOF troop transport helicopters had repeatedly been inserted into a heavily defended LZ without adequate preplanned air cover.[107] Indeed, one high-level compilation of Air Force briefing charts went so far as to suggest that those responsible for Anaconda had "intentionally" and "deliberately" excluded the air component from the operation's planning.[108]

Nevertheless, despite the undeniable early setbacks that Anaconda experienced as a result of the land component's initial planning oversights, it appeared for a time that broadly accepted rules of interservice etiquette would preclude any serious public Monday-morning quarterbacking of the various factors that occasioned those setbacks. The floodgates were eventually opened for a heated post-Anaconda contretemps between the Air Force and Army, however, by some sharp criticisms of Air Force CAS performance that were levied in a published interview in September 2002 by none other than General

---

[106] Rowan Scarborough, "Military Officers Criticize Rush to Use Ground Troops," *Washington Times*, March 7, 2002.

[107] Roundtable discussion with Air Force participants in Operation Enduring Freedom, Air Command and Staff College, Maxwell AFB, Alabama, November 17, 2003.

[108] "Joint Air-Ground Operations: Operation Anaconda Background," Directorate of Plans and Programs, Headquarters Air Combat Command, Langley AFB, Virginia, undated briefing charts.

Hagenbeck himself.[109] In his interview remarks, General Hagenbeck stated that because of the rough terrain in the target area and the uncooperative weather at the scheduled time of Anaconda's start, overhead ISR systems had been unable to locate and identify the enemy's cave complexes, thus necessitating an insertion of ground troops to find the caves. He added that some preparatory bombing had taken place 20 minutes before the first assault team entered the area, but that he "did not want to attack the dozens and dozens of cave complexes arbitrarily without having some sense of what was in them. . . . So without knowing what was in those caves, we did not want to have air strikes on them until we could assess them."[110] On the asserted premise that because U.S. forces had only "so many of those precision munitions [presumably LGBs and JDAMs]," he elected instead to use "mortars and machine guns to kill [the al Qaeda combatants] outright. . . . We got a number of kills with close air support, but they were *primarily* [emphasis added] because our mortars and machine guns kept the al Qaeda from getting up and running back into their caves."[111]

General Hagenbeck went on to claim that the most effective CAS asset he had available to him "was the Apache, hands down. The Apaches were extraordinary—they were lethal and survivable"—a statement that did not reflect the Apache's actual combat performance in Anaconda. He granted that fixed-wing aviation also provided praiseworthy CAS but then hastened to add that "our fixed-wing pilots faced some procedural and maneuvering challenges." In a clear, if implied, deprecation of Air Force aggressiveness under fire, he remarked that "the Navy and Marine Corps fighter pilots routinely flew as low to the ground as they could to achieve the effects, even when it

---

[109] Robert H. McElroy, "Interview: Fire Support for Operation Anaconda," *Field Artillery Journal,* September–October 2002.

[110] It bears stressing on this point that the primary mission of Operation Anaconda was *not* to collect intelligence on al Qaeda but rather to seek out and capture or kill any al Qaeda fighters who may have been holed up in the Shah-i-Kot hinterland.

[111] In fact, by the time Anaconda kicked off in early March 2002, an effort initiated in late 2001 to replenish Air Force and Navy JDAM stocks had provided CENTCOM with a more than ample supply of those munitions.

was below what was deemed safe distance," and that "they were terrific," whereas "the Air Force had to work through airspace management," with aircraft "stacked up to the ceiling" such that they "could only be flown in a few numbers."[112] Furthermore, he added, whereas Air Force aircrews turned in "some" CAS successes, "it took anywhere from 26 minutes to hours (on occasion) for the precision munitions to hit the targets." In contrast, he said, the Army's mortars "performed superbly."

General Hagenbeck further suggested that "we have a huge procedural and training issue we've got to work through with our Air Force friends" centering on the presumed fact that because of the "complexity" of precision weapons, the Air Force will not employ JDAMs "without either a GFAC [ground forward air controller] or ETAC calling them in."[113] He commented, correctly, that "there are not enough GFACS or ETACs in [the Air Force's] inventory to support every ground maneuver element," an admitted shortfall that prompted him to suggest that, as a result, the Army has a valid need for its own certified ground controllers to call in JDAM strikes. He also remarked that because on-scene Predator UAVs sometimes were moved by the CAOC out of a particular area where he desired to look and because a request for Predator support had to go through channels for him to redirect the drone's search, "the UAV operator needs to be sitting next to the ground tactical commander."

In that same forum, one of Hagenbeck's former subordinates, the deputy fire support coordinator for Anaconda, went further yet by suggesting that although more than 30 U.S. ground troops in direct contact with the enemy had been effectively supported by CAS missions during the first 24 hours of Anaconda, "we must not extol the efforts of fixed-wing support alone," since the "time constraint"

[112] This was the case not just for Air Force air assets but for all CENTCOM fixed-wing and rotary-wing air, including that of the Army, Navy, and Marine Corps.

[113] It was not the complexity of the weapons themselves (which are, in fact, anything but complex) that was at issue here so much as the complexity of the tactical situation in which they were used. GFACs and ETACs were required by CENTCOM and Washington to provide positive target identification in many cases to avoid inadvertent fratricide or collateral damage.

allegedly placed on CJTF Mountain for the planning of Anaconda "hindered the responsiveness of the targeting process" because of the alleged fact that "the ATO [air tasking order] required aviation assets [to] be coordinated 36 hours out."[114] After conceding that the ATO remained the best available mechanism for coordinating large-force air operations, this lieutenant colonel charged that "it is . . . inflexible and not well-suited to support a nonlinear, asymmetrical battlefield." Revealing a lack of familiarity with even the basics of the ATO development and execution process, he added that it "must be flexible enough to change aircraft and munitions packages as the intelligence picture changes by the minute." He further asserted, likewise without foundation, that "in some cases, the inabilities [sic] of aircraft to break self-imposed USAF altitude restrictions, slow their strike speed down or strafe the battlefield (the latter in the case of the bombers) restricted these aircraft's [sic] abilities to deliver timely munitions in close support of troops on the ground."

Clearly blindsided by these untoward Army charges, Air Force Chief of Staff General John Jumper promptly initiated a top-level review, in conjunction with the Army staff, of Air Force CAS delivery in Anaconda to get to the bottom of them, adding that he was "taking this on personally."[115] That review, conducted in substantial part by the service's Air Combat Command at Langley AFB, Virginia, focused on five charges, in particular, that were levied against the Air Force in the course of the criticisms outlined above. They centered on (1) CAS response time, (2) airspace congestion and management, (3) an alleged reluctance of Air Force aircrews, unlike their supposedly more courageous Navy and Marine Corps counterparts, to descend into the enemy's AAA and infrared SAM envelopes to provide on-call CAS, (4) an unsatisfactory use of combat controllers and ETACs, and (5) an insufficiently helpful contribution by the RQ-1 Predator drone. In each case, the review found that the complaints reflected

---

[114] Lieutenant Colonel Christopher F. Bentley, USA, "Afghanistan: Joint and Coalition Fire Support in Operation Anaconda," *Field Artillery Journal*, September–October 2002.

[115] Grossman, "Left in the Dark for Most Anaconda Planning, Air Force Opens New Probe."

not only widely divergent Army and Air Force perspectives on CAS in general but, more important, numerous Army assumptions about CAS delivery by all services in Anaconda that were simply unfounded.

To take the response-time issue first, once the CAOC was fully integrated into CJTF Mountain's battle plan, the actual time delay from initial CAS request to ordnance on target was reported to have been, on average, as little as five minutes, according to those in the CAOC who kept detailed records of CAS performance by all aircraft in all services on a sortie-by-sortie basis.[116] Those responses that were said to have been "26 minutes to hours (on occasion)" in coming took the amount of time they did for a number of valid reasons.

To begin with, the implied charge of excessively slow response time erroneously conflated CAS and interdiction attacks. In so doing, it misled readers to believe that fixed-wing air support to allied troops in contact with the enemy was unreasonably delayed. In fact, enemy forces in direct contact with friendly forces did not require positive target identification and were usually engaged upon request very quickly. The targeting process for interdiction attacks, however, typically took longer because it required positive target identification first. That process, moreover, was not Air Force–determined, but rather was a CENTCOM process established and enforced at Pentagon and White House insistence, the main goal of which was target destruction with no fratricide and minimal collateral damage. From the perspective of CJTF Mountain, the entire Shah-i-Kot valley and its approaches lay within enemy mortar range, seemingly rendering any identified enemy firing positions legitimate CAS targets. Yet many of

---

[116] "Joint Air-Ground Operations: Operation Anaconda Background." This asserted average delay, however, suggests that some CAS responses took *less* than five minutes. That would allow scant time for deconfliction and whatever procedural measures that may have been required to get the shooter on target. The Air Force air liaison officer (ALO) assigned to TF Rakkasan who called in most of the initial CAS attacks later reported that the average CAS response time was more on the order of five to 15 minutes, depending on how many target-servicing requests were being processed simultaneously. (Comments on an earlier draft by my RAND colleague Bruce Pirnie.) The latter suggested time frame seems more realistic than a five-minute average. What matters, however, is that the requested fire support was uniformly timely enough to produce the desired effect.

the targets in that confined battlespace fell into the separate categories of time-sensitive or interdiction targets rather than CAS targets because of the need to deconflict the former from possible nearby noncombatants. That need caused them to be governed by standing rules of engagement that required prior CENTCOM approval for them to be attacked, since al Qaeda fighters in the valley were often commingled with Afghan civilians, with reports that some had offered local residents money for the use of their homes.[117]

Significantly, there was no fire-support coordination line in Anaconda because the battlespace was too fluid and nonlinear for there to have been one with any meaning. All requested air strikes against enemy targets on the eastern ridgeline were treated and coded as CAS strikes, which could be called in directly by on-scene ground commanders. Requested attacks in the valley and on the western ridgeline just a few miles away, however, were defined and treated as TST strikes. The latter required CENTCOM approval and thus often involved associated delays, even though enemy forces may have been firing at U.S. troops from those locations as well. That requirement necessarily affected response times in those cases.

The need to secure prior CENTCOM clearance for attacking non-CAS interdiction-coded targets in Anaconda was not the only source of delay in requested target servicing. Other factors included the need to prioritize CAS requests, local air traffic control requirements in the tightly confined battlespace, deconflicting and managing the ingress and egress of multiple aircraft in common airspace, visual target acquisition problems from the air, and an absence of proper radios on the ground in some circumstances for quickly communicating CAS requests. Still others had to do with terrain features that complicated or precluded multiple concurrent attacks in common airspace.

In addition, terminal attack controllers had to pick a weapon match that was appropriate to the target before committing an aircraft to drop on it. In the case of a JDAM attack, the munition re-

---

[117] Rebecca Grant, "The Air Power of Anaconda," *Air Force Magazine*, September 2002, p. 62.

quires mensurated target coordinates (including not only latitude and longitude but also elevation) to be effective. The manual entering of those coordinates into the aircraft's weapons computer takes time and, in at least some instances, caused a nominal additional delay in response time. On this point, Rear Admiral Matthew Moffit, the commander of the Naval Strike and Air Warfare Center at NAS Fallon, Nevada, noted that "satellite-guided weapons . . . are not ideally suited for time-critical strikes. The process of getting the GPS-guided bombs ready for firing takes longer than it would take for an aviator to spot a target with his sensor pod, beam a laser, and release a laser-guided bomb."[118] Finally, there were times when it was simply not advantageous to use an air asset against a minor fleeting target, such as a hit-and-run mortar team with only three or four enemy personnel on the move.

Once fixed-wing air power entered the battle flow in full force, however, the execution of specific requested target-servicing missions was almost always more than sufficiently responsive, indicating that they would have been more than sufficiently responsive from the start had a more timely engagement of the air component been enlisted by Anaconda's planners. In all, hundreds of targets nominated by CJTF Mountain were successfully attacked within minutes, irrespective of the allegedly overlong and rigid ATO cycle. (The ATO does, of necessity, detail specific aircraft to specific missions, areas, and times and indeed requires 48 to 72 hours to plan starting from scratch. Yet specific changes in the ATO's execution can be made and carried out in mere minutes as the needs of the moment may dictate. More to the point, the ATO schedules aircraft to go where and when planners anticipate they will be needed but does not specify their targets in cases of on-call CAS. What those aircraft strike and when is determined by the needs of ground maneuver-force commanders, conveyed to on-call aircrews via those commanders' terminal attack controllers.) In more than one instance, the CAOC managed to conduct

---

[118] Quoted in Brigadier General David L. Grange, USA (Ret.), and others, "The Close Air Support Imperative: Failings in Afghanistan Highlight Deficiencies in U.S. Air Force Doctrine and Equipment," *Armed Forces Journal International,* December 2002, p. 15.

as many as six simultaneous CAS engagements within airspace confines that could only accommodate two at any time safely.

To expand on this point, although the 72-hour air-tasking cycle itself was not flexible, the air employment scheduled *within* that cycle was infinitely flexible. The Master Air Attack Plan (MAAP) and ATO became the point of departure for all daily Enduring Freedom missions flown, including during Operation Anaconda. According to one CAOC staffer who participated in this process, "the plans division was not happy with the number of changes that occurred, but the operations division did a great job in responding to changing requests on the ground. We used to make the joke that the ops division should take the MAAP and throw it up against the wall, and whatever stuck would be flown as scheduled. Not much stuck to the wall."[119] As for the assertion that the ATO must be sufficiently flexible to alter in real time not only aircraft taskings but also "munitions packages as the intelligence picture changes by the minute," it is an inescapable fact of life that no aircraft operated by *any* service can have its weapons loadout changed once the aircraft is airborne. That said, those Air Force, Navy, and Marine Corps aircraft that were dedicated to CAS missions in the ATO almost invariably launched with a sufficient variety of weapons to deliver the desired effect requested by ground commanders.

In sum, the complaint that it took "26 minutes to hours" to get requested enemy targets attacked made no account of the distinction between CAS-coded and interdiction-coded targets. It also reflected unfamiliarity with CENTCOM's target approval process; lumped together CAS requests for aircraft checking in from all operating locations, including from as far away as Kuwait, Manas airfield in Kyrgyzstan, Diego Garcia, and the Navy's carriers at sea; and excluded AC-130s (which were separate SOF assets not under General Moseley's operational and tactical control). Once the AC-130s were

---

[119] Comments on an earlier draft by Major Charles Hogan, USAF, December 22, 2003.

factored in, the average response time for CAS in Anaconda eventually turned out to have been as low as five minutes.[120]

As for the charge that "the Air Force had to work through airspace management" with aircraft "stacked up to the ceiling" such that they "could only be flown in a few numbers," the hard fact was that Anaconda's area of operations centered on the Shah-i-Kot valley floor, which was only some 15 square miles in area (about the same size, as General Moseley noted, of the American Civil War's Battle of Chancellorsville) and which was surrounded by 11,000-foot-high mountains.[121] Its unusual compactness necessarily constrained the use of fixed-wing aircraft. Yet despite these constraints, aircraft were repeatedly flown in and through that confined and crowded airspace not in "only . . . a few numbers," as the complaint suggested, but in dangerously *large* numbers, and at considerable risk to the personal safety of their aircrews, to provide needed on-call support to CJTF Mountain's troops.

In addition, because of the involvement not only of conventional U.S. ground troops but also of covert SOF units and CIA paramilitary forces, fire support coordination measures necessarily required the declaring of restricted fire areas and no-fire areas (NFAs) at various times and places to deconflict compartmented activities within those areas from the operations of other forces that were participating in Anaconda. Some SOF units had tactical control of helicopters and AC-130s that they presumed were dedicated SOF assets rather than CAS assets available for use as necessary by the CAOC.[122] Others, notably those operated by JSOC and by so-called other government agencies, often appeared to be working from a separate playbook altogether and were ill-disposed to communicate their intentions with more mainstream players in the unfolding offensive. As one informed observer later recalled in this regard, "in the beginning,

---

[120] "Joint Air-Ground Operations: Operation Anaconda Background."

[121] Conversation with General T. Michael Moseley, USAF, Headquarters United States Air Force, Washington, D.C., June 30, 2004.

[122] Fleri and others, "Operation Anaconda Case Study," p. 25.

the ASOC had a lot of problems coordinating with the 'special guys' who don't traditionally like to talk about their planned missions." In a telling testament to the absence of open communications that frequently plagued the interaction between those entities early on, this commentator cited a government agency that owned one particular designated NFA in the embattled area and whose representative on the ground resisted coordinating his actions with those of TF-11, which the ASOC was supporting. According to this account, after the ASOC was hung up on once at a crucial moment by that representative during an ongoing battle, the latter was radioed again by the ASOC and summarily told: "I'm about to drop a [expletive deleted] load of 2,000-lb bombs inside your [expletive deleted] NFA whether you say so or not. Now, do you want to talk, or do you want to hang up again, you [expletive deleted]?!"[123] The coordination was said to have gone better after that seminal exchange of words.

There also were communications challenges occasioned by the complex terrain and by the great distance to higher headquarters that compounded both the IFF (identification friend or foe) problem and airspace and target deconfliction. The crowded nature of the airspace over the immediate combat zone demanded unusually close coordination among the CAOC, the E-3 AWACS, the ASOC, terminal attack controllers, and aircrews. This naturally and predictably limited how quickly allied fixed-wing air power could respond to impromptu calls for fire support in some cases. Aircraft run-in headings were also restricted because of the confined battlespace, with multiple strike aircraft operating simultaneously in the same airspace and with friendly ground forces in close proximity to enemy targets, both of which dictated specific attack headings to avoid fratricide from weapons effects. Moreover, many targets were cave entrances situated on steep slopes, which limited the available run-in headings for effectively delivering ordnance. The good news in all of this was that there was no midair collision or other aircraft mishap throughout Operation Anaconda. In at least one case, however, a B-52 had to be directed not to drop

---

[123] Major Kenneth Barker, USAF, "The ASOC," unpublished paper, August 27, 2002, p. 9.

its bombs because a SOF AC-130 gunship was orbiting directly beneath it.

With respect to the intimation, seemingly informed by a belief that low altitude equals greater effectiveness, that Air Force pilots lacked the aggressiveness to fly as low as Navy and Marine Corps pilots, in fact *all* services were required to adhere to assigned special instructions (SPINs) and rules of engagement established by the CENTCOM commander with the goal of protecting his assets. The altitude floor was set by General Moseley in accordance with the assessed threat, and it applied to *all* aircraft operating within the ATO.[124] The infrared SAM threat dictated an altitude floor of 10,000 feet over the valley and over ridgelines unless compelling circumstances demanded lower flight. Legitimate concern about the infrared SAM threat from the high Shah-i-Kot mountaintops sometimes forced U.S. aircraft to operate at altitudes that made more difficult the visual identification of small targets that had been called out by friendly ground forces. For its part, as noted above, the AC-130 operated *only* at night because it also was governed by the assessed threat and by its established tactics, techniques, and procedures. The assessed threat throughout Anaconda was that infrared SAMs fired from mountaintops could easily reach the AC-130's normal tactical operating altitude. This required that AC-130 crews not expose themselves during daylight hours when the aircraft could be seen by the enemy and easily targeted by those weapons.[125] Finally, it bears noting here that many precision and near-precision weapon engagement parameters often require greater distances from the target for the weapon to arm and guide properly.[126]

---

[124] Email to the author from then–Brigadier General Robert J. Elder, USAF, Deputy Commander, 9th Air Force, October 3, 2002.

[125] During Operation Desert Storm, an AC-130 was downed by an Iraqi infrared SAM shortly after daybreak, with the loss of 14 crewmembers.

[126] Ever since Vietnam, when CAS missions were routinely and frequently flown by Air Force fighters in support of Army combat operations on the ground, Army servicemen have come to expect to see Air Force aircraft at low altitudes overhead conducting bombing and strafing missions in their direct support. This has engendered something of an "out of sight, out of mind" syndrome within the ground-warrior culture, whereby combat aircraft operat-

Despite these valid rules, General Moseley never denied a legitimate request for lower attacks whenever they were deemed necessary to provide adequate CAS. Since the Air Force operated far fewer fighters in Anaconda than did the carrier-based Navy and Marine Corps because of the former's more distant forward bases in the Persian Gulf, those fighters were naturally less often overhead supporting U.S. ground troops in the battle area. However, Air Force altitude procedures were no different from those for the other services. The rules applied uniformly to *all* aircraft tasked by the ATO, and all air component assets were cleared to descend to near-ground level whenever a need arose.[127] Furthermore, every strafe-capable Air Force aircraft strafed whenever there was a requirement for it. As General Moseley later declared, all aircraft were under his control as Enduring Freedom's ultimate airspace control authority, and there were no "separate SPINs for each element. Multiple times flight leads [were] cleared to the surface before takeoff."[128] Air Force F-15Es flew below their normal operating altitude to support the imperiled U.S. SOF troops and aircrews who had been aboard the downed Army MH-47 helicopters on Roberts Ridge, and F-16s strafed enemy positions there under the direction of Air Force controllers to provide the pinned-down U.S. combatants further relief from the nonstop enemy fire. On more than one occasion when U.S. ground forces were under direct fire and when urgent CAS was required, Air Force aircrews

---

ing at higher altitudes where they cannot be seen by troops on the ground must, almost by definition, not be providing satisfactory CAS. This common misconception overlooks today's lethal combination of bombers and fighters at medium to high altitudes dropping LGBs or GPS-aided weapons with great accuracy on CAS targets—even targets in close proximity to friendly forces—under the direction of Air Force terminal attack controllers on the ground.

[127] Air Force General Charles F. Wald, for example, who had been the CFACC at the start of Enduring Freedom, commented that he had been the first to put into place the altitude rules and that they expressly allowed that "if we ever needed [fighters] to go below [15,000 feet], you can do that in a heartbeat. We'll tell you. You can just ask, or if the situation warrants, do it. The rule was always [that] you'll always go down to whatever altitude you need to [when] under duress, particularly if there's a U.S. person down there [in need]. And they did." (Elaine Grossman, "Army Anaconda Commander Revisits Remarks About Air Power Lapses," *Inside the Pentagon*, November 7, 2002, p. 3.)

[128] "Joint Air-Ground Operations: Operation Anaconda Background."

would willingly provide needed air support, even where there was no assurance of finding a tanker and over mountainous terrain where they were exposed to infrared SAM fire.[129]

With respect to the suggestion that the Army should cultivate its own cadre of terminal attack controllers, the job involves more than merely designating targets and calling in air strikes. Terminal attack controllers do not just provide target coordinates to combat aircraft. They also are trained to manage the overall on-scene air operation, most notably the flow of aircraft into and out of the battlespace, as de facto air traffic controllers.[130] Since Operation Enduring Freedom represented the first combat experience in which JDAMs were targeted via ground-controller input, there was naturally considerable real-time learning and improvisation as Anaconda unfolded. Yet the Air Force has *not* insisted as a matter of doctrine and practice that only Air Force personnel can control JDAM use. However, CENTCOM established a rule calling for JDAMs to be used in Enduring Freedom—by *any* attacking aircraft, not just by Air Force aircraft—only under positive ground control. The rule was written in such a way that nonqualified personnel could make an emergency CAS request. It was then up to the CAS requester to notify the aircrew that he was not a trained terminal attack controller, and up to the aircrew dropping the weapon to have eyes or sensors on the target or target area to confirm its validity before releasing the weapon.[131]

Although at a service-wide level, the Air Force has had recurrent difficulty filling out all of its air liaison officer and terminal attack controller billets, there was never a case in which needed air support was denied to CJTF Mountain because of a lack of enough Air Force controllers. Nevertheless, General Hagenbeck raised a valid issue in spotlighting the Army's need for more controllers at lower levels in its

[129] Bowden, "The Kabul-Ki Dance," p. 78.

[130] For further details on combat controller capabilities and required training, see Glenn W. Goodman, Jr., "Warriors Training Warriors: New Entry Training for USAF Combat Controllers Is Paying Off," *Armed Forces Journal International*, September 2002, pp. 82–84.

[131] Information provided by then-Brigadier General Robert J. Elder, USAF, Deputy Commander, 9th Air Force, email to the author, October 3, 2002.

organizational structure. Partly in response to that valid observation, the Army since Enduring Freedom has articulated a high ETAC requirement to the Air Force—2,100 or more for conventional forces and 800 for SOF units—in a clear testament to the fact that future combat situations will increasingly call for terminal attack controllers at the company level or below rather than just at the division and corps levels as was the case in past conflicts.

In the main, however, the charges addressed above reflected frustration over some early tactical-level execution problems in Anaconda that were largely occasioned by the land component's failure to have made adequate prior arrangements for the possibility of needed CAS in the first place. Many of those problems could have been avoided had a contingency need for CAS been foreseen and had airmen been included in CJTF Mountain's and the covert SOF community's planning processes from the very start. In the subsequent assessment of one Air Force participant in Anaconda, "there was little capability built into the system [at first] to handle high-volume, extremely close air support." Furthermore, because of the failure of the theater air control system and Army air-ground system to make the most of the opportunities that CENTCOM's air component could have provided, "there was a lack of shared information and joint planning prior to the operation." That, in turn, resulted in such preventable shortcomings as "no mission brief; no idea where friendly forces were; no check-in briefing and update; TACPs arguing over who gets CAS; not enough contact points for holding and deconfliction; and deconfliction of CAS assets in the target area. All of these issues could have been solved by planning for and setting up a healthy ASOC within radio range of the Shah-i-Kot valley. . . . The initial deconfliction problem should have been the job of the ASOC and the CAOC, not the TACP on the battlefield."[132]

For all the recriminations that have since been heard over Anaconda from various protagonists on all sides of the issues addressed above, it is important not to lose sight of the overriding fact that the

---

[132] Neuenswander, "JCAS in Operation Anaconda."

operation in the end was an unqualified success, thanks in substantial part to what a senior Air Force A-10 pilot called "the frantic work of many tireless airmen who pulled together a tactical air control system on the fly."[133] To cite just two examples of such real-time improvisation, once a dire need for A-10s became apparent on Anaconda's first day, General Moseley directed the 74th Expeditionary Fighter Squadron (EFS) stationed at al Jaber Air Base in Kuwait to rush five of those aircraft to a forward location within easy reach of the Anaconda fighting. (A-10s had not previously been required for Enduring Freedom's air operations.) That unit deployed the first aircraft within 12 hours of having been notified on the night of March 3, and it had its forward detachment in place and ready to provide on-call CAS barely more than a day after notification by the CAOC. The A-10s conducted CAS and FAC-A missions in support of Anaconda and at times also fulfilled the ABCCC function. Their pilots aided significantly in target acquisition and target-area deconfliction as well as in the terminal control of other CAS aircraft. At one point during Anaconda, that unit provided 21 continuous hours of CAS and FAC-A support with only four aircraft.[134]

In a similar illustration of effective air component improvisation on the fly, on March 5, members of the 74th EFS, working closely with elements of the 18th Air Support Operations Group (ASOG) and the CAOC, developed a kill box deconfliction scheme to manage the airspace over the Shah-i-Kot valley that enabled A-10, F-14, and F-16 FAC-As to control that airspace with less trepidation than before over the danger of midair collisions or inadvertent fratricide incidents. By the night of March 6, General Moseley had built an effective command-and-control system that solved most of the problems that had occurred during the preceding four days of the operation. The following day, the new kill box arrangement was fully in place and operational. FAC-As were in constant radio contact with CJTF

---

[133] Neuenswander, "JCAS in Operation Anaconda."

[134] Neuenswander, "JCAS in Operation Anaconda." Once the runway at Bagram was improved to a point where it could enable full-length operations, the 74th EFS redeployed there to support the remainder of Enduring Freedom.

Mountain's air liaison officers at Bagram and were routinely undertaking CAS missions with current friendly and enemy positions marked on their maps. Moreover, as noted above, General Moseley had arranged through the 18th ASOG commander, Colonel Longoria, the implementation of a plan to put fighter aircrews aboard the E-8 Joint STARS aircraft to fulfill both the command-and-control and deconfliction functions normally provided by the ABCCC. This innovation was in place by March 6 and proved crucial in determining the ultimate success of the operation. The original plan for Anaconda did not envisage any need for high-intensity CAS. When that need suddenly arose, the CAOC within just four days tripled the number of land- and carrier-based strike aircraft available on immediate notice for on-call CAS. A senior Air Force participant in those operations rightly called them "as close to a maximum effort as many of us will ever see."[135]

Finally, as for the suggestion that the Predator controller be collocated with the ground commander so that the latter might have more assured access to the UAV, such an arrangement would be completely impractical, since Predator controllers can only fly the aircraft from an operating complex that cannot be easily and quickly relocated. After Anaconda, other Army officers complained that not enough UAVs had been available to Army field commanders. On that point, the chief of Army intelligence, Lieutenant General Robert Noonan, suggested that had the Army been able to maintain "more UAVs on landing zones prior to us going in there, we would not have had this problem [of battlefield surprise]." Be that as it may, the Army chose not to send its own limited inventory of Hunter UAVs to Afghanistan, leaving CJTF Mountain instead to rely on the Air Force's RQ-1 Predator, which, unfortunately was committed, first and foremost, to providing higher-priority theater-level support in response to CENTCOM and CIA tasking. Complained Noonan: "The Predators are searching for high-value targets throughout Afghanistan, and although they were tasked to support Anaconda, they

---

[135] Neuenswander, "JCAS in Operation Anaconda."

were also searching for other targets." That led him to conclude that the Army needs more organic UAVs of its own.[136] That is something quite different from the issue of where the Predator controller should sit and suggests a bona fide requirement the Army might usefully pursue as a part of its transformation plan.

Toward Better Air-Ground Coordination

In their initial planning workups for Anaconda, both CJTF Mountain and the covert SOF community failed to make the most of the potential synergy of land and air power that was available to them in principle from CENTCOM's air component. That failure, moreover, was anything but preordained. By way of illustrating how planning for Anaconda might have been more effectively approached, the first major ground operation in Enduring Freedom, namely, the Ranger and Delta Force raid on Mullah Omar's compound the previous October 21, featured well-integrated joint air-ground planning and execution. Although that operation proved in the end to have yielded little of strategic value, at least the desired effects had been clearly relayed in full detail by the operation's planners to the air component commander at the time, then–Lieutenant General Charles Wald. That, in turn, enabled the CAOC to build and execute an air plan designed to help achieve those effects at minimum cost in time and risk to friendly lives.[137]

As another contrasting example of how the planning for Anaconda might have been approached more effectively, in the case of Marine Corps infantry operations out of FOB Rhino, there was regular and close contact between TF-58 at Rhino and the Marine Aviation Liaison Officer (MARLO) in the CAOC. Indeed, according to one knowledgeable Marine Corps aviator who served on the TF-58 staff at Rhino during the early part of Enduring Freedom, "because of

[136] Marc Strass, "More SIGINT, UAVs and HUMINT Top Army Intel Needs from Afghanistan," *Defense Daily*, April 11, 2002, p. 1.

[137] "Joint Air-Ground Operations: Operation Anaconda Background."

our good communications and MARLO in the CAOC, we decided not to take artillery with us because TF-58 was confident that 'big' fires can come from the air, and they did when needed." In contrast, it was his clear impression that the Army did not routinely avail itself of the Air Force's massive ISR pipeline and that in marked contrast to the "priceless" role played by the MARLO in keeping the CAOC fed, Army units in the war zone would not communicate directly to their own BCD in the CAOC, but instead would typically send any input of note to the land component's forward headquarters, "where it would stay in the black hole." If this impression was representative of more general Army practice, it suggests that at least some of the information that the CAOC badly needed regarding essential details on the eve of Anaconda may have been routinely forwarded instead to General Mikolashek's headquarters in Kuwait, where it offered the air component little help.[138]

Because of the initial absence of a full-up ASOC at Bagram equipped to translate General Hagenbeck's commander's intent into a systematic CAS prioritization scheme, friction and confusion ensued at first as terminal attack controllers on the ground competed for limited CAS assets on an ad hoc basis over a single tactical air direction frequency.[139] (As explained later by Colonel Longoria, the 18th ASOG commander, the controllers were left with but a single tactical frequency because CENTCOM had devoted most of its available bandwidth to SOF operators, given the latter's predominant role during the initial months of Enduring Freedom, and because the air component learned of Operation Anaconda and its potential needs too late to request an adequate frequency reallocation in sufficient time.) In addition, no Control-Point (CP) and Initial-Point (IP) matrix was provided for managing the flow of CAS assets and creating

---

[138] Comments on an earlier draft by Lieutenant Colonel Robert T. Charette, USMC, Commander, Marine Fighter/Attack Squadron 323, MCAS Miramar, California, January 26, 2004.

[139] Elaine M. Grossman, "Operation Anaconda: Object Lesson in Poor Planning or Triumph of Improvisation?" InsideDefense.com, August 12, 2004.

an optimal geometry for attack run-in headings.[140] As a result, near-pandemonium ensued in the congested airspace over the Shah-i-Kot area as numerous aircraft of all types literally were forced to dodge one another (as well as one another's falling bombs) as they simultaneously serviced multiple urgent requests for CAS. A near-tragedy occurred when poor coordination almost occasioned a friendly fire incident when a U.S. SOF team was barely missed by a 2,000-lb bomb dropped by a French Mirage 2000D fighter whose pilot had not been briefed about the team's presence on the ground. Eventually, an eleventh-hour effort was made to cobble together a usable set of Initial Points (that is, assigned run-in start points for individual aircraft target attacks) that might help smooth out this predictable result of the land component's failure to engage the CAOC at the outset of planning for Anaconda. However, that did not occur until well into the operation, and the terminal attack controllers on the ground never used them.[141]

It bears repeating here that although General Hagenbeck was assigned control over all of the conventional U.S. Army and overt SOF units engaged in Anaconda, he was *not* given control over those SOF teams that reported up a separate chain of command to JSOC. As a result, some ground combatants whose leaders reported up a chain of command other than CENTCOM's operated within CJTF Mountain's battlespace but not under Hagenbeck's operational or tactical control. That was, to say the least, a highly suboptimal arrangement for what turned out to be a complex and costly joint and combined operation. Further compounding the problem was the fact that before the start of Enduring Freedom, the SOF community had not been accustomed to integrating conventional air power into its plans and operations and instead typically worked only with such familiar SOF air assets as the AC-130. As a result, it rarely trained in scenarios that

---

[140] Lieutenant Colonel John M. Jansen, USA, and others, "The Tower of Babel: Joint Close Air Support Performance at the Operational Level," *Marine Corps Gazette*, March 2003, p. 34.

[141] Lieutenant Colonel John M. Jansen, USA, and others, "'Lines One Through Three . . . N/A,'" *Marine Corps Gazette*, April 2003, p. 34.

required extensive fighter and bomber integration and accordingly may not have given much thought to its likely need for those assets.[142]

To make matters worse yet, the SOF liaison element in the CAOC remained highly compartmented throughout Enduring Freedom, and only a few select select members of the CAOC staff (perhaps as few as three) had access to covert SOF information. Even the CAOC's director of combat plans was not read into the missions that were being conducted by some SOF units. As one informed assessment observed on this point, as Enduring Freedom's battle flow transitioned from mainly SOF to conventional ground operations, "the SOLE did not adjust operations and, as a result, most SOF operations still remained [compartmented], which ultimately increased the likelihood of poor integration among the components."[143] Nevertheless, because the CAOC was not actively engaged in Anaconda's planning from the very start, CENTCOM's air component was not integrated into the plan, even though it proved in the end to have provided the overwhelming preponderance of force application for CJTF Mountain. Had it been integrated from the outset of planning, Anaconda might have been wrapped up more quickly and with fewer casualties.

Asked two years after the operation why CJTF Mountain remained in such a hurry to proceed with the execution of Anaconda even after the operation's air support needs had become fully apparent to all and after General Moseley and the CAOC had become fully involved in the last-minute planning details, General Hagenbeck replied that it had been of crucial importance, in his judgment, to gain tactical surprise over the al Qaeda forces holed up in the Shah-i-Kot valley and surrounding mountains, even though CENTCOM had long since lost the elements of operational and strategic surprise thanks to leaks from al Qaeda spies in the ranks of the Northern Alliance. He also noted that the weather in eastern Afghanistan during

---

[142] Davis, p. 43.

[143] Davis, p. 43.

that time of the year was unpredictable and that it made sense for that reason as well to move out earlier rather than later.[144] As it turned out, however, the al Qaeda forces in the Shah-i-Kot valley were well-entrenched and ready for a fight. Had the land component been willing to slip the scheduled start of Anaconda by merely the week or so that would have been needed for the CAOC to prepare itself fully for any contingency needs, General Moseley and his staff could have designed and implemented any number of measures to ensure that the operation would have the fullest support from CENTCOM's air assets in all services. Such measures would have included a prepositioning of all needed aircraft and materiel before the start of the operation, including the forward deployment of A-10s to Bagram in ample time for them to be ready from the outset. It also would have included preparation of the air component's infrastructure and the determination of sustainment requirements, such as the number of needed AC-130s and proper crew-to-aircraft ratios for all platforms; the use of all available ISR assets to map out known enemy cave locations; the establishment of tanker requirements and preplanning of airborne tanker tracks in the operating area; the development of aircraft stacking arrangements and deconfliction schemes above the various assigned helicopter LZs; a land component fully fleshed out in its representation in the CAOC; and the development of a proper command-and-control arrangement, including the timely provision of a full-up air operations center assigned to CJTF Mountain's field headquarters at Bagram. Once those arrangements had been duly attended to, General Moseley and the CAOC staff could then have "chair-flown" the entire operation beforehand with all involved air component principals, not only the mission commanders and flight leaders but every other key participant as well, right down to the combat controllers and ETACs.[145] Concurrently, since the CAOC had far better access to all-source intelligence inputs than did CJTF

[144] Conversation with Lieutenant General Franklin L. Hagenbeck, USA, Headquarters United States Army, Washington, D.C., July 1, 2004.

[145] Conversation with General T. Michael Moseley, USAF, Headquarters United States Air Force, Washington, D.C., February 12, 2004.

Mountain, the latter could have tapped into the CAOC's extensive ISR resources to good effect in its final planning for Anaconda. The al Qaeda holdouts who had concentrated in the Shah-i-Kot hinterland might have slipped away during that period, but their behavior once attacked suggested that they were not likely to have ceded the ground without a fight.

As the Anaconda experience fades from memory, urban legends persist about the initially flawed operation, with one report in late 2002 noting how Anaconda somehow revealed "technology's shortcomings," when, in fact, the causative shortcomings were entirely process- and procedures-related.[146] As a result of the previous six months of generally successful force application, General Moseley had gained intimate familiarity with Enduring Freedom's war process; with what worked and what did not; with CENTCOM's rules of engagement; with distances and airspace limitations; and with the needed enabling effects to achieve an optimum air-ground synergy. Yet that expertise was not drawn upon in Anaconda planning by CJTF Mountain and by the land component more generally. Worse yet, even after Moseley had become more fully apprised of what was about to unfold, his subsequent concerns regarding the absence of a CAS coordination plan, adequate command and control, adequate logistics and sustainment provisions, and adequate medical evacuation planning were never addressed by those responsible for the execution of Anaconda. That resulted in a requirement at the last minute to insert a dangerously large number of aircraft into a small area at the same time once CJTF Mountain faced an urgent need to put out a Mayday call for CAS.

In the end, fixed-wing air power did most of the work originally envisaged for organic Army fires. On Anaconda's first day, Air Force terminal attack controllers had to call in F-15Es and an AC-130 to provide urgent CAS when the Army's Apaches proved unable to perform the mission on their own. The vast majority of al Qaeda terrorists killed throughout Anaconda were attributable to CENTCOM's

---

[146] Greg Jaffe, "New Battle Theory Would Be Tested in an Iraqi Invasion," *Wall Street Journal*, November 27, 2002.

air component, thanks primarily to the pivotal role played by Air Force ground controllers in providing U.S. aircraft with consistently accurate target designation. Once the fight was on, friendly ground forces were often used in a support role for air power by fixing enemy forces in position for air attacks or at least drawing enemy fire.

In the course of pursuing his post-Anaconda inquiry into Air Force CAS performance noted above, General Jumper pointedly included Anaconda CAS operations as a priority issue for discussion in a closed session of the annual high-level Army-Air Force warfighter talks in October 2002. The Air Force chief indicated that the two services concurred that a breakdown in communications between CENTCOM's land and air components had contributed materially to the eight U.S. fatalities and numerous additional battle wounds that had been incurred on Roberts Ridge and in the lower valley engagements. He added that the service leaders were working together "to fix [problems] through adjustments in the way we train together on a daily basis." He further noted that the chiefs and vice chiefs of the two services were now "going out to our war colleges, standing on the stage together, and talking very directly about Anaconda, but also about the things we have to do to have a better [mutual] appreciation."[147]

If this initiative maintains its momentum, it can only help ensure better Army cooperation with the Air Force, and vice versa, in getting the most out of the nation's current air and ground capabilities. Such cooperation could usefully start with more peacetime composite force training to help both services know and understand better the other's operating practices and needs so as to ensure more effective future joint operations under fire. It also could benefit from more institutionalized cross-fertilization between the two services at the senior planning level. Significantly in this latter respect, the two services agreed in February 2003 to establish a new senior Air Force wartime presence within CENTCOM's land component headquarters to facilitate better communication between the two components

---

[147] Elaine Grossman, "Jumper: Army, Air Force Work to Avoid Repeat of Anaconda Lapses," *Inside the Pentagon*, February 27, 2003, p. 1.

at the operational level so as to reduce the likelihood of future planning failures of the sort that were exemplified in Anaconda from its very start. That decision had a clear and significant payoff in Operation Iraqi Freedom that ensued the following month.[148]

To be sure, in all likelihood there were elements of accountability to be shared all around for the initial complications that were experienced in Anaconda. For example, even Air Force officers have conceded more than once that with the hardest part of Enduring Freedom having been concluded more than two months before in December 2001, the CAOC was operating in a more relaxed mode during the weeks that preceded Anaconda and that its most experienced staff members had rotated back to the United States and had been replaced by relative newcomers who were still learning the ropes. Furthermore, General Moseley, by that time preoccupied with initial planning for a possible war against Iraq in the year to come, was on the road visiting potential Gulf-region coalition partners with that concern uppermost in his mind. That being so, one may wonder whether, in that comparatively desultory phase of Enduring Freedom, in-boxes in the CAOC did not tend to fill up, especially during times when General Moseley was away, and whether, as a result, some messages did not get noted for their possible significance in a timely way.

This in no way, to be sure, exonerates the land component and covert SOF leadership for having failed to communicate their intentions and Anaconda's likely air support needs to the air component more clearly and fully from the very start of their planning. However, it does suggest that the CAOC might have better anticipated Anaconda's needs had its sensors that filtered and prioritized the land component's inputs been more finely attuned. That said, it would be an overreach to conclude from this, as one assessment of Anaconda maintained, that there was "a serious information flow problem

---

[148] For a fuller discussion of needed remedies highlighted by the Anaconda experience and of subsequent progress that has been made between the Air Force and Army on the CAS front, see Bruce R. Pirnie, Alan J. Vick, Adam Grissom, Karl P. Mueller, and David T. Orletsky, *Beyond Close Air Support: Forging a New Air-Ground Partnership*, Santa Monica, Calif.: RAND Corporation, MG-301-AF, 2005.

within the CAOC organization" emanating from the purported fact that General Moseley, in the wake of the air war's earlier successes, had "allowed his organization to atrophy to a point where it became combat ineffective for planning purposes."[149] It would be even more misplaced to suggest that, on the mere basis of having received the Anaconda operations order via the BCD a week before the operation's scheduled start, and with no accompanying formal tasking from the land component whatsoever, "General Moseley and his staff did not adequately seek out or ascertain the needs of Major General Hagenbeck in a timely fashion."[150] Quite to the contrary, by this same assessment's own admission, no one in the CAOC was in the least aware of the potential importance of the information on Anaconda that was routinely flowing to the BCD from CJTF Mountain. To them, "it was just another Army operation that did not necessarily require CAOC coordination"—all the more so since the preceding six months of Enduring Freedom had entailed operations that did not require extensive air-ground cooperation.[151] In those circumstances, it was scarcely incumbent on either General Corley or General Moseley to have contacted the land component's principals "to ask for clarification or complain about being excluded from the operation" when both were completely taken by surprise by the CAOC's eleventh-hour receipt of the operations order and had never once been engaged at any time in its development during the preceding month.[152] As for the suggestion that the CAOC had somehow fallen asleep at the wheel in this regard, the manner in which it rose to the challenge of providing emergency CAS when Anaconda began to falter and in crafting and executing on the fly a complex air support plan for the remainder of the operation pointed to *anything but* the performance of an organization that had been allowed "to atrophy to a point where

---

[149] Davis, pp. 88, 91. This groundless allegation is also made in Naylor, p. 271.

[150] Davis, p. 90.

[151] Davis, p. 85.

[152] Davis, p. 88.

it became ineffective for combat planning purposes."[153] On the contrary, in reflecting later on the prodigious efforts that were exerted not only by the CAOC but also by brave and able warriors at the execution level from all services to make the operation a success in the end, General Moseley rightly remarked that "the essence of American air power came to bear in Anaconda."[154]

In sum, although there is no evidence to suggest that the CAOC was deliberately cut out of the planning for Anaconda by the land component, numerous faulty going-in assumptions nonetheless resulted in CJTF Mountain's being only barely covered by needed air support once the first insertion on Day One encountered surprise resistance and the going got unexpectedly rough. For one thing, since no one in the land component evidently believed that Anaconda would be as intense as it turned out to be, there was a widespread tendency throughout CJTF Mountain not to take the air-ground coordination issue all that seriously. For another, since the air component had maintained a constant and effective presence of orbiting bombers and fighters over Afghanistan ever since the first night of Enduring Freedom, there may have been a tendency on the part of CJTF Mountain's planners to be lulled into the complacent belief that coalition air power, if needed, would always be responsive without detailed planning and coordination. As General Hagenbeck freely conceded two years later, "we weren't idiots, but we weren't asking the questions we needed to."[155] He further remarked: "Now that we're all experienced, and as we look in the rear-view mirror, we surely would have done some [things differently] and asked some

---

[153] General Moseley categorically rejected the charge when informed of it: "That's not true. We were focused on Afghanistan because that's where we were fighting." (Grossman, "Operation Anaconda: Object Lesson in Poor Planning or Triumph of Improvisation?")

[154] Conversation with General T. Michael Moseley, USAF, Headquarters United States Air Force, Washington, D.C., February 12, 2004.

[155] Conversation with Lieutenant General Franklin L. Hagenbeck, USA, Headquarters United States Army, Washington, D.C., July 1, 2004.

harder questions of each other at that point."[156] In reflecting on all of this, the former CAOC director during the first phase of Enduring Freedom aptly concluded: "The message that needs to come out of this issue is that to optimize air-ground synergy, the air component must be included in all phases of planning surface operations and vice versa. That is what went awry in Anaconda, not CAS."[157]

---

[156] Grossman, "Operation Anaconda: Object Lesson in Poor Planning or Triumph of Improvisation?"

[157] Comments on an earlier draft by Major General David A. Deptula, USAF, Director of Operations, Pacific Air Forces, October 4, 2002.

Terrorists declare war. The attacks conducted against the United States by al Qaeda on September 11, 2001, starkly defined the face of early 21st-century conflict. Here emergency first aid is being administered to one of the many people who were injured when American Airlines Flight 77, a Boeing 757, was flown into the southwest side of the Pentagon that fateful morning.

Noble duty. Immediately after the terrorist attacks occurred, a round-the-clock combat air patrol code-named Operation Noble Eagle was established over New York, Washington, D.C., and 28 other key American cities. This F-15A from the 102nd Fighter Wing of the Massachusetts Air National Guard based on Cape Cod and armed with live missiles orbits high above New York City, with Manhattan Island to the north.

Trouble for the Taliban. A munitions technician prepares a pallet of 2000-lb GBU-31 satellite-aided JDAMs for loading into one of the bomb bays of this B-1B bomber operating against Taliban and al Qaeda targets out of Diego Garcia in the Indian Ocean. Over the course of Operation Enduring Freedom, B-1Bs dropped more than twice as many JDAMs as all other U.S. combat aircraft combined.

Bread bomber. President Bush was determined from the start of Enduring Freedom that the bombing portion of the campaign be matched by a concurrent aid effort in support of Afghan civilian refugees. These containers, each holding a total of 420 individual humanitarian daily ration packages, are being loaded aboard a C-17 for night air delivery over selected drop zones in Afghanistan.

Cocked and ready. This F/A-18C armed with GBU-31 JDAMs and attached to Marine Fighter/Attack Squadron 314 aboard the aircraft carrier USS *John C. Stennis* is poised on the catapult moments before being launched on a mission into Afghanistan that could last as long as eight hours. Marine Corps strike fighter aviation is now almost fully integrated into the Navy's 10 carrier air wings.

Long-distance runners. A B-1B assigned to the Air Force's 7th Bomb Wing at Dyess AFB, Texas, approaches touchdown at Diego Garcia after a mission into Afghanistan as a B-52 from the 2nd Bomb Wing at Barksdale AFB, Louisiana, taxies out for takeoff. These heavy bombers dropped roughly 80 percent of the ordnance, including the majority of JDAMs, delivered in Enduring Freedom.

KABUL DARULAMAN BARRACKS, AFGHANISTAN
PRE STRIKE

Fort

First targets in the war on terror. Among the many target categories attacked with precision-guided weapons by Air Force heavy bombers and Navy and Marine Corps strike fighters during Enduring Freedom's opening night were Taliban early warning radars, military headquarters buildings, and barracks facilities such as those depicted in this prestrike overhead reconnaissance image.

KABUL DARULAMAN BARRACKS, AFGHANISTAN
POST STRIKE

Fort

Initial results. The effectiveness of modern precision ordnance in cleanly eliminating specific targeted objectives while causing no collateral damage to adjacent structures is graphically shown in this post-attack battle-damage assessment image indicating how a number of well-placed laser-guided bombs completely destroyed four preselected Taliban barracks buildings.

Nerve center for the air war. CENTCOM's Combined Air Operations Center at Prince Sultan Air Base, Saudi Arabia, was the hub of all command-and-control activity for the Enduring Freedom air war. This 70,000-square-foot facility with multiple large-screen displays, a profusion of computer stations, and nearly 100 high-speed T-1 Internet lines allowed for fully integrated coalition air operations.

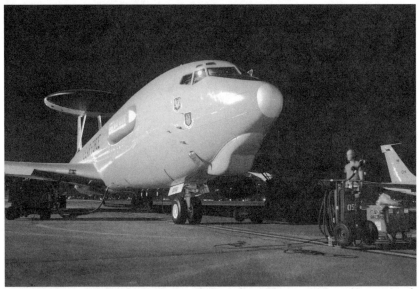

The big-picture provider. Air Combat Command's E-3 Airborne Warning and Control System aircraft maintained a constant airborne presence in the Afghan theater of operations. They served both as close-in battle-management platforms for deconflicting multiple concurrent air operations over Afghanistan and as the main source of comprehensive Blue Force tracking for the CAOC.

Nowhere to hide. An F-15E weapons systems officer makes a final preflight check of a 2,000-lb laser-guided bomb designed especially for penetrating hard structures such as al Qaeda cave hideouts. Strike Eagles began conducting long-range missions into Afghanistan from al Jaber Air Base in Kuwait on October 17, 2001, with one setting a record of 15.8 hours as the longest fighter mission ever.

Ready for tasking. This F-15E en route to an assigned holding area over Afghanistan pulls off a KC-10 tanker after having completed an inflight refueling. Like most aircraft that participated in Enduring Freedom after the first week of engaging fixed targets, it took off without predetermined target assignments and was on-call for attacking time-sensitive targets as they emerged.

The heart and soul of CAS. Air Force air liaison officers like this B-52 pilot on a two-year tour of duty with the Army supervise teams of enlisted tactical air controllers in providing target information to strike aircrews orbiting overhead. Such teams were indispensable in providing the needed ground-based coordination for conducting close air support during Operation Anaconda.

Special operator. Air Force Special Operations Command MH-53 Pave Low helicopters performed numerous critical missions throughout the seven months of major fighting in Afghanistan, including the insertion of overt and covert SOF teams and the extraction of injured personnel under fire. The one shown here with extended-range fuel tanks is being refueled in flight.

Loaded for bear. AFSOC AC-130 gunships, nine of which were committed to Enduring Freedom, operated at night in cleaning out concentrations of enemy fighters who falsely thought that they were protected by darkness. Equipped with thermal imaging gear and cued by live UAV video, they used their computer-aimed 105mm and 40mm cannons and 25mm Gatling guns to consistently lethal effect.

Killer drone. In the first deadly use of an unmanned aircraft in combat, MQ-1 Predator UAVs operated by the CIA fired a total of 40 Hellfire missiles against high-value Taliban and al Qaeda targets during Enduring Freedom. This Air Force variant shows a Hellfire mounted on the aircraft's left wing pylon. The drone also performed vital surveillance and target-identification functions throughout the war.

The latest in persistent surveillance. The Air Force's RQ-4 Global Hawk high-altitude UAV was still not operational when it was introduced into the Afghan theater of operations on November 13, 2001. Operating out of a base in the United Arab Emirates, the drone was able to remain airborne for up to 36 hours at a height of 65,000 feet and to identify targets as far as 30 miles away with its onboard sensor suite.

Precision-guided weapon. An A-10 pilot preflights an AGM-65 Maverick air-to-ground missile before launching from a forward-deployed location on a mission to provide CAS for embattled U.S. troops during Operation Anaconda. The imaging infrared sensor installed on the missile allows it to home on both fixed and moving targets with unerringly lethal accuracy.

A band of brothers. Two A-10 pilots engage in light banter with a crew chief as the LGB-equipped aircraft beside them is readied for a CAS mission. A-10s were introduced into the combat support flow only when Operation Anaconda began to falter on its first day. They did not commence routine day and night operations from Bagram Air Base inside Afghanistan until the major fighting was over.

Where the old met the new. In a remarkable confluence of 19th- and 21st-century styles of warfare, Air Force combat controllers equipped with laptop computers, laser range-finders, and UHF radios joined forces, sometimes on horseback for the first time in their lives, with indigenous Afghan Northern Alliance fighters in organizing and directing prompt air attacks against emerging Taliban targets.

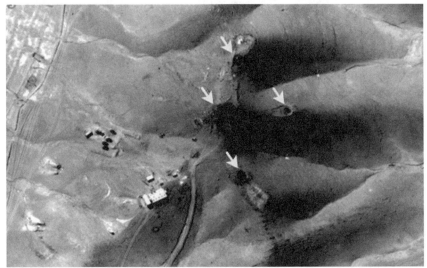

Multiple kills per sortie. One of the many distinguishing features of transformed American air power is that the main measure of combat efficiency is no longer how many aircraft it takes to attack a single target, but how many aim points can be serviced by a single aircraft. With targeting assistance from combat controllers on the ground, B-52 and B-1B crews could engage four or more targets on one pass.

Getting the word out. Six EC-130 Commando Solo aircraft operated by the Air National Guard's 193rd Special Operations Wing were used to beam messages into Afghanistan as a part of a focused psychological operations effort against the enemy. A number of captured al Qaeda prisoners later admitted that they had surrendered during Operation Anaconda after hearing such radio transmissions.

Great weapon, wrong use. The Army's AH-64 Apache attack helicopter is a fearsome instrument of deep attack and CAS if afforded the protection of prior suppressive fire. Because such suppression was not provided by fixed-wing air power at the start of Operation Anaconda, however, the seven Apaches that were committed to the fight were quickly rendered ineffective by intense al Qaeda fire.

Stranger in a strange land. A Navy Seabee provides perimeter security for an Air Force C-17 airlifter at Bagram Air Base in Afghanistan after his unit installed a crude runway and electrical power at the undeveloped facility. Once Bagram was rendered easily accessible by air, C-17s became Enduring Freedom's logistical workhorse for providing needed materiel and humanitarian relief supplies.

Tomcat tender. F-14s like this one aboard the USS *Enterprise* being readied for a flight by a deck crewman were versatile assets in the Afghan air war thanks to their ability to conduct precision strikes from medium altitude using their infrared LANTIRN targeting pod, to carry mixed loads of LGBs and JDAMs, to fulfill the FAC-A role, and to provide real-time tactical imagery with their TARPS pod.

246

Vital support from a close ally. Strike fighters operating from the four Navy carriers committed to Enduring Freedom could not have carried out their indispensable deep-attack function without the help of nonorganic tanking provided by Air Force KC-135s and KC-10s and by British Royal Air Force Tristars and VC-10s (one of the latter shown here refueling two F/A-18s).

Viper power. Air Force, Air National Guard, and Air Force Reserve F-16s also saw service in Enduring Freedom, especially in support of embattled Army and SOF troops during Operation Anadonda. The one depicted here with a load of 2,000-lb LGBs is being preflighted by its pilot before launching on a long-range mission into Afghanistan from remote al Jaber Air Base in Kuwait.

CHAPTER SIX

Distinctive Aspects and Achievements

Even before the Enduring Freedom air war was largely over, one account in early December 2001 described the precision bombing that had brought down the Taliban as possibly "the most significant victory for air power since before the 1991 Gulf War."[1] That characterization overreached not only because Desert Storm was a more historic air power achievement than was CENTCOM's Afghan success, but also because the war against the Taliban and al Qaeda was not a victory by air power alone.[2] It would have been entirely appropriate, however, to conclude that Operation Enduring Freedom constituted a SOF-centric application of joint air power that, in the end, added up to a new way of war for the United States. Among other things, even more than in the case of Desert Storm, the campaign's results showed the ability of the United States to conduct successful force projection from land bases located thousands of miles away from the target area, as well as from carrier operating stations positioned farther away from a landlocked combat zone than ever before in the history of naval air warfare.

As indicated by statistics compiled by the CAOC during the 76 days of bombing between October 7, when Enduring Freedom began, and December 23, when the first phase of the war ended after

---

[1] Peterson.

[2] In terms of scale alone, only around 200 sorties at most were flown per day during Operation Enduring Freedom, compared to as many as 3,000 a day during the height of Desert Storm.

the collapse of the Taliban, some 6,500 strike sorties were flown by CENTCOM forces altogether, out of which approximately 17,500 munitions were dropped on more than 120 fixed targets, 400 vehicles and artillery pieces, and a profusion of concentrations of Taliban and al Qaeda combatants. Of the total number of allied munitions expended, 57 percent were precision-guided munitions. U.S. carrier-based strike fighters accounted for 4,900 of the strike sorties flown during that period, making up 75 percent of the total (see Figure 6.1). More than half of those sorties were flown by Navy and Marine Corps F/A-18s (see Figure 6.2).

Perhaps the three most pivotal ingredients that made this achievement possible were long-range precision air power managed by an unprecedentedly sophisticated and capable CAOC, consistently good real-time tactical intelligence, and mobile SOF teams on the ground working in close concert with indigenous Afghan resistance forces and equipped with enough organic firepower and electronic

Figure 6.1
Strike Sorties Through December 2001 by Service

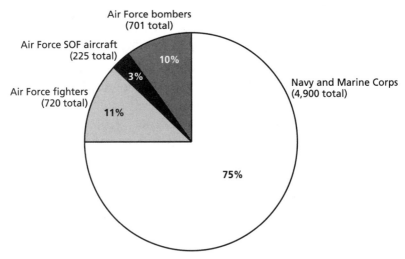

SOURCE: *Sea Power*, March 2002.

Figure 6.2
Strike Sorties Through December 2001 by Aircraft Type

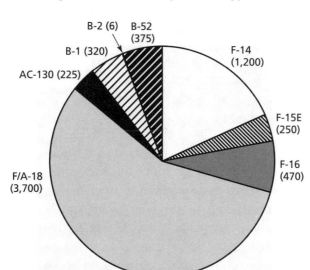

SOURCE: *Sea Power*, March 2002.

support to maintain situation awareness, operate independently, and avoid enemy ambushes. Units from different services with little or no prior joint warfighting experience performed under fire as though they had trained and operated together for years. In the aggregate, Enduring Freedom was uniquely emblematic of the quality and resourcefulness of today's American military personnel.

After the air war essentially ended following the successful conclusion of Operation Anaconda, Pentagon sources reported that around 75 percent of all munitions employed throughout Enduring Freedom had hit their intended targets and achieved the desired result, compared to around 45 percent in both Desert Storm and Allied Force. Laser-guided bombs and JDAMs accounted for 60 percent of the 22,434 bombs, missiles, and other munitions expended altogether, with the B-1 dropping twice as many JDAMs as all other U.S. aircraft combined. In all, some 6,500 JDAMs were dropped throughout the campaign at an assessed effectiveness rate of 90 percent.[3] A slightly higher percentage of precision munitions was dropped by Navy and Marine Corps fighters operating off carriers in the North Arabian Sea, whereas Air Force bombers dropped the vast majority of unguided bombs. The accuracy of the latter munitions improved dramatically in Enduring Freedom over that in previous conflicts, thanks to better onboard radars and better computers to manage weapons ballistics.[4]

Despite their relatively small number (only eight B-1s and 10 B-52s) compared to the overall commitment of combat aircraft to Enduring Freedom, the two Air Force heavy bomber types were able to maintain a constant armed presence over Afghanistan, typically flying missions that lasted from 12 to 15 hours. Depending on the mission profile, the B-1 carried up to 84 Mk 82 free-fall bombs, or 30 CBUs, or 24 JDAMs. The B-52 usually carried a mixed load of 12 JDAMs and 27 Mk 82 general-purpose bombs or 16 CBU-103/CBU-87 wind-corrected munitions dispenser (WCMD) canisters and 27 Mk 82s. The CBU-103 was configured to dispense 202 BLU/97B combined-effects submunitions accurately against soft area targets from high altitude.[5]

---

[3] Eric Schmitt, "Improved U.S. Accuracy Claimed in Afghan Air War," *New York Times*, April 9, 2002, and John Hendren, "Afghanistan Yields Lessons for Pentagon's Next Targets," *Los Angeles Times*, January 21, 2002. Of these early reported numbers, Air Force Major General John Rosa of the Joint Staff cautioned media representatives to be "very careful" about accepting specific effectiveness claims before all the returns were in. Hunter Keeter, "Pentagon Downplays Preliminary Look at Weapons Accuracy in Afghanistan," *Defense Daily*, April 10, 2002, p. 7.

[4] Schmitt, "Improved U.S. Accuracy Claimed in Afghan Air War."

[5] "Afghanistan Sees First Combat Use of New Bomb," *Aviation Week and Space Technology*, December 10, 2001, p. 40, and "Wind-Corrected Munitions Dispenser in First Combat Use, Program Office Director Says," *Aerospace Daily*, December 5, 2001. The Wind-Corrected Munitions Dispenser (WCMD) system is designed to make corrections for wide variations in wind direction and velocity as the weapon free-falls from a release altitude of 39,000 feet or higher. It was used in combat for the first time in Enduring Freedom. WCMD comes in three varieties—the CBU-103/CBU-87 combined-effects munition (CEM), the CBU-104/CBU-89 Gator (which was not used in Enduring Freedom), and the CBU-105/CBU-97 sensor-fused weapon (SWF).

In addition to the high-profile strike sorties that were flown to deliver these munitions, nearly 4,800 airlift missions moved more than 125,000 tons of materiel from the United States to the Afghan theater. Moreover, more than 8,000 USAF, Navy, and RAF tanker missions were flown altogether in support of aircraft from all services.[6] There were more than 1,300 ISR-related sorties, including those flown by the Predator and Global Hawk UAVs, the RC-135 Rivet Joint, the U-2, the E-3 AWACS, the E-8 JSTARS, and the EC-130 Compass Call. Coalition partners flew more than 3,300 missions of all sorts. In Operation Noble Eagle, the concurrent homeland air defense effort, more than 20,000 fighter, tanker, and AWACS sorties were flown during the first six months after September 11. In that operation, more than 250 aircraft were committed to the homeland defense mission, and more than 300 alert scrambles and combat air patrol diverts were conducted in response to actual events.[7]

As for air warfare "firsts" registered during Operation Enduring Freedom, apart from the initial combat use of WCMD noted above, the war saw the first combat employment of the RQ-4 Global Hawk high-altitude UAV, as well as the first operational use of MQ-1 Predators armed with Hellfire missiles and the first combat employment of JDAM by the B-1 and B-52. (During Operation Allied Force, only the B-2 had been configured to deliver that satellite-aided weapon.) Notably, although erroneous target coordinates were occasionally programmed into JDAMs because of various causes, there were no true JDAM aim-point misses in Enduring Freedom. That was a remarkable achievement for a mere $18,000 modification to a simple free-fall bomb. The integration of combat controllers on the ground with heavy bombers for enabling precision attacks on emerging targets was also novel, as was the use, for the first time, of the

---

[6] This point bears emphasizing. The projection of offensive force into landlocked Afghanistan would simply not have been been possible without the support of long-range tankers. The Navy, in particular, was especially dependent on Air Force and RAF tanking and made excellent daily use of it in a superb case example of interservice synergy that contrasted tellingly with the absence of the same during the lead-up to Operation Anaconda.

[7] "USAF Talking Points: The War on Terrorism," SAF/PA, March 21, 2002.

vastly improved CAOC at Prince Sultan Air Base in Saudi Arabia and the provision of live Predator UAV video feed directly to orbiting AC-130 gunship crews.[8]

Finally, Operation Enduring Freedom saw a continuation of some important trends that were first set in motion during the Gulf War a decade earlier. Precision weapons accounted for only 9 percent of the munitions expended during Desert Storm, yet they totaled 29 percent in Allied Force and nearly 60 percent in Enduring Freedom. That overall percentage can be expected to continue to grow in future contingencies as precision-guided munitions (PGMs) become ever more plentiful and, as a result, as even small groups of combatants, such as a handful of enemy troops manning a mortar position, may eventually be deemed worthy of a PGM in some circumstances.[9] As a result of the increased PGM availability and increase in the number of combat aircraft capable of delivering them, the number of PGMs expended per combat sortie flown has steadily grown. In Desert Storm, that number was 0.32. In Allied Force, it was 0.73. In Enduring Freedom, it was 1.66. That dramatic improvement in overall force leverage reaffirmed that one now can speak routinely not of the number of sorties required to engage a given target but rather of how many targets can be successfully engaged by a single sortie.[10]

Yet another trend that continued in Enduring Freedom had to do with extended-range operations. In Desert Storm, the percentage

---

[8] Before the war started, differences of view within the Pentagon had emerged over whether to deploy Predator immediately or to wait for impending communications upgrades that would make it interoperable with the other services. (It takes about 30 days to make a Predator operational in theater.) At that time, the Air Force had taken delivery of 50 Predators since 1994, of which 19 had crashed, with 11 assessed as combat losses. In the end, Predator saw an early commitment to the war effort. Icing was suspected of having caused at least two of three Predator losses in Enduring Freedom as of early November. (Fulghum, "Afghanistan Crash Reveals U.S. Intel Operation," p. 28, and also by David Fulghum, "U.S. Girds for Demands of Long Winter War," *Aviation Week and Space Technology*, November 12, 2001, p. 34.)

[9] Fulghum, "U.S. Girds for Demands of Long Winter War," p. 34.

[10] Christopher J. Bowie, Robert P. Haffa, Jr., and Robert E. Mullins, *Future War: What Trends in America's Post-Cold War Military Conflicts Tell Us About Early 21st Century Warfare*, Arlington, Va.: Northrop Grumman Analysis Center, January 2003, p. 60.

of tanker sorties among the total number of air sorties flown was 12 percent. In Allied Force, it was 20 percent. In Enduring Freedom, it was 27 percent. By the same token, long-range bombers have delivered a steadily increasing percentage of overall numbers of weapons expended throughout the succession of U.S. combat engagements since Desert Storm. In the Gulf War, it was 32 percent. In Allied Force, it was roughly 50 percent. In Enduring Freedom, it was about 70 percent.[11]

Data Fusion Comes of Age

For the first time in the history of modern warfare, Operation Enduring Freedom was conducted under an overarching intelligence, surveillance, and reconnaissance (ISR) umbrella that stared down relentlessly in search of enemy activity. That umbrella was formed by a constellation of overlapping multispectral sensor platforms. It also included the E-3 AWACS, the E-8 Joint STARS with its SAR and moving-target indicator (MTI) radars, the RC-135 Rivet Joint SIGINT aircraft, the Navy's EP-3, and the RQ-1 Predator and RQ-4 Global Hawk UAVs (the latter of which was still in testing at the time and had not yet been approved for full-scale production). Finally, it included the U-2 mounting a synthetic-aperture radar and a new SIGINT package, the EA-6B, the ES-3 surveillance aircraft equipped with a SAR able to provide rough geolocation coordinates for targets as far away as 60 miles on either side, and the F-14, F-15E, and Block 30 F-16C+ with their Low-Altitude Navigation and Targeting Infrared for Night (LANTIRN) (or, in the case of the F-16C+, Litening II) infrared target imaging pods, plus the Tactical Aerial Reconnaissance Pod System (TARPS) in the case of the F-14. The RAF's contribution included a Nimrod R1 electronic intelligence (ELINT) aircraft, Canberra PR9 reconnaissance aircraft, and an

---

[11] Bowie and others, p. 4.

E-3D AWACS. The French Air Force contributed Mirage IV reconnaissance aircraft, and the CIA made use of its I-Gnat UAV.[12]

This multiplicity of interlinked and mutually supporting sensors enabled a greatly increased refinement of ISR input over that which had been available during earlier conflicts. It also permitted a degree of ISR fusion that distinguished Enduring Freedom from all previous air campaigns. The extent of progress that had been registered in this respect was showcased by the merging of multiple sources of information and the channeling of the resulting product into the cockpits of armed aircraft ready to act on it. That progress allowed for greater connectivity not only between sensors and shooters, but also between those with execution authority at the point of contact with the enemy and more senior decisionmakers at all echelons up the chain of command. The RQ-1 Predator, for example, could provide live video not only to the AC-130, but also to the CAOC, to CENTCOM headquarters in Florida, and to the Pentagon, the CIA, and even the White House in Washington.[13] The Joint Tactical Information Distribution System (JTIDS) carried by the F-15E used Link 16 to provide connectivity between ground forward air controllers (GFACs) and airborne platforms.[14] Link 16 allowed aircrews to acquire a real-time air picture indicating the location and status of all friendly aircraft, as well as to receive target information in five to 10 seconds via data link rather than having it painstakingly read over secure radio by an AWACS operator. The Navy's Link 11 system performed a similar function.

---

[12] The I-Gnat has a range of 400 to 500 miles and mounts a miniature SAR called Lynx that, in its spotlight mode, can image details as small as four inches in diameter (including tire tracks in sand and footprints in mud) as far as 16 miles away both through the weather and around the clock. It also can detect moving targets and small scene changes from one pass to the next and can be upgraded for three-dimensional imaging and aerial identification of targets marked by special operations forces. One downside is that it cannot fly as high (above 20,000 feet) or remain airborne as long (up to 12 hours) as the Predator. (Fulghum, "Afghanistan Crash Reveals U.S. Intel Operation," p. 28.)

[13] Daniel Goure, "Location, Location, Location," *Jane's Defense Weekly*, February 27, 2002.

[14] Some JTIDS terminals that were initially destined for installation in F-15Cs were diverted for use in the F-15Es that were flying combat missions over Afghanistan.

Numerous ISR fusion scenarios were rendered possible by this confluence of capabilities. For example, a satellite might detect an area of interest for JSTARS to search, which, in turn, would cue an RQ-1 Predator orbiting near the area to provide targeting-quality imagery for strike platforms. Using JSTARS to cue Predator proved to be highly effective. The slower-flying Predator might be calibrated and launched to take its narrow-field-of-view sensors to an area of interest. Upon arriving in the target area, it would relieve the E-8, which would then resume its wide-area search for new targets while the Predator provided refined target coordinates to an AC-130 or a strike aircraft orbiting nearby. The Predator, which can remain airborne for up to 16 hours, mounts a digital video camera, infrared sensors, and a SAR capable of detecting and identifying targets through smoke and clouds. Through the intervention of Big Safari, the Air Force's special-projects operation, a radio was installed on Predator allowing its ground-based pilot and sensor operator to talk to other aircraft and to targeteers in the CAOC. Eventually, the ability to transfer real-time Predator video was added, allowing AC-130 aircrews to be briefed with live imagery well before arriving in the target area. Because the CAOC was the one locale that had a complete picture of the air campaign, its hands-on involvement was essential to making all of this work.

In a different scenario, SIGINT aircraft would note a spike in communications traffic coming from a known Taliban location. An RQ-1 Predator would then be sent to the vicinity of the source for a closer look, streaming real-time video of the building to targeteers in the CAOC in Saudi Arabia and at CENTCOM headquarters in Tampa, Florida. An F-14 crew loitering nearby would look for additional signs of activity and would visually confirm the presumed target to be the correct one. Targeteers would then develop mensurated target geolocation coordinates and would pass those coordinates both directly to the F-14 and to the AWACS via CAOC personnel who communicated with the latter. With precise target coordinates and CAOC clearance to drop in hand, the F-14's radar intercept officer (RIO) would then target a JDAM or LGB for the building. F-14s were also equipped with an FTI (fast tactical imagery) capability that enabled aircrews to store an image taken by the aircraft's LANTIRN forward-looking infrared (FLIR) pod and send it by data link to the CAOC via the aircraft carrier in near-real-time for prompt target assessment and approval.[15]

These experiences and others like them reflected a broader and continuing effort to close the links in the kill chain across service lines both vertically and horizontally. The intent, as Air Force Chief of Staff General John Jumper put it, was to "let the digits do the talking" between manned and unmanned systems and satellites. General Franks went out of his way to lend his personal support to this admittedly experimental effort. As Secretary of the Air Force James Roche later observed, "what General Franks has done is give us the opportunity . . . to put in a number of these [ISR] assets and learn how they work together and how to do that better over time." That latitude granted by Franks occasioned what Roche called a "cultural breakthrough" in solidifying widespread acceptance of the value of UAVs.[16] Roche further noted how Predator was initially used to help provide target acquisition by AC-130 gunship crews by illuminating a target with a laser spot so that the gunners' eyes could be talked onto the target by the Predator's ground operator.[17] When that arrangement proved so effective that the gunship crews asked if they could receive live Predator video feed directly aboard the AC-130, the requested capability was provided to them within six days.[18]

General Jumper likewise applauded General Franks's support of this effort: "[He] let us put these things together in the course of battle—many of these techniques unproven—and they have been

[15] Robert Wall, "F-14s Add Missions in Anti-Taliban Effort," *Aviation Week and Space Technology*, November 19, 2001, p. 38 and Frank Wolfe, "Navy F-14s Able to Transmit, Receive Imagery from Green Berets," *Defense Daily*, August 1, 2002, p. 1.

[16] Michael Sirak, "Interview: James Roche—Secretary of the U.S. Air Force," *Jane's Defense Weekly*, January 9, 2002.

[17] At General Jumper's urging, laser designators had been installed on the Predator, which enabled AC-130 gunners wearing night-vision goggles (NVGs) to attack ground targets that had been marked by the beam.

[18] "Q and A with Air Force Secretary James Roche," *Business Week* online, February 1, 2002.

extremely successful."[19] Close to 500 megabits per second (Mbps) of bandwidth were leased commercially by CENTCOM and other agencies for Enduring Freedom to help facilitate it, since the Air Force had not fielded enough Link 16 wideband data links to provide real-time target data to all strikers. In some aircraft, notably the heavy bombers, the ability to receive email in the cockpit allowed aim-point coordinates to be received and acted on nearly as quickly as targets could be generated and approved. B-52 crews repeatedly used target data provided by SOF personnel on the ground to drop long sticks of bombs precisely into 1,000-yard-long boxes. The air component commander during the opening weeks of Enduring Freedom, Lieutenant General Charles Wald, later commented that "when history is written, it will show that three or four guys up there [in the north] made the difference in this conflict. When Mazar-i-Sharif started falling, it was basically because of them."[20]

In this regard, thought was given for a time to sending some B-2s back to the war after their initial use during the first few nights, not to participate in the bombing effort but rather to employ the aircraft's high-resolution SAR for pinpointing the location of small targets such as cave entrances and transferring the target information in real time to JDAM-armed orbiting bombers through a satellite data link.[21] By mid-November, cloudy weather had begun to limit the ability of electro-optical sensors aboard the U-2 and other aircraft to provide imagery of critical surveillance and target areas, thus increasing the importance of SAR-equipped aircraft in the theater. The essence of joint operations was spotlighted when an Air Force Predator below cloud cover used its laser designator to cue Navy fighter aircrews at medium altitudes to drop LGBs accurately through the weather while SOF units on the ground provided updated target co-

---

[19] David A. Fulghum and Robert Wall, "Heavy Bomber Attacks Dominate Afghan War," *Aviation Week and Space Technology*, December 3, 2001.

[20] Thomas E. Ricks, "Bull's-Eye War: Pinpoint Bombing Shifts Role of GI Joe," *Washington Post*, December 2, 2001.

[21] Fulghum and Wall, "Heavy Bomber Attacks Dominate Afghan War." Eventually that option was determined to be unnecessary.

ordinates to Navy and Air Force strike aircraft orbiting overhead for JDAM attacks. Said General Jumper: "The turning point came . . . when all these systems began to come together at the 30- to 40-day point, so that your accuracy and precision improved greatly."[22]

Other breakthrough areas in ISR fusion came in the form of greater sensor persistence on areas and objects of interest to the CAOC, integration of information from multiple sources at the operational and tactical levels, and greatly improved management of data collection. If certain sensors could not communicate directly with one another, their product could at least be fused through information links in the CAOC. As the director of ISR on the Air Staff, Major General Glen Shaffer, put it, "we understand how to control [ISR] better than ever, people have better tools, and we learned a lot of lessons in Operation Allied Force. In the past, command and control of ISR started only after someone found a target on the ground."[23]

A New Air-Ground Synergy

Another notable innovation pioneered during Operation Enduring Freedom was the uniquely close synchronization of air and land power that dominated the war effort. SOF teams performed three major missions throughout the campaign. First, they marshaled and gave direction to the unorganized forces of the Northern Alliance. Second, they built small armies out of Pashtun tribesmen in the south. Third, they provided accurate and validated target information to U.S. aircrews for conducting precision air attacks. These roles were highly improvised, and they involved a new relationship between the military and the CIA. The Army's Special Forces contribution to the Enduring Freedom SOF effort totaled just 316 Special Forces troops divided up into 18 12-man A-Teams, four company-level units, and

---

[22] Ricks, "Bull's-Eye War: Pinpoint Bombing Shifts Role of GI Joe."

[23] David A. Fulghum, "Intel Emerging as Key Weapon in Afghanistan," *Aviation Week and Space Technology*, March 11, 2002, p. 24.

three battalion-level commands. All of these reported to the Joint Special Operations Task Force (JSOTF) North at Karshi-Khanabad Air Base in Uzbekistan 100 miles north of the Afghan border.

Nearly every SOF team included one or two CIA paramilitary operatives and an AFSOC combat controller. Air Force controllers from the 23rd Special Tactics Unit home-based at Hurlburt Field, Florida, joined the initial Special Forces A-Teams that were inserted into Afghanistan. They used laser spot markers to indicate targets and determine their geolocational coordinates. This information was then fed into a GPS device that transmitted the target coordinates to aircrews for JDAM targeting via a multiband hand-held radio. As the campaign shifted from attacking fixed targets to engaging emerging time-sensitive targets, aircrews would routinely launch without preassigned targets. By the time the air war was over, some 80 percent of all targets attacked by allied aircrews had not been preplanned but rather were assigned while their aircraft were en route to their assigned holding points over Afghanistan.

The Tactical Air Control Party (TACP) was typically a SOF team's only link to allied air support. Each TACP member carried up to 120 lb of equipment and was widely considered colloquially to be the team's American Express card ("don't leave home without him"). Using a hand-held GPS receiver and laser target marker, a GFAC could designate extremely precise aim points, allowing fighters to deliver ordnance against enemy troop concentrations positioned dangerously close to friendly forces. Strike pilots would be asked to drop ordnance under these conditions only when the urgency of the situation demanded such a drastic resort.[24] Many argued that as borne out by the pivotal contribution of TACPs to the success of Enduring Freedom, they should be considered and treated as weapons systems, just as important to producing desired combat outcomes as attack aircraft and precision munitions. Although chronically underfunded,

---

[24] Dangerously close for the AC-130's 40mm cannon is 120 meters. It is 200 meters for the aircraft's 105mm howitzer, 425 meters for a 500-lb Mk 82 LGB, and 500 meters for the 2,000-lb JDAM. (Bacon, p. 14.)

said one grateful beneficiary of their service, "they go out there with their maps and their skills and have done a phenomenal job."[25]

This integration of Air Force controllers with Army Special Forces A-Teams and Navy SEAL detachments was arguably the greatest tactical innovation of the war. Some Air Force TACPs called in air strikes for 25 days straight, averaging 10 to 30 target attacks per day.[26] These controllers would rack and stack a dozen or more fighters and bombers like layers of a wedding cake over a segment of the battlefield and then talk pilots' eyes onto specific targets in a process called terminal attack. In that manner, they could engage six separate designated mean points of impact (DMPIs) with six JDAMs in a single drop.

The SOF teams were supported by two Air Force EC-130H Compass Call electronic warfare aircraft operated by the 41st Electronic Combat Squadron based at Davis-Monthan AFB, Arizona. The EC-130s were deployed to the theater during the last week of September 2001. Ultimately, they flew 108 missions devoted to jamming communications, with the goal of disrupting Taliban and al Qaeda activities. The aircraft were capable of suppressing enemy radio signals without interfering with friendly frequencies. Because of the high mountains, they operated closer to enemy positions than they normally would have. In several instances, EC-130 aircrews exposed themselves to AAA fire and knowingly positioned themselves within Stinger infrared SAM range.[27]

Army and Navy SOF teams continually discovered new ways to communicate target coordinates and other tactical information to airborne combat aircrews. A revealing demonstration of the shortened kill chain was provided in late November 2001, when a Special Forces A-Team member was given a target requested by General Dos-

---

[25] Bacon, p. 14.

[26] Vernon Loeb, "An Unlikely Super-Warrior Emerges in Afghan War," *Washington Post*, May 19, 2002.

[27] Glenn W. Goodman, Jr., "Invisible Support: Air Force Communications-Jamming Aircraft Aided U.S. Special Operations Forces in Afghanistan," *Armed Forces Journal International*, August 2002, pp. 70–71.

tum personally. The team's TACP examined the requested target; recorded its coordinates with a device featuring a digital map display, a portable laser range finder, and a GPS receiver; and transmitted the coordinates to the CAOC via a satellite data link. Since the target was in an already established and approved engagement zone, the CAOC assigned the target to a B-52 orbiting nearby. Only 19 minutes later, the B-52 destroyed the target—a Taliban tank and troop formation massing on a ridge more than a mile from Kunduz—with 16 CBUs.[28] Dostum, who had been hoping for a response within 24 hours, was singularly impressed.[29] Using similar cueing, a Navy F/A-18 pilot was able to skip a laser-guided Maverick missile under a bridge, killing the enemy forces who had taken cover when they heard the approaching aircraft while leaving the bridge itself undamaged.[30] In a related case, Navy SEALs on the ground observed women and children commingled with a targeted group of Taliban and fortunately aborted, at the last minute, a TST attack by an inbound B-52 whose crew had not coordinated the attack with the SEALs who had been working in the target area.[31]

As presaged earlier during Operation Allied Force, when NATO aircrews on several occasions toward the war's end received target information about Serbian troop positions indirectly from Kosovo Liberation Army (KLA) ground spotters, Operation Enduring Freedom showed once again that air power can be more effective in many circumstances if it is teamed with ground elements that can identify and, in the case of Afghanistan, shape, flush out, and concentrate en-

---

[28] Greg Jaffe, Chip Cummings, and Anne Marie Squeo, "Accidental Bombing of Friendly Forces May Be Avoidable with Minor Fixes," *Wall Street Journal,* December 6, 2001.

[29] Eric Schmitt and James Dao, "Use of Pinpoint Air Power Comes of Age in New War," *New York Times,* December 24, 2001.

[30] Vernon Loeb, "Afghan War Is a Lab for U.S. Innovation," *Washington Post,* March 26, 2002.

[31] Briefing by Captain Robert S. Harward, USN, "Operation Enduring Freedom: Special Reconnaissance and Direct Action Operations in Afghanistan, October 6, 2001–March 30, 2002," Santa Monica, Calif.: RAND Corporation, August 19, 2002.

emy forces.[32] Enduring Freedom was far more successful in this regard, showing the need not only for ground forward observers but also for friendly ground forces robust enough to force the enemy to concentrate and expose itself, which the KLA could not normally do in Kosovo. What was demonstrated in Afghanistan was not classic close air support but rather something closer to ground-enabled precision strike. The latter was distinguished by ground forces supporting air power rather than the other way around through the provision of targeting and combat identification in the same manner that such support to air operators is provided by other offboard sensors and methods. Navy carrier pilots freely praised the role played by the Air Force's terminal attack controllers in this newly emergent concept of operations, stressing that the presence of those controllers was "extremely helpful, especially in identifying ground targets as hostile and guiding us into them. They relieved us of tremendous responsibility."[33] Of this continuous process of adaptation, General Jumper later remarked that "we are inventing . . . tactics more or less in the course of battle."[34] The experience gained in coordinating orbiting strike aircraft and ground target spotters in Enduring Freedom has since been integrated into the training syllabus at the USAF Air-Ground Operations School at Nellis AFB, Nevada.

---

[32] For abundant good reason, not least of which was a determination to avoid even a hint of appearing to legitimize the KLA's independent activities, NATO had no interest in serving as the KLA's de facto air force and refused to provide it with the equipment it would have needed for its troops to have performed directly as forward controllers. However, it did benefit from KLA-provided target information at least a few times during the KLA's Operation Arrow against Serbian forces at Mount Pastrik toward the Kosovo war's end. For more on this, see Benjamin S. Lambeth, *NATO's Air War for Kosovo: A Strategic and Operational Assessment*, Santa Monica, Calif.: RAND Corporation, MR-1365-AF, 2001, pp. 53–55.

[33] Zoran Kusovac, "Carrier Aircraft Are 'Crucial Factor,'" *Jane's Defense Weekly*, November 21, 2001.

[34] Sue C. Payton, "Fast-Tracking Innovative Technologies: DoD's ACTD Program Supports the War on Terrorism," *Armed Forces Journal International*, April 2002, p. 28.

Humanitarian Relief and Force Sustainment

For all the recent spotlighting of the new mode of air-ground coop-eration sketched out above, Operation Enduring Freedom was more than just a SOF and JDAM story. It also featured an air mobility component that was no less indispensable for ensuring the campaign's success. Indeed, the campaign saw the third most massive air trans-port effort ever after the Berlin airlift of 1948–49 and Operation De-sert Shield in 1990–91. That air mobility effort began on October 6 and ended roughly six months later at about the time Operation Ana-conda was concluded.

Even before the initial options planning for Enduring Freedom had begun to crystallize, United States Air Forces in Europe (USAFE) began playing a key role in this respect. Immediately after the second tower of the WTC was struck on September 11, 2001, a crisis action team was activated at USAFE headquarters at Ramstein Air Base, Germany. USAFE's 3rd Air Force headquartered at RAF Mildenhall, England, similarly activated a contingency response cell, and USAFE's 16th Air Force at Aviano Air Base, Italy, activated a regional operations center there in anticipation of the delivery challenges that would soon follow. For its part, EUCOM activated a theater command-and-control center at its headquarters in Stuttgart, Ger-many, to monitor events, and NATO increased its capability at Sigonella Air Base in Sardinia, Italy, to support the air bridge from Europe to Afghanistan that would be eventually created. Across the board, the alert level throughout USAFE rose to Force Protection Condition Delta—the highest lockdown state—for a time beginning on September 11.

On September 15, a Theater Air and Space Operations Support Center was activated at Ramstein in preparation for USAFE's partici-pation in Enduring Freedom support activities soon to follow. Five days later, on September 20, USAFE's commander was directed by the Joint Staff through EUCOM to request support from Air Mobil-ity Command (AMC) to provide a director of mobility forces (DIRMOBFOR) to manage the lift component of Enduring Free-dom. On September 24, the chairman of the JCS, General Richard

Myers, issued a deployment order directing USAFE to provide medical support to CENTCOM at RAF Lakenheath, England, and at Incirlik Air Base, Turkey. Rhein-Main Air Base, Germany, became the principal airlift node, with Moron Air Base, Spain selected as the tanker hub and Sigonella as the C-17 hub. Together, these facilities enabled the southern air bridge to Afghanistan and its environs, a link that soon found itself worked to full capacity. To sustain and manage this link, the commander of USAFE became the de facto Commander of Air Force Forces (COMAFFOR) for the mobility portion of Enduring Freedom.

On September 28, the Joint Staff tasked EUCOM to enlist USAFE as Operation Enduring Freedom's "bread-bombing" entity.[35] Two days later, on September 30, General Myers issued a deployment order for humanitarian assistance. On October 1, U.S. Transportation Command (TRANSCOM) was directed by the Joint Staff to begin moving HDRs to Ramstein for prompt delivery to Afghan refugees and other needy civilians once combat operations against the Taliban and al Qaeda began. The next day, USAFE was tasked to execute the effort. On October 6, four C-17s were committed and made ready for the mission, with 200,000 HDRs in the initial delivery package. This preparation was all planned and put into place in just a little over a week.[36]

On the night of October 7, less than an hour after the commencement of bombing operations, two C-17s air-dropped 34,400 HDRs from an altitude of 29,000 feet into an area southeast of Kabul within a mile-wide and three-mile-long patch of flat terrain that was heavily populated by displaced Afghan civilians. The aircraft were accompanied by an Air Force fighter escort provided by CENTCOM and launched from Incirlik. The HDRs were packed inside seven-

---

[35] General Gregory S. Martin, USAF, "Operation Enduring Freedom: Humanitarian Relief and Force Sustainment Operations," briefing to the author, Headquarters USAFE, Ramstein Air Base, Germany, September 24, 2002.

[36] Such preparation was pioneered earlier by USAFE during Operation Allied Force when testing was done in anticipation of possible air delivery of humanitarian aid (which, in the end, proved unnecessary) to isolated Kosovar Albanians.

foot-high cardboard containers that had been loaded into the C-17s on special pallets. As each container left the aircraft, a lanyard ripped off the cord holding it together and the slipstream pulled away the cardboard, releasing the food packs which then free-fell to the ground.[37] The outside air temperature was below zero, and aircrews were required to prebreathe 100-percent oxygen two hours before the drop to minimize their risk of contracting the bends. C-17 pilots were guided to their release points by GPS, in radio silence and with their navigation lights out.[38]

The following night, two more C-17s dropped the same number of HDRs in the same area. The HDR deliveries the first two nights took the long route from Ramstein via Saudi Arabia and Pakistan, making a total of 23 missions in 24 hours. While this was taking place, USAFE deployed F-15Cs, F-15Es, F-16CJs, and tankers to Incirlik and Rhein-Main to support the force-package coverage that included Operation Northern Watch KC-135s and RC-135s to support the C-17s out of Ramstein. This humanitarian aid operation, which was initially supposed to last only five days but which ultimately continued for many weeks, was a personal creation of President Bush, who had proposed early during the planning of Enduring Freedom that food be dropped in the north and south concurrently with the initial bombing attacks because he wanted the United States to be perceived as a liberator.[39]

By November 12, barely a month after the campaign had begun, AMC had flown nearly 1,500 transport and tanker missions in sup-

---

[37] The packets were developed in 1993 as a civilian alternative to military Meals Ready to Eat (MREs), offering 2,200 calories instead of the MRE's 4,400 calories so as to be better tailored to the needs of refugees weakened by travel and hunger. Each HDR weighs 30 ounces and comes in a bright yellow pouch made of thick plastic strong enough to withstand high-altitude drops and extreme environmental conditions. According to the CIA's Jawbreaker team leader who was on the receiving end of this initial delivery, many of the HDR packets burst open on impact with the ground, pointing to a serious packaging deficiency that needed fixing. (Schroen, p. 168.)

[38] Steven Komarow, "Air Force Delivers Aid with Attitude," USA Today, November 9, 2001.

[39] Woodward, pp. 130–131.

port of Enduring Freedom. Some 200 C-17s and C-5s were committed to getting materiel transported to some two dozen overseas bases, many of which had the barest of operational support facilities and that offered living conditions that could rightly be described as abysmal. AMC's commander, General Tony Robertson, said of that commitment level that "if there was another war, there might come a point where I call the [regional combatant commanders] and say I'm maxed out—what's your priority?"[40]

The attempt to provide fighter escorts for these missions was a new experience for USAFE's Air Mobility Operations Control Center (AMOCC) at Ramstein. Accordingly, securing the needed diplomatic clearances for such missions proved uniquely challenging. Toward that end, the AMOCC looked not only to USAFE's assigned political adviser but also to EUCOM's directorate of plans (J-5) for guidance and support. Because the Navy's carrier-based fighters in the North Arabian Sea were too far south to provide escort service to airlifters entering Afghan airspace from the north, Air Force fighters were instead prepositioned at Incirlik for that purpose. A blanket diplomatic clearance arrangement for fighter escort up to the Black Sea was eventually secured, but only one HDR delivery mission with an armed two-ship escort was actually flown in the end because the Uzbek government disapproved any further transit of armed American fighters through Uzbek airspace.

Nevertheless, the humanitarian aid and sustainment missions would not have been possible without the overflight and basing support that was provided by a number of coalition partners and other willing countries.[41] To facilitate that support, the Department of State in the early aftermath of September 11 assembled a crisis action team that included USAF representation. Shortly thereafter, EUCOM also staffed a contingency response team that assumed responsibility for calling U.S. defense attachés in the concerned coun-

---

[40] "Keeping the Birds Aloft," *U.S. News and World Report*, November 12, 2001.

[41] Switzerland actually *asked* that U.S. aircraft transit its airspace en route to Afghanistan so that it could project an appearance of being an actively involved player.

tries as circumstances required. Bulgaria, in particular, bent every effort to cooperate, and it found itself high on the list of appreciated allies as a result. The Bulgarian government approved every overflight, transit, and presence request submitted by Washington and made available its Burgas airfield as a staging base for Air Force tankers in an arrangement that became completely comfortable and routine not long after KC-135R operations began there on November 23. Incirlik also became a huge air mobility hub in support of Enduring Freedom. With its preexisting commitment to Operation Northern Watch on top of the added flow of AMC staging, its ramp space soon became saturated.

The new bases that had been established and opened up in the former Soviet Central Asian republics also figured prominently in the Enduring Freedom mobility story. Air Force Red Horse civil-engineering units graded 190,000 square yards of new ramp space (the equivalent of 30 football fields) at nine such expeditionary airfields, described by one account as a "network of new U.S. bases that have sprung up like dragon's teeth across Central Asia and the Middle East."[42] The Partnership for Peace experience provided an institutional foundation for much of this support. The personal contacts that had been established throughout the region by the Supreme Allied Commander for Europe, Air Force General Joseph Ralston, also helped greatly in further facilitating it.[43]

Much of the initial concept development for the humanitarian aid and sustainment missions was done literally on the backs of envelopes at Ramstein. To facilitate the flow of aid packages and other cargo into Afghanistan, General Martin on November 1 was designated EUCOM's air component commander for the airdrop effort, at which time the 32nd Air Operations Group at Ramstein became the

---

[42] William M. Arkin, "Building a War: As Some Argue, Supply Lines Fill Up," *Los Angeles Times,* November 10, 2002.

[43] In one notable temporary hiccup, because of fears of possible Taliban reprisal, Turkmenistan for two nights denied the United States diplomatic clearance for overflight, as a result of which allied transports could not transit Turkmen airspace en route to geographically contiguous Afghanistan.

CAOC for the mobility mission. All humanitarian relief missions emanated from Ramstein, were included on General Moseley's daily Air Tasking Order (ATO) for Enduring Freedom, and were coordinated by a C-17 cell in the CAOC in Saudi Arabia. As for the flow process itself, the HDRs were delivered to Ramstein from the United States by AMC. German ramp workers at Ramstein then built up the HDR packages, which in turn were delivered to Incirlik by German Air Force C-160 Transalls for transshipment into Afghanistan by C-17s. All of the air-delivered logistics support to the SOF teams and Northern Alliance opposition groups was also marshaled at Ramstein and flown from there to Incirlik, where it was transferred (and sometimes reconfigured) to AFSOC MC-130s for delivery into Northern Afghanistan. After the first three or four weeks, almost all of the support sorties from Ramstein to Incirlik were flown by German Transalls.

The airdrop of HDRs used the tri-wall aerial delivery (TRIAD) system. Each TRIAD, about the size of a refrigerator box, contained around 420 HDRs. A single C-17 could carry as many as 42 TRIAD packages, all of which were dropped on GPS coordinates. In each case, the drop zone was arranged for and assigned by CENTCOM's JSOTF North, with the final go-no go decision being made by the CAOC. Drop zone coordinates would often be changed during the course of an ongoing mission. On October 31, the millionth HDR was dropped on Afghanistan during the 61st C-17 humanitarian aid sortie.[44] By November 30, two million HDRs had been delivered by 127 C-17 missions.

A similar form of precision delivery was provided for supplying U.S. SOF teams in Afghanistan by means of containerized delivery system (CDS) air drops. Unlike HDRs, which relied on free-fall,

---

[44] As noted in Chapter Three, one problem was that the original HDRs were the same yellow color as CBU submunitions. The CBU-87 contains 202 submunitions, each roughly the size of soda can. One CBU can spread these submunitions over an area 100 by 50 meters. About 7 percent of them fail to detonate. The resulting duds were deadly objects for children and any other unsuspecting passersby who might pick one up out of curiosity. CENTCOM finally decided to change the color of the HDR packets from yellow to blue to avoid any further confusion and unintended harm.

CDS packages required parachute delivery. The latter were packed either with standard, nonstandard, or lethal materiel, depending on the nature and source of the requests. All were assembled and rigged by Task Force Firepower, an effort mounted by the 29th Support Group of the Army's 21st Theater Support Command (TSC) at the Rhine Ordnance Barracks adjacent to Ramstein. The 21st TSC provided packaging and rigging support both to the Air Force and to the CIA and various covert SOF operations. Taskings for air refueling, air drop, and resupply missions typically came by telephone call, email message, or ATO tasking, as often as not with little notice.

The transshipment of CDS packages began on October 22 once the initial SOF teams were in place on the ground in Afghanistan. Those teams made itemized requests for airdrops of virtually everything, from weapons and ammunition to boots, blankets, oats for horse and donkey feed, and even vaseline to treat saddle sores. (Airdrop is usually a last resort for the Army, but it was the only resort in this case because Afghanistan was landlocked and surface access was not yet available.) The packages were flown from Ramstein to Incirlik and then transloaded there for delivery into Afghanistan twice daily by Special Operations Command Europe (SOCEUR) via MC-130H, with each mission carrying eight CDS bundles and with USAFE providing KC-135R support for inflight refueling. In more than a few cases, a timely precision delivery of such badly needed supplies to an opposition-group leader via a Special Forces A-Team converted an Afghan skeptic into a friend. Radar imagery showed that most CDS drops landed within 100 meters of their intended aim point, although many reportedly ended up landing more like a thousand meters away from their assigned coordinates. Some CDS bundles, as one would expect, broke open on impact and had their contents damaged or destroyed as they rolled down rocky hillsides.[45]

Because of the compartmented nature of some of the SOF supply requests, some taskings were transmitted via special channels,

---

[45] Moore, p. 68.

which made execution unusually complicated.[46] The good news was that the customers never complained about the service provided. The Army component indicated that it had been impressed by USAFE's cooperativeness and willingness to be flexible in the interest of getting the job done.[47]

Diplomatic clearances for overflight of certain countries also continued to be a challenge, given the need to coordinate with nine countries and to transit two regional joint-command AORs to make the humanitarian assistance mission work. At the outset, C-17s operated from unimproved strips as they brought heavy equipment into Afghanistan to help the Marines set up FOB Rhino. C-17s carried fuel in fuel bladders in their cargo bays. In all, 59 C-17 sorties delivered various CDS packages, many to SOF units for delivery to opposition-group leaders, as well as additional HDRs.[48] The last HDR delivery mission was flown on December 21, not long after the Taliban regime was finally brought down. The following January 10, the first hard-core Taliban and al Qaeda detainees were moved from Afghanistan to Incirlik by C-17s and from there transferred via C-141s under intense security to a holding facility at the U.S. naval base at Guantanamo Bay, Cuba. General Myers said of some of those detainees: "These people would gnaw hydraulic lines in the back of a C-17 to bring it down. These are very, very dangerous people, and that's how they're being treated."[49]

Apart from the clear physical threat to C-17 and C-130 operations presented by enemy AAA and man-portable infrared SAMs, especially during the early phase of the Afghan campaign, the single

---

[46] "Talking Paper on 3rd Aerospace Expeditionary Task Force Lessons Learned," Headquarters 86th Airlift Wing/XP, Ramstein Air Base, Germany, September 19, 2002.

[47] Conversation with 21st TSC staff at Rhine Ordnance Barracks, Germany, September 26, 2002.

[48] "Talking Paper on Operation Enduring Freedom 3rd Aerospace Expeditionary Task Force A-4 and Logistics Readiness Cell Perspective," Headquarters USAFE/LGTR, September 20, 2002.

[49] Comment by General Richard Myers, USAF, January 11, 2002, quoted in "USAF Talking Points: The War on Terrorism," SAF/PA, January 16, 2002.

greatest challenge associated with the mobility portion of Enduring Freedom was organizational and had to do with the overlapping lines and boxes that connected the various involved unified and specified commands. The recurring friction that ensued from those organizational complications suggested a need for a more focused dialogue before the next such major tasking among the commanders of USAFE, AMC, and the involved SOF organizations to ensure better coordination on cargo and passenger transshipment execution at the lowest levels.[50]

The unexpectedly early fall of Mazar-i-Sharif further contributed to friction in the mobility effort because of the new and different lift demands it created. After a slow start, the air campaign began registering successes against the Taliban far sooner than had been anticipated. Ensuing mission creep and shifts in mission complexion made for still additional problems. Some associated issues included security compartmentation in connection with SOF support, such as the identity of the customer and the nature of the materiel being shipped. Although the HDR packages were unclassified, the CDS packages that had been assembled at Ramstein for delivery to SOF teams were classified because of the nature of their contents. That fact occasioned a profusion of clandestine meetings and frequent arguments between suppliers and aircrews over unspecified cargo that might include explosives. The principal source of this friction was the customer, who often would change his mind hourly regarding his needs.[51]

In light of this experience, General Martin later spotlighted a need to better organize, resource, and structure the conduct of forward operations from rear-area locations in the interest of making them more effective as well as to improve staff coordination across regional combatant command boundaries toward that end.[52] Absent

---

[50] Conversation with General Gregory S. Martin at Headquarters USAFE, Ramstein Air Base, Germany, September 24, 2002.

[51] Roundtable discussion with staff officers at Headquarters USAFE, Ramstein Air Base, Germany, September 25, 2002.

[52] Conversation with General Gregory S. Martin at Headquarters USAFE, Ramstein Air Base, Germany, September 24, 2002.

such formal and institutionalized arrangements, simple email transactions helped considerably toward making things happen more quickly. Once trust relationships were established, "ad hoc-ery" became the name of the game, and networking proved pivotal in facilitating the prompt achievement of desired outcomes.[53]

In the end, Operation Enduring Freedom was the first American campaign in which, for several months, everything the military used, including fuel, had to be airlifted into Afghanistan because the country was landlocked. Until the land route from Uzbekistan was finally opened on December 9, everything that went into or out of Afghanistan went by air. This requirement forced TRANSCOM to come up with new ideas continuously, since even something as simple as the absence of a compatible front-end loader to unload arriving aircraft could quickly bring an entire operation to a state of gridlock. Despite the manifold difficulties that were encountered along the way, however, the successful execution of the lift portion of Enduring Freedom spotlighted the value of logistics as a weapon system, as well as the fact that effects-based operations entail materiel delivery as well as bombing.[54]

Special credit for the success of the Enduring Freedom lift achievement should be given to recent developments aimed at stressing and improving asset tracking. These helped the United States build a presence quickly in a part of the world where it previously lacked any foothold. One of the many distinctive challenges of preparing for Enduring Freedom was that the prospective combat zone was far removed from all permanent U.S. bases worldwide, which necessitated establishing new bare-base operating locations essentially

---

[53] Roundtable discussion with staff officers at Headquarters USAFE, Ramstein Air Base, Germany, September 25, 2002.

[54] One of the least-known facts of the Enduring Freedom logistics story is that *after* this land bridge was opened, the preponderance of shipments to U.S. forces in Afghanistan used rail lines through Russia, starting from the Russian Arctic, the Black Sea, and Vladivostok in the Russian Far East. By the time those surface routes were fully operational, they were handling 92 percent of all military materiel going into Afghanistan. Air delivery of the first 1.4 million humanitarian daily rations cost more than $7 per HDR. Sending the next million by surface transport reduced the cost to only 15 cents per ration.

from scratch. The Air Force's Deputy Chief of Staff for Installations and Logistics, Lieutenant General Michael Zettler, later recalled that "every one of those [missions] was a recipe for failure," since just about everything was needed at an unimproved site from which American military personnel had never before operated.[55] Yet allied forces were able to operate out of those bases within less than two weeks after the initial establishment of a U.S. presence.

It was not as easy as it may have appeared by any means. Both operators and support personnel had to be innovative in meeting accelerated taskings before the required materiel and infrastructure basics were in place. The earlier experience of Operation Allied Force in 1999 had revealed some severe shortcomings in the Air Force's asset-tracking capabilities. In response, an improved tracking capability that had been put into place by the time of Enduring Freedom turned asset visibility into a force multiplier by allowing inventories to be kept more closely to ideal levels without the need to over-order or cannibalize parts, even though the in-transit visibility of shipments remained disturbingly deficient early in the campaign.[56] General Zettler said that the Air Force now understands better what it takes to go into a bare base, such as those in Central Asia, and operate any kinds of forces. He added that the Air Expeditionary Force (AEF) concept had been "taken to a very high level of fidelity" in Enduring Freedom, even though there remain kinks in the process that still need ironing out.

On balance, USAFE's experience as the de facto mobility AFFOR brought to light some major challenges in managing an organization of cross-functional participants having little common experience and no shared operating environment, such as EUCOM, the U.S. Army in Europe (USAREUR), SOCEUR, the Defense Logistics Agency, TRANSCOM, the German Air Force, the CIA, and the various nongovernmental organizations that were involved in pro-

---

[55] Adam J. Hebert, "Supply Chain Visibility: U.S. Air Force Adapts to War in Afghanistan and Learns Logistics Lessons," *Armed Forces Journal International,* April 2002, p. 30.

[56] Comments on an earlier draft by my RAND colleague Carl Rhodes, January 17, 2004.

viding humanitarian relief. Timelines for acquiring and moving needed items were often highly compressed. Tankers had to deploy to multiple locations because of an absence of large beddown bases, as a result of which tanker dispersal often exceeded the availability of needed spare parts. Nevertheless, leadership at all levels compensated as well as it could in the absence of an established, proof-tested, synchronized, coordinated, and integrated logistics pipeline tailored to the specific needs of Enduring Freedom.[57]

Space Support to Force Employers

Various satellites in earth orbit were key parts of the ISR umbrella over Afghanistan described above. They proved pivotal in providing real-time situation awareness to all Enduring Freedom players at both the command and execution levels. By one account, a third KH-11 imaging satellite was launched two days before the start of Enduring Freedom to join two others that had been placed on orbit in 1995 and 1996. Although that launch had been scheduled for some time, it reportedly was moved up because of the additional KH-11's obvious value to the operations that were about to begin in Afghanistan. By that same account, a new Operational Support Office was established in the National Reconnaissance Office (NRO), the principal operator of U.S. intelligence-gathering satellites, in time for Enduring Freedom to make NRO's assets more reponsive to the needs of field commanders.[58] In all, nearly 100 satellites contributed either directly or indirectly to allied military operations, and a brigadier general from Air Force Space Command was assigned to the CAOC to ensure that CENTCOM got what it needed from U.S. space resources.

In channeling space support to the CAOC and to other force employers, 14th Air Force's space operations center located at Van-

---

[57] "Talking Paper on Push and Pull Logistics Lessons Learned," Headquarters USAFE/ LGXX, September 19, 2002.

[58] Norman Friedman, *Terrorism, Afghanistan, and America's New Way of War*, Annapolis, Md.: Naval Institute Press, 2003, pp. 290–291.

denberg AFB, California, was fully manned around the clock and played an indispensable role through its many activities to synchronize the planning, tasking, and direction of satellite operations in service to the war effort. Of special importance, it produced the daily Space Tasking Order (STO), 14th Air Force's space counterpart to the CAOC's ATO, that allowed for the provision of such space effects as enhanced GPS accuracy, area watch for infrared events, and other initiatives to support such critical CENTCOM missions as special operations and CSAR.[59] The space AOC's daily space-tasking cycle was closely integrated with the CAOC's daily air-tasking cycle to optimize space support by balancing space assets against global and theater requirements and by deconflicting those requirements to the greatest extent possible. The space AOC and CAOC ran similar and parallel daily organizational processes, including Guidance, Apportionment, and Targeting (GAT) and Master Air Attack Planning (MAAP). Moreover, just like the ATO, the STO allowed for short-notice retasking of space assets as necessary within its 24-hour execution cycle to meet late-arising needs of the supported commander. After receiving the ATO each day and ensuring that the STO reflected ATO tasking, the commander of 14th Air Force, as the main provider of space support to warfighters, approved the STO and disseminated it to all users, first and foremost to the CAOC.[60]

In lending force enhancement support to the CAOC throughout Enduring Freedom, the space AOC also provided such services as near- and longer-term GPS performance predictions for strike planning and advance notification of potentially hostile overhead satellites for use in special operations mission planning. The space AOC also managed the repositioning of defense communications satellites to increase the amount of bandwidth available to CENTCOM as well as the provision of space-based infrared support to postattack mission

---

[59] Comments on an earlier draft by Major Mark Main, USAF, Headquarters 14th Air Force, Vandenberg AFB, California, March 8, 2004.

[60] "Space Tasking Order (STO)," Doctrine Watch No. 21, Air Force Doctrine Center, Maxwell AFB, Alabama, undated paper provided to the author by the office of the Commander, 14th Air Force, Vandenberg AFB, California.

analysis and assessment. In its crucial reach-back role, it answered more than a hundred requests for information on satellite support, force protection, and operational planning issues not only from the CAOC but also from CENTCOM, the Air Staff in Washington, Air Force Space Command, and the unified U.S. Space Command.[61]

The still-embryonic Mission Management Center for space support to the CAOC at the USAF Space Warfare Center (SWC) at Schriever AFB, Colorado, was also manned 24 hours a day and tracked friendly forces throughout the entire area of operations. SWC's commander, Major General Thomas Goslin, reported that SWC's greatest contribution was probably the movement of information to support CSAR. Space assets also were able to confirm when occasional collateral damage incidents caused only minimal actual harm to noncombatants and Afghan infrastructure. Although Goslin noted that the specifics of that ability remain classified, he indicated that they involve fusing multiple data streams to "improve knowledge of where the bombs landed. It gives us a better awareness of how the strike went—where weapons actually hit as compared to where we wanted them to go."[62]

A prototype system called BRITE (for Broadcast Request Imagery Technology Experiment) enabled operators, for the first time, to view satellite imagery in near-real-time. Designed to be carried in the field and operated with a laptop computer, the system enabled ground forces to relay the coordinates of objects of interest to satellites, which would then image the site and transmit high-resolution imagery, such as a photograph of a suspected camp on the other side of a ridgeline, back down to the ground units. Electro-optical imaging was used during daylight hours, with radar imaging being used at

---

[61] Captain Scott J. Galaydick, USAF, "Bullet Background Paper on Space AOC Support for Operation Enduring Freedom," 614th Space Operations Squadron, Vandenberg AFB, California, March 19, 2004.

[62] William B. Scott, "Improved Milspace Key to Antiterrorism War," *Aviation Week and Space Technology*, December 10, 2001, p. 36. As just one example, the Defense Support Program (DSP) satellite constellation was used in Enduring Freedom to determine whether bombs produced high-order detonations.

night and through all kinds of weather.[63] In a related space application, Air Force Predators were flown over Afghanistan from a ground station hundreds of miles away in Pakistan. The UAV's ground-based pilots could talk directly to the crews of combat aircraft operating in the same general area by means of a satellite link. Near-real-time Predator video feed was also transmitted via satellites to identify and track targets of interest on the ground, even though there might not be a friendly soldier there within miles.[64]

Air and maritime operations also benefited from commercial, National Aeronautics and Space Administration (NASA), and National Oceanic and Atmospheric Administration (NOAA) weather satellite information provided to the Navy, which reprocessed the information for military use, combined it with classified data derived from military space systems, and transmitted it to fleet and other users. To note some examples, NASA's Quick Scatterometer (Quikscat) spacecraft provided detailed reporting on sea surface wind speed and direction.[65] Similarly, SeaWiFS and Modis spacecraft monitored wind, fog, dust, and cloud conditions at specific altitudes and geographic locations so that planners and aircrews might determine best altitudes and angles for weapons release. Those satellites also were able to detect and monitor the dust storms that hampered the initial attempts to insert U.S. SOF teams into Afghanistan. SeaWiFS, in particular, was only recently used for the first time in providing such tactical information to military consumers.

Information on dust conditions was also of interest to the four carrier battle groups, which needed to remain clear of dust so as to avoid the congestion and other problems it would cause for ships and aircraft. Such space-derived information was used in one case to steer

---

[63] Tim Friend, "Search for Bin Laden Extends to Earth Orbit," *USA Today*, October 5, 2001.

[64] In some parts of Afghanistan, satellite coverage was spotty, as a result of which video feed from UAVs would fade in and out.

[65] Concern was voiced by some that this growing role of NASA in providing such real-time operational support to the military could raise questions in Congress about NASA's compliance with its civil charter.

USS *Independence* away from a severe dust plume in sufficient time to prevent the carrier's being enveloped by it. Weather satellites were also able to differentiate low clouds from fog, the latter of which was a key consideration in low-level helicopter operations in isolated valleys of Afghanistan. The Navy's accuracy in reporting atmospheric conditions by such means enabled safer helicopter operations in dynamic weather states. It also helped to determine whether laser or GPS-guided weapons would be more suitable for a specific target at any given time. SeaWiFS-derived information of special usefulness to SOF personnel included temperature variations and the characteristics of snow in mountainous areas.[66] Also in direct support of Enduring Freedom, the National Geospatial Intelligence Agency extended for 30 days an agreement with a commercial firm, Space Imaging, for exclusive imaging for military use in Afghanistan.[67] Additional space contributions included an unprecedentedly efficient use of bandwidth in downloading weather satellite information, which enabled more frequent updates to terrestrial weather forecasts.[68]

The extremely high demand for bandwidth was a big part of the Enduring Freedom space story. Predator and Global Hawk were by far the most voracious consumers of military bandwidth. Once the capability of Predator was expanded to include providing real-time imagery directly to the AC-130 and other users, the demand for that capability predictably soared, with an ensuing overtaxing of available bandwidth. For its part, a single Global Hawk consumed around 500 megabits of bandwidth per second when it was operating, about five times the total bandwidth consumed by the entire U.S. military during Operation Desert Storm at its peak. Because of the bandwidth squeeze, Global Hawk pilots were often forced to turn off some of the

---

[66] Craig Covault, "Navy Enlists NASA in the War on Terror," *Aviation Week and Space Technology*, April 8, 2002, p. 30.

[67] Kerry Gildea, "NIMA Extends Deal with Space Imaging for Exclusive Imagery Over Afghanistan," *Defense Daily*, November 7, 2001.

[68] William B. Scott, "'Space' Enhances War on Terrorists," *Aviation Week and Space Technology*, January 21, 2002, p. 31.

UAV's sensors and to transmit lower-resolution imagery to provide real-time video without overwhelming the system. In all, six Predators and two Global Hawks were available for operations over Afghanistan. Thanks to an acute bandwidth limitation, however, it was possible to keep only two Predators and one Global Hawk airborne simultaneously.

Moreover, Predator and Global Hawk operated in the commercial frequency band, requiring U.S. Space Command (SPACECOM) to lease an unprecedented amount of commercial satellite support. In the face of this demand, SPACECOM was able to double the bandwidth that was made available to CENTCOM partly through the purchase of additional commercial support and partly by taking bandwidth away from other regional combatant commanders worldwide. SPACECOM also provided CENTCOM with such highly refined GPS accuracy that the JDAM's average miss distance was half again better than the design criteria stipulated in the munition's operational requirements documents.[69]

In all, the demand for space support to warfighters in Operation Enduring Freedom spotlighted a growing need to manage available bandwidth better. For example, any satellite capacity that was devoted exclusively to Predator or Global Hawk went wasted when those aircraft were not flying and the capacity was not made available to other systems that could have used it. Accordingly, a search is now under way for technology that will enable several systems to share bandwidth from a single satellite transponder.[70] On the plus side, space systems enabled a greatly enhanced collection, processing, and distribution of time-sensitive information in Enduring Freedom, with one Marine Corps general stating that space "has made the big difference in this war. We used to measure our support with a calendar, and now we're using a stopwatch."[71]

---

[69] Peter Grier, "The Combination That Worked," *Air Force Magazine*, April 2002, p. 32.

[70] Greg Jaffe, "Military Feels Bandwidth Squeeze as the Satellite Industry Sputters," *Wall Street Journal*, April 10, 2002.

[71] William B. Scott, "Milspace Comes of Age in Fighting Terror," *Aviation Week and Space Technology*, April 8, 2002, pp. 77–78.

CAOC Operations

As noted above, the air portion of Operation Enduring Freedom was conducted by the air component commander and his staff from CENTCOM's new CAOC at Prince Sultan Air Base Saudi Arabia. That recently opened 70,000-square-foot battle-management facility enabled fully integrated coalition air operations.[72] The CAOC's construction began in July 2000. The complex reached initial operational capability in the spring of 2001 and became fully operational shortly thereafter. First under General Wald and then under General Moseley (the two successive air component commanders for the campaign), all Enduring Freedom air operations—including mobility, space, information warfare, intelligence, and precision bombing—were melded in the CAOC without any stovepipes blocking cross-communication among the many team players.

The Prince Sultan Air Base CAOC was the most capable and sophisticated command-and-control system anywhere in the world when Enduring Freedom kicked off. In marked contrast to the cramped and makeshift CAOC in Vicenza, Italy, during Operation Allied Force, it more closely resembled how war rooms are depicted in Hollywood movies. Huge screens displayed the exact location of every aircraft over Afghanistan and Iraq at any given moment. Other situation displays included live feed from various ISR sensors over the battlefield, and numerous computer stations provided links to information sources all around the world through nearly 100 high-speed T-1 Internet lines that were available for simultaneous use. The air commander himself occupied a battle cab above the large operations floor with his most senior staff, including the CAOC director and ISR director. General Wald said that the information available to him during the first days of Enduring Freedom had been equal to that available a decade earlier to General Horner only after six months of preparation for Desert Storm.[73]

---

[72] Lieutenant General Charles F. Wald, USAF, "Command Brief," 9th Air Force Headquarters, Shaw AFB, South Carolina, January 25, 2001.

[73] John Tirpak, "Enduring Freedom," *Air Force Magazine*, February 2002.

Activities coordinated in the CAOC by the air commander went extremely well in most cases. As but one example, there was not the least apparent discord between Navy and Air Force personnel over the CAOC's operations. One report affirmed that the Navy was "fully committed to the [ATO] concept and [was] a full participant in the targeting process."[74] The first CAOC director for Enduring Freedom, Air Force Major General David Deptula, later reported that throughout the campaign, there was "a coherent and cooperative group of planners from all the services, working together with a common goal and perspective" because they were all operating under one roof without barriers. "It just jelled," he said, in terms of personalities, adding that "we were all working together as an air component, not as individual services."[75] Moreover, the Prince Sultan Air Base CAOC showed a greater degree of efficiency than had ever before been experienced in such a facility. Despite a cap on U.S. military personnel imposed by the Saudi government that kept the CAOC's manning at a lower than ideal level, the facility's performance throughout Enduring Freedom reflected, in the words of General Wald, a "significant improvement" over that of the Vicenza CAOC during Operation Allied Force two years earlier.[76]

Some problems were encountered, however, in integrating new systems and operational approaches into the CAOC's preexisting command-and-control arrangement. To begin with, the CAOC was configured with a floor plan, equipment, and operating procedures intended principally to support the conduct of OSW by CENTCOM's Joint Task Force Southwest Asia (JTF-SWA). It opened just in time to provide the air component with the wherewithal to command the very different Operation Enduring Freedom. That created dynamics that were inappropriate for Enduring Free-

[74] John G. Roos, "Turning Up the Heat: Taliban Became Firm Believers in Effects-Based Operations," *Armed Forces Journal International*, February 2002, p. 37.

[75] Quoted in Rebecca Grant, "The War Nobody Expected," *Air Force Magazine*, April 2002, p. 36.

[76] Lieutenant General Charles F. Wald, USAF, "Enabling the PSAB CAOC Weapon System: Roadmap for the Future," briefing to Corona Top '02, n.d.

dom, since the differing demands of those two separate and highly dissimilar operations yielded an ad hoc organization in the CAOC that was optimized for neither.[77]

From September 11 to October 7, the CAOC underwent a major ramp-up from its relatively modest OSW monitoring function to becoming the nerve center for a major air war. At first, fewer than 40 percent of the arriving personnel sent to Prince Sultan Air Base for CAOC duties were trained in specific operating procedures pertinent to the CAOC. The remaining 60 percent spent their first days simply getting familiar with the CAOC's systems, a process further complicated by the fact that there were ever fewer in-house experts available over time to show them the ropes because of the standard 90-day AEF rotation cycle. That practice created a pronounced inconsistency in the discipline and knowledge level in the CAOC's various divisions, cells, and operating areas. To make matters worse, the CAOC staff was grossly overburdened with 14- to 19-hour work days and no time off for 60 days at a stretch.[78]

In addition, the CAOC staff worked under the combined requirements and pressures of OSW and Enduring Freedom, with multiple (and sometimes conflicting) lines of control and poorly defined relationships for fully synchronizing the CAOC's daily flow pattern with the air commander's immediate operational needs. When the initial planning for Enduring Freedom was set in motion after the terrorist attacks on September 11, 2001, additional personnel for that impending campaign began streaming into the CAOC on top of an existing CAOC organization that had been configured wholly and exclusively for OSW. The CENTCOM staff at MacDill AFB was also oriented primarily by an OSW mindset, which involved different goals, a different coalition, and—for good reason—different and highly exacting and controlled targeting processes. Not surprisingly, the additional personnel sent to the CAOC to plan and execute the

---

[77] Discussion with CAOC staff members, Headquarters CENTAF, Shaw AFB, South Carolina, December 11, 2003.

[78] Discussion with CAOC staff members, December 11, 2003.

air campaign portion of Enduring Freedom did not integrate smoothly with the preexisting process.

To be sure, CENTAF's "Dash One" (modeled after standardized operating manuals for military aircraft) containing agreed and validated procedures for the CAOC was, at no less than 620 pages in length, perfectly reflective of what was called for as a manual for employing the CAOC as a weapon system. Yet with few exceptions, those procedures were not taught to or followed by the CAOC staff in the actual execution of Enduring Freedom. Many of the CAOC's high-technology systems went unused because assigned personnel were unfamiliar with their operation and functions. As a result, the daily process of generating the ATO was handled in a more primitive and manual way than it needed to be. That shortcoming did not present insurmountable problems for an operation like Enduring Freedom, with its relatively low daily sortie rate even at the height of activity. It would clearly have been unsatisfactory, however, in a higher-intensity air war like Operation Iraqi Freedom, which followed not long thereafter.[79]

Moreover, in Operation Enduring Freedom, the combined CAOC and Air Forces Forward (AFFOR) staffs were smaller than those for Allied Force in part because of the Saudi cap of 350 U.S. military personnel. That arbitrary and artificial limitation prevented the deployment of the fuller contingent of personnel who could have extracted more leverage from the CAOC's systems. After the busiest phase of the air war subsided in late December 2001, many of the semi-CAOC functions that had evolved at Prince Sultan Air Base began to migrate back to CENTCOM headquarters in Tampa, Florida. Accordingly, the CAOC at Prince Sultan Air Base did not meet the fullest promise of a CAOC as a true weapon system at any time during Enduring Freedom. Although General Wald affirmed that the Prince Sultan Air Base CAOC "actually [represented] the state of the art for command and control at the operational level of war," numerous discontinuities, jury-rigged arrangements, and ad hoc arrange-

---

[79] Discussion with CAOC staff members, December 11, 2003.

ments persisted. As a result, the CAOC remained inadequately configured for a major theater war. Its systems were outstanding, but they were not manned with enough properly trained and qualified personnel. For those reasons among others, said General Wald in hindsight, "we still have a long way to go before we can say with confidence that the CAOC is a weapon system."[80]

In sum, the high personnel tempo of Operation Enduring Freedom inescapably occasioned the sending of untrained personnel to the CAOC, which, in turn, inescapably undermined the continuity of the team that was already in place there. The CAOC's preexisting focus on supporting JTF-SWA for OSW also created a problem in that that focus was not fully meshed with standing CENTCOM policies and procedures for major theater wars. Incessant "reach-forward" demands for immediate information from the CAOC by CENTCOM staffers in Tampa drove an increased and arguably unnecessary requirement for additional CAOC manning. Furthermore, CENTCOM's landmark standard operating procedures that had been optimized for major theater wars were not used as templates for day-to-day OSW operations. It naturally followed, given the OSW template that was applied to Enduring Freedom, that they also were not used in that more important and high-stakes campaign. Of this major deficiency in the exploitation of an otherwise state-of-the-art facility, General Wald concluded: "If we expect CFACCs [Combined Force Air Component Commanders] to rely on reach-back for their stressing operational requirements, we need to clearly define the command relationships that spell out the level of control we want the CFACC to have," a process that "should be codified in an order of some sort so there are no mistakes in the heat of battle as to who works for whom."[81]

---

[80] Wald, "Enabling the PSAB CAOC Weapon System: Roadmap for the Future."

[81] Wald, "Enabling the PSAB CAOC Weapon System: Roadmap for the Future."

The Buildup at Manas

Not long after the terrorist attacks of September 11, 2001, U.S. military tent cities sprang up at 13 sites in nine countries from Bulgaria and Kuwait all the way to Uzbekistan and beyond. These new outposts eventually came to embrace more than 60,000 U.S. military personnel who supported hundreds of allied aircraft operating out of forward expeditionary airfields in those countries. In so doing, they greatly extended the preexisting U.S. overseas basing network and presence.[82]

Of the 13 new expeditionary airfields that were set up in the region by the Air Force, Manas airport in Kyrgyzstan was by far the most prominent and path-breaking. Situated near Bishkek, less than 1,000 miles north of Khandahar, it featured a 13,800-foot-long runway that had originally been built to accommodate Soviet long-range bombers. In a move that presaged the opening of a sustained intratheater airhead into Afghanistan, EUCOM on December 12 directed USAFE to deploy the 86th Contingency Response Group (CRG) based at Ramstein Air Base, Germany, to Manas after much prior diplomatic preparation and logistical planning. Immediately thereafter, the base's commander-to-be, Air Force Brigadier General Christopher Kelly, took a vanguard of 26 Air Force personnel into the badly rundown former Soviet Air Force base, whereupon members of his contingent from the 86th CRG established a preliminary tent city.

In the course of its diplomatic efforts to gain greater forward access in the early aftermath of the September 11 attacks, the Bush administration succeeded in negotiating a one-year status of forces agreement for the use of the base, which soon emerged as a key coalition facility for conducting CSAR, refueling, and strike operations. At first, the country's former Soviet air defense system, with its still-intact and functioning SAM and AAA inventory, presented a real and serious concern to U.S. planners. As elsewhere, zero risk was sought

---

[82] William M. Arkin, "U.S. Air Bases Forge Double-Edged Sword," *Los Angeles Times*, January 6, 2002.

for U.S. operations in Kyrgyzstan. As a result, the first few nights of U.S. aircrews gingerly entering and flying through Kyrgyz airspace en route to Manas proved highly reminiscent of flying "in the corridor" through Soviet-controlled airspace during the Berlin airlift of 1948–49. The Kyrgyz air traffic control bureaucracy was also very demanding and adamantly insisted on on-time arrivals.[83]

As these and other wrinkles were being ironed out, the 86th CRG worked overtime at opening up the Manas airport, which was renamed Peter Ganci Air Base after a New York City fireman who had perished during the WTC rescue effort on September 11. The allied footprint at Manas quickly reached 650 American and 250 French military personnel, with a final goal of 2,000 personnel in all. By May 2002, some 2,000 coalition military personnel were temporarily stationed at Manas, around half of whom were Americans.[84] Force protection was provided by allied security guards who patrolled a four-mile perimeter that surrounded the base.[85]

Manas supported operations by USAF C-130s and C-141s, French and Turkish tankers, commercial Boeing 747s and Russian An-225 heavy airlifters, and Marine F/A-18D and French Mirage 2000D strike fighters, the latter of which arrived just in time to provide air support to Operation Anaconda.[86] Three Norwegian-led C-130Hs also established a joint airlift presence at Manas consisting of Norwegian, Danish, and Dutch aircraft deployed to support both Enduring Freedom and the International Security Assistance Force in Afghanistan. Those three countries further announced an intention to send six Dutch, four Danish, and four Norwegian F-16 midlife-update (MLU) fighters to eventually replace the detachment of French Mirage 2000Ds that operated alongside U.S. combat aircraft at Manas. (The Netherlands also sent a KC-10 tanker and 30 person-

---

[83] Roundtable discussion with staff officers at Headquarters USAFE, Ramstein AB, Germany, September 25, 2002.

[84] John Hendren, "Beddown in Bishkek," *Air Force Magazine*, July 2002, pp. 57–60.

[85] John Hendren, "U.S. Base Looks a Lot Like Home," *Los Angeles Times*, April 4, 2002.

[86] Since the base only had available space on its taxiways for parking four C-5s or C-17s, overnight stays by those large aircraft types was discouraged.

nel to al Udeid Air Base in Qatar to bolster a U.S. tanker task force operating out of that facility in support of Enduring Freedom.)[87]

The Kyrgyz government warmly welcomed the economic and diplomatic benefits of the allied presence, suggesting that the United States may remain there on a low-profile basis for some time. The declared intent was for the United States to use its military presence at Manas as, among other things, a medium for flowing more than $40 million into the weak Kyrgyz economy. No permanent U.S. military presence is planned for Manas, but the airfield will remain available for allied operations on-call.

New Technology Applications

As in previous U.S. air campaigns since the end of the Cold War, Operation Enduring Freedom provided a live-fire setting in which to validate not only new concepts of operations but also a variety of new weapons and ISR technologies. To note some of the latter briefly, the various weapon innovations that were proof-tested in Afghanistan were led by the use of armed MQ-1 Predator UAVs already addressed in chapters above. The CIA's Predators reportedly began operating out of a base in Uzbekistan near the Afghan border long before the start of the campaign, despite Uzbek fears of an adverse Russian reaction were that fact to become public knowledge. That operation, which began in September 2000 and which reportedly had Osama bin Laden in its sights more than once, used Predators owned by the Air Force that had been loaned to the CIA.[88]

Several months earlier, the CIA had looked into arming its Predators with air-to-ground munitions and discovered along the way that General Jumper, then the commander of Air Combat Command, had already been tackling that problem. The CIA conse-

---

[87] Joris Jannsen Lok, "Europe Strengthens Support for Enduring Freedom," *Jane's Defense Weekly*, April 17, 2002.

[88] Neil King, Jr., and David S. Cloud, "A Year Before September 11, U.S. Drones Spotted bin Laden in His Camps, But Couldn't Shoot," *Wall Street Journal*, November 23, 2001.

quently brought its loaned Predators back to Indian Springs Auxiliary Airfield near Nellis AFB, Nevada, where the Air Force's Predator squadrons were based, to be equipped with Hellfire missiles using Air Force assistance. By August 2001, the armed Predators were ready for action. A debate subsequently arose concerning what to do next and who was in charge. The debate continued unresolved until the terrorist attacks of September 11, at which time the now-armed CIA Predators remained in the United States waiting to be returned to the theater.[89] The issue was reportedly settled in the early aftermath of September 11 by a memorandum of understanding between the Air Force and the CIA, later said by some to have been inadequate, whereby the CIA would be free to fire at a list of selected terrorist target categories and the military would retain responsibility for all other targets.[90] In all, more than 40 Hellfire missiles were eventually fired from CIA Predators during the course of the campaign.

The use of mountain cave hideouts by al Qaeda forces also provided an incentive for the rapid development of new earth-penetrator weapons. One such adaptation was the AGM-86D, an air-launched cruise missile with its nuclear warhead replaced by a slender, heavy conventional warhead. Another was a modified GBU-24 LGB called the advanced unitary penetrator offering twice the hard-target capability of its parent munition. It featured a long, slender centroid made of a heavy, hard alloy of nickel, cobalt, and steel, shielded by a conventional aluminum casing that stripped away as the munition hit the target. A related innovation was a computer-controlled hard-target smart fuse capable of distinguishing between rock, concrete, and soil as the weapon penetrated a buried target. That same fuse was similarly capable of counting off the number of ceilings or walls in a building as it approached the desired detonation point during penetration.

---

[89] King and Cloud.

[90] Judith Miller and Eric Schmitt, "Ugly Duckling Turns Out to Be Formidable in the Air," *New York Times*, November 23, 2001.

Another weapon development prompted by the unique needs of Enduring Freedom was the BLU-118B, a hard-target thermobaric device intended to create a high overpressure inside enemy tunnel hideouts.[91] Its penetrator body can be mated with the GBU-15, GBU-24, and AGM-130. Before being shipped to the theater, the weapon was tested with a GBU-24 in the Nellis range complex by the Air Force's 422nd Test and Evaluation Squadron in December 2001. It showed a longer burn time and greater overpressure potential than previous such munitions. Ten were provided to CENTCOM for potential use in Enduring Freedom.[92] The first and only one actually employed in the campaign was delivered at the start of Operation Anaconda by an F-15E against what General Myers called a "tactically significant" cave.[93] (A procedural error in the delivery caused the munition to land short, however, rendering it ineffective even though it detonated properly.)

In the category of ISR sensors and targeting aids, the Litening II infrared imaging and targeting pod, which was carried only by Air Force Reserve Command and Air National Guard F-16C+s because of prior service procurement decisions, allowed laser marking and laser spot tracking and was said to have all but eliminated the potential for misidentifying targets. It also contributed to minimizing the potential for collateral damage, unintended casualties, and fratricide when bombs were dropped close to friendly forces or enemy infrastructure. The system can acquire targets from an altitude as high as 40,000 feet, 15,000 feet higher than the maximum target-servicing range of the older LANTIRN targeting pod.[94] (Actually, the LANTIRN pod can acquire targets well above 25,000 feet, but its laser is software-inhibited above that altitude such that LGBs cannot be guided to their intended targets. Although the Litening pod is

---

[91] Andrew C. Revkin, "U.S. Making Weapons to Blast Underground Hideouts," *New York Times*, December 3, 2001.

[92] Frank Wolfe, "Thermobaric Weapons Shipped for Possible Use in Operation Enduring Freedom," *Defense Daily*, January 9, 2002.

[93] Loeb, "Afghan War Is a Lab for U.S. Innovation."

[94] Vernon Loeb, "Up in Arms," *Washington Post*, January 11, 2002.

slightly more effective than the LANTIRN pod in its infrared mode, it features, in addition, an electro-optical mode for daytime use that is a substantial improvement over the infrared mode. Moreover, beyond the laser marker and laser spot search-and-track capability offered by the Litening pod, the F-16C+ had a Situation Awareness Data Link, or SADL for short, that enabled very rapid digital communications between F-16s equipped with that capability.)[95]

In a related targeting improvement, the B-2's SAR showed its ability to improve the accuracy of the satellite-aided GBU-31 JDAM considerably, as it did previously during Operation Allied Force over Serbia and Kosovo. The difference between an aim point's uncorrected GPS location and its actual location can cause up to a 30-foot miss distance by a JDAM. To compensate and correct for this, the B-2 would fly an arc to generate a relative bearing change of at least 25 degrees between successive SAR readings for more precise target triangulation. As each SAR image was made, an automatic target re-designation algorithm updated the target location, allowing final miss distances against fixed targets of less than 10 feet from 40,000 feet.[96]

Operation Enduring Freedom also featured an increased use of MASINT (measurement and signature intelligence), such as foliage-penetrating radar sensors, hyperspectral imaging, and technologies enabling the tracking of pattern changes over time. Relatedly, aircraft-mounted infrared sensors that work best in cold weather were used to detect warmth escaping from tunnel and cave entrances from airborne platforms miles away. Scanners that can detect extremely weak magnetic fields emanating from metal equipment buried 100 feet or more underground and from electrical wiring used to provide lighting to tunnels were also used. Gravity-measuring instruments were used to search for underground bunkers.[97] The integration of Link 16 into the F-15E brought that aircraft into the fused mosaic of

---

[95] Comments on an earlier draft by Lieutenant Colonel Mark Cline, USAF, CENTAF A-3/DOXP, Shaw AFB, South Carolina, August 13, 2003.

[96] Andrew C. Revkin, "New Sensors Report, 'I Know They're In There, I Can See Them Breathing,'" *New York Times,* November 22, 2001.

[97] Revkin, "New Sensors Report, 'I Know They're In There, I Can See Them Breathing.'"

target information, as did the SADL system installed in the F-16C+. Finally, R&D efforts were accelerated in the areas of micro-drones, microwave antipersonnel guns that stun rather than maim or kill, and a nuclear quadropole resonance sensor that can detect bulk explosive materials in trucks and shipping containers. All were put to use in support of the global war on terror.[98]

It bears noting here that the RQ-1 Predator, one of the Defense Department's first ACTD efforts, was but one of 30 such products employed in Operations Enduring Freedom and Noble Eagle. This series of programs sometimes involved integrating off-the-shelf technologies with a platform like Predator and inserting new technology into an existing system to work emergent operational problems. It also included:

- The RQ-4 Global Hawk UAV
- An ACTD called adaptive joint planning offering automated planning tools and software for use in a unified command and its subordinate commands
- Unattended ground sensors
- A Link 16 product called Rosetta, which was used as a translator between data links, transmitting air and ground imagery and fusing them into a single picture
- An ACTD called the automated deep operations coordination system that establishes priorities among time-sensitive targets and that deconflicts and manages targeting in designated kill zones
- Personnel recovery mission software that gathers and integrates information used for CSAR, such as overhead imagery, personnel locator signals, and threat information.[99]

---

[98] Payton, "Fast-Tracking Innovative Technologies: DoD's ACTD Program Supports the War on Terrorism."

[99] Payton, "Fast-Tracking Innovative Technologies: DoD's ACTD Program Supports the War on Terrorism."

CHAPTER SEVEN
Problems in Execution

By every measure that matters, the first phase of Operation Enduring Freedom from October 7, 2001, through March 2002 was a resounding success as far as it went, considering that CENTCOM's combat involvement in Afghanistan continues as a lower-intensity counterinsurgency effort and that the allied struggle against residual Taliban forces attempting a rearguard comeback remains far from over. Never before in modern times had the United States fought an expeditionary war so far removed from its base structure. The tyranny of distance that dominated the campaign redefined the meaning of endurance in air warfare and was an unprecedented test of American combat flexibility. One B-2 sortie lasted 44.3 hours from takeoff to landing, becoming the longest-duration air combat mission flown in history. Similarly, an F-15E sortie lasted 15.5 hours to become the longest-duration fighter combat mission ever flown. It was not uncommon for fighter sorties to last 10 hours or more. Indeed, the war saw the longest-range carrier-based strike operations conducted in the history of naval air warfare. People rather than equipment constituted the main limiting factor in CENTCOM's ability to maintain a persistent combat presence over Afghanistan.

Beyond that, the United States commenced operations against the Taliban and al Qaeda from a standing start with less than a month's time to plan and marshal forces for the impending war. The campaign saw an unprecedented reliance on SOF, in which a unique synergy flowed from the unconventional enabling of precision air power by allied SOF and indigenous friendly ground forces. Each force element amplified the inherent leverage of the other, with SOF teams allowing air power to be effective against elusive targets and air power permitting allied SOF units to work more efficiently with opposition groups in close-quarters land combat against Taliban and al Qaeda forces in the initial phase with a complete absence of involvement by conventional U.S. ground forces. Apart from occasional instances of human error or mechanical failure, air-delivered laser-guided and satellite-aided munitions consistently went where they were directed to go, keeping unintended collateral damage to a tolerable minimum. The decision to rely on SOF units rather than on heavier conventional ground forces also greatly eased the logistics burden on CENTCOM.[1]

At the same time, Enduring Freedom was not without inefficiencies and friction points. Much as in the previous Operation Allied Force against Serbia, some severe shortcomings in target approval under tight time constraints were revealed.[2] Thanks to the revolution in global communications and ISR fusion described in the preceding chapter, sensor-to-shooter data cycle time (known more colloquially as the "kill chain") was reduced from hours—or even days—often to single-digit minutes. Yet an oversubscribed target-approval process often nullified the potential effects of that breakthrough by extending decision timelines, making the human factor rather than the command, control, communications, and computers (C4)/ISR system the principal rate-limiter.

Many of the problems in execution that were encountered by CENTCOM during Enduring Freedom, most notably those concerning rules of engagement, collateral damage avoidance, and target approval, were almost inseparably intertwined. However, they can be

---

[1] It is not clear whether it would have been possible for CENTCOM to insert and sustain a large U.S. ground presence into Afghanistan in any event, at least during the most pivotal early months, given the primitiveness of the country's airfield and logistics infrastructure and the fact that neither had been secured.

[2] For more on the many execution problems associated with Operation Allied Force, see Lambeth, *NATO's Air War for Kosovo: A Strategic and Operational Assessment*, especially pp. 101–218.

broken out for analytical purposes into three broadly discernible categories: (1) unusually tense intracommand relations within CENTCOM, particularly during the first two months of the war; (2) unusually restrictive rules of engagement that flowed from the highest levels of the U.S. government; and (3) a tendency toward both centralized adaptive planning and centralized execution of operations by CENTCOM that was made possible by the unprecedented worldwide sensor and communications connectivity, both horizontal and vertical, that dominated the role played by C4/ISR in the war. Other problems included a sometimes less-than-seamless integration of the CIA into combat operations and the burdens that the war's demands for personnel and equipment placed on combatant commanders in other theaters around the world.

Early Tensions Between the CAOC and CENTCOM

In some respects even more than during Operation Allied Force in 1999, tensions emerged almost from the war's very first moments between the CAOC at Prince Sultan Air Base in Saudi Arabia and the higher combatant command staff situated to the rear in Tampa, Florida. This difficult intracommand relationship, which the first air component commander for Enduring Freedom, then–Lieutenant General General Charles Wald, referred to discreetly as the "other dynamic," persisted for a time despite efforts on both sides to work out their various differences.[3] A variety of factors occasioned this discomfiting situation, not the least being the campaign's unprecedentedly exacting rules of engagement overlaid on a strategy that was unclear at the war's start and that evolved rapidly once combat operations against the Taliban and al Qaeda were under way. The first and most important causal factor, however, in the retrospective opinion of both air component commanders who oversaw the air war, was CENTCOM's selection of a suboptimal and inappropriate

---

[3] Conversation with Lieutenant General Charles F. Wald, USAF, Headquarters United States Air Force, Washington, D.C., May 15, 2002.

approach to the planning and conduct of air operations over Afghanistan.

Adopting the familiar repertoire to which it had been habituated for 10 years, CENTCOM elected to conduct Operation Enduring Freedom in the same manner and using roughly the same procedures as those of the very different and far more routinized Operation Southern Watch, the enforcement of the UN-imposed no-fly zone over southern Iraq.[4] In the latter operation, typically only one military response option, on average, was implemented each week, within a draconian rules-of-engagement environment in which the CAOC had to ask CENTCOM (and, on occasion, higher authority) for permission to do virtually *anything*. In contrast, Enduring Freedom was to be a full-fledged war against the Taliban and al Qaeda, in which one would expect that the goals, incentive structure, and operational imperatives would naturally be driven by the demands of a fight to the finish rather than by those of an international policing action. All the same, CENTCOM had become so accustomed to maintaining close control over the day-to-day operations of the CAOC that General Franks did not include General Wald in any of the initial planning decisions when he briefed Secretary Rumsfeld and General Myers on the air attack plan for the first night of Enduring Freedom.[5] It was entirely predictable that problems would develop in the conduct of Enduring Freedom once Tampa opted to impose onto the Afghan war a Southern Watch–like operations flow, with the latter's strict rules-of-engagement interpretation and SPINs and target vetting procedures, all dominated by heavy hands-on involvement by senior leadership that exhibited highly centralized control and execution.

---

[4] Conversations with Lieutenant General T. Michael Moseley, USAF, Nellis AFB, Nevada, August 8, 2002, and Lieutenant General Charles F. Wald, USAF, Headquarters United States Air Force, Washington, D.C., October 15, 2002.

[5] As the CAOC's director of combat plans at that time, Colonel Rick Anderson, recalled the essential facts on this point: "We [CENTAF] had no input to targets or strategy. All we were was a conduit to attack the targets that CENTCOM sent down to us. . . . That's against doctrine, but that is the way it happened. . . . We were the executor of a multi-thousand line MAAP." (Quoted in Davis, p. 36.)

When enforcing the no-fly zone was, in the words of Air Combat Command's Staff Judge Advocate, "literally the only game in town," the relatively genteel pace of that operation naturally allowed CENTCOM to insinuate itself over time into the most intimate details of daily Southern Watch operations, with recurrent grumbling but not much serious resistance by senior Air Force airmen.[6] There was no real harm done to the mission of JTF/SWA by this CENTCOM practice. Indeed, the latter arguably even provided a modest measure of value-added by way of imposing an extra layer of discipline and insurance against errors atop a continuing operation that entailed obvious political sensitivities. However, CENTCOM's subsequent tasking for Enduring Freedom came so suddenly and so forcefully that shifting rapidly from the unique and even almost familial JTF/SWA mode of operations into the more orthodox and doctrinally pure one that wartime circumstances required for Afghanistan proved to be extremely challenging to all concerned, to say the least.

That challenge was further exacerbated by the fact that by tradition and culture, CENTCOM was and remains an Army-styled organization that, given the nature of high-intensity land warfare, requires processes that are inherently more conservative and structured than those followed by airmen when there are large and potentially unwieldy formations on the ground at immediate risk. In light of that fact, a clash of professional cultures between the CENTCOM staff in Tampa and the air component headquartered eight time zones forward in the CAOC was all but inevitable, since time did not permit a collegial reconciliation of differing approaches before the start of Enduring Freedom. As a result, the visionary manner in which airmen in the CAOC wanted to use air power against the Taliban and al Qaeda, an approach to force employment that differed fundamentally from the template that CENTCOM had imprinted on the air component throughout the preceding decade of JTF/SWA, could not be readily

---

[6] Comments on an earlier draft by Brigadier General Charles J. Dunlap, Jr., USAF, Staff Judge Advocate, Air Combat Command, Langley AFB, Virginia, December 27, 2003.

absorbed in the compressed timeline dictated by operational exigencies.

Instead, even though Enduring Freedom was fated to be entirely different from Southern Watch in both its nature and its goals, CENTCOM's leaders almost reflexively opted to do what they knew best, despite the fact that Enduring Freedom was a new situation with demands that were in no way anticipated by any of CENTCOM's preexisting contingency plans. Interestingly, General Wald seemed to anticipate the Southern Watch template overlay problem more than a year *before* the terrorist attacks of September 11 when he commented, in an all-hands memorandum to CENTAF staff, that "although OSW is our daily focus, the specter of a larger conflict is ever-present in the background," requiring that CENTAF "as an air component must prepare for that likelihood. We do not have the luxury of rethinking a major OPLAN [operations plan] during execution."[7]

Beyond the fact that CENTCOM's leading air authorities believed that the command had approached the planning of Enduring Freedom with the wrong template to begin with, there were conflicting schools of thought within CENTCOM when it came to how best to conduct the war. On the one hand, there were those, mainly at CENTCOM headquarters in Tampa, whose principals believed that the insertion of a heavy ground-force presence into Afghanistan was an essential precondition for achieving decisive results.[8] On the other hand, there were those, mainly Air Force airmen in the CAOC, who believed that air power, in conjunction with SOF and indigenous Afghan ground forces, would suffice to achieve CENTCOM's declared objectives. This contrast in outlooks reflected, at bottom, a

---

[7] Lieutenant General Charles F. Wald, USAF, "Memorandum for All USCENTAF Personnel, Subject: Commander's Intent," Headquarters U.S. Central Command Air Forces, Shaw AFB, South Carolina, May 18, 2000.

[8] Comments on an earlier draft by Pat A. Pentland, Science Applications International Corporation (SAIC), May 28, 2003. In an anticipation of that possibility, Operation Bright Star was used by CENTCOM to take advantage of that scheduled U.S.-Egyptian combined annual training event to move a large number of U.S. ground combatants into the AOR. (Conversation with Lieutenant General Charles F. Wald, USAF, Headquarters United States Air Force, Washington, D.C., May 15, 2002.)

choice between a traditional attrition-oriented approach and what the CAOC's airmen held to be a more modern effects-based campaign. The more outspoken among the latter even went so far as to suggest that the attrition-based approach that was predominantly applied throughout Enduring Freedom actually hampered mission accomplishment and needlessly prolonged the campaign.[9] According to the CAOC director during the critical first six weeks of Enduring Freedom, Air Force Major General David Deptula, some of the friction between the CAOC and CENTCOM headquarters stemmed from the fact that CENTCOM's staffers, despite their avowed concerns to limit collateral damage as a first order of business, were directing weapon selections, fuse settings, and target-attack tactics that promised to be *more* destructive than necessary because those staffers had never before planned any action larger than those that defined OSW and accordingly were insufficiently appreciative of the potential of effects-based operations and what it took to accomplish them.[10]

There also were differing views within CENTCOM over the extent of destructiveness that should be sought by the air war as well as over the desired pace of operations. Those in the CAOC during the war's early days genuinely believed that they commanded a comparative edge in proximity to the action and in depth of air power expertise. They were convinced that they were the best equipped to determine the most appropriate force employment options at the operational and tactical levels. They further felt that many at CENTCOM headquarters were dominated by a ground-warfare view of the world that failed to appreciate what modern air power could accomplish if used to its fullest potential. "Reach forward," a phenomenon experienced in full flourish for the first time in Enduring Freedom, had crossed the bounds of reason, in their view, when those to the rear repeatedly acted as though they had a "better idea" for getting the most out of air power. Ultimately, within just hours of the

---

[9] Comments on an earlier draft by Major General David A. Deptula, USAF, Director of Plans and Programs, Air Combat Command, Langley AFB, Virginia, January 24, 2004.

[10] Comments on an earlier draft by Major General David A. Deptula.

start of Enduring Freedom, as one Air Force observer of this process suggested in hindsight, the relationship between the CAOC's leaders and their counterparts in Tampa degenerated into a situation in which "great Americans with strong views unfortunately tended to talk past each other at times."[11]

In one of the first signs of tension between the CAOC and CENTCOM headquarters, General Wald asked for a commitment of E-8 JSTARS aircraft to the buildup for the impending war only a day after the terrorist attacks of September 11, well before his departure for Saudi Arabia and the onset of serious planning for Enduring Freedom. He encountered repeated resistance early on from the CENTCOM staff, whose principals balked at first at deploying that aircraft to the theater.[12] No learning was said to have occurred with respect to the potential offered by JSTARS for locating and fixing enemy ground vehicles, even though the aircraft had performed superbly in that role in both Operations Desert Storm and Allied Force. In the end, JSTARS arrived in the war zone only late in November, after the heaviest part of the Enduring Freedom air war was nearly over. As but one suggestive indicator of the possible costs exacted by this delay, there were massive Taliban convoys that the E-8 could have detected. At least a few of those convoys may have been missed by the E-8's absence until too late. To be sure, standing rules of engagement emphasized the need for confirmation that the convoys were military, something that the sensors aboard the E-8 could not do on their own with sufficient confidence. Yet at the same time, one provision of the rules of engagement was that if allied aircraft drew enemy fire, they could drop bombs on the source of the fire in return. It took the Taliban more than a few days to figure that out. Nevertheless, the retreat of the Taliban from Mazar-i-Sharif to Kunduz could have been interdicted more effectively had the E-8 been avail-

---

[11] Comments on an earlier draft by an Air Force general who prefers to remain anonymous.

[12] Conversation with Lieutenant General Charles F. Wald, USAF, Headquarters United States Air Force, Washington, D.C., October 15, 2002.

able to the CAOC at the time. As it was, JSTARS arrived late to the fight and was never used to its fullest potential.[13]

For their part, some senior leaders at CENTCOM headquarters reportedly felt that the leading airmen in the CAOC were overly service-centric in their orientation and were seeking, in effect, to fight their own private air war.[14] Yet whatever the ultimate explanation for the intracommand tension may have been, it is a safe conclusion from the sources on which this assessment is based that those in the CAOC were striving to use air power to achieve the campaign's declared goals—such as a denial of enemy freedom to operate at will either on the ground or in the air—with the least possible expenditure of time, effort, and firepower, whereas most on the CENTCOM staff remained wedded instead to more attrition-oriented thinking that insisted on the confirmed physical destruction of all known and targetable enemy ground and air assets, irrespective of whether those assets presented any threat to CENTCOM's timely achievement of the campaign's objectives.

In a telling illustration of the practical effects of this difference in outlook, uncontested allied air control over Afghanistan was essentially established almost immediately after the initial attacks the first night of Enduring Freedom. Yet in assembling its after-action report, CENTCOM's intelligence staff in Tampa built a stoplight briefing chart of attacked targets, without CAOC input, that showed multiple "reds" indicating targets on which no BDA had been performed because of an absence of timely imagery that the intelligence staff's BDA rules required. CENTCOM's director of intelligence insisted

---

[13] Comments on an earlier draft by Major Charles Hogan, USAF, December 22, 2003. Major Hogan served in the CAOC after October 13, 2001, both in the ISR cell and on the operations floor. In fairness to CENTCOM, there was a serious constraint-based airlift prioritization issue in late September and early October, and even some Air Force staffers both at CENTCOM headquarters and in the CAOC felt that JSTARS would initially be of little practical value, given the mountainous Afghan terrain and the absence of a significant Taliban mechanized force. In hindsight, however, the main lesson to be learned here would seem to be to bring all the desired equipment items to begin with and send home those that turned out to be either unneeded or unhelpful.

[14] Comments on an earlier draft by Pat A. Pentland, SAIC, who contributed to the Air Force's Task Force Enduring Look assessment of Operation Enduring Freedom.

that he could confirm only five valid enemy aircraft kills on the ground because of insufficient BDA information on all other claimed kills. Red markers were accordingly assigned to the remaining claimed kills, even though no Taliban radars had emitted after the first hours of the campaign, no Taliban aircraft had been observed flying, and the Taliban SA-3 threat had been essentially neutralized, all of which gave CENTCOM de facto ownership of the sky above 15,000 feet from the campaign's very outset. The ensuing briefing was given to Secretary Rumsfeld, who understandably was discomfited by the image, misleading, as it turned out to be, of faltering progress in the air war that it conveyed. Nevertheless, acceptable confirmation of targets destroyed, a prerogative that was exclusively owned by CENTCOM, became the air campaign's sole measure of success for the next four days. In the prevailing CAOC view, the effect of that needlessly exacting BDA rule was to deny the very success of CENTCOM's air operations to date.[15] The desired effect, complete control of the air, had been readily achieved within the first hour—as attested by the fact that USAF and RAF E-3 AWACS aircraft began operating with high confidence inside Afghan airspace as early as the campaign's third night.[16] Yet Navy fighters and Air Force bombers were directed to attack the same air-defense-related targets again and again until CENTCOM's BDA requirement could be satisfied.[17] It was the opinion of those in the CAOC that the BDA process should seek more realistically to determine actual strike *effects* on enemy behavior rather than simply focus on observable physical damage to objects.

Instead, when questioned by General Franks as to the effectiveness of a given target attack, CENTCOM's director of intelligence would repeatedly answer that he did not have "total certainty" about

---

[15] Conversation with Lieutenant General Charles F. Wald, USAF, Headquarters United States Air Force, Washington, D.C., October 15, 2002.

[16] Comments on an earlier draft by Lieutenant Colonel Mark Cline, USAF, CENTAF A-3/DOXP, Shaw AFB, South Carolina, August 13, 2003.

[17] Conversation with Lieutenant General Charles F. Wald, USAF, Headquarters United States Air Force, Washington, D.C., October 15, 2002.

the attack's results.[18] That, in turn, occasioned a diversion of strike assets to reattack targets already written off by the CAOC as destroyed simply to satisfy the CENTCOM intelligence staff's BDA reporting requirements. The effect of this insistence on such certainty was reflected more than once when a just-attacked target was positively assessed by real-time Predator imagery as having been successfully engaged, only to be disallowed in the BDA accounting as a target destroyed until an ostensibly better source of information confirming that assessment could be provided. Franks later reported at the Air Force Association's 2002 Air Warfare Symposium that virtually the entire enemy early warning and air defense system had been taken down within two weeks.[19] Yet that system redefined the meaning of rudimentary. General Wald, for his part, remarked that all of the essentials of that takedown had been attended to within the air war's first 15 minutes and that too many subsequent sorties had been flown and costly precision munitions expended on further attacks against Taliban air defenses over the ensuing two weeks just to satisfy the CENTCOM intelligence directorate's's BDA requirements.[20]

Similarly, an often literal CENTCOM response to the Pentagon's ban, at White House direction, on "infrastructure" attacks sometimes hindered the CAOC's efforts to interdict roads. The argument given by CENTCOM was that all roads needed to be left intact, since incoming nongovernmental organizations would eventually require their use in connection with their humanitarian relief efforts. The problem, however, was that the category of "infrastructure" was so vaguely defined that it could be said to include virtually anything.[21]

---

[18] Thomas E. Ricks, "Target Approval Delays Cost Air Force Key Hits," *Washington Post,* November 18, 2001.

[19] Grier, "The Combination That Worked."

[20] Conversation with Lieutenant General Charles F. Wald, USAF, Headquarters USAF, Washington, D.C., October 15, 2002.

[21] Conversation with Lieutenant General T. Michael Moseley, USAF, Nellis AFB, Nevada, August 8, 2002.

All of this was further aggravated by the pronounced geographic separation between CENTCOM headquarters and the CAOC, a distance that covered eight time zones. As in Operation Allied Force and quite unlike the contrasting case of Desert Storm, the combatant commander and his air component commander were not collocated. On top of that, staff personnel at all levels were spread so far and wide that many often did not know exactly for whom they worked at any given moment. The conduct of the war relied heavily on a process called "reach-back," which entailed leaving many key command and support personnel behind at CENTCOM headquarters in Florida and relying on a massive communications pipeline to move information and orders from the rear-echelon headquarters to the CAOC in Saudi Arabia, from which the campaign's air operations were principally directed and controlled. Only this time, those wielding the approval authority were often asleep when the combat action was at its peak because of the time difference. Much the same as in Allied Force, VTCs often turned into daily staff meetings.

In addressing this dispersion of command elements, General Franks commented after the war ended that "the technology available to us here [in Tampa] allows us to do things we have never been able to do, and we wouldn't necessarily have that if we moved [the headquarters] forward."[22] That statement was certainly correct as far as it went, but it also may have entailed making a virtue of necessity, at least at the margins. To begin with, it was clear from the start that Secretary Rumsfeld was determined to maintain close control of the war process from Washington. In light of that, it was thought by some that General Franks had been kept in Tampa rather than deployed forward at least in part because the Bush administration did not want a high-visibility combatant commander in the war zone conducting press conferences like those staged by General Norman Schwarzkopf from Riyadh during Operation Desert Storm. Not only that, Franks himself was more than content to fulfill his combatant commander duties behind the scenes and was said by a former subor-

---

[22] Ron Martz, "From Tampa, Franks on Top of the War," *Atlanta Journal and Constitution,* April 18, 2002.

dinate to have felt that Schwarzkopf had "cut way too high a profile during the Gulf War."[23]

There also may have been something in the eleventh-hour deal that Rumsfeld struck with the Saudis for the use of the CAOC at Prince Sultan Air Base that prevented Franks from moving his headquarters to that venue from Tampa. Despite much public reporting that the Saudis were being helpful, the Saudi government in fact would not let General Franks activate and use his forward headquarters at Eskan Village, nor would they allow him to bring his headquarters into the CAOC. Furthermore, as recalled by CENTCOM's director of operations throughout Enduring Freedom, other Gulf state leaders were likewise reluctant to permit the beddown of a CENTCOM forward headquarters in their countries, either because they lacked suitable facilities, were preoccupied with major exercises (as was the case with Oman), or felt themselves vulnerable to Saudi economic and political pressure.[24] For all of these reasons, there was simply no usable forward headquarters in the war zone into which General Franks and his principal staff subordinates could have readily moved. On top of that, it was rightly believed by both CENTCOM and the Department of Defense that the loss of momentum that would have been occasioned by unplugging the CENTCOM staff from Tampa and reconnecting it a few weeks later at a more forward location would, in any case, have created an unacceptable gap in what turned out to be a short and intense planning cycle that demanded nearly daily interaction with the Joint Staff, Secretary Rumsfeld, and ultimately President Bush.[25]

Be that as it may, much counterproductive friction between the forward and rear components of CENTCOM nonetheless ensued from the resultant separation of command elements. In light of that, it seems reasonable to suggest in hindsight that in the absence of a

---

[23] Michael Duffy and Mark Thompson, "Straight Shooter," *Time*, March 17, 2003.

[24] Comments on an earlier draft by Lieutenant General Victor E. Renuart, USAF, Vice Commander, Pacific Air Forces, Hickam AFB, Hawaii, February 14, 2004.

[25] Comments on an earlier draft by Lieutenant General Victor E. Renuart.

suitable way for General Franks and his key subordinates to have deployed forward so as to have been more closely collocated with the air component commander around the clock, the latter could instead have been collocated with General Franks at CENTCOM headquarters and delegated the execution of CAOC functions to the CAOC director. Alternatively, had the air component commander been able to provide a senior general-officer representative at CENTCOM headquarters as his personal emissary to General Franks and had Franks done likewise in return, perhaps much of the early tension that occurred between the front and rear could have been alleviated— or prevented altogether.

Further compounding the tension within CENTCOM at the most senior staff level, the combatant commander's intent was sometimes less than crystal clear because it was not always communicated straightforwardly. General Franks himself fully understood the political and strategic imperatives of the campaign. Yet by the recollections not only of senior CAOC staffers but also of General Mikolashek, the land component commander, and General Hagenbeck, the commander of CJTF Mountain, it was his preferred leadership style not to deal with his component commanders directly as a rule but rather to interact with them through his principal subordinates, usually his deputy, Marine Corps Lieutenant General Michael DeLong.[26] That practice reportedly occasioned much selective interpretation by subordinate staffers of what they *thought* General Franks's intent was, as some of the more senior members stopped being staff officers and tried to become ersatz commanders, and as senior staff "translations" became de facto "guidance." Beyond that, there was an asymmetry of information that sometimes contributed indirectly to strained intra-CENTCOM command relations. For example, the CAOC never received some of the most important national-source intelligence con-

---

[26] The recollections of Generals Mikolashek and Hagenbeck are cited in Davis, p. 36. During the critical first 60 days of Enduring Freedom, General Franks was present at only around six of the daily component commander VTC meetings. (Comments on an earlier draft by Major General David A. Deptula, USAF, Director of Plans and Programs, Air Combat Command, Langley AFB, Virginia, January 24, 2004.)

trolled primarily by the CIA and National Security Agency, since those originating agencies refused to let that information go outside the continental United States. That meant that CENTCOM headquarters in Tampa often had a better all-source picture than did the CAOC. Those in the CAOC, for their part, were never aware of that because, by definition, they could not know what they did not know.[27] As a result, what was often thought to have been the "common operating picture" made possible by expanded global ISR and communications connectivity was, at least in some circumstances, only a *perception* of a common operating picture. For example, thanks to its comparative advantage in access to the most sensitive details of Operation Enduring Freedom, the CENTCOM staff had a better picture of covert SOF and CIA operations, whereas the CAOC, because of its closer proximity to the fight and its clear advantage in air power expertise, had a better picture of conventional SOF and air operations. This often produced a rivalry of sorts in which both those in the CAOC and those on the CENTCOM staff in Tampa each genuinely believed that they had the "best" operational picture when, in fact, they were frequently talking about different things.[28]

Moreover, the air component commander and his staff were isolated, sometimes to a discomfiting degree, not only from the CENTCOM mainstream but also from Washington. As a telling testament to this, as noted earlier in this chapter, CENTCOM's initial air operations plan (which essentially entailed the use of B-52s and TLAMs) was briefed to the JCS and Secretary of Defense, after which it went to the president, who approved it. General Wald, the air component commander at the time, provided no input into that plan and never saw it.[29] Later, in at least one instance Navy F/A-18s were cleared to drop ordnance by an outside authority, with General Wald remaining wholly out of the loop with respect to it and, in effect, not

---

[27] Comments on an earlier draft by Pat A. Pentland.

[28] Comments on an earlier draft by Major Charles Hogan.

[29] Conversation with Lieutenant General Charles F. Wald, USAF, Headquarters United States Air Force, Washington, D.C., October 15, 2002.

being entirely in command of his assigned airspace.[30] Largely because of the intra-CENTCOM command relations that ultimately prevailed, the air commander, at least during the initial weeks of Enduring Freedom, was denied the freedom to use the CAOC as it was designed to be used.

The most persistent and onerous thorn in the side of the CAOC's airmen during Enduring Freedom was the fact that the development of the Joint Integrated and Prioritized Target List (JIPTL) and all target selection were done at CENTCOM headquarters rather than within the CAOC itself, as had been the case in the vaunted "Black Hole" of then–Lieutenant General Charles Horner's air component throughout Operation Desert Storm. According to joint doctrine, the air component commander oversees a daily air tasking cycle that takes the combatant commander's intent and assigned rules of engagement as points of departure and proceeds through a systematic process beginning with strategy and measure-of-effectiveness input; moving next to guidance, apportionment, and target selection; then to MAAP creation; and finally to production, dissemination, and execution, segueing smoothly and naturally from that point into the next day's cycle, beginning anew with assessment and strategy input. Yet in the case of Enduring Freedom, far more in keeping with the flawed precedent of Operation Allied Force, a key element of this cycle was preempted by CENTCOM—to such an extent that the air component had only *one* targeteer at a time working on the JIPTL alongside CENTCOM's targeteers.

More to the point, the CAOC's daily strategy input did not go directly to the air component commander and to the guidance and apportionment cell within the CAOC, as joint doctrine and practice would normally direct, but rather to General Franks, whose staff handed it off to CENTCOM intelligence in Tampa, where the JIPTL for the day's operations was built and then forwarded to the CAOC as the planning basis for the next day's MAAP. This selection process was chaired by CENTCOM's director of operations, but

---

[30] Conversation with Lieutenant General Charles F. Wald.

the director of intelligence all too often was the driving force. Weaponeering also was done in Tampa rather than in the CAOC. To support it, CENTCOM's Joint Intelligence Center commandeered all of the air component's targeteers who ordinarily would have been in the CAOC, running the number of targeteers at CENTCOM up from 600 to 1,200—which, if it was going to produce the daily JIPTL, it genuinely needed.[31]

In addition, a Saudi-imposed manning cap precluded the full CAOC staffing that would have been required to run the target development and JIPTL processes. One plausible solution to this problem would have been to have the responsibility for the daily JIPTL process assigned to the CAOC, yet with the latter's strategy and guidance, apportionment, and targeting cells collocated either with the air component commander himself or with his appointed senior representative back in Tampa at CENTCOM headquarters—all the more so considering that CENTCOM had direct access to the national intelligence community and to rapidly changing White House and Pentagon guidance. Because so little prewar study of Afghanistan had been accomplished, the target development process would have been slow even in the best of circumstances. That said, under the alternative arrangement sketched out above, the JIPTL and MAAP processes could have been moved forward in a way that both worked and engaged the participation of the air component commander directly, even if it offered less than an optimal solution. Moreover, CENTCOM could have retained the prerogative of producing the Joint Target List (JTL), the No-Strike List (NSL), and the Restricted Target List (RTL), leaving it to the CAOC to produce the JIPTL for all targets on the approved JTL based on CENTCOM's strategy and guidance for the day. As it was, the preemption of the JIPTL's daily development by CENTCOM took the strategy-to-task process out of the air component commander's hands, making the CAOC planning staff little more than mission schedulers, to all intents and purposes, while their operations counterparts on the floor did good execution

---

[31] Conversation with then–Brigadier General Robert Elder, USAF, Vice Commander, U.S. Central Command Air Forces, Maxwell AFB, Alabama, August 14, 2002.

work.[32] In those circumstances, it is hardly surprising that the CAOC staff felt so frustrated by the extent of oversight imposed by their superiors at CENTCOM headquarters back in Tampa.[33] In a candid expression of this frustration, the first CAOC director, Major General Deptula, commented shortly after his return to Washington in late November 2001: "You have an Army one-star J-2 [director of intelligence] and an Army one-star deputy J-2 and an Army 0-6 [colonel] assistant deputy, who is an Army engineer on his first tour in intelligence, back at CENTCOM doing target selection and DMPI selection and weapon selection, in some cases, until we told them: 'Hey, you've got to stop doing this.' Micromanagement is not the right word to describe what went on. It was ten times worse, and that significantly inhibited the campaign's effectiveness."[34]

On this bone of contention, General Wald later commented that it was his personal belief that during the first few weeks of the air war, "because of a lack of understanding of what we could do [in the CAOC], we lost opportunities that . . . kept us in Afghanistan overtime, longer than we would have had to be. And that's a tragedy. I

---

[32] Conversation with Lieutenant Colonel Mark Cline, USAF, CENTAF A-3/DOXP, at Nellis AFB, Nevada, July 8, 2003. This is not, to be sure, to denigrate the continued difficulty of creating the daily MAAP, which remained a complex and labor-intensive task in its own right.

[33] In his memoirs published nearly three years later, General Franks made only one passing allusion to these tensions, in reference to what he described as "the unpleasant news" that three designated Taliban and al Qaeda targets—a helicopter pad from which the Taliban flew their few airworthy Mi-8s, an airstrip long enough to handle twin-engine Soviet-era An-26 turboprops, and a bunker complex—had not been hit during the first night's air attacks. When informed of this, Franks said: "Furious, I called [Major General] Gene Renuart and [Lieutenant General] Rifle DeLong aside. Keeping my voice even, I made my point. 'Pass this on to Chuck Wald in the CAOC. In the future, pay attention to *my* priorities—priorities based on the needs of the joint team, not the desire of a single service.'" (Franks, p. 288, emphasis in the original.) Why it would have been in the interest of a "single service" (plainly the Air Force, in this case) not to have attacked those targets as directed by CENTCOM was left unanswered by Franks. However, his comment bore ample witness to his inclination to interact with his component commanders through his staff rather than directly.

[34] Conversation with General Deptula at Headquarters United States Air Force, Washington, D.C., November 23, 2001.

think some day that will all come out."[35] Yet as valid as that lament may have been as far as it went, the fact remains that there will *always* be the potential for tense intracommand and interservice relations at the most senior leadership levels simply by virtue of the fact that the top echelons of military organizations are populated by smart, strong-willed, and opinionated people. The core leadership challenge here lies in managing such perennial tensions. They do not seem to have been managed optimally during the initial weeks of Enduring Freedom. They began to be eased perceptibly, however, once the campaign finally hit its stride.

The Impact of Rules-of-Engagement Constraints

Operation Enduring Freedom also set a new record for strict rules of engagement and target-approval criteria, even compared to the also heavily rule-governed Operation Allied Force that preceded it in 1999, despite much prewar expectation that "the gloves would finally come off this time" thanks to the unprecedented heinousness of the September 11 terrorist attacks against the United States.[36] When the bombing first began, Secretary Rumsfeld retained the right to give final approval for attacks on any and all targets deemed to be "sensitive." Such targets were defined and specified in a set of rules of engagement called Serial One issued by the JCS chairman on October 6, 2001. They included a category labeled "infrastructure," which embraced electrical power, roads, and "industry," such as it was in Afghanistan, as well as any targets associated with the Taliban leadership on which an attack could be said to have "political implica-

---

[35] Lieutenant General Charles F. Wald, USAF, Deputy Chief of Staff for Air and Space Operations, Headquarters United States Air Force, quoted in John T. Correll, "Verbatim," *Air Force Magazine*, August 2002, p. 9.

[36] By "rules of engagement," the discussion here refers not simply to the formal written rules themselves, but rather more to a generic amalgam of rules of engagement, special instructions, laws of armed conflict, targeteering and weaponeering guidance, commander's intent, and related mandated constraints on the use of force.

tions."[37] Attacks on mosques were banned, even if a mosque was known to house enemy military personnel.

By the end of the campaign's second day, it was decided that this approval arrangement was unworkable, whereupon approval authority over most so-called sensitive targets was delegated to General Franks. The rules still stipulated, however, that no target classed as "significant," namely, one that involved any chance of causing a collateral damage incident, could be delegated to the air component commander for his approval but rather had to be approved by either CENTCOM or Washington.[38] That often meant waking people up in the middle of the night to secure a go or no-go decision, since CENTCOM headquarters and the Pentagon were eight hours behind the CAOC in Saudi Arabia—one more reason why CENTCOM was more comfortable holding the JIPTL process in Tampa.

Once allied SOF teams were finally on the ground in Afghanistan and the campaign had shifted from attacking fixed targets to engaging emerging time-sensitive targets, the rules of engagement required that at least one SOF team member have eyes on the target before the target could be struck, with no slack allowed for presumptions or blind judgment calls. A second SOF team member also was required to double-check and confirm all target coordinates before they were passed to the assigned strike aircraft.[39] Later in November, General Franks received permission to delegate sensitive-target approval authority yet a further step downward to his director of operations at CENTCOM headquarters. Such approval authority, however, was never delegated to the air component commander at any time during the campaign.

From the first night onward, the exceptional stringency of the target vetting process led to a target approval bottleneck at CENTCOM that allowed a number of fleeting attack opportunities

---

[37] William M. Arkin, "The Rules of Engagement," *Washington Post*, April 21, 2002.

[38] Arkin, "The Rules of Engagement."

[39] Kirk Spitzer, "Green Berets Outfought, Outthought the Taliban," *USA Today*, January 7, 2002.

to slip away. To cite a particularly notable case in point, during the campaign's opening night on October 7, 2001, a CIA-operated MQ-1 Predator UAV armed with Hellfire missiles observed a column of vehicles leaving a known Taliban compound near the Kandahar airport. The column was so long that intelligence experts in the CAOC thought that it might contain top Taliban or al Qaeda leaders. The convoy made its way into Kandahar and stopped in front of what one expert saw as a mosque and another saw as a private residence. Mullah Omar himself was thought by some to have been observed disembarking from the lead vehicle.[40] At that point, the Predator had the presumed Omar in its targeting cursor, and a prompt attack on the convoy was requested by the CAOC.

General Franks was reportedly inclined to approve pulling the trigger based on the live Predator video imagery alone. However, he demurred after his Judge Advocate General (JAG) suggested that the column might be an enemy ruse to create a collateral damage incident, voiced concern about the rules of engagement, and pointed to the potential danger of killing innocent Afghan civilians.[41] The standing rule in such an event was for the CAOC to secure approval to attack not only from General Franks but also from Washington. A call accordingly went from CENTCOM headquarters to the Pentagon. Secretary Rumsfeld immediately approved the attack and called the president to alert him of it. By the time Rumsfeld's approval was secured, however, the would-be Omar had disappeared from the scene. The Predator fired a Hellfire at those who remained, to no

---

[40] Michael R. Gordon and Tim Weiner, "Taliban Leader Is Target in U.S. Air Campaign," *New York Times*, October 16, 2001, and Thomas E. Ricks, "U.S. Arms Unmanned Aircraft," *Washington Post*, October 18, 2001. The Hellfire missile had been test-fired for the first time only the previous February. It was launched from a Predator at Indian Springs Auxiliary Air Field near Nellis AFB, Nevada, the home of the Air Force's Predator squadrons. The aircraft had been fitted with a laser designator that illuminated the target and enabled the Hellfire to guide on it. Of 16 Hellfires fired in this test, 12 scored direct hits on old tank carcasses. ("Send in the Drones," *The Economist*, November 10, 2001, p. 73.)

[41] Gordon and Weiner, "Taliban Is Target in U.S. Air Campaign," Vernon Loeb, "U.S. Intensifies Airstrikes on Taliban," *Washington Post*, October 16, 2001, and Richard J. Newman, "The Little Predator That Could," *Air Force Magazine*, March 2002, p. 53.

apparent strategic effect.[42] Secretary Rumsfeld was said to have been highly displeased upon learning of that possible lost opportunity.[43]

Later in October, CENTCOM reportedly lost another fleeting opportunity to kill hundreds of Taliban combatants in one stroke as a result of a last-minute change in assigned DMPI placement. The CAOC's plan was to drop a single 15,000-lb BLU-82 daisy cutter from an AC-130 onto a concentration of enemy forces that had moved into a civilian neighborhood and turned its buildings into a bivouac area. During his final approach to the target, however, the AC-130 pilot was given new coordinates for an impact point where "no confirmed Taliban existed," according to one official. Critics later charged that the intended detonation point had been changed as the result of an order from Washington driven by concern over the possibility of killing civilians, even though the original intended target had been studied for days beforehand and confirmed to be wholly military in nature.[44]

In yet another case in connection with the battle for Mazar-i-Sharif, a convoy of 1,500 estimated enemy combatants was detected. General Franks granted approval for the CAOC to attack the convoy if it could be positively shown to consist solely of enemy military personnel. On closer inspection, it turned out to number only 500 people, and it could not be determined whether they were uniformly enemy forces.[45] They eventually dispersed. In all, the CAOC reportedly had top Taliban and al Qaeda leaders in the cursor as many as 10 times during the war's first six weeks but could never get a sufficiently timely clearance from CENTCOM to attack them. As one senior Air Force officer later remarked, "we knew we had some of the big boys.

---

[42] Miller and Schmitt.

[43] J. Michael Waller, "Rumsfeld: Plagues of Biblical Job," *Insight Magazine*, December 10, 2001.

[44] Rowan Scarborough, "Change of Target Saved Hundreds of Taliban Soldiers," *Washington Times*, November 21, 2001.

[45] Conversation with Lieutenant General T. Michael Moseley, USAF, Nellis AFB, Nevada, August 8, 2002.

The process [was] so slow that by the time we got the clearances and everybody put in their two cents, we called it off."[46]

The repeated escape of Taliban and al Qaeda leaders as a result of delays in securing target approval was a consequence not so much of rules that had been imposed from above by Washington but more directly of a cumbersome target vetting process *within* CENTCOM that had been fashioned after the one used in OSW, with which CENTCOM was both familiar and comfortable, instead of being tailored to meet the different and more high-stakes demands of the global war on terror. That process was dominated by an overwhelming determination to avoid causing even a single civilian casualty. According to one CAOC staffer, any target that could create even one noncombatant casualty if attacked with less than perfect precision and discrimination had to be briefed first to CENTCOM by the CAOC and then reviewed by General Franks. That requirement entailed a time-consuming process of briefing preparation that often undermined the effectiveness of the CAOC's air effort.[47]

In an instructive example of this concern, the opposition warlord General Dostum learned during the battle for Mazar-i-Sharif that a former house of his in the area had since been commandeered by the Taliban and was being used as a headquarters by the regional Taliban commander. A Predator located the house and provided the necessary targeting information, after which an attack aircraft could have been called in to destroy it within minutes. CENTCOM's intelligence director, however, insisted on a second-source confirmation that it was the right house, so he faxed overhead photographs of the proposed target to the theater to be taken to Dostum himself for con-

---

[46] Ricks, "Target Approval Delays Cost Air Force Key Hits."

[47] Comments on an earlier draft by Major Charles Hogan, USAF, December 22, 2003. It bears adding here that targets throughout Enduring Freedom were weaponeered not for assured destruction but to avoid collateral damage. For example, if a 2,000-lb bomb was deemed necessary to achieve 30-percent destruction of a building yet was assessed by CENTCOM to be too large for collateral-damage reasons, the CAOC would have to revert to a smaller bomb. In this major culture change from the way weaponeering has traditionally been done, the weapon was selected not for its desired effect but rather to honor collateral-damage considerations.

firmation. Those photographs were not delivered to Dostum until three days later. Dostum confirmed that the photographs were indeed of his former house. By that time, however, the Taliban command unit had already moved on.[48] In another reported instance, SOF units on the ground were required to get CENTCOM approval before firing directly on fleeing enemy combatants in Tora Bora by first describing how many personnel were involved, which way they were moving, and why they were suspected to be al Qaeda.[49] (It might be noted in passing here that in addition to the stringent rules of engagement, an entirely sensible edict from an operator's perspective was that all missions be flown such that there be virtually *no* chance of U.S. aircrews being taken by the enemy, since it was clear to all from the outset that any captured Americans would be tortured and killed. Because the consequences of failure in that regard were prohibitively high, combat missions were flown very conservatively in the presence of known or presumed enemy air defenses.)[50]

Not surprisingly, many airmen complained bitterly about the seeming stranglehold imposed by the rules of engagement, CENTCOM's unwaveringly strict constructionism in interpreting them, and what the latter was doing to prolong target approval times. General Wald raised the issue within CENTCOM channels more than a dozen times after the campaign commenced, not only to no avail but without even getting a response.[51] In the midst of it all, an

---

[48] Richard J. Newman, "From Up in the Sky," *U.S. News and World Report*, February 25, 2002, p. 19. In fairness to CENTCOM, Dostum had, on several occasions, sought to use U.S. air power to settle scores with rival warlords. In several instances, the air liaison officer to JSOTF North discovered that Dostum was trying to call in air strikes on other Northern Alliance tribal chiefs who happened to be collocated with U.S. Army Special Forces A-Teams. For that reason, he was considered to be highly untrustworthy, and CENTCOM's leaders were reluctant to hit targets that had been unilaterally nominated by him. That said, a three-day turnaround time to make good on the CAOC's target-approval request was excessive by any measure, given today's global communications connectivity.

[49] Newman, "From Up in the Sky,"

[50] Conversation with Lieutenant General T. Michael Moseley, USAF, Nellis AFB, Nevada, August 8, 2002.

[51] Conversation with Lieutenant General Charles F. Wald, USAF, Headquarters United States Air Force, Washington, D.C., October 15, 2002.

active-duty four-star general spoke openly of micromanagement of the war by the Pentagon's most senior civilians, calling the war's execution "military amateur hour. The worst thing is the lack of trust at the senior leadership level."[52] This perception of a return to seeming Vietnam-era practices, what another unnamed senior officer derisively called "back to the future," was without question a case of close control from the rear, even more so in terms of restrictiveness than was the case throughout the Vietnam War in most respects. It suggested that senior leadership involvement and organizational caution had now become the main sources of drag and delay in time-sensitive targeting.

There also was an allied overlay when it came to constraints on force employment. In particular, U.S. aircraft that were based in the United Kingdom operated under more restrictive rules than did U.S. aircraft based elsewhere. The British government insisted on approving any target nominated for attack by U.S. bombers operating out of Britain's island protectorate of Diego Garcia in the Indian Ocean. Its approvals—or, more to the point, disapprovals—at times came so late as to cause major ripples in the ATO. In addition, the British on more than one occasion wielded a "red card" against proposed time-sensitive leadership target attacks by U.S. aircraft that had just refueled from an RAF tanker. To be sure, approval authority for some targets over which the United Kingdom exercised control was delegated to the senior three-star British military representative to CENTCOM, RAF Air Marshal Jock Stirrup. Few such targets were so delegated at the outset, however, and Air Marshal Stirrup frequently had to consult with the attorney general at the British Ministry of Defense before he could grant approval for targets scheduled for attack by USAF bombers operating out of Diego Garcia. The time difference between Tampa and London was a key factor in precipitating an eventual change in this practice, as London officials

---

[52] Arkin, "The Rules of Engagement."

finally tired of being awakened at 0400 and ultimately agreed to delegate expanded approval authority to Stirrup.[53]

Some such complaints about the rules of engagement and about target-approval restrictions appeared to be well founded. There is no question, for example, that some sources of friction and delay in the target-approval process, such as the heavy JAG and other senior rear-echelon staff involvement, were occasioned by CENTCOM's conscious choice of an OSW template for conducting Enduring Freedom, with all of that template's preexisting target vetting and approval procedures. Among other things, the approval delays eventually made it necessary for SOF troops to hunt down enemy leaders on the ground who might have been killed earlier by air attacks had such strikes been authorized in a sufficiently timely manner. The effect of those delays was undeniably to prolong the campaign.

At the same time, it is important for critics of this process to understand where the rules of engagement came from and what considerations underlay them. The fact is that they emanated from the highest level of the U.S. government and were anything but arbitrary. On the contrary, President Bush was personally determined to avoid any untoward occurrence in Operation Enduring Freedom that might even remotely suggest that the campaign was an indiscriminate war against the Afghan people or against Islam. That determination led to a political requirement for a minimally destructive air campaign using force-employment tactics that would not risk alienating the Afghan rank and file, further damaging an already weak Afghan economy and infrastructure, and inflaming popular passions elsewhere in the Arab world. For that reason, infrastructure targets were expressly excluded from attack. Moreover, a relentless effort was made in target assessment to ensure that the amount and type of force employed was proportionate to the target's value.

In addition to that, there was the paramount need to maintain a rules-of-engagement regime keyed to the avoidance of inadvertent fratricide, given the persistent difficulty of distinguishing Northern

---

[53] Conversation with Air Marshal Sir Jock Stirrup, RAF, senior British military representative to CENTCOM, Whitehall, London, England, July 23, 2002.

Alliance, SOF, and other friendly personnel on the ground from the enemy. These and related constraints were accurately characterized by CENTCOM's director of operations as having been as exacting as any in the history of warfare.[54] Yet at the same time, to give credit where due, American airmen had long since become accustomed to operating within highly restrictive rules of engagement both during Operation Allied Force and throughout 10 years of Operations Northern and Southern Watch. Those rules were not only well understood but also fully appreciated and embraced by the leaders and senior staff in the CAOC. The problem was never with the rules of engagement themselves, which those in the CAOC readily accepted as legitimate and appropriate, so much as with the fact that decisions about their application were not delegated to the air component in accordance with joint doctrine and practice.

In light of the president's personal concerns in this respect, however, Secretary Rumsfeld was the de facto combatant commander, to all intents and purposes, when it came to the most important decisions about how the war would be conducted. Rumsfeld later admitted freely that he had become deeply involved in the target-approval and rules-of-engagement generation processes. He spoke with General Franks so many times each day that some saw him as running the war himself from his office in the Pentagon. As Rumsfeld put it: "In the early part of an activity, particularly an activity that's not a set piece, which this certainly wasn't, there's no road map. We were figuring out what we ought to do." That resulted in interaction between himself and Franks that he characterized as "extensive."[55]

As reflections of that extensive top-down leadership involvement, an internal Pentagon memorandum noted that certain target attacks or specific weapon uses might be prohibited "so as not to needlessly shame or antagonize the enemy, tilt allied or U.S. public

---

[54] Conversation with Major General Victor E. Renuart, USAF, CENTCOM J-3, Washington, D.C., September 5, 2003.

[55] Ricks, "Rumsfeld's Hands-On War."

opinion in a particular direction, or escalate hostilities."[56] The rules of engagement were also shaped, as noted above, by a common-sense determination to avoid telegraphing any impression that the United States was at war with Islam as a whole, as opposed to the Taliban dictatorship and the al Qaeda terrorist network that it was harboring. No less valid was the concern at CENTCOM and in Washington that destroying Afghan infrastructure would hinder postwar reconstruction and add needlessly to civilian suffering. Toward that end, collateral damage mitigation procedures were not made up arbitrarily at CENTCOM but rather came straight from the most pertinent Joint Munitions Effectiveness Manuals (JMEMs). Also, CENTCOM had ready access to the Joint Warfare Analysis Center and its ability to provide weaponeering support as necessary to prevent collateral damage against the most sensitive targets.[57]

A notable problem here, however, was that the methodology used by CENTCOM for collateral damage expectancy (CDE) assessment itself was inadequate. It was based on damage rings that CENTCOM had "validated" over the course of its 11-year experience of bombing targets in Iraq in OSW. Each munition and weapon weight class had a circle associated with it, starting in the high hundreds of feet and scaled down based on CENTCOM's interpretation of the JMEM fragmentation manual's delivery accuracy ascribed to each weapon. The process did not allow for bomb burial, delayed fusing, or shielding, whereby terrain or an object would block the fragmentation pattern. It also often did not allow common sense to be applied. For example, one proposed target compound had multiple buildings closely backed up against one another around the four sides, with a mosque situated in the middle. CENTCOM's proffered solution was a 500-lb bomb, which would have required a LGB, since 500-lb JDAMs were not yet available. The CAOC had argued for a delayed-fused 2,000-lb JDAM out of a conviction that there was a greater chance for collateral damage with an LGB because of either

---

[56] Arkin, "The Rules of Engagement."

[57] Comments on an earlier draft by Pat A. Pentland.

aircrew error or a weapon "no-guide." Moreover, most Afghan buildings were inside walled compounds. CAOC staffers watched with interest as CENTCOM's rings were placed on desired targets and the fragmentation rings fell outside the targeted compounds. Yet, as anticipated, poststrike BDA would repeatedly show that the compounds' walls had absorbed all of the weapon fragmentation, leaving the buildings in the adjoining walled compound undamaged. It was this sort of inflexible application of an inadequate CDE methodology that understandably discomfited the CAOC's air warfare professionals. Moreover, it appeared in the CAOC as though many at CENTCOM had forgotten that attacking a high CDE target in a situation of bona fide military necessity was well within the laws of armed conflict and that the call to do so was properly a commander's call, not a staff's or a JAG's call.[58] In fact, as discomfiting as some of those calls may have been to the CAOC's airmen, they were invariably made by General Franks rather than by any of his staff advisers. It also is pertinent here that Enduring Freedom was the first combat experience of the new Bush administration. As such, its most senior leaders from the president on down were learning some important lessons with regard to the benefits and pitfalls of centralized execution that were taken to heart and applied to good effect in Operation Iraqi Freedom a year later.[59]

In and of itself, the exacting rules-of-engagement regime that was imposed on the Pentagon and on CENTCOM by the White House from the very start of Enduring Freedom was entirely warranted by the situation, considering the possibility that the effort could have been completely derailed had those rules not been assiduously followed. To cite but one case in point, significant attacks against Afghan infrastructure and a high incidence of civilian fatalities could easily have caused Pakistan to withdraw its support for the war, thus denying the United States the use of Pakistani airspace and pos-

---

[58] Comments on an earlier draft by Lieutenant Colonel Mark Cline, USAF, CENTAF A-3/DOXP, Shaw AFB, South Carolina, August 13, 2003.

[59] Comments on an earlier draft by Lieutenant General Victor E. Renuart, USAF, Vice Commander, Pacific Air Forces, Hickam AFB, Hawaii, February 14, 2004.

sibly sparking a popular anti-American uprising. They also could have caused other Gulf states to withdraw their approval for the stationing of U.S. support assets in those countries. Either development could have been an Enduring Freedom show-stopper.

At issue here is not whether the restrictions applied by the Bush administration were appropriate in and of themselves but rather whether their enforcement necessarily required the slow and inefficient target-approval process that ultimately was developed and used by CENTCOM. For one thing, although CENTCOM's CDE rings were easy enough to apply to a potential target if an adequate image of the target was available, there was an inevitable and unavoidable sensor-to-shooter delay if an image of the proposed target had to be located and acquired. Beyond that, rampant concern at the highest levels over even an outside chance of causing collateral damage arguably led to an excess of caution at lower CENTCOM echelons, where legal advisers would appear to play devil's advocate with every proposed time-sensitive target. Sometimes concern about causing collateral damage was the *only* factor occasioning a no-strike decision. In some cases that concern may have emanated not from direct command guidance but merely from a tendency for each subordinate level down the chain of command to interpret its guidance and to overlay the approval process with additional safety firewalls.

To cite a telling example, Air Force generals and other military lawyers in the Enduring Freedom loop reported that CENTCOM's JAG hesitated to recommend attacking the convoy believed to be transporting Omar on the first night of the war in part because the Geneva Convention prohibits government-sponsored assassinations and because Omar could be considered a "foreign leader." Pentagon rules further stipulated that any weapon slated for use must first be deemed not "unnecessarily cruel" or able to cause "disproportionate damage," and the Hellfire missile carried by the CIA's armed Predator had not previously been vetted by CENTCOM's legal staff for use as a weapon.[60] It is entirely fair to ask why these kinds of issues

---

[60] Esther Schrader, "War, on Advice of Counsel," *Los Angeles Times*, February 15, 2002.

and concerns were not duly identified and resolved during the three weeks of preparation before the first bomb was dropped.

As it turned out, in what amounted to preemptive surrender to the darkest interpretation of the rules of engagement, the approach followed by CENTCOM led to a tendency on the part of CAOC staffers to be gun-shy in proposing targets out of anticipatory fear of CENTCOM disapproval on grounds of collateral damage sensitivities. This tendency forced General Wald almost every day during his six weeks as air component commander to remind the CAOC staff of what the campaign was ultimately about: "We're here because of dead Americans."[61] All the same, thanks to their overriding sensitivity to collateral damage, however legitimate and proper in and of itself, CENTCOM and its Pentagon and White House superiors did themselves out of many lucrative attack options, such as interdicting moving vehicles, because of the power that that sensitivity conferred on overly cautious implementers at lower levels to invoke such considerations as a nearby civilian structure or the inability to see inside a truck as excuses for disapproving a requested target attack. At times, matters got to a point where mission accomplishment took a back seat to collateral damage avoidance. As one Air Force officer rightly noted in this regard, when CAOC leaders and staff knew beforehand that every reported incident would be autopsied to the last verifiable detail, collateral damage avoidance became not just an important planning consideration but "the first thing people [thought] about."[62]

Clearly it is the rightful prerogative of national leaders to impose collateral damage constraints in the interest of achieving broad objectives and avoiding undesirable turns of events. But those leaders must be mindful of the consequences that their choices can produce. Although President Bush and Secretary Rumsfeld had made running down Taliban and al Qaeda leaders a top campaign priority, inordinate delays in target approval at lower levels were nonetheless allowed

---

[61] William M. Arkin, "Fear of Civilian Deaths May Have Undermined Effort," *Los Angeles Times*, January 16, 2002.

[62] Arkin, "Fear of Civilian Deaths May Have Undermined Effort."

to occur. There was a tendency at all levels to forget that information on time-sensitive targets is highly perishable and often must be acted on within minutes to produce desired results. Beyond that, part of the slowness in target approval was often because senior leaders, both military and civilian, did not fully understand the accuracy and reliability of munitions, their destructive effects, and their ability to mitigate collateral damage when used properly. That led to fears of collateral damage on their part that were groundless and that imposed needless delays in target approval. A key missing ingredient in engaging emerging targets involving special political sensitivities was refined, fused, and actionable target information made available to decisionmakers in a sufficiently timely way.

The Trend Toward Centralized Execution

More than any previous war, Operation Enduring Freedom saw not only centralized planning but also a pronounced expansion of centralized execution that reached from the highest levels of government all the way down to engaged combatants at the point of contact with the enemy. The greatly expanded global ISR and communications connectivity described in the preceding chapter not only provided heightened real-time situation awareness at all levels of the chain of command but also enabled what some have called "command at a distance." That global connectivity allowed sensor-to-shooter links to be shortened from hours to minutes, in some cases. But it also resulted in an oversubscribed target-approval process that had the effect of lengthening rather than shortening the kill chain. Because of the eight time-zone geographic separation between the CAOC and the United States, it further contributed to aggravated intra-CENTCOM tensions that had their roots in related but different problems discussed above. The expanded workday length of 14 to 16 hours in the CAOC was largely occasioned by the need for CAOC principals and their subordinates to interact extensively with staff personnel in Tampa and Washington.

How did such a situation develop? A pronounced downside of the expanded bandwidth and situation awareness at all levels that have evolved since Desert Storm is that at the same time they have made possible far more efficient and timely operations than ever before, they also have increasingly come to enable direct senior leadership involvement in the finest details of force employment. Even before the terrorist attacks of September 11, 2001, the traditional command-and-control arrangement had already been transformed into what the Air Force's Task Force Enduring Look called a "meshwork" of communications linkages yielding "metastasized command and control," wherein virtually any element could talk to any other element irrespective of its placement in the chain of command.[63] It was simply a new reality, and senior leaders exploited it to the limit in Enduring Freedom because they both felt a need to and, more to the point, were *able* to. One observer said that such top-down direction and control of events was both "a blessing and a curse of instant communications. . . . The guys can micromanage things that are happening on the ground in Afghanistan."[64]

Such senior leadership hands-on involvement was defensible up to a point. The strategy goals of Enduring Freedom, after all, called for exceedingly precise control at all levels of force employment. Otherwise, the campaign could have failed disastrously. Senior decisionmakers accordingly had legitimate concerns for imposing needed discipline on operations. It naturally followed that the heightened rules-of-engagement restrictions required a richer shared awareness picture at all levels of the chain of command. The ability of the metastasized command-and-control system to provide more real-time information to senior leaders allowed them to make more target-approval decisions.

This connectivity, however, cut both ways. Although it was a good thing in some respects, it often resulted in gridlock. It gave

---

[63] Comments on an earlier draft by Pat A. Pentland, SAIC, May 28, 2003.

[64] Rowan Scarborough, "U.S. Rules Let al Qaeda Flee," *Washington Times*, December 21, 2001.

highly refined situation awareness to senior commanders when it was available. Yet it also tended to make them err on the side of excessive caution when information was deemed to be insufficient. As good as it was, information availability was often inadequate to enable timely adaptive planning to meet the required cycle time for engaging time-sensitive targets. Needed mechanisms and procedures were also not in place for that demanding task. One four-star general complained that the growing propensity of higher staffs to bear down on lower ones had become a major hindrance to greater operational efficiency: "It's insatiable, and it really is a downside of instant communication."[65] A Marine Corps "lessons learned" study prompted by the Enduring Freedom experience similarly portrayed rear-echelon headquarters intrusions as a source of unnecessary friction.[66]

To note a case in point, the ability to transmit live Predator video from the war zone in Afghanistan to Tampa and Washington eight time zones to the rear generally provided senior commanders with little useful information bearing on their strategic-level concerns yet often made for irresistible distractions and, at the same time, encouraged higher-level staffs to try to micromanage the fighting. A pernicious result was to cause those senior players to get overly focused on what they could actually see through the equivalent of a drinking straw and to neglect what they could *not* see, even though events occurring elsewhere in Afghanistan might have been far more important to them at any given moment.[67] Ultimately, senior decisionmakers often intervened in execution at the tactical level not be-

---

[65] Thomas E. Ricks, "Un-Central Command Criticized," *Washington Post*, June 3, 2002.

[66] Ricks, "Un-Central Command Criticized."

[67] On this point, CAOC action officers soon came to refer to live Predator feed as "Predator crack" (as in crack cocaine) because of its propensity to instill a perceived need for ever more—and ever more frequent—"fixes" among senior players inclined to spend long periods of time looking at it. As one knowledgeable CAOC staffer recalled in this respect, "Some senior officers would do their own initial photo interpretation and ask the Predator imagery personnel to look for a cave entrance because 'I saw a person on that goat while Predator was panning through that valley and I don't see where he went to.' That was bad. Predator provides a great soda straw through which to see what is going on, but it is only a soda straw." (Comments on an earlier draft by Major Charles Hogan, USAF, December 22, 2003.)

cause political or operational circumstances required it but simply because they *could*. All of this raised a valid question in the minds of many about the appropriateness of having live Predator feed (or, for that matter, *any* real-time sensor feed) at the combatant command headquarters, at the Pentagon, and in the White House.[68]

A related unwelcome aspect of the expanded communications connectivity and battlespace awareness that predominated throughout Enduring Freedom was the rise in tension and frustration created by the emergence of powerful distributed organizations, all of whose principals wanted to be hands-on players. The systems and capabilities that have evolved since Desert Storm to give every interested principal, in effect, a common operating picture demand an unprecedented degree of discipline by commanders and senior leaders to ensure that innovations intended to speed up operations do not end up instead being brakes on those operations. This calls for command and support relationships aimed at enabling and ensuring flexibility and rapidity of action instead of the opposite if the component commanders are to be properly empowered to be commanders in fact as well as in name.

Yet another downside of expanded communications connectivity is that "reach-back," a good thing in and of itself when used only as necessary and with due discrimination, metamorphosed into what came to be called "reach forward" as rear headquarters staffs—notably including very senior staff personnel—began to ask for information from the CAOC and then to use that information to try to influence events in the war zone from the rear. The inevitable result was the involvement of too many layers of supervision and too many influential outside players to make the most of what the CAOC had to offer as a weapon system.

Even General Hagenbeck of Operation Anaconda renown admitted that "it proved at first to be disruptive" as observers in the Persian Gulf, at CENTCOM headquarters in Tampa, and in the Penta-

---

[68] One report said that President Bush himself had constant access to live Predator feed in the White House. Peter Pae, "Future Is Now for Creator of Predator," *Los Angeles Times*, January 3, 2002.

gon, prompted by real-time Predator imagery that they were watching at the same time as he was, would barrage him with questions from the rear as he monitored the flow of ground operations from his forward command post at Bagram. During the first days of Anaconda, he said, "people on other staffs at higher levels would call all the way down to my staff and get information or make suggestions, or they were pulling information for details that they presumed their bosses would want to know." The solution to this unwelcome and unhelpful proclivity, he suggested, was to anticipate such questions from the rear and to try to answer them in advance by posting detailed battle reports several times daily on the Secure Internet Protocol Router Network (SIPRNET). After his subordinates began doing that, he said, the higher staffs "started backing off."[69]

Some argue that centralized execution of the sort that predominated in Operation Enduring Freedom may by now have become an irreversible fact of early 21st-century military life. In that respect, three defense analysts subsequently commented that "owing to the high political content of armed conflict in a world of high-speed information and the capability to transmit information over global distances in the blink of an eye, there is a high probability that centralized execution . . . may be here to stay."[70] That may or may not have become an accomplished fact just yet, but it certainly seems to be the direction in which recent trends have pointed. Insofar as that is the case, it bodes ill for the long-term interests of U.S. security if it is accepted uncritically and simply surrendered to by operators without being challenged.

Some kinds of operations in which the political content and consequences of failure are exceptionally high will continue to require both stringent rules of engagement and centralized execution. However, national leaders need to remain mindful of the potential effect of such constraints. Centralized execution worked in spite of itself in a small war like Operation Enduring Freedom. But a larger war re-

---

[69] Thomas E. Ricks, "Beaming the Battlefield Home," *Washington Post*, March 26, 2002.

[70] Bowie, Haffa, and Mullins, p. 35.

quiring a thousand or more combat sorties a day could not handle it. Time-sensitive targeting will continue to be the wave of the future in many circumstances. Yet the nation needs a faster way of getting timely approval for such targeting on a large scale. Senior leaders and commanders cannot expect to approve every DMPI placement when thousands are being attacked every day.

To sum up, there is an inherent tension between the imperatives of political control and those of efficient execution in the new C4/ISR environment that senior operators and decisionmakers need to understand and deal with. If centralized execution is increasingly going to be the norm at least for certain kinds of conflicts, the system needs a way to process and integrate incoming battlespace information more quickly and efficiently. Beyond that, senior leaders both in and out of uniform need to remain focused on their proper level of war and to know when their hands-on involvement is appropriate and when it is not. For most situations, the proven leadership rule of thumb espoused by a former commander of the Air Force's Tactical Air Command, the late General Bill Creech, called NIFO (for "nose in, fingers out") would seem to make greatest sense as the abiding governing mechanism.[71]

Even though the American military command-and-control meshwork has now evolved to a point where centralized execution has become routinely possible in principle, decentralized execution remains both the preeminent virtue of American military culture and the one feature that distinguishes it from its polar opposite, namely, the inflexible and discredited top-down approach of the former Soviet High Command.[72] As the former air commander during the 1991 Persian Gulf War, retired Air Force General Charles Horner, bluntly observed, "the most dangerous thing we face [as a result of increased ISR and communications connectivity worldwide] is the 8,000-mile

---

[71] Bill Creech, *The Five Pillars of TQM*, New York: Dutton, 1994, p. 281.

[72] For further discussion of how the Soviet approach to command and control stifled initiative and hampered the flexibility of Soviet forces at the operational and tactical levels, see Lambeth, *Russia's Air Power in Crisis*, pp. 71–109.

screwdriver simply because it is possible."[73] Without question, current operational doctrine, standard procedures, and agreed practices have yet to catch up with the new command, control, and communications (C3) reality, and the increasingly widespread profusion of real-time information both horizontally and vertically has enabled senior players who are entirely indifferent to the way things used to be done in a simpler past to insert themselves into the execution process. This bears out the long-standing aphorism that a problem without a solution is no longer a problem but a fact to be dealt with. Doctrine and practice must accordingly recognize this new reality and find a way to address it preemptively lest that reality be allowed, by operator default, to undermine and ultimately destroy one of the nation's most preeminent military advantages.

Integrating Other Government Agencies

Still another source of friction for CENTCOM and for its air component in particular was the pursuit of a parallel and compartmented mini-war conducted by the CIA with its Hellfire-armed Predators. That activity did not figure in the air component's daily ATO, yet it nonetheless entailed the firing of more than 40 Hellfires over the course of the campaign, causing recurrent surprises and deconfliction challenges for the CAOC in the process. The problem first manifested itself during the campaign's opening night, when the CIA fired a Hellfire from a Predator that had not been included in the ATO. On later investigation, it turned out that CENTCOM's director of intelligence had given the agency clearance to fire straight from Tampa, short-circuiting the air component commander and the CAOC.[74]

There were subsequent complaints from some in the Air Force that the CIA had repeatedly failed to share information about its ac-

---

[73] Comments on an earlier draft by General Horner, January 8, 2004.

[74] Conversation with Lieutenant General Charles F. Wald, USAF, Headquarters United States Air Force, Washington, D.C., October 15, 2002.

tivities in Afghanistan, although General Wald rejected that charge, saying that "the relationship with the agency [was] fantastic. I don't see that as a problem."[75] Nevertheless, to all intents and purposes, the CIA's involvement in Enduring Freedom was tantamount to that of a fifth warfighting service. Because of its long-standing secrecy and compartmentation practices, to say nothing of its near-total lack of experience at working in close and regular operational concert with the U.S. armed forces, it often was not clear at any moment where units of what were euphemistically called "other government agencies" (OGAs) were on the ground in Afghanistan or what they were doing. At a minimum, that shortcoming raised some fundamental concerns about battlespace safety that call for further reflection, as well as suggesting a case for an addendum to existing air doctrine that addresses the special requirements of integrating secrecy-driven OGAs into conventional combat operations. Beyond that, on the long-accepted premise that military organizations fight like they train, it spotlighted a need for all services to exercise more frequently with such OGAs in peacetime to help ensure better mutual support in future contingencies.

The Costs of the High Operating Tempo

After the rude awakening the nation received during Operation Allied Force in 1999, it came as little surprise when Operation Enduring Freedom once again showed the extent to which the post–Cold War force drawdown had increased the burdens placed on the American defense establishment across the board, most notably in the realm of personnel, low-density/high-demand (LD/HD) platforms, and precision munitions stocks.[76] The unavailability of forward land bases within easy operating range from the war zone placed an unusual burden on Navy carriers, an extension of their deployments beyond

---

[75] Conversation with General Wald.

[76] For further discussion of the overcommitment burdens experienced during Operation Allied Force, see Lambeth, *NATO's Air War for Kosovo*, pp. 170–177.

their normal schedules, and a substantial spike in their daily operating tempo, with combat and support sorties being launched from carrier flight decks at three to five times the Navy's normal peacetime training rate. The need to commit four carrier battle groups to the campaign forced some painful juggling elsewhere. The commander of U.S. Pacific Command, Admiral Dennis Blair, told the House Armed Services Committee that as a result of the demands of Operation Enduring Freedom, "we do not have adequate forces to carry out our missions in the Pacific if the operations [in Afghanistan] continue." Admiral Blair noted that the Western Pacific had been without a carrier battle group during the war's early days, a rare shortfall that was compensated for by temporarily deploying Air Force fighters from Alaska to Korea. "We can mitigate for a while," he said, "but there are shortages of naval forces, of intelligence, surveillance and reconnaissance forces, in particular, that have to be made up for if we are to continue the current level of operations in Central Command."[77]

The Supreme Allied Commander in Europe and combatant commander of EUCOM, Air Force General Joseph Ralston, similarly reported that he did "not have the forces in EUCOM today to carry out [obligated] missions" in the 91 countries in his area of responsibility. Ralston added that if further demands were imposed, he would "come back to the chairman of the Joint Chiefs and the Secretary of Defense and ask for additional forces. They are going to have to come up with a choice: Where are they going to take them away from?" Ralston admitted that he had not had a Marine Corps amphibious ready group, the primary unit he would use to evacuate noncombatant Americans in the event of a crisis somewhere in EUCOM's area of responsibility, on-call since October 2001 and had not had an aircraft carrier available to him in months, other than for the few days it took a carrier battle group to transit the Mediterranean Sea en route elsewhere. Asked about the effect of another carrier decommissioning,

---

[77] "Top Brass: Military Spread Too Thin," *Washington Times*, March 21, 2002.

General Ralston replied: "I'm already at zero. With one less, I can't be any worse than zero."[78]

The high operating tempo of Enduring Freedom also drained Air Force and Navy munitions inventories and accelerated the aging of many aircraft in both services. Admiral Robert Natter, the commander of the Navy's Atlantic Fleet, reported that the Navy nearly ran out of JDAMs. He complimented the Air Force for having helped the Navy maintain adequate JDAM stocks aboard the participating carriers for the duration of Enduring Freedom. He also said that he had phoned contractors to request that they ramp up their JDAM production rate for the Navy.[79] In a notable related burden on equipment and personnel, the unusual mission length dictated by the remoteness of the Afghan area of operations meant that a tanker mission was flown almost for every strike mission. That contributed to a gradual exhaustion of tanker aircrews who had begun the campaign with only a one-to-one crew-to-aircraft ratio.[80]

As for LD/HD assets, Admiral Blair said in congressional testimony that Enduring Freedom had exacerbated a preexisting EP-3, U-2, and Rivet Joint shortage to which he had already testified two years earlier.[81] The admiral did not provide hard numbers, but he indicated that the collection rate of required intelligence in the Pacific as a result of the shortfall in critical ISR assets was "dangerously low."[82] Secretary of the Air Force James Roche expressed similar concern that the high utilization rate of C-17s was such that the aircraft's maintenance might not be getting enough attention. Secretary of the

---

[78] "Top Brass: Military Spread Too Thin."

[79] Dale Eisman, "Navy Says It Nearly Ran Out of Bombs," *Norfolk Virginian-Pilot*, March 1, 2002.

[80] David A. Fulghum, "Bombing Costs Escalate in Afghanistan Operations," *Aviation Week and Space Technology*, December 10, 2001, p. 38.

[81] As Secretary Rumsfeld pointed out, LD/HD is a fancy term for "those things we didn't buy enough of." Mark Mazetti, Thomas Omestad, and Richard J. Newman, "The Thin Green Line," *U.S. News and World Report*, April 8, 2002.

[82] "U.S. Pacific Command Needs Missile Defense, More Aircraft, CINC Says," *Aerospace Daily*, March 6, 2002. See also Robert Wall, "War Costs Overextend Pentagon Purse, Gear," *Aviation Week and Space Technology*, March 25, 2002, p. 31.

Navy Gordon England testified before the Senate Armed Services Committee that the F/A-18 was being flown well in excess of its planned utilization rates, as were F-14s, SH-60 helicopters, and other aircraft.[83] The commander of Pacific Air Forces, General William Begert, confirmed that the drawdown of ISR assets in the Pacific was where the U.S. military was hurting the most. That included a disruption in the routine use of the E-8 JSTARS to monitor North Korean military exercises.[84]

The unified Special Operations Command also bore heavy costs of the heightened operating tempo, sustaining several high-profile accidents involving the Army's MH-47 helicopter. Also, an AFSOC MC-130 Combat Shadow was lost during the campaign (although not to hostile fire), and three AFSOC MH-53 Pave Low helicopters sustained major mishaps. The commander of SOCOM, Air Force General Charles Holland, declared that "we are concerned about the battle-damaged and destroyed aircraft now missing from this fleet and how quickly they can be recapitalized."[85] In an overview statement, Army General William Kernan, commander of Joint Forces Command, said in congressional testimony that U.S. forces across the board were overextended and exhausted.[86] Kernan told the House Armed Services Committee on March 20: "We are stretched. It is manageable right now, but we are stretched." Asked about Kernan's statement that U.S. forces were "overextended and exhausted," a rankled Rumsfeld replied: "It's a disservice to [U.S. military personnel] to leave that impression, in my view."[87] Be that as it may, however, the commander of U.S. Air Forces in Europe (USAFE), Air Force

---

[83] Robert Wall, "War Drains Military's Aircraft and Munitions," *Aviation Week and Space Technology*, February 18, 2002, p. 31.

[84] Robert Wall, "Afghanistan Alters USAF Posture in Asia," *Aviation Week and Space Technology*, September 2, 2002, pp. 39–40.

[85] Robert Wall, "Counterterror Combat Shrinks Special Ops Inventory," *Aviation Week and Space Technology*, March 18, 2002, p. 28.

[86] "Top Brass: Military Spread Too Thin."

[87] Thom Shanker, "Addressing Worries, Pentagon Says It Can Fight Wider War," *New York Times,* March 29, 2002.

General Gregory Martin, emphasized that Operation Enduring Freedom was only a part of the overall global war on terror. Across the board, Martin said, "we have going on right now probably the largest planning effort since World War II. We're doing about six major theaters of war's worth of planning and using about three MTWs [Major Theater Wars] of people. When you look at the whole system, that's what's happening."[88]

---

[88] David A. Fulghum, "After the Taliban: What Next?" *Aviation Week and Space Technology,* October 29, 2001, p. 40.

CHAPTER EIGHT

Conclusions

Operation Enduring Freedom was the first major war of the 21st century. It also was a defining moment for the still-nascent presidency of George W. Bush. Its outcome in bringing down the Taliban and destroying al Qaeda's terrorist infrastructure in Afghanistan validated the president's decision to avoid leaping into a precipitous response to the terrorist attacks of September 11, 2001, even though the initial inclination, as Secretary of Defense Rumsfeld noted early on, had been to lash out reflexively.[1] Instead, the Bush administration laid the groundwork for retaliation systematically and carefully, exercising in the process what *The Economist* called "considerable amounts of skill, subtlety, leadership, and, above all, intelligence" both in building a coalition and in planning and conducting the campaign.[2] In so doing, it surprised both its critics and, most likely, the terrorists as well, the latter of whom were, for the first time, put on the defensive and thrust into a reactive mode. The simultaneous initiation of strike and humanitarian relief operations helped contribute to a popular Afghan view of the United States as a liberator rather than an invader. It also helped prevent the emergence of a significant Afghan insurgent resistance to the U.S. military presence.

---

[1] Anne Scott Tyson, "Why U.S. Is Moving So Deliberately," *Christian Science Monitor*, October 4, 2001.

[2] "Closing In," *The Economist*, September 29, 2001, p. 11.

Planning for Enduring Freedom began as an exercise in coercion, with a view toward persuading the Taliban to turn over Osama bin Laden and his chief al Qaeda deputies. Soon thereafter, however, it became an exercise in brute-force regime takedown and active pursuit of Taliban and al Qaeda fanatics to the bitter end as it became clear that the Taliban leaders would remain unyielding in this regard. As the war commenced on October 7, 2001, President Bush urged CENTCOM to "take high risks and push the envelope in prosecuting this campaign."[3] Although the war got off to a slow start due to weather-driven delays in inserting U.S. SOF teams into Afghanistan, the Taliban crumbled so rapidly in the end that the air offensive did not have discernible phases once its collaborative work with those teams began in earnest. Foreign affairs commentator Fareed Zakaria flatly concluded from the experience that "American air power today is an amazing weapon of war."[4]

After the initial bombing ended and the interim Karzai government had been installed, it became clear to many that the war had indeed been another air power success story, as were Operations Desert Storm, Deliberate Force, and Allied Force before it. Many lessons from the earlier Allied Force experience were duly honored and incorporated, particularly the synergistic effect of using friendly ground forces for shaping enemy troop movement and cueing allied air power. By the end of Operation Anaconda in mid-March 2002, Enduring Freedom had become the longest-running combat operation the United States had been involved in since Vietnam. Thanks to its persistence, however, according to one reflective account, the terrorists had finally become "the hunted, not the hunters."[5]

---

[3] Wald, "Operation Enduring Freedom: The CFACC Viewpoint."

[4] Fareed Zakaria, "Face the Facts: Bombing Works," *Newsweek*, December 3, 2001.

[5] "Six Months On," *The Economist*, March 9, 2002, p. 11.

Innovations in Force Employment

In addition to its overarching role as the first military move in the global war on terror, Operation Enduring Freedom was also a battle laboratory for testing, in a live combat setting, some of the most significant air power developments to have appeared in more than two decades. Among other things, the war saw the first use of an unmanned ISR platform, the MQ-1 Predator, as a precision-attack weapon. It also represented the first major occasion in which "other government agencies," notably the CIA, were directly integrated into air combat operations. Its dominant features were persistence of pressure on the enemy and rapidity of execution, thanks to the improved data fusion enabled by new technologies, a better-managed CAOC, more help from space, and smarter concepts of operations. Much of the persistent pressure stemmed from the widespread availability of precision weapons. During Allied Force, only the B-2 was configured to drop JDAMs. In Enduring Freedom, nearly every U.S. strike platform was equipped with that capability.

Many tactics, techniques, and procedures (TTPs) were improvised in the heat of battle by allied combatants, who were often the first to identify needed improvements in such areas as communications, organizational arrangements, and ways of using force. Perhaps the most notable innovation was the much-improved integration of precision air power with friendly ground forces, in this case heavy bombers and fighters armed with JDAMs and LGBs and allied SOF teams aided by Air Force terminal attack controllers. Particularly in the case of Operation Anaconda, it was this combination of air assets in all services and highly qualified combat controllers and ETACs on the ground that saved the day for CJTF Mountain despite the latter's ill-planned start of the operation.

The success of this combination was due not so much to the technologies employed as to the way they were fused together into a novel concept of operations. The war's first air component commander, Air Force Lieutenant General Charles Wald, later recalled that the rapid progress of the Northern Alliance in early November 2001 had been enabled by the targeting support provided by just "three or four [SOF] guys on the ground."[6] In the end, little more than 300 U.S. SOF combatants proved pivotal in bringing down the Taliban by allowing allied air power to deliver to its fullest potential. The measured and discriminate use of force that was a signature feature of Enduring Freedom emanated from what Secretary of the Navy Gordon England called "targeting truth," namely, knowing that a desired target is "an authorized target, a target that you can go hit," as well as understanding "the collateral [damage] consequences of those targets . . . and then, of course, the validity of the bomb damage assessment."[7]

Attempts at effects-based operations depended heavily on accurate and real-time target information. The major breakthroughs here were not in aircraft or munitions but rather in the realm of ISR fusion enabled by linking the inputs of Predator, the RC-135, the U-2, the E-8, and other sensors around the clock. The result was far better than that two years earlier during Operation Allied Force. Greater communications connectivity and more available bandwidth enabled constant surveillance of enemy activity and contributed significantly to shortening the kill chain. Predator and, even more, Global Hawk offered a major improvement in this regard in that they could loiter over the battlefield continuously for long periods without the high absenteeism rate of satellites. They also did not represent a national asset like a satellite and hence bore no requirement for the air component commander to request tasking.[8]

---

[6] Ricks, "Bull's-Eye War: Pinpoint Bombing Shifts Role of GI Joe."

[7] "Precision Weapons, Networks Trump Navy's Need for New Ships, England Says," *Aerospace Daily*, October 17, 2002.

[8] A second Global Hawk crashed on July 10, 2002, into friendly territory in Pakistan on a routine mission while supporting CENTCOM's mopping-up operations in Afghanistan. That loss left Air Combat Command with only one of five developmental aircraft remaining from the original demonstration effort. Earlier in June, Northrop Grumman announced that Global Hawk had passed the 1,000-hour flight milestone while supporting Enduring Freedom. Amy Butler, "Flight Testing Halts After OEF Claims Second Global Hawk in Crash," *Inside the Air Force*, July 12, 2002, p. 1, and "U.S. Grounds Spy Plane," *Washington Post*, July 13, 2002.

With respect to this persistent ISR, Secretary of the Air Force Roche said: "I think we're almost there."[9] The capability was so effective in part because a UAV can now remain on station for a long time, enabling the elusive goal of near-instantaneous attack by finding a target, matching it with a weapon, releasing the weapon, and observing the resultant effects. Through such highly leveraged use, UAVs were a major part of the Enduring Freedom success story, demonstrating in the process a clear need for more of such capability. Compared to orbital assets, they provided longer dwell time, more rapid revisit rates, and the ability to be tasked to a specific need far more quickly.

In addition, a new concept of offensive air employment against enemy ground forces was successfully tested in Enduring Freedom. Although often mistakenly equated with close air support (CAS), it was, in fact, something fundamentally new by way of air power application that entailed direct air attacks against fielded enemy forces who were *not* in direct contact with friendly troops.[10] That novel use of air power needs to be further thought through and codified in joint-service doctrine and TTPs so that it can become more fully institutionalized and integrated into the four services' force-employment repertoires. Better doctrine and concepts of operations are also needed for using fused air power and friendly SOF teams in conjunction with indigenous forces like the Afghan anti-Taliban groups. Beyond that, a need was shown for doctrinal improvements aimed at accommodating operational relationships with other government agencies, notably the CIA. Still other operational innovations that helped account for Enduring Freedom's success included a reduction in the GPS signal error by 50 percent and a demonstration of CENTAF's CAOC as the world's most powerful command center,

---

[9] Frank Tiboni, "Instantaneous Attack Capability Near for U.S.," *Defense News*, January 7–13, 2002, p. 1.

[10] For more on this new approach to the use of air power in land warfare, see Major General David A. Deptula, USAF, Colonel Gary Crowder, USAF, and Major George L. Stamper, USAF, "Direct Attack: Enhancing Counterland Doctrine and Joint Air-Ground Operations, *Air and Space Power Journal*, Winter 2003, pp. 5–12.

enabling the full integration of space operations into mission planning and an unprecedented rapidity of execution.

Overall, the most salient features of the Afghan air war by way of innovations in force employment included:

- A new synergy between SOF spotters and air power
- Sensor-to-shooter technical links reduced to minutes
- A continuous ISR umbrella permitting on-call day and night, all-weather precision JDAM capability that enabled lethality on demand throughout the theater
- Multisensor ISR directly available to the warfighting component
- A near-seamless integration of space, mobility, and information in the CAOC
- A high-bandwidth capability in the CAOC that provided significantly improved situation awareness and theaterwide connectivity
- A near-real-time capability in the CAOC, offered by Predator, for aiding targeteers in deriving mensurated coordinates in minutes in support of fused precision time-sensitive targeting[11]
- Better integration than ever before of service component contributions in the CAOC
- Integrated real-time, loitering hunter-killer operations.[12]

---

[11] Predator provided the CAOC with target coordinates through its video display, but those coordinates were not accurate enough in and of themselves to enable the precision dropping of a JDAM. Targeteers either in the CAOC or at CENTCOM provided the actually mensurated coordinates using the RAINDROP point mensuration based on the National Imagery and Mapping Agency's Digital Point Precision Data Base (DPPDB), a three-dimensional display of most of the world from which GPS-quality coordinates and elevation can be derived for GPS-aided bombs. (Comments on an earlier draft by Major Charles Hogan, USAF, December 22, 2003.)

[12] These points were all drawn from Major General David A. Deptula, USAF, "Operation Enduring Freedom—Highlights, Challenges, and Potential Implications: Some Observations from the First 60 Days," unpublished briefing charts. General Deptula was the CAOC director for Operation Enduring Freedom from September 23 to November 23, 2002.

Persistent Problems in Need of Attention

Notwithstanding the innovations outlined above, Operation Enduring Freedom also embodied some more controversial features. As noted in Chapter 7, those developments included a pronounced tendency toward not only centralized planning but also centralized execution of force employment. That, in turn, led to an implementation of the rules of engagement in often ad hoc and dysfunctional ways, thanks to the war's domination both at CENTCOM and in Washington by leaders strongly inclined toward detailed oversight and unwilling either to trust their subordinates or, if they were not trustworthy, to replace them. The more controversial aspects referred to here also included some revealed shortcomings in ISR capability, overly convoluted command arrangements with respect to special operations forces, and a less-than-ideal relationship between the combatant commander and the air component commander from a *structural* viewpoint, irrespective of the personalities involved. Each of these shortcomings offered useful grist for the defense community's "lessons learned" mill. In some combination, they may have contributed to the unnecessary escape of some top Taliban and al Qaeda leaders.

As for collateral damage avoidance, it is now an entrenched fact of life that as American air power has become ever more accurate, lethal, and effective, it also has come under ever more intense public attention, scrutiny, and questioning, even as it has, at the same time, heightened not only the nation's political imperatives but also a legal need to be more discriminate in the use of force. Moreover, as concern for avoiding enemy noncombatant casualties has steadily risen in recent years, it has spawned an increasingly stringent rules-of-engagement regime aimed at minimizing the incidence of collateral damage. During Desert Storm, the rules of engagement were certainly a factor in inhibiting air operations on occasion, as was the natural inclination of leaders and planners to avoid causing collateral damage whenever possible even when the rules were not so constraining. The rules of engagement were more restrictive in Allied Force, however, and they were unprecedentedly restrictive in the case of Enduring Freedom. Indeed, the determination by CENTCOM to avoid collateral damage irrespective of that effort's effect on mission accomplishment was so prepossessing that CENTAF, to its credit, created a special collateral damage reaction cell in the CAOC to look into allegations of civilian fatalities and other unintended damage by examining target data, pilot reports, and aerial reconnaissance photography. This was a salutary development that needs to be formally incorporated into doctrine and practice. One useful lesson taught by both Enduring Freedom and Allied Force was the compelling need for an institutionalized ability in the CAOC to gather information quickly and determine causes when things go wrong, as they inevitably will from time to time, not only for collateral damage situations, but even more so when friendly fire incidents demand quick, honest, and convincing explanations.

In reviewing several scores of such allegations, that CAOC reaction cell confirmed but a handful of weapon malfunctions or DMPI placement errors that actually caused unintended casualties.[13] A later report based on an Associated Press review of hospital records, interviews, and visits of bombed sites indicated that the civilian death toll in Afghanistan was less than that registered two years earlier in Serbia and Kosovo during Operation Allied Force, the latter of which was on the order of 500 to 600.[14] Shortly after the campaign ended, an American organization called Global Exchange sent a field team into Afghanistan to assess reported collateral damage incidents, after which it compiled a list indicating that 812 civilians had been killed by errant attacks. One explanation offered by the group was that U.S. SOF teams relied excessively on faulty information provided by Afghan opposition groups. In response to that report, Secretary of the Air Force Roche admitted that mistakes had been made, singling out in particular the failed battery in an Air Force combat controller's GPS receiver that resulted in the controller's own position being bombed and Hamid Karzai almost getting killed. The Afghan provi-

---

[13] Barry Bearak, "Uncertain Toll in the Fog of War: Civilian Deaths in Afghanistan," *New York Times*, February 10, 2002.

[14] Laura King, "Civilian Toll in Afghan War Likely Lower," *Philadelphia Inquirer*, February 12, 2002.

sional government eventually estimated that fewer than 500 Afghan civilians had been killed by errant bombs.[15]

Some airmen maintained that the collateral damage constraints in Enduring Freedom that emanated from CENTCOM or above severely hindered effective combat operations. For example, those constraints may have contributed to the escape of Mullah Omar on the first night, a possibility that has not been confirmed beyond doubt. But without question, the heightened aversion to the potential costs of unintended consequences that pervaded the chain of command from the White House on down allowed numerous other similarly lucrative but fleeting opportunities to kill enemy leaders to slip away. There was abundant good reason for that CENTCOM aversion to collateral damage in principle, however, and such cases of missed chances were fortunately exceptions to the rule. On this important point, the air commander during Operation Desert Storm, General Horner, rightly noted that in Enduring Freedom, "collateral damage concerns [indeed] became more important than mission success. But then, in part, mission success depended on avoiding collateral damage."[16] In general, as Australian air power historian Alan Stephens has pointed out, "the need to balance operational opportunities against international political sensibilities seems to have been reasonably well managed . . . certainly better managed than was the case during Allied Force."[17]

Some critics charged that even while the war was under way, General Franks had been overly influenced by his JAG, who was said to have repeatedly held forth with a thumbs-down opinion on CAOC target nominations, even though the proposed targets were clearly military in nature. It was she, for example, who reportedly recommended against approving the CAOC's requested attack on a convoy thought to contain Omar the first night out of concern that

---

[15] Dexter Filkins, "Flaws in U.S. Air War Left Hundreds of Civilians Dead," *New York Times,* July 21, 2002.

[16] Comments on an earlier draft by General Horner, January 8, 2004.

[17] Alan Stephens, "Afghanistan and the Australian Way of War," unpublished paper, p. 6.

the convoy might involve a trick to sucker in a strike against commingled civilians. In fairness to the approval process, however, she was only doing her job in questioning the legal basis for the requested attack. Enforcement of rules of engagement is not the JAG's responsibility. The rules-of-engagement issue is quintessentially an operational issue. Pentagon spokesman Rear Admiral Craig Quigley was on solid ground in reminding the critics that CENTCOM's JAG "was never in a position to 'stop' any attack (nor is any JAG anywhere). That is the prerogative of Franks and other operational commanders alone."[18] The commander's responsibility is to determine how much risk he is prepared to take. The military lawyer's job, in turn, is to bend every effort to keep the commander from becoming a war criminal as a result of his actions. It is up to commanders, in turn, to use their JAGs proactively and not allow them to veto force-employment options by defaulting to their opinions to the exclusion of all other considerations.[19]

Notably, most of the inadvertent civilian fatalities in Enduring Freedom occurred *after* Tora Bora and Zhawar Kili and the end of the war against the Taliban in mid-December 2001. As the effort metamorphosed into a counterinsurgency operation, it demanded ever more exacting enforcement of rules to avoid collateral damage to avert even an occasional undisciplined or trigger-happy force-employment event. Of the highly publicized incident in which festive small-arms fire at an Afghan wedding drew a lethal response from an AC-130 orbiting nearby, one observer rightly called it "more than a

---

[18] Schrader, "War, on Advice of Counsel."

[19] Conversation with Lieutenant General Ronald Keys, USAF, Commander, 16th Air Force, at Maxwell AFB, Alabama, August 14, 2002. It should be added here that most JAGs, once engaged, do not take long to make decisions about targeting recommendations, even when those decisions are unwelcome. Moreover, insofar as JAGs may have been responsible at times for injecting friction into the mission execution process, that friction has arguably been a good thing rather than an impediment to efficient conduct of the campaign in most cases. As one of the Air Force's most operationally minded JAGs has remarked on this point, "a lot of agony for a lot of people could have been avoided had a JAG been able to inject a little 'friction' into the AC-130 wedding-party attack and other friendly fire incidents." (Comments on an earlier draft by Brigadier General Charles J. Dunlap, Jr., USAF, Staff Judge Advocate, Air Combat Command, Langley AFB, Virginia, December 27, 2003.)

mistake: It is a major political error, and the more errors there are, the less awe and the more resistance American power will awaken."[20] That incident starkly dramatized the need for collateral damage avoidance standards to become ever more exacting, at least in the most politically sensitive circumstances, if the United States is to prevail in the propaganda war.

Timely and accurate intelligence has become increasingly paramount for providing top leaders the needed confidence to approve attacks against time-sensitive targets. Such high-quality intelligence will come only from multiple sources and consistently good analysis. It is now a given that clever adversaries will use the international laws of armed conflict as a weapon, in what the current Staff Judge Advocate at Air Combat Command has aptly referred to as "lawfare."[21] A proven asymmetric counter to our technology advantages available to unprincipled opponents like the Taliban is to attack the legitimacy of American combat involvement by creating collateral damage incidents and then forcing *us*, in effect, to prove our freedom from guilt. The further one goes down the scale of conflict, the more this potential counter becomes a problem. Such a propaganda ploy might not matter so much in a counteroffensive war for high stakes against North Korea. But in Afghanistan, the Taliban's exaggerations of civilian casualties as a result of alleged U.S. bombing errors created a serious perceptions-management problem for U.S. leaders.

As that problem attests, getting better at information warfare is a major challenge for the United States. Much as in the earlier case of Allied Force against Slobodan Milosevic, the Afghan experience highlighted the need to be aggressively proactive rather than reactive in dealing with enemy uses of the media. Perception management in some cases can be as important as the shooting war, which suggests a

---

[20] Michael Ignatieff, "Nation-Building Lite," *New York Times Magazine*, July 28, 2002, p. 30.

[21] Brigadier General Charles J. Dunlap, Jr., USAF, "Air and Information Operations: A Perspective on the Rise of 'Lawfare' in Modern Conflicts," presentation at a conference on Current Issues in the Law of Armed Conflict, Naval War College, Newport, Rhode Island, June 2003.

need for a much better-organized set of procedures and information operations to help shape third-party perceptions in ways that facilitate rather than undermine the war effort.[22] A related challenge, which cuts against the grain of this worthy goal, entails ensuring that collateral damage considerations are properly balanced against the no less important interests of mission accomplishment. Collateral damage in warfare is manageable. Unintended consequences are not. Efforts to avoid the latter by controlling the former to a fault can put an excessive burden on the war effort at the expense of early mission accomplishment.[23]

Yet another challenge that was raised by Enduring Freedom is ensuring that centralized control of military operations does not degenerate, without compelling reason, into centralized execution and that "reach back," a laudable resort in principle, does not devolve into "reach forward," namely, a situation in which staffers to the rear seek real-time information from the CAOC and then attempt to use that information to micromanage tactical operations from afar.[24] As in the earlier case of NATO's air war for Kosovo, Operation Enduring Freedom featured command elements that were widely dispersed geographically. In the latter case, however, the situation was compounded by the fact that such geographic separation spanned eight time zones. Although the kill chain has become shortened from hours to minutes, that shortened cycle time was often negated by the added length of the decision cycle for securing target approvals, with the result that the human factor has now become the chief limiting factor impeding more effective time-critical targeting.

A big part of this conundrum, as described in Chapter 7, has been a natural outgrowth of expanded global communications connectivity in all directions. Lieutenant General Ronald Keys, then–

---

[22] A problem here, it should be noted, is that democracies are not characteristically very good at this because of their great virtue of societal openness.

[23] Deptula, "Operation Enduring Freedom—Highlights, Challenges, and Potential Implications."

[24] Deptula, "Operation Enduring Freedom—Highlights, Challenges, and Potential Implications."

commander of 16th Air Force, frankly described the rear-area monitoring of live Predator feed by senior leaders as insidious "cyber-rubbernecking." He noted that it indeed enabled senior leaders to ask questions more easily and faster but countered with a reminder that providing good answers continues to take time.[25] For his part, Vice Admiral John Nathman, then–commander of U.S. naval air forces, stressed that the steady creep toward the elevation of target-approval decisions to ever higher authority inevitably slowed air power's responsiveness whenever emerging targets were detected. At times, the resultant air traffic control bottlenecks were severe, with numerous aircraft in the flow stacked up waiting for targets to be identified and approved so they could be attacked. Nathman concluded: "I think we need to put [the decision authority] back in the cockpit if we are going to enable time-critical strike."[26]

BDA response times in Enduring Freedom were nearly as long as they were in Desert Storm. There as well, too many organizational divides persisted as obstructions to faster performance, and poor coordination between widely dispersed elements of CENTCOM continued to abound. Moreover, assessments were still based on measurable attrition rather than on observed effects, and BDA teams continued to assess only what they could measure, not necessarily the results that mattered most. For example, those in the CAOC who were striving for an effects-based targeting approach complained that the IADS drawdown goal of 100 percent of SAM equipment destroyed was a needlessly high performance criterion that wasted sorties and added to the campaign's duration. Viewed from this perspective, the real issue at hand was not assessment per se but rather CENTCOM's failure to arrive at an agreed determination of desired effects and goals before the actual assessment process ever began.

Reduced to basics, the sensor-to-shooter cycle entails finding, fixing, tracking, targeting, deciding, engaging, and assessing the re-

---

[25] Conversation with Lieutenant General Ronald Keys, USAF, Commander, Allied Air Forces South, at Maxwell AFB, Alabama, August 14, 2002.

[26] Robert Wall, "War Expansion May Require New Operational Techniques," *Aviation Week and Space Technology*, April 29, 2002, p. 55.

sults. Compared to Desert Storm, in Enduring Freedom each of these functions required steadily less time, with the singular exception of deciding. That function grew substantially in required time because of the nature of the war itself and of the target-approval process that was enabled by modern C4/ISR.[27] A core challenge now facing the warfighting community entails ensuring that the greatly reduced TST execution timeline, now down to minutes, does not continue to be negated by lengthier decision cycles occasioned by higher headquarters intervention, in which an oversubscribed target vetting process can completely wipe out our technological improvements.

The most fundamental issue with respect to time-sensitive targeting concerns the level at which specific target-approval decisions should be made. The cumulative experiences of Desert Storm, Allied Force, and Enduring Freedom showed plainly that approval time is a direct function of the political sensitivity of the target, collateral damage possibilities, and the reliability of the intelligence put forward to support the recommended attack. What worked in Enduring Freedom despite manifold inefficiencies will not work without high cost in a more demanding scenario involving many more combat sorties and DMPIs. On this count, it remains to be seen whether senior commanders and their civilian superiors will eventually learn to discipline themselves to remain at their appropriate level of war and not insert themselves into tactical-level decisionmaking just because technology now permits it.

As for the campaign's achievements, Enduring Freedom brought down the Taliban in less time than had been expected. Yet CENTCOM did not deal quickly enough with the ability of al Qaeda's top leaders to elude capture. In fairness to CENTCOM, General Franks was the combatant commander in an unusually difficult situation and had to adapt continually to ever-changing de-

---

[27] As Rear Admiral Mark Fitzgerald, who commanded the USS *Theodore Roosevelt* carrier battle group during Enduring Freedom, put it to me, the "D" in the so-called OODA (for observe, orient, decide, and act) loop is now the limiting factor in expeditious time-sensitive targeting. (Conversation in the Office of the Chief of Naval Operations, Washington, D.C., May 14, 2003.)

mands. Those most critical of his alleged micromanagement from Tampa may have insufficiently appreciated the very limited flexibility that he was given by the leadership in Washington.[28] Secretary Rumsfeld was a key player in the chain of command, after all, and Franks was most definitely responding to pressures on him, both real and perceived, from above. He was said to have been especially concerned to avoid projecting even a hint of the American military presence on the ground in Afghanistan as being an occupying force. Accordingly, he elected to rely heavily on Afghan opposition groups to do most of the searching for bin Laden, with allied SOF teams providing help but little direct involvement. The price of the Bush administration's collective decision to use Afghan proxies rather than U.S. forces in the battles of Tora Bora and Zhawar Kili was a failure to capture or kill many al Qaeda combatants, including, most notably, its top leaders.

Defenders of that decision insist that it was not a fear within CENTCOM of sustaining U.S. casualties so much as a determination to avoid provoking an anti-American insurgency among the Afghan opposition elements. Yet be that as it may, the administration's choice of relying on the opposition groups during the Tora Bora and Zhawar Kili operations rather than on bringing a sufficient number of American ground troops to do the demanding work of locating and hunting down the enemy created an unsatisfactory mix. The Afghan resistance fighters had their own agendas, were not eager to comb caves in search of the enemy, and were wholly willing to smuggle al Qaeda fighters across the border into Pakistan in return for bribes. The result was a complete failure to entrap any of the the enemy's top leaders. In hindsight, as CENTCOM's director of operations, Air Force Major General Victor Renuart, later reflected on this point, planners would probably have been better advised to rely more on allied SOF units than on Afghan opposition groups for intelligence as well as to focus more heavily on the paths that led above the

---

[28] Comments on an earlier draft by Lieutenant General Victor E. Renuart, USAF, Vice Commander, Pacific Air Forces, February 14, 2004.

Tora Bora valley into Pakistan and on the secret escape and supply routes that led off to the southwest.[29]

On the ISR front, Enduring Freedom was the most bandwidth-intensive war in history. Yet there never seemed to be enough capacity to meet user demands. This suggests that there must be a Parkinson's Law for bandwidth waiting to be defined and articulated.[30] The good news was the nearly seamless cooperation between the air component and SOF teams on the ground and the use of near-precision GPS-aided weapons that made even the B-52 a de facto strike fighter. A more discouraging bad-news story was the slowness of Link 16 to emerge, which delayed the much-needed shift from analog to digital communications on which shorter response times and greater force efficiency heavily depend. The services have been less than fully focused in installing that capability in their aircraft, and each service continues to operate its own version of it. On this point, the former commander of U.S. Joint Forces Command, retired Admiral Harold Gehman, commented that "only in America could we allow each of three services their own Link 16 systems."[31] Similarly, the chairman of the JCS, General Richard Myers, remarked that for all the improvement in ISR fusion and communications connectivity that had taken place since Desert Storm, access to needed information by field components at the tactical level remains "widely different among the components . . . and that is unacceptable. . . . We have to get better at joint warfighting and integrating our services' capabilities, and . . . the C4/ISR piece is the key to that."[32]

Another emerging issue spotlighted during the course of Enduring Freedom entailed the CIA's operation of armed Predators out-

---

[29] William M. Arkin, "The Risky Business of Modern War: A Top U.S. Military Leader Shares His Thoughts About Armed Conflict in a Post-9/11 World," *Los Angeles Times*, September 21, 2003.

[30] Parkinson's Law, of course, stipulates that the volume of work to be done expands to fill the available time in which to do it.

[31] Jaffe, Cummings, and Squeo.

[32] Hunter Keeter, "Myers: Command and Control Interoperability Problems Persist," *Defense Daily*, June 12, 2002, p. 6.

side the ATO context and in ways about which the air component commander was often in the dark. Thanks to their compartmentation practices and long habits of secrecy, covert SOF and OGA teams conducted activities that were often opaque to the CAOC. More than a few airmen complained that without greater transparency and cross-communication between those entities and the more mainstream components of CENTCOM's command structure, such practices will eventually get friendly combatants needlessly killed by inadvertent fratricide. As matters stood, a command-and-control Byzantium ensued from the need to integrate overt SOF, covert SOF, OGA, coalition, and indigenous opposition-group players into a coherent and deconflicted plan of operations. That convoluted arrangement necessitated the placement of an exorbitant number of liaison officers from all communities at both CENTCOM headquarters and in the CAOC as well as in the various JSOTF field headquarters that were scattered throughout the war zone.

Finally, it seems clear in hindsight that the combatant commander and his air component commander should have at least been in the same time zone, if not physically collocated—an anomaly that was finally corrected in the subsequent Operation Iraqi Freedom, when General Franks deployed his headquarters forward from Tampa to Qatar as General Moseley continued to operate out of the CAOC in Saudi Arabia. As the dust of Enduring Freedom was settling, Franks commented that he had been able to remain in Tampa for that war "because of technology assists, which provide 24/7 situational awareness," and good communications that "have permitted us to provide intent and guidance without doing the tactical work of subordinate commanders." Franks further expounded: "We have actually incredible situational awareness of what's going on in Afghanistan. . . . I'd like to be closer to the troops. On the other hand, it's a big thing and it's a very hard thing to move a large combatant headquarters into a theater. Post-9/11, we had an amount of energy available to us, and I could either use the energy available to us to wrap our arms around the problem we faced and the mission that we wanted to get after, or I could focus my attention on moving this headquarters forward, and it very simply was and remains more important to us to focus our energy on what we're doing in support of and command of our components, who in fact are forward. . . . I think there are some fights . . . where I would want this headquarters to be right in the thick of it. There are other fights where we have been blessed by technology to an extent that we can command and control a fight in an offset way, and my belief is we need to be able to do both."[33]

A reasonable argument can be made that this was, while true enough as a statement of fact, also something of a rationalization after the fact. Access, credibility, and trust are all essential preconditions for success among the most senior players in a joint- and combined-operations setting. In particular, there must be a solid trust relationship between the combatant commander and his air component commander if air power is to be put to its best and fullest use. Ideally, the air commander should be able to *command* air and space power, not simply manage air operations by direction from above. As it was, friction points were allowed to develop between CENTCOM's component commanders because of the absence of close proximity to one another and the intimate daily dialogue and mutual understanding that would naturally have gone with it. For example, AFSOC got numerous land component requests during Anaconda for AC-130 support to beleaguered small units during daylight, which was not only an improper but a downright foolhardy use of that asset. It was commendable that Army leaders so valued the quality of the fire support that the AC-130 provided. Yet such requests showed little appreciation of the aircraft's vulnerabilities when observable from the ground within the engagement envelopes of enemy infrared SAMs and AAA.[34] Closer proximity and dialogue between the land component commander and his SOF counterpart might have prevented such well-meaning yet uninformed and time-wasting requests.

---

[33] Ron Martz, "Q&A with General Tommy Franks," *Atlanta Journal and Constitution*, April 7, 2002.

[34] Conversation with Lieutenant General Paul Hester, USAF, Commander, Air Force Special Operations Command, at Maxwell AFB, Alabama, August 13, 2002.

The air component commander, no less than the land and maritime component commanders, should want to avoid at every reasonable cost going to the combatant commander with a complaint about another component. To prevent any such perceived need from arising, all components should be represented in the CAOC to ensure proper awareness of all available options, and all component commanders should be in continual face-to-face or VTC dialogue in a way that only being in the same time zone, at a minimum, would permit. On this point, retired Air Force General Charles Horner, the air commander during Desert Storm, was emphatic on the importance of the component commanders' ability to work harmoniously in producing that war's successful outcome. During a 10-year Gulf War retrospective colloquy among the participating component commanders, he said: "The one thing you need to understand if you're going to understand Desert Storm is that the relationship among the four people at this table—[Admiral Stanley] Arthur, [General Walter] Boomer, [Lieutenant General John] Yeosock, and me—was highly unusual. Such a relationship probably has never existed before, and it probably won't exist in the future. The trust and respect we had for one another was unbelievable. This was a function of personality as much as a desire to get the job done. Unless you understand our relationships, then you really won't understand what went on in Desert Storm, all the good and bad—and there was plenty of each."[35]

Not only would having had the air component commander in closer proximity and interaction with the combatant commander have enabled better time management, it also would have helped ensure that CENTCOM's best air and space expertise was always on tap and available at any moment. The issue here is not whether General Franks should have built a wartime headquarters and moved it forward in sufficient time before the start of Enduring Freedom but that CENTCOM should have established a forward headquarters years before as all of its components (air, maritime, and land) had done.

---

[35] "Ten Years After," *Proceedings*, January 2001, p. 65.

Throughout the preceding decade during which Operation Southern Watch was conducted, CENTAF staffers routinely took 90-day rotations to Prince Sultan Air Base to conduct that operation, whereas CENTCOM staffers rarely, if ever, went forward on such a rotation. As a result of that arguably shortsighted prior planning, they never really came to understand fully how their theater and their components worked in actual practice.

As it was, with CENTCOM headquarters and the CAOC situated eight time zones away from one another, staffers at both ends were so heavily overworked that many became walking zombies. This suggests that the CAOC, in particular, may have been seriously understaffed given the tasks it had to perform. A nontrivial lesson to be learned here might well be that without at least six hours of sleep a night, a staff officer—particularly one with here-and-now combat-support responsibilities—is of little use to anyone. Another might be that as the CAOC moves increasingly toward General Jumper's vision of it as a weapon system, its adoption of crew-rest rules just like those of any flying unit will inevitably be required. The issue of staff stress and exhaustion warrants further analytical attention. Although rarely addressed in detail in after-action reports, it was a factor of more than a little significance in Enduring Freedom and represents an inherent flaw in any arrangement that spreads headquarters across multiple time zones. It also raises a valid question as to how far the Air Force should go in trying to reduce the personnel footprint of the CAOC, especially for operations that last for a month or longer. As the Staff Judge Advocate of Air Combat Command insightfully observed on this point, "we get no gold stars for scrimping on manpower if, as could easily happen, the end result is one bad decision with strategic effects."[36]

---

[36] Comments on an earlier draft by Brigadier General Charles J. Dunlap, Jr., USAF, December 22, 2003.

On Balance

In all, Operation Enduring Freedom earned far more by way of deserved accolades than demerits. Once again, as in the earlier cases of Desert Storm and Allied Force, the chronic doubters of air power's capability and potential were proven wrong. Before the war was even a month old, such critics spoke ominously of an impending "quagmire" and complained that CENTCOM's air strategy was "not working."[37] In the end, however, Enduring Freedom showed the overwhelming preeminence of American military power. Its success in routing the Taliban and putting al Qaeda on the run with the help of indigenous Afghan ground forces and a substantial worldwide coalition also reaffirmed that when the United States leads, others follow. As *The Economist* put it, President Bush "matched forcefulness in Afghanistan with an unexpected delicacy in statecraft" and achieved a military success without doing so in a way that would turn others away.[38]

Although the average combat sortie rate in Enduring Freedom (around 80 to 90 a day, with a high of around 120 during any 24-hour period) was quite low compared to both Operations Desert Storm and Allied Force, no CAOC request for target servicing ever went unmet, and no designated target in need of servicing ever went unstruck for lack of an available sortie. On the contrary, CENTCOM's air component did what it needed to do, even if it could have generated more strike sorties with the aircraft and munitions stocks that were available in principle in the theater of operations. Indeed, it bears recalling on this point General Wald's complaint early on during the war's first two weeks that the CAOC was *wasting* valuable sorties and munitions and putting U.S. aircrews at needless repetitive risk by continued reattacks against Taliban air-defense-related targets that had already been deemed destroyed or otherwise put out of the fight, thanks to CENTCOM's BDA rule

---

[37] Apple, "Quagmire Recalled: Afghanistan as Vietnam," and Pape.

[38] "Six Months On," p. 11.

that required electro-optical imagery confirmation of destructive effects. It further bears recalling the tyranny of distance that dominated the majority of Enduring Freedom's air operations. The average bomber mission from Diego Garcia lasted 12 to 15 hours. Typical carrier-based strike fighter missions from the North Arabian Sea lasted four to six hours, with some lasting as long as 10 hours. Typical land-based fighter sorties out of the Persian Gulf lasted 10 hours or more. Those unusual sortie lengths were profoundly stressful on the aircrews who flew them, and it was demanding enough on the involved units to sustain the sortie numbers that the air component generated in the circumstances. Each carrier air wing operated at a fairly desultory pace compared to the sortie intensity generated during peacetime surge training operations, however, because that was all that the air component commander asked of them. They could have flown more, and they had the needed munitions and aviation fuel reserves to fly more.

As to the charge that CENTCOM's initial air strategy was "not working" and that early air operations had less influence on the war's course and outcome than did later operations, it was deemed essential by CENTCOM and the CAOC to achieve control of the air and the ensuing ability to operate with impunity above 10,000 feet first before doing anything else, which was what many of the first week's air attacks were all about. No one at CENTCOM or in Washington ever expected that those attacks would rout the Taliban and win the war in and of themselves. It also was a part of the war plan to go after fixed military targets of note and to render those unusable before putting Taliban and al Qaeda forces on the run and going after them in detail. That was just sensible, straightforward, conservative military planning, and no one at CENTCOM was in any rush at that point to get Enduring Freedom over with. It also explains why the complaint voiced just two weeks into the war that CENTCOM was pursuing a bankrupt air strategy was so fundamentally misinformed. There was also the fact that weather complications kept CENTCOM from getting a significant SOF presence on the ground to work with the Northern Alliance and enable precision attacks against emerging targets until around the third week of October. In sum, both the initial attacks against fixed Taliban command-and-control and air defense targets (which some complained were "not working") and those that followed against Taliban and al Qaeda forces on the move were equally essential to CENTCOM's ultimate military success. It was not as though CENTCOM tried one approach that failed to work and accordingly then tried an alternate approach that did work in the end.[39]

The war experience further showed that one can now command military operations from anywhere in the world and that the United States can go it alone, if need be, for the hardest part of at least some challenges to its security, however undesirable such a resort may be as a matter of general practice. True enough, the nation relied heavily on basing and overflight rights to achieve its success in Enduring Freedom, including operating from parts of the former Soviet Union in a manner that would have been inconceivable just a few years before.[40] It also had the twin advantages of Northern Alliance support and an enemy that blended pathetic incompetence with a willingness to fight the United States. Nevertheless, as *The Economist* observed, "the chief lesson of Afghanistan, for America, is that it can fight its wars by itself," even though it remains equally true that it can scarcely do so in isolation from any external support whatever.[41]

Granted, one must take care not to overgeneralize from Operation Enduring Freedom. Much like Desert Storm, Deliberate Force, and Allied Force before it, the war was, at bottom, a one-sided application of space-enabled air power to produce a desired outcome, one in which the enemy really never had a chance to counter allied offensive operations. Taliban air defenses, with so few antiaircraft weapons of any reliability, were all but nonexistent. The resultant control of the air commanded by the coalition almost from the war's opening moments enabled both the persistence of allied air strikes and much

---

[39] I am indebted to Kenneth Pollack of the Brookings Institution for having urged me to develop and include these important points.

[40] Conversation with Air Chief Marshal Sir John Day, RAF, Commander in Chief, RAF Strike Command, RAF High Wycombe, England, July 23, 2002.

[41] "Satellites and Horsemen," *The Economist*, March 9, 2002, p. 29.

of the constant, staring ISR that supported them. Predator and Global Hawk could operate essentially unmolested. Coalition assets at sea likewise faced no threat, and the enemy had no means of interfering with our computer networks. Moreover, the number of fixed Taliban and al Qaeda targets of any importance was small, and the coalition never presented sizable targets for the enemy.

For these reasons and more, the war said little about how the United States might fare against a more capable and worthy opponent. Although the nation's pronounced edge in technology, tactics, and training figured importantly in producing the successful outcome, Anthony Cordesman sounded an appropriate note of caution in suggesting that "anyone who rushes out to draw dramatic lessons about the decisive impact of technology, new tactics, or the revolution in military affairs should take a very long, hard look at this list of unique conditions."[42] Much of what worked so impressively in Afghanistan would not be similarly effective in a more demanding threat setting. Mindful of that fact, the commander of Air Combat Command, General Hal Hornburg, warned that "we are in danger of learning the wrong lessons from Afghanistan."[43] The Taliban did not present a robust air defense threat for allied forces to contend with, as would North Korea and other parts of the world where the United States could find itself forced to engage some day. As a result, there was no need to fight for air supremacy. In a Korean scenario, in contrast, far more challenging work would be required to take down the enemy's air defenses and command-and-control network. Noting only one example of the difference, Secretary Roche pointed out that one of the most important lessons that Enduring Freedom taught the Air Force was the growing operational importance of UAVs. At the same time, he cautioned against expecting that UAVs can do everything, adding that the success of Predator over Afghanistan "is not something that is going to work in heavy air defenses," especially in

---

[42] Cordesman, p. 10.

[43] Tony Capaccio, "Afghan Lessons Don't Apply to 'Axis,' Generals Say," Bloomberg.com, February 20, 2002.

the case of UAVs that operate at lower altitudes.[44] As the Chief of Naval Operations, Admiral Vern Clark, concluded in this respect: "It is going to be different in every scenario. . . . The last one wasn't like this one, and the next one won't be like this one. . . ."[45]

That said, the campaign represented a unique blend of air power, allied SOF, and indigenous Afghan opposition-group combatants on the ground. It was further marked by a complete absence of heavy-maneuver U.S. ground forces. Notwithstanding the later involvement of a large number of conventional ground troops in Operation Anaconda, the campaign was not a land war but a SOF-centric air war that largely accounted for the ultimate successes of the Afghan resistance forces. SOF teams and air power produced a unique synergy in which each enabled the other. The SOF units rendered air power more effective than it would have been otherwise, and air power enabled the SOF teams to succeed with opposition groups in land operations against Taliban and al Qaeda forces in a fashion that otherwise would not have been possible. Consistently accurate air attacks against Taliban positions also allowed SOF teams to convince opposition-group leaders that air power had immediate effects and that American combat controllers and ETACs were a swing factor in making that possible. Ground spotters made air power more effective by identifying and designating enemy combatants after Northern Alliance forces flushed them out of hiding and exposed them to direct attack. They also minimized not only unintended collateral damage but also friendly fire incidents. For their part, U.S. fighter aircrews showed commendable discipline in honoring collateral damage avoidance restrictions.[46]

---

[44] Ron Lorenzo, "Air Force Secretary Teaches Lessons of Afghanistan," *Defense Week,* July 8, 2002, pp. 1–2. It bears noting that Predator and Global Hawk are not unpiloted; their pilots are simply not aboard the aircraft. They still require pilot skills and pilot judgment to be operated effectively.

[45] Ricks, "Bull's-Eye War: Pinpoint Bombing Shifts Role of GI Joe."

[46] As a case in point, in one reported instance, an F-15E weapon system operator became temporarily disoriented while his LGB was guiding. He accordingly directed the weapon into a dirt field rather than allow it to continue guiding on what may have been an unapproved target. Bowden, "The Kabul-Ki Dance," p. 76.

SOF units on the ground further enabled a patient waiting process of monitoring potential targets, acquiring precise geolocation and target characterization information, holding out for the best possible time to attack, and then calling in strikes when the enemy was most exposed. In this, the SOF presence was critical to Enduring Freedom's outcome. After Mazar-i-Sharif and Kabul were finally taken, the Army's Vice Chief of Staff, General John Keane, said in an interview: "Those population centers toppled as a result of a combined-arms team: U.S. air power and a combination of special forces and Afghan troops."[47] The commander of USAREUR, General Montgomery Meigs, added in a similar spirit: "It takes a ground force to make the precision weapons more effective. . . . If you want your precision weapons to be most effective, use your ground forces to force them out of their holes."[48] Neither air power alone nor air power in support of conventional ground troops could have produced the same results. Yet the integration of SOF operations with strike aviation turned the enemy's cave redoubts from safe hideaways into death traps. Navy SEALs and other U.S. SOF personnel are now most definitely a part of the air power equation. Thanks to their involvement, Operation Enduring Freedom saw more kills per sortie than ever before. Many CAS targets were taken out with a single munition.

Cooperation within the SOF community was also superb, as was the integration of the space component with SOF-supported air operations. For example, when Knife 3, the MH-53 Pave Low helicopter that launched to rescue an ill SOF combatant in northern Afghanistan, went down in bad weather early during the campaign, space and SOF involvement made the ensuing CSAR effort possible. Space weapons officers in the CAOC and air leaders willing to incorporate space as an equal partner in the CAOC helped to break down

---

[47] Quoted in Grant, "An Air War Like No Other," p. 40.

[48] Ann Roosevelt, "Ground Forces Help Make Precision Weapons Precise," *Defense Week Daily Update*, April 9, 2002.

both intra-Air Force and interservice organizational firewalls toward that end.

Enduring Freedom further showed the force-multiplier effect of having trained eyes on the ground to locate, identify, and validate targets. Those SOF eyes represented, in effect, yet another class of up-close sensors able to quickly detect, identify, and assess fast-moving targets. Confidence in the ability of SOF teams to do this consistently well allowed senior decisionmakers to more confidently transfer target approval authority to on-scene commanders for many target categories. SOF personnel can also provide immediate BDA after an attack that may not be available from other forward air controllers (FACs). At bottom, the effective integration of air power with SOF units, urged from the very outset by Secretary of Defense Rumsfeld, constituted the break point in the war and was what ultimately made it work. As Rumsfeld concluded: "The air war enabled the ground war to succeed."[49] That would suggest that the time has come for all services to begin institutionalizing such connections more thoroughly in their respective doctrines and TTPs.[50]

The war also achieved a new high in joint-service cooperation. There were grumblings early on from some quarters in the Navy alleging that the Air Force was dragging its heels on providing needed JDAM kits to the Navy. Those charges, however, were later refuted authoritatively by both service chiefs.[51] Also, some Navy and Air Force advocates for a time got into a parochial "who did what" exchange over bomb tonnage dropped versus combat sorties flown that was totally unhelpful to a correct understanding of the synergy that produced the successful outcome of Enduring Freedom. The overarching fact that matters most is that each service brought a comparative advantage to the fight. Air Force bombers flew only around 10

---

[49] Quoted in Robert S. Dudney, "Beat the Devil," *Air Force Magazine*, October 2002.

[50] For more on this point, see Philip S. Meilinger, "Preparing for the Next Little War: Operation Enduring Freedom Points to New Ways of Warfighting," *Armed Forces Journal International*, April 2002, pp. 38–41.

[51] "Report of Air Force, Navy Wrangling Misses the Mark," *Washington Times*, November 13, 2001.

percent of the sortie total but dropped 80 percent of the ordnance, including a large number of accurate JDAMs. Also, the Navy needed land-based Air Force and RAF tankers to be mission-effective in Enduring Freedom. Yet its carrier air wings proved indispensable to CENTCOM in a part of the world where the Air Force lacked the needed access to operate its fighters most effectively. Both air component commanders, then–Lieutenant Generals Wald and Moseley, reported that Air Force and Navy cooperation was outstanding in every respect. For its part, the Marine Corps, characteristically thought of as an over-the-beach amphibious force, projected its power and influence more than 600 miles inland.

As in the earlier Operations Deliberate Force and Allied Force, there was no need in Enduring Freedom for massed U.S. ground forces to seize and hold enemy territory. Of course, going in light on the ground in Afghanistan was essential in any case to avoid creating any false impression that the allied military presence was an invading force. That said, it seems clear that the day of more or less equally matched infantry and armor clashes on a close battlefield may be near over, at least against an adversary like the United States with the capacity to demolish anything it can see by means of precision standoff air attack. Of course, there is no assurance that the United States will never again need heavy ground forces in large numbers, starting with a worst-case scenario in Korea. Because many countries have invested in heavy conventional forces, they will use them to the best of their ability. Consequently, the United States will very likely engage in more conventional battles in the future. Yet as long as it controls the air and has good standoff weapons in all services, it will continue to win victories in any conventional conflict. It also almost surely will never again have to sustain a high incidence of ground-force casualties in conventional single-battle situations if it makes the most of its comparative advantages in the air, space, and information arenas. Retired Army Major General Robert Scales captured this point well when he suggested that the long-familiar Army mission of "closing with and destroying the enemy" is no longer pertinent, at least in most conceivable circumstances, and that friendly armies should now be thought of mainly as "finding and fixing force[s] whose purpose is to verify the exact composition and location of the enemy and hold him in place long enough for precision fires to do the killing with efficiency, discretion, and dispatch—from a distance."[52] That said, the continued attrition that has been experienced by U.S. ground forces in counterinsurgency and urban fighting since the end of large-scale offensive operations in Afghanistan demonstrates the effectiveness of asymmetric tactics undertaken by those who understand and fear the capacity of American air power.

If there was anything "transformational" about the way Operation Enduring Freedom was conducted, it was the dominance of fused information over platforms and munitions as the principal enabler of the campaign's success in the end. That new dynamic made all other major aspects of the war possible, including the integration of SOF with precision-strike air power, the minimization of target-location error, collateral damage avoidance, and command from the rear. The use of SOF teams as human ISR sensors for applying air power in a manner and for a purpose far different from traditional notions of CAS was a novel concept that touched the heart of the always-sensitive SOF-conventional Army relationship. It may have accounted, at least in part, for some of the friction encountered in Operation Anaconda once the conventional Army got involved in what the SOF world had come to regard as "its" battlespace. In all events, thanks to real-time imagery and increased communications connectivity, the kill chain was shorter than ever, and target-attack accuracy was truly phenomenal. Throughout Enduring Freedom, persistent ISR and precision attack gave CENTCOM the ability to deny the enemy sanctuary both day and night. Such network-centric operations are now the cutting edge of an ongoing paradigm shift in American combat style that may be of greater potential moment than was the introduction of the tank at the beginning of the 20th century. Even before the war was over, President Bush declared that this

---

[52] Major General Robert L. Scales, "Checkmate by Operational Maneuver," *Armed Forces Journal International*, October 2001, pp. 38–42. Scales further points out that effects-based planning and execution, information operations, network-centric approaches, rapid maneuver, and precision attack need not be the exclusive roles of any single service.

emerging paradigm shift "promises to change the face of battle" and that "Afghanistan has been the proving ground for this approach."[53]

As for the downside, however, continuing a trend that had been set earlier in both Operations Deliberate Force and Allied Force, the unprecedented global communications connectivity and ISR fusion that distinguished Enduring Freedom was matched by unprecedented emphasis on avoiding collateral damage and an unprecedented dominance of senior civilian leadership in shaping target approvals. Although by definition war is about politics, the political considerations in this case were so overriding that strict rules-of-engagement enforcement was deemed absolutely essential by the Bush administration. Just as centralized execution was made possible by modern communications technology, it also was driven by perceived national leadership needs. The proverbial 8,000-mile screwdriver, however, is *not*, at least in most circumstances, a recommended tool for conducting modern combat operations. Clearer rules of engagement before the fact, along with constant updates of approved targets and empowerment of the components for execution, have become indispensable for effective time-sensitive targeting.

The Enduring Freedom experience pointed up some new facts of life about likely future American combat involvement in coming years. First, it showed that positive target identification and avoiding civilian casualties have become deeply ingrained features of the emerging American way of war. Second, it suggested that senior leadership will continue to guard its authority to make strike approval decisions for target attacks that entail a high risk of inflicting civilian casualties. Approval time and TST timelines will increasingly be determined by rules of engagement and target approval criteria. Accordingly, airmen must get away from the "one size fits all" approach to targeting doctrine. Because quick-response attack against emerging targets has become the new reality, airmen need to create new operating concepts and TTPs to accommodate it. They also need to begin forging a new doctrine for handling the downside effects of improved

---

[53] Quoted in Peter J. Boyer, "A Different War: Is the Army Becoming Irrelevant?" *The New Yorker*, July 1, 2002, p. 65.

C4/ISR fusion, including, most notably, such issues as "reach forward" and centralized execution.

Although they could scarcely have known so at the time, those who participated in Enduring Freedom at both the command and execution levels were engaged in what, in hindsight, turned out to have been a fortuitous dress rehearsal for the subsequent three-week conventional campaign against Iraq that CENTCOM initiated barely a year later, almost to the day, after the dust from Operation Anaconda had settled. As eager as military organizations have repeatedly been throughout the years since Desert Storm to extract instant "lessons learned" from conflicts like Enduring Freedom, such lessons all too often are merely indicated rather than truly "learned," since only rarely are they reflected by due changes in resource apportionment and operational conduct. Moreover, since the successive conflicts experienced by the U.S. military since the 1991 Gulf War have each been planned and led by almost entirely different groups of principals at all levels, the course and outcome of each have been heavily, if not wholly, direct outgrowths of the personalities who occupied the key decisionmaking positions. Operations Desert Storm, Allied Force, and Enduring Freedom, to note only the three most significant of those conflicts, each saw central roles played by the president, his national security adviser, the Secretary of Defense, the chairman of the Joint Chiefs of Staff, a regional combatant commander, and an air component commander, among others. To that extent, each could be said to have featured a common organizational chart. Yet each also saw profoundly different personalities occupying those key positions, some strong and decisive and others less so. As a result, the ensuing chemistry between and among those singular combinations of players tended to yield outcomes that were equally unique and idiosyncratic, irrespective of any would-be "lessons" that should have been drawn and applied from one conflict to the next.

Operations Enduring Freedom and Iraqi Freedom, in marked contrast, differed from the earlier U.S. conflicts of the 1990s in that they took place in such close temporal proximity to one another that each was conducted by the same principal players, from the White House and Pentagon in Washington through CENTCOM headquarters in Tampa to the CAOC in Saudi Arabia and even, in many cases, at the shooter level in all services. Accordingly, if there was ever to be any opportunity in principle for "lessons learned" from one experience to be applied in a second, one would think that Operation Iraqi Freedom would have presented precisely such an opportunity. As of mid-2005, most official accounts of the Iraqi Freedom experience by those who participated in the first three weeks of major combat were still not publicly available.[54] Nevertheless, it has already become clear that many of the most nagging frustrations of Enduring Freedom identified and assessed in this study were *not* encountered, by and large, by those in the CAOC who ran the subsequent air war over Iraq.

For example, in the latter case there were far fewer approval delays encountered in time-critical targeting, and only rarely did General Moseley have to seek target approvals from higher authority.[55] Moreover, the combatant commander and air component commander were now, although still not physically collocated, at least forward-deployed in the same time zone. That allowed much easier communication between those two principals as needed. By the same token, in contrast to the case in Enduring Freedom, the air component commander had *total* control over the JIPTL. And a two-star Air Force general was attached to the land component for the war's duration, not only to ensure closer coordination between the air and land components but also, at least implicitly, to help guard against any recurrence of another untoward experience like Anaconda. Most important of all, the close interaction between and among the most

---

[54] To cite two especially notable examples, CENTAF organized and led a comprehensive classified effort to record all essential details of the Iraqi Freedom air war by convening a two-week conference of more than 250 of the air war's participants from all services at Nellis AFB, Nevada, beginning on July 7, 2003. The Naval Strike and Air Warfare Center conducted a similar, though less ambitious, one-day classified event with appropriate Navy and CENTAF representation to capture essential Navy contributions and conclusions at Naval Air Station (NAS) Fallon, Nevada, on September 18, 2003.

[55] Conversations with Brigadier General Daniel Darnell, USAF, senior CAOC director during Operation Iraqi Freedom, and Lieutenant General Victor E. Renuart, USAF, CENTCOM J-3, Washington, D.C., September 4–5, 2003.

senior principals in CENTCOM and in Washington during the period spanning the wars in Afghanistan and Iraq, with the air component commander, General Moseley, playing a leading and pivotal role, enabled team-building and the development of trust relationships that gave the CAOC control of the JIPTL and much greater collateral damage management authority. All of that proved indispensable in shaping the early successful outcome of Iraqi Freedom in toppling the regime of Saddam Hussein.

To be sure, the conduct of Iraqi Freedom also saw a rise of new frustrations in strategy execution yet to be documented that undoubtedly will require senior leadership attention and action. Yet when the full history of that campaign is eventually written, it almost surely will show that the war's initial conduct was made both easier and more effective by the applied learning of its principals and their respective staffs in correcting mistakes made over the course of Enduring Freedom. That, in and of itself, may be among the most salient and memorable teachings of CENTCOM's war against the Taliban and al Qaeda in Afghanistan.

Bibliography

Books

Anderson, Jon Lee, *The Lion's Grave: Dispatches from Afghanistan*, New York: Grove Press, 2002.

Bowden, Mark, *Black Hawk Down: A Story of Modern War*, New York: Penguin Books, 1999.

Creech, Bill, *The Five Pillars of TQM*, New York: Dutton, 1994.

Franks, General Tommy, *American Soldier*, New York: Regan Books, 2004.

Friedman, Norman, *Terrorism, Afghanistan, and America's New Way of War*, Annapolis, Md.: Naval Institute Press, 2003.

Huntington, Samuel P., *The Clash of Civilizations and the Remaking of World Order*, New York: Simon and Schuster, 1996.

Lambeth, Benjamin S., *Russia's Air Power in Crisis*, Washington, D.C.: Smithsonian Institution Press, 1999.

Moore, Robin, *The Hunt for bin Laden: Task Force Dagger*, New York: Random House, 2003.

Naylor, Sean, *Not a Good Day to Die: The Untold Story of Operation Anaconda*, New York: Berkley Books, 2005.

Pollack, Kenneth M., *The Threatening Storm: The Case for Invading Iraq*, New York: Random House, 2002.

Priest, Dana, *The Mission: Waging War and Keeping Peace with America's Military*, New York: W. W. Norton & Company, 2003.

Schroen, Gary C., *First In: An Insider's Account of How the CIA Spearheaded the War on Terror in Afghanistan*, New York: Ballantine Books, 2005.

The 9/11 Commission Report: Final Report of the National Commission on Terrorist Attacks Upon the United States, New York: W. W. Norton & Company, 2004.

Woodward, Bob, *Bush at War*, New York: Simon and Schuster, 2002.

Monographs and Reports

Bensahel, Nora, *The Counterterror Coalitions: Cooperation with Europe, NATO, and the European Union*, Santa Monica, Calif.: RAND Corporation, MR-1746-AF, 2003.

Bowie, Christopher J., Robert P. Haffa, Jr., and Robert E. Mullins, *Future War: What Trends in America's Post-Cold War Military Conflicts Tell Us About Early 21st Century Warfare*, Arlington, Va.: Northrop Grumman Analysis Center, January 2003.

Cordesman, Anthony, *The Lessons of Afghanistan: Warfighting, Intelligence, Force Transformation, Counter-Proliferation, and Arms Control*, Washington, D.C.: Center for Strategic and International Studies, June 28, 2002.

Lambeth, Benjamin S., *NATO's Air War for Kosovo: A Strategic and Operational Assessment*, Santa Monica, Calif.: RAND Corporation, MR-1365-AF, 2001.

Pirnie, Bruce R., Alan J. Vick, Adam Grissom, Karl P. Mueller, and David T. Orletsky, *Beyond Close Air Support: Forging a New Air-Ground Partnership*, Santa Monica, Calif.: RAND Corporation, MG-301-AF, 2005.

Journal and Periodical Articles

"Afghan Air War Continues for Second Month," *Air International*, December 2001.

"Afghanistan Sees First Combat Use of New Bomb," *Aviation Week and Space Technology*, December 10, 2001.

"Allies in Search of a Strategy," *The Economist*, September 22, 2001.

Arostegui, Martin, "The Search for bin Laden," *Insight Magazine*, September 2, 2002.

Asker, James R., "Washington Outlook," *Aviation Week and Space Technology*, September 7, 2001.

————, "Washington Outlook," *Aviation Week and Space Technology*, October 8, 2001.

Bacon, Lance M., "Secret Weapons: The Airmen Who Are Winning the Ground War," *Air Force Times*, April 8, 2002.

Barrie, Douglas, and Michael A. Taverna, "European Forces in Afghanistan Buildup," *Aviation Week and Space Technology*, January 21, 2002.

"A Battle on Many Fronts," *The Economist*, October 6, 2001.

Bentley, Lieutenant Colonel Christopher F., USA, "Afghanistan: Joint and Coalition Fire Support in Operation Anaconda," *Field Artillery*, September–October 2002.

Billingsley, Dodge, "Choppers in the Coils: Operation Anaconda Was a 'Back to Basics' Campaign for U.S. Combat Helicopters," *Journal of Electronic Defense*, September 2002.

Bowden, Mark, "The Kabul-Ki Dance," *The Atlantic Monthly*, November 2002.

Boyer, Peter J., "A Different War: Is the Army Becoming Irrelevant?" *The New Yorker*, July 1, 2002.

Brookes, Andrew, "The Air War in Afghanistan," *Air International*, August 2002.

Butler, Amy, "Global Hawk UAV Crash Claims Program's Only Infrared Camera," *Inside the Air Force*, January 4, 2002.

————, "Flight Testing Halts After OEF Claims Second Global Hawk in Crash," *Inside the Air Force*, July 12, 2002.

Carney, James, and John F. Dickerson, "Inside the War Room," *Time*, December 31, 2001–January 7, 2002.

"Closing In," *The Economist*, September 29, 2001.

Correll, John T., "Verbatim," *Air Force Magazine*, August 2002.

Covault, Craig, "Navy Enlists NASA in the War on Terror," *Aviation Week and Space Technology*, April 8, 2002.

"The Day the World Changed," *The Economist*, September 15, 2001.

Deptula, Major General David A., USAF, Colonel Gary Crowder, USAF, and Major George L. Stamper, USAF, "Direct Attack: Enhancing Counterland Doctrine and Joint Air-Ground Operations, *Air and Space Power Journal*, Winter 2003.

Dudney, Robert S., "Beat the Devil," *Air Force Magazine*, October 2002.

Duffy, Michael, "War on All Fronts," *Time*, October 15, 2001.

Duffy, Michael, and Mark Thompson, "Straight Shooter," *Time*, March 17, 2003.

Dusch, Major Charles D., Jr., USAF, "Anaconda Offers Lessons in Close Air Support," *Proceedings*, March 2003.

Elliott, Michael, "'We're at War," *Time*, September 24, 2001.

————, "'We Will Not Fail,'" *Time*, October 1, 2001.

Erwin, Sandra I., "Naval Aviation: Lessons from the War," *National Defense*, June 2002.

Fang, Bay, "Waiting on the Mountain," *U.S. News and World Report*, November 12, 2001.

Fineman, Howard, "Bush's 'Phase One,'" *Newsweek*, October 15, 2001.

Fulghum, David A., "War Plans, Defense Buildup Take Shape," *Aviation Week and Space Technology*, September 17, 2001.

————, "Pentagon Anticipates No Shopping Spree," *Aviation Week and Space Technology*, September 24, 2001.

————, "Afghanistan Crash Reveals U.S. Intel Operation," *Aviation Week and Space Technology*, October 1, 2001.

————, "After the Taliban: What Next?" *Aviation Week and Space Technology*, October 29, 2001.

————, "Airdrop in a Crowded Sky," *Aviation Week and Space Technology*, October 29, 2001.

————, "Big Bomb Batters Taliban Troops," *Aviation Week and Space Technology*, November 12, 2001.

————, "U.S. Girds for Demands of Long Winter War," *Aviation Week and Space Technology*, November 12, 2001.

————, "Big Bomb Strikes Kandahar Defenses," *Aviation Week and Space Technology*, December 3, 2001.

————, "Aircraft Close on Battlefield," *Aviation Week and Space Technology*, December 10, 2001.

————, "Bombing Costs Escalate in Afghanistan Operations," *Aviation Week and Space Technology*, December 10, 2001.

————, "Navy Exploits P-3 in Overland Recce Role," *Aviation Week and Space Technology*, March 4, 2002.

————, "Intel Emerging as Key Weapon in Afghanistan," *Aviation Week and Space Technology*, March 11, 2002.

————, "U.S. Troops Confront al Qaeda in Vicious Mountain Battle," *Aviation Week and Space Technology*, March 11, 2002.

Fulghum, David A., and Robert Wall, "Military Aids Inquiry, Plans for Retribution," *Aviation Week and Space Technology*, September 17, 2001.

————, "U.S. to Move First, Plan Details Later," *Aviation Week and Space Technology*," September 24, 2001.

————, "U.S. Stalks Taliban with New Air Scheme," *Aviation Week and Space Technology*, October 15, 2001.

————, "Global Hawk, J-STARS Head for Afghanistan," *Aviation Week and Space Technology*, November 5, 2001.

————, "Heavy Bomber Attacks Dominate Afghan War," *Aviation Week and Space Technology*, December 3, 2001.

Fulghum, David A., Robert Wall, and David M. North, "Navy Priorities Are UAVs, Data Links, Persistence," *Aviation Week and Space Technology*, December 24/31, 2001.

Gildea, Kerry, "NIMA Extends Deal with Space Imaging for Exclusive Imagery Over Afghanistan," *Defense Daily*, November 7, 2001.

"Global Hawk Back in the Fight After Post-Crash Stand-Down," *Inside the Air Force*, March 15, 2002.

Goodman, Glenn W., Jr., "Invisible Support: Air Force Communications-Jamming Aircraft Aided U.S. Special Operations Forces in Afghanistan," *Armed Forces Journal International*, August 2002.

———, "Warriors Training Warriors: New Entry Regime for USAF Combat Controllers Is Paying Off," *Armed Forces Journal International*, September 2002.

Goure, Daniel, "Location, Location, Location," *Jane's Defense Weekly*, February 27, 2002.

Grange, Brigadier General David L., USA (Ret.), Lieutenant Colonel Walter Bjorneby, USAF, Captain Kelly Sullivan, Air National Guard, Lieutenant Mike Sparks, U.S. Army Reserve, and Chuck Myers, "The Close Air Support Imperative: Failings in Afghanistan Highlight Deficiencies in U.S. Air Force Doctrine and Equipment," *Armed Forces Journal International*, December 2002.

Grant, Rebecca, "The War Nobody Expected," *Air Force Magazine*, April 2002.

———, "The Air Power of Anaconda," *Air Force Magazine*, September 2002.

———, "An Air War Like No Other," *Air Force Magazine*, November 2002.

———, "The Clash About CAS," *Air Force Magazine*, January 2003.

Grier, Peter, "The Combination That Worked," *Air Force Magazine*, April 2002.

———, "The Strength of the Force," *Air Force Magazine*, April 2002.

Grossman, Elaine, "Military Is Embroiled in Debate Over Who Should Guard the United States," *Inside the Pentagon*, September 20, 2001.

————, "Jumper: Army, Air Force Work to Avoid Repeat of Anaconda Lapses," *Inside the Pentagon*, February 27, 2002.

————, "Left in the Dark for Most Anaconda Planning, Air Force Opens New Probe," *Inside the Pentagon*, October 3, 2002.

————, "Army Anaconda Commander Revisits Remarks About Air Power Lapses," *Inside the Pentagon*, November 7, 2002.

————, "Was Operation Anaconda Ill-Fated from the Start? Army Analyst Blames Afghan Battle Failings on Bad Command Set-Up," *Inside the Pentagon*, July 29, 2004.

Hammer, Joshua, and John Barry, "A Win in the Fog of War," *Newsweek*, November 19, 2001.

Hebert, Adam J., "Supply Chain Visibility: U.S. Air Force Adapts to War in Afghanistan and Learns Logistics Lessons," *Armed Forces Journal International*, April 2002.

Hendren, John, "Beddown in Bishkek," *Air Force Magazine*, July 2002.

Hersh, Seymour M., "Manhunt: The Bush Administration's New Strategy in the War Against Terrorism," *The New Yorker*, December 23/30, 2002.

Hirsh, Michael, and Roy Gutman, "Powell in the Middle," *Newsweek*, October 1, 2001.

Hirsh, Michael, and John Barry, "Behind America's Attack on Afghanistan," *Newsweek*, October 7, 2001.

Hodge, Nathan, "Predator Helps Coalition Estimate Body Count," *Defense Week Daily Update*, March 19, 2002.

Ignatieff, Michael, "Nation-Building Lite," *New York Times Magazine*, July 28, 2002.

Jansen, Lieutenant Colonel John M., USA; Lieutenant Commander Nicholas Dienna, USN; Majors William T. Bufkin and James B. Sisler, USAF; and Majors Thomas R. Di Tomasso and David I. Oclander, USA, "The Tower of Babel: Joint Close Air Support

Performance at the Operational Level, *Marine Corps Gazette*, March 2003.

———, "'Lines One Through Three . . . N/A,'" *Marine Corps Gazette*, April 2003.

Kaplan, Lawrence F., "Troop Movement: How the Army Ditched the Powell Doctrine," *New Republic*, March 25, 2002.

"Keeping the Birds Aloft," *U.S. News and World Report*, November 12, 2001.

Keeter, Hunter, "PGM Funding May Top List for Short-Term Military Spending Increase," *Defense Daily*, September 20, 2001.

———, "Pentagon Downplays Preliminary Look at Weapons Accuracy in Afghanistan," *Defense Daily*, April 10, 2002.

———, "Myers: Command and Control Interoperability Problems Persist," *Defense Daily*, June 12, 2002

———, "Key Navy Lessons from Afghanistan: Invest in SOF, PGMs, Sea Basing," *Defense Daily*, July 9, 2002.

Kusovac, Zoran, "Carrier Aircraft Are 'Crucial Factor,'" *Jane's Defense Weekly*, November 21, 2001.

"A Leader Is Born," *The Economist*, September 22, 2001.

Lesure, Marie, "The 'Market Price' of Terrorism: U.S. Allies Add to Toll Paid by Taliban and al Qaeda," *Armed Forces Journal International*, June 2002.

Lewis, Paul, "Russia Opens Way for U.S. Attack," *Flight International*, October 2–8, 2001.

Lok, Joris Jannsen, "Europe Strengthens Support for Enduring Freedom," *Jane's Defense Weekly*, April 17, 2002.

Lorenzo, Ron, "Air Force Secretary Teaches Lessons of Afghanistan," *Defense Week*, July 8, 2002.

Lowe, Christian, "Relevance of QDR in Question," *Defense Week*, September 24, 2001.

Mazetti, Mark, "Now, It's Eyeball to Eyeball," *U.S. News and World Report*, November 19, 2001.

Mazetti, Mark, and Richard J. Newman, "Fight to the Finish," *U.S. News and World Report*, October 22, 2001.

———, "Rumsfeld's Way," *U.S. News and World Report*, December 17, 2001.

Mazetti, Mark, Thomas Omestad, and Richard J. Newman, "The Thin Green Line," *U.S. News and World Report*, April 8, 2002.

Morring, Frank, Jr., "NASA Test Satellite Collects War Imagery," *Aviation Week and Space Technology*, January 21, 2002.

McElroy, Robert H., "Interview: Fire Support for Operation Anaconda," *Field Artillery*, September–October 2002.

McGeary, Johanna, "Hunting Osama," *Time*, December 10, 2001.

Meilinger, Philip S, "Preparing for the Next Little War: Operation Enduring Freedom Points to New Ways of Warfighting," *Armed Forces Journal International*, April 2002.

Muradian, Vago, "DoD Asks Industry to Prepare for Surge; Focus on Precision Munitions, Spares," *Defense Daily*, September 17, 2001.

Nathman, Vice Admiral John B., USN, "'We Were Great': Navy Air in Afghanistan," *Proceedings*, March 2002.

Naylor, Sean D., "In Shah-i-Kot, Apaches Save the Day—and Their Reputation, *Army Times*, March 25, 2002.

———, "Officers: Air Force Policy Left Ground Troops High and Dry," *Army Times*, September 30, 2002.

Newman, Richard J., "From Up in the Sky," *U.S. News and World Report*, February 25, 2002.

———, "The Little Predator That Could," *Air Force Magazine*, March 2002.

"The Next Phase," *The Economist*, October 13, 2001.

"Notes from NDIA's 2002 Space Policy and Architecture Symposium, February 26–27, Falls Church, Virginia," *Inside the Air Force*, March 1, 2002.

Neuenswander, Colonel Matt, USAF, "JCAS in Operation Anaconda: It's Not All Bad News," *Field Artillery*, May–June 2003.

"Old Friends, Best Friends," *The Economist*, September 15, 2001.

Payton, Sue C., "Fast-Tracking Innovative Technologies: DoD's ACTD Program Supports the War on Terrorism," *Armed Forces Journal International*, April 2002.

"Precision Weapons, Networks Trump Navy's Need for New Ships, England Says," *Aerospace Daily*, October 17, 2002.

"Q and A with Air Force Secretary James Roche," *Business Week* online, February 1, 2002.

Ramo, Joshua Cooper, "In Hot Pursuit," *Time*, October 8, 2001.

Ratnesar, Romesh, "Grading the Other War," *Time*, October 14, 2002.

———, "The Ground War: Into the Fray," *Time*, October 29, 2001.

Roos, John G., "Turning Up the Heat: Taliban Became Firm Believers in Effects-Based Operations," *Armed Forces Journal International*, February 2002.

Roosevelt, Ann, "Ground Forces Help Make Precision Weapons Precise," *Defense Week Daily Update*, April 9, 2002.

"Satellites and Horsemen," *The Economist*, March 9, 2002.

Scales, Major General Robert L., "Checkmate by Operational Maneuver," *Armed Forces Journal International*, October 2001.

Scott, William B., "Domestic Air Patrols Tax Tankers, AWACS," *Aviation Week and Space Technology*, October 8, 2001.

———, "Improved Milspace Key to Antiterrorism War," *Aviation Week and Space Technology*, December 10, 2001.

———, "'Space' Enhances War on Terrorists," *Aviation Week and Space Technology*, January 21, 2002.

———, "U.S. Reassesses Protective Flights," *Aviation Week and Space Technology*, January 21, 2002.

———, "Milspace Comes of Age in Fighting Terror," *Aviation Week and Space Technology*, April 8, 2002.

———, "F-16 Pilots Considered Ramming Flight 93," *Aviation Week and Space Technology*, September 9, 2002.

———, "NORAD, Fighters on High Domestic Alert," *Aviation Week and Space Technology*, October 1, 2002.

"Send in the Drones," *The Economist*, November 20, 2001.

Sirak, Michael, "Interview: James Roche—Secretary of the U.S. Air Force," *Jane's Defense Weekly*, January 9, 2002.

"Six Months On," *The Economist*, March 9, 2002.

Strass, Marc, "More SIGINT, UAVs and HUMINT Top Army Intel Needs from Afghanistan," *Defense Daily*, April 11, 2002.

Taverna, Michael, "Europeans Bolster Antiterrorism Role," *Aviation Week and Space Technology*, December 3, 2001.

"Ten Years After," *Proceedings*, January 2001.

"Testing Intelligence," *The Economist*, October 6, 2001.

Thomas, Evan, "Gunning for bin Laden," *Newsweek*, November 26, 2001.

Thomas, Evan, and Melinda Liu, "Warlords: For Sale or Rent," *Newsweek*, November 5, 2001.

Tiboni, Frank, "Instantaneous Attack Capability Near for U.S.," *Defense News*, January 7–13, 2002.

Tirpak, John, "Enduring Freedom," *Air Force Magazine*, February 2002.

"U.S. Air Force Flies Combat Patrols Over Dozens of American Cities," *Inside the Pentagon*, September 13, 2001.

"U.S. Pacific Command Needs Missile Defense, More Aircraft, CINC Says," *Aerospace Daily*, March 6, 2002.

Vego, Milan, "What Can We Learn from Enduring Freedom?" *Proceedings*, July 2002.

Wall, Robert, "Taliban Air Defenses Target U.S. Weakness," *Aviation Week and Space Technology*, October 15, 2001.

———, "Targeting, Weapon Supply Encumber Air Campaign," *Aviation Week and Space Technology*, October 22, 2001.

———, "EA-6B Crews Recast Their Infowar Role," *Aviation Week and Space Technology*, November 19, 2001.

———, "F-14s Add Missions in Anti-Taliban Effort," *Aviation Week and Space Technology*, November 19, 2001.

————, "Navy Adapts Operations for Afghan War Hurdles," *Aviation Week and Space Technology*, November 19, 2001.

————, "Battle Management Dominates E-2C Combat Operations," *Aviation Week and Space Technology*, November 26, 2001.

————, "Big Bomb Strikes Kandahar Defenses," *Aviation Week and Space Technology*, December 3, 2001.

————, "War Drains U.S. Military's Aircraft and Munitions," *Aviation Week and Space Technology*, February 18, 2002.

————, "Counterterror Combat Shrinks Special Ops Inventory," *Aviation Week and Space Technology*, March 18, 2002.

————, "War Costs Overextend Pentagon Purse, Gear," *Aviation Week and Space Technology*, March 25, 2002.

————, "Army Seeks to Fill Intelligence 'Gap,'" *Aviation Week and Space Technology*, April 15, 2002.

————, "MH-47 Crews Detail Conflict's Exploits, Woes," *Aviation Week and Space Technology*, April 15, 2002.

————, "Military Assesses War Strengths, Shortfalls," *Aviation Week and Space Technology*, April 15, 2002.

————, "War Expansion May Require New Operational Techniques," *Aviation Week and Space Technology*, April 29, 2002.

————, "USAF to Bolster Pilot Rescue Ability," *Aviation Week and Space Technology*, August 12, 2002.

————, "Afghanistan Alters USAF Posture in Asia," *Aviation Week and Space Technology*, September 2, 2002.

"Washington Outlook," *Aviation Week and Space Technology*, September 17, 2001.

"Washington Outlook," *Aviation Week and Space Technology*, October 8, 2001.

"Washington Outlook," *Aviation Week and Space Technology*, March 18, 2002.

Waller, J. Michael, "Rumsfeld: Plagues of Biblical Job," *Insight Magazine*, December 10, 2001.

"Wind-Corrected Munitions Dispenser in First Combat Use, Program Office Director Says," *Aerospace Daily*, December 5, 2001.

Winograd, Erin Q., "Additional Apaches Arrive in Afghanistan for Anti-Terror Campaign," *Inside the Army*, March 18, 2002.

Wisecup, Captain Phil, and Lieutenant Tom Williams, USN, "Enduring Freedom: Making Coalition Naval Warfare Work," *Proceedings*, September 2002.

"World News Roundup," *Aviation Week and Space Technology*, December 3, 2001.

Wolfe, Frank, "Thermobaric Weapons Shipped for Possible Use in Operation Enduring Freedom," *Defense Daily*, January 9, 2002.

————, "Navy F-14s Able to Transmit, Receive Imagery from Green Berets in Afghanistan," *Defense Daily*, August 1, 2002.

Zakaria, Fareed, "Face the Facts: Bombing Works," *Newsweek*, December 3, 2001.

Newspaper Articles

Allen, Mike, "Quietly, Cheney Again Takes a Prominent Role," *Washington Post*, September 17, 2001.

Allen, Mike, and Bill Miller, "President Releases Tally of Progress Against Terrorism," *Washington Post*, October 2, 2001.

Anderson, John Ward, "Pentagon Denies Role in Explosions in Afghan Capital," *Washington Post*, September 12, 2001.

"Angered Putin Calls for Coordinated Response," *Moscow Times*, September 12, 2001.

Apple, R. W., Jr., "Aides Say Bush Was Target of Hijacked Jet," *New York Times*, September 13, 2001.

————, "No Middle Ground," *New York Times*, September 14, 2001.

————, "Quagmire Recalled: Afghanistan as Vietnam," *New York Times*, October 31, 2001.

Aris, Ben, "Russian Troops Are Put on Alert," *London Daily Telegraph*, September 17, 2001.

Arkin, William M., "A Week of Air War," *Washington Post*, October 14, 2001.

———, "U.S. Air Bases Forge Double-Edged Sword," *Los Angeles Times*, January 6, 2002.

———, "Fear of Civilian Deaths May Have Undermined Effort," *Los Angeles Times*, January 16, 2002.

———, "Old-Timers Prove Invaluable in Afghanistan Air Campaign," *Los Angeles Times*, February 10, 2002.

———, "The Rules of Engagement," *Washington Post*, April 21, 2002.

———, "Building a War: As Some Argue, Supply Lines Fill Up," *Los Angeles Times,* November 10, 2002.

———, "The Risky Business of Modern War: A Top U.S. Military Leader Shares His Thoughts About Armed Conflict in a Post-9/11 World," *Los Angeles Times*, September 21, 2003.

Baker, Peter, "Uzbeks Eager to Join U.S. Alliance," *Washington Post*, September 17, 2001.

———, "Tense Tajikistan Braces for Instability," *Washington Post*, September 19, 2001.

———, "Taliban Preparing Capital for War," *Washington Post*, October 4, 2001.

———, "Kabul and Kandahar Hit in Attacks Through the Night," *Washington Post*, October 8, 2001.

———, "Afghans Bolster U.S.-Led Force," *Washington Post*, March 8, 2002.

———, "British Forces Lead New Afghan Mission," *Washington Post*, April 17, 2002.

Baker, Peter, and Molly Moore, "Anti-Taliban Rebels Eager to Join U.S. Retaliation," *Washington Post*, September 24, 2001.

Baker, Peter, and Steve Vogel, "Large U.S. Force Battles al Qaeda Fighters," *Washington Post*, March 4, 2002.

Balz, Dan, "U.S. Strikes Again at Afghan Targets; Americans Told to Be Alert to Attacks," *Washington Post*, October 9, 2001.

Balz, Dan, and Bob Woodward, "A Day to Speak of Anger and Grief," *Washington Post*, January 30, 2002.

Barber, Ben, "Taliban Threatens to Invade Pakistan," *Washington Times*, September 16, 2001.

Bearak, Barry, "Uncertain Toll in the Fog of War: Civilian Deaths in Afghanistan," *New York Times*, February 10, 2002.

Beeston, Richard, and Helen Rumbelow, "Allies Defend Cluster Bombs," *London Times*, October 29, 2001.

Bender, Bryan, "U.S. Shifts Command to Kuwait," *Boston Globe*, December 10, 2001.

Berke, Richard L., "Poll Finds a Majority Back Use of Military," *New York Times,* September 16, 2001.

Blair, David, and Toby Harnden, "U.S. Troops Will Stay in Afghanistan 'Until We Win,'" *London Daily Telegraph*, October 8, 2002.

Boot, Max, "This Victory May Haunt Us," *Wall Street Journal,* November 14, 2001.

Branigin, William, "U.S. Team Visits Rebel Commanders," *Washington Post*, October 22, 2001.

Branigin, William, and Doug Struck, "U.S. Intensifies Bombing," *Washington Post*, November 1, 2001.

Branigin, William, and Keith B. Richburg, "Alliance Surges Across North," *Washington Post*, November 12, 2001.

Brown, Adam, "Afghans Seek Curb on U.S. Operations," *Chicago Tribune*, July 13, 2002.

Bumiller, Elisabeth, and Jane Perlez, "A Vow to Erase Terrorist Networks—bin Laden Is Singled Out," *New York Times*, September 14, 2001.

Burns, John F., "U.S. Demands Air and Land Access to Pakistan," *New York Times*, September 15, 2001.

———, "Pakistani Team Giving Afghans an Ultimatum," *New York Times*, September 17, 2001.

————, "Taliban Reject Pakistan's Call for bin Laden," *New York Times*, September 18, 2001.

————, "Bin Laden Taunts U.S. and Praises Hijackers," *New York Times*, October 8, 2001.

————, "Taliban Figure Asks Bombing Halt to Make Deal on bin Laden," *New York Times*, October 16, 2001.

————, "Alliance in Kabul Will Share Power, U.S. Envoy Reports," *New York Times*, November 20, 2001.

————, "In a Shift, U.S. Uses Airstrikes to Help Kabul," *New York Times*, February 19, 2002.

————, "U.S. Planes Pound Enemy as Troops Face Tough Fight," *New York Times*, March 4, 2002.

————, "U.S. Adds Troops and Helicopters in Afghan Battle," *New York Times*, March 7, 2002.

————, "Saying Battle Is Effectively Over, U.S. Sends Troops Back to Base," *New York Times*, March 11, 2002.

————, "U.S. Planning New Operations to Root Out Scattered Afghan Holdouts," *New York Times*, March 18, 2002.

Butcher, Tim, "British Muscle and U.S. Jets Arrive in Jittery Islamabad," *London Daily Telegraph*, September 19, 2001.

Carter, Tom, "Rival Alliance Offers Help to Hunt Down bin Laden," *Washington Times*, September 20, 2001.

Chandrasekaran, Rajiv, "Afghan Clerics Suggest That bin Laden Leave," *Washington Post*, September 21, 2001.

————, "Taliban Rejects U.S. Demand, Vows a 'Showdown of Might,'" *Washington Post*, September 22, 2001.

Chivers, C. J., "Second Wave of Troops Arrives in Uzbekistan," *New York Times*, October 8, 2001.

Clark, James, Tony Allen-Mills, and Stephen Grey, "SAS Troops Clash with Taliban Unit Deep Inside Afghanistan," *London Sunday Times*, September 23, 2001.

Cooper, Richard T., "Fierce Fight in Afghan Valley Tests U.S. Soldiers and Strategy," *Los Angeles Times*, March 24, 2002.

Cox, Margaret, "U.S. Role Is Far from Over," *Atlanta Journal and Constitution*, October 6, 2002.

Crawley, James W., "Caves of Zhawar Kili Yield Arsenal for Terror," *San Diego Union-Tribune*, January 17, 2002.

Cummings, Jeanne, "Bush Recruits International Leaders in Effort to Build Antiterror Alliance," *Wall Street Journal*, September 19, 2001.

Cummings, Jeanne, and Neil King, Jr., "Military Response by U.S. Is Broader Than Plan Initially Proposed to Bush," *Wall Street Journal*, October 8, 2001.

Cummins, Chip, "U.S. Repositions Up to 1800 Soldiers as Eastern Afghanistan Battle Rages," *Wall Street Journal*, March 6, 2002.

Curl, Joseph, "U.S. Can Go to War with Any Enemies," *Washington Times*, September 13, 2001.

Cushman, John H., Jr., "More Reserves Called Up," *New York Times*, September 23, 2001.

Daley, Suzanne, "For First Time, NATO Invokes Pact With U.S.," *New York Times*, September 13, 2001.

Daniszewski, John, "More U.S. Troops in bin Laden Hunt; Hideouts Bombed," *New York Times*, November 19, 2001.

————, "Afghans Advance Toward al Qaeda, Taliban Holdouts," *Los Angeles Times*, March 13, 2002.

Daniszewski, John, and Thom Shanker, "Americans Rescue Soldier Who Fell Ill," *New York Times*, November 5, 2001.

Daniszewski, John, and Eric Schmitt, "Bin Laden Hunted in Caves; Errant U.S. Bomb Kills Three GIs," *New York Times*, December 6, 2001.

Daniszewski, John, and Geoffrey Mohan, "Afghans Set Off to Root Out al Qaeda, Taliban Holdouts," *Los Angeles Times*, March 12, 2002.

Dao, James, "More U.S. Troops in bin Laden Hunt; Hideouts Bombed," *New York Times*, November 19, 2001.

Dao, James, and Thom Shanker, "Americans Rescue Soldier Who Fell Ill," *New York Times*, November 5, 2001.

Dao, James, and Eric Schmitt, "Bin Laden Hunted in Caves; Errant U.S. Bomb Kills Three GIs," *New York Times*, December 6, 2001.

DeYoung, Karen, and Marc Kaufman, "Bombs, Lawlessness Threaten Aid Efforts," *Washington Post*, October 17, 2001.

DeYoung, Karen, and Vernon Loeb, "Land-Based Fighters Join Airstrikes in Afghanistan," *Washington Post*, October 18, 2001.

Dobbins, James, "Afghanistan's Faltering Reconstruction," *New York Times*, September 12, 2002.

Drinkard, Jim, "America Ready to Sacrifice," *USA Today*, September 17, 2001.

———, "U.S. Hits Troops Near Kabul," *USA Today*, October 22, 2001.

Eggen, Dan, and Vernon Loeb, "U.S. Intelligence Points to Bin Laden Network," *Washington Post*, September 12, 2001.

Eisman, Dale, "U.S. War in Afghanistan Reaffirms Critical Role Played by Navy's Carriers," *Norfolk Virginian-Pilot*, November 11, 2001.

———, "Navy Says It Nearly Ran Out of Bombs," *Norfolk Virginian-Pilot*, March 1, 2002.

Erlanger, Steven, "Germany Ready to Send Force of 3900," *New York Times*, November 7, 2001.

Evans, Michael, "Britain Offers Military Planning Team," *London Times*, September 14, 2001.

———, "Coalition Troops Set for Covert Action," *London Times*, September 22, 2001.

———, "Britain May Send Forces to Central Asia This Week," *London Times*, September 24, 2001.

———, "U.S. Plans for Battle on Multiple Fronts," *London Times*, October 1, 2001.

———, "U.S. Troops and Helicopters Set for Ground War," *London Times*, October 11, 2001.

———, "Special Forces' Reach Curbed by Flight Time," *London Times*, November 8, 2001.

————, "British Special Forces to Join Cave Assault," *London Times*, December 3, 2001.

————, "'Precision Weapons' Fail to Prevent Mass Civilian Casualties," *London Times*, January 2, 2002.

Evans-Pritchard, Ambrose, "EU Calls for 'Intelligent and Targeted' Response," *London Daily Telegraph*, September 15, 2001.

————, "EU Leaders Demand a Place in the Front Line," *London Daily Telegraph*, November 7, 2001.

Farrell, Stephen, and Michael Evans, "SAS Searches 'bin Laden' Cave System," *London Times*, December 4, 2001.

Filkins, Dexter, "Flaws in U.S. Air War Left Hundreds of Civilians Dead," *New York Times*, July 21, 2002.

Filkins, Dexter, with James Dao, "Afghan Battle Declared Over and Successful," *New York Times*, March 19, 2002.

Fitchett, Joseph, "NATO Unity, But What Next?" *International Herald Tribune*, September 14, 2001.

————, "AC-130 Use Signals Start of Attack on Troops," *International Herald Tribune*, October 17, 2001.

————, "Major Drive Seen for Afghan Cities," *International Herald Tribune*, October 31, 2001.

Frantz, Douglas, "Murky Picture Emerges of Life Under Bombardment," *New York Times*, October 11, 2001.

————, "Hundreds of al Qaeda Fighters Slip into Pakistan," *New York Times*, December 19, 2001.

Friend, Tim, "Search for Bin Laden Extends to Earth Orbit," *USA Today*, October 5, 2001.

Gellman, Barton, and Mike Allen, "The Week That Redefined the Bush Presidency," *Washington Post*, September 23, 2001.

Gellman, Barton, and Susan Schmidt, "Shadow Government Is at Work in Secret," *Washington Post*, March 1, 2002.

Gellman, Barton, and Thomas E. Ricks, "U.S. Concludes bin Laden Escaped at Tora Bora," *Washington Post*, April 17, 2002.

Gerstenzang, James, "Bush Offers New Vision of Military," *Los Angeles Times*, December 12, 2001.

Gerstenzang, James, and Paul Richter, "Jets Had OK to Down Airliners," *Los Angeles Times*, September 17, 2001.

Gertz, Bill, "Fearful, Iran and Iraq Hunker Down," *Washington Times*, September 17, 2001.

————, "Precision Bombing Is the Weapon of Choice," *Washington Times*, October 8, 2001.

————, "Afghanistan Hits Will Continue Until Taliban Is Ousted," *Washington Times*, October 9, 2001.

————, "General Happy with Campaign's Progress," *Washington Times*, November 9, 2001.

————, "Forces Tighten the Noose on bin Laden," *Washington Times*, November 16, 2001.

————, "Nine U.S. Soldiers Killed in Afghanistan," *Washington Times*, March 5, 2002.

————, "Rumsfeld Says Afghan Battle's End Near," *Washington Times*, March 8, 2002.

Gertz, Bill, and Rowan Scarborough, "Pentagon to Send Fourth Carrier to Afghanistan," *Washington Times*, November 8, 2001.

Glasser, Susan B., "Russia Rejects Joint Military Action with United States," *Washington Post*, September 15, 2001.

————, "First U.S. Planes Land at Uzbek Air Base," *Washington Post*, September 23, 2001.

————, "Putin Confers with Bush, Central Asian Presidents," *Washington Post*, September 24, 2001.

————, "Al Qaeda Aides Killed in Raids," *Washington Post*, December 5, 2001.

————, "U.S. Attacks on al Qaeda Intensify," *Washington Post*, December 10, 2001.

————, "The Battle of Tora Bora: Secrets, Money, Mistrust," *Washington Post*, February 10, 2002.

————, "U.S. Challenged to Define Role in Afghanistan," *Washington Post*, August 3, 2002.

Glasser, Susan B., and Peter Baker, "Bush and Putin Discuss Response to Terrorism," *Washington Post*, September 13, 2002.

Gordon, Michael R., "Scarcity of Afghan Targets Leads U.S. to Revise Strategy," *New York Times*, September 19, 2001.

————, "Rumsfeld Meets Saudis and Says He's Satisfied with Level of Support," *New York Times*, October 4, 2001.

————, "U.S. Hopes to Break the Taliban with Pounding from the Air," *New York Times*, October 17, 2001.

————, "Alliance of Convenience," *New York Times*, October 23, 2001.

————, "This Time, American Soldiers Join the Fray," *New York Times*, March 4, 2002.

Gordon, Michael R., and Eric Schmitt, "Pentagon Tries to Avoid Using Pakistan Bases," *New York Times*, October 3, 2001.

Gordon, Michael R., and Tim Weiner, "Taliban Is Target in U.S. Air Campaign," *New York Times*, October 16, 2001.

Gordon, Michael R., and Steven Lee Myers, "U.S. Will Increase Number of Advisers in Afghanistan," *New York Times*, November 1, 2001.

Gordon, Michael R., with Eric Schmitt, "Troops May Scour Caves for Qaeda, U.S. General Says," *New York Times*, December 20, 2001.

Graham, Bradley, "Fighter Response After Attacks Questioned," *Washington Post*, September 14, 2001.

————, "Military Alerted Before Attacks," *Washington Post*, September 15, 2001.

————, "Bravery and Breakdowns in a Ridgetop Battle," *Washington Post*, May 24, 2002.

Graham, Bradley, and Dan Balz, "U.S. Controls Skies, Hunts New Targets and Encourages Anti-Taliban Forces," *Washington Post*, October 10, 2001.

Graham, Bradley, and Vernon Loeb, "Cave Complexes Smashed by Bombs," *Washington Post,* October 12, 2001.

————, "Taliban Dispersal Slows U.S.," *Washington Post,* November 6, 2001.

Graham, Bradley, and Thomas E. Ricks, "Rumsfeld Says War Far From Over," *Washington Post,* December 8, 2001.

Graves, David, "Allies in the Gulf Guarantee Supplies of Fuel," *London Daily Telegraph,* September 18, 2001.

Grunwald, Michael, "Terrorists Hijack Four Airliners, Destroy World Trade Center, Hit Pentagon; Hundreds Dead," *Washington Post,* September 12, 2001.

Hall, Mimi, "Poll: USA Less Optimistic on War," *USA Today,* May 31, 2002.

Harnden, Tony, "Rumsfeld Spells Out What U.S. Victory Will Mean," *London Daily Telegraph,* September 24, 2001.

Harris, John F., "Bush Gets More International Support," *Washington Post,* September 17, 2001.

Harris, John F., and Mike Allen, "President Outlines War on Terrorism, Demands bin Laden Be Turned Over," *Washington Post,* September 21, 2001.

Helmer, Kendra, "General Franks, in Uzbekistan, Says Fight Against Terrorism Has Not Stalled," *European Stars and Stripes,* October 31, 2001.

Hendren, John, "Afghanistan Yields Lessons for Pentagon's Next Targets," *Los Angeles Times,* January 21, 2002.

————, "U.S. Base Looks a Lot Like Home," *Los Angeles Times,* April 4, 2002.

Hendren, John, and John Daniszewski, "Seven U.S. Troops Are Killed in Assault on Enemy Fighters," *Los Angeles Times,* March 5, 2002.

————, "Navy SEAL Was Captured and Killed," *Los Angeles Times,* March 6, 2002.

Hendren, John, and Maura Reynolds, "The U.S. Bomb That Nearly Killed Karzai," *Los Angeles Times,* March 27, 2002.

Hoagland, Jim, "Bush's Week of Truth," *Washington Post*, November 14, 2001.

"In a Desert Outpost, Afghan War Was Won: U.S. Firepower Decimated Taliban at Tarin Kot," *Washington Post*, December 31, 2001.

"India Says It Gave U.S. Secret Data," *Washington Times*, September 17, 2001.

Jaffe, Greg, "U.S. Armed Forces Are Put on the Highest State of Alert," *Wall Street Journal*, September 12, 2001.

———, "As More Forces Head to Region, U.S. Seeks Greater Access to Bases Ringing Afghanistan," *Wall Street Journal*, September 24, 2001.

———, "U.S. Offensive in Afghanistan Enters Riskier Phase of Commando Raids," *Wall Street Journal*, October 22, 2001.

———, "Military Feels Bandwidth Squeeze as the Satellite Industry Sputters," *Wall Street Journal*, April 10, 2002.

———, "New Battle Theory Would Be Tested in an Iraq Invasion, *Wall Street Journal*, November 27, 2002.

Jaffe, Greg, and Alan Cullison, "Tajikistan Offers U.S. Military Three Airfields to Use in Intensifying Its Bombing Campaign," *Wall Street Journal*, November 8, 2001.

Jaffe, Greg, Chip Cummings, and Anne Marie Squeo, "Accidental Bombing of Friendly Forces May Be Avoidable with Minor Fixes," *Wall Street Journal*, December 6, 2001.

Jones, George, "We Will Help Hunt Down Evil Culprits, Says Blair," *London Daily Telegraph*, September 12, 2001.

Jones, George, and Anton La Guardia, "War Will Begin Within Days," *London Daily Telegraph*, September 26, 2001.

Keen, Judy, "Bush Lauds New Partnership with Pakistan," *Washington Post*, February 14, 2002.

Kelly, Jack, "U.S. IDs Possible Sites for Retaliation," *USA Today*, September 17, 2001.

Khan, Kamran and Molly Moore, "Pakistani Leaders Agree on Measures to Assist U.S.," *Washington Post*, September 15, 2001.

Kifner, John, "Anti-Taliban Troops Take Up Positions on Mountainsides," *New York Times*, December 12, 2001.

Kifner, John, and Eric Schmitt, "Fierce al Qaeda Defense Seen as a Sign of Terror Leader's Proximity," *New York Times*, December 14, 2001.

King, Laura, "Civilian Toll in Afghan War Likely Lower," *Philadelphia Inquirer*, February 12, 2002.

King, Neil, Jr., and Greg Jaffe, "U.S. Plans to Use a Bombing Campaign to End Taliban Protection of bin Laden," *Wall Street Journal*, October 5, 2001.

King, Neil, Jr., and David S. Cloud, "A Year Before September 11, U.S. Drones Spotted bin Laden in His Camps, But Couldn't Shoot," *Wall Street Journal*, November 23, 2001.

Knickmeyer, Ellen, "Taliban Offers to Surrender Kunduz," *Washington Times*, November 19, 2001.

Knowlton, Brian, "Taliban Say They Are Hiding bin Laden; Saudi Must Be 'Purged,' U.S. Warns," *International Herald Tribune*, October 1, 2001.

————, "Anti-Taliban Forces Continue Their March," *International Herald Tribune*, November 12, 2001.

————, "Fight Enters 'Dangerous Phase' in Kandahar," *International Herald Tribune*, December 3, 2001.

Komarow, Steven, "Air Force Delivers Aid with Attitude," *USA Today*, November 9, 2001.

Krauthammer, Charles, "To War, Not to Court," *Washington Post*, September 12, 2001.

Laville, Sandra, and Michael Smith, "Bin Laden's Henchman 'Killed in Bomb Raid,'" *London Daily Telegraph*, October 19, 2001.

Loeb, Vernon, "Rules Governing Downing Airliners," *Washington Post*, September 28, 2001.

————, "U.S. Intensifies Airstrikes on Taliban," *Washington Post*, October 16, 2001.

————, "Pentagon Eyes Use of Tajikistan Air Base," *Washington Post*, November 13, 2001.

————, "Up in Arms," *Washington Post*, January 11, 2002.

————, "Footprints in Steppes of Central Asia," *Washington Post*, February 9, 2002.

————, "'Friendly Fire' Deaths Traced to Dead Battery," *Washington Post*, March 24, 2002.

————, "Afghan War Is a Lab for U.S. Innovation," *Washington Post*, March 26, 2002.

————, "'Friendly Fire' Probed in Death," *Washington Post*, March 30, 2002.

————, "An Unlikely Super-Warrior Emerges in Afghan War," *Washington Post*, May 19, 2002.

Loeb, Vernon, and Dana Priest, "Retaliatory Options Are Under Study," *Washington Post*, September 13, 2001.

————, "Saudis Balk at Use of Key Facility," *Washington Post*, September 22, 2001.

Loeb, Vernon, and Thomas E. Ricks, "U.S. Sends Troops to Ex-Soviet Republics," *Washington Post*, October 3, 2001.

————, "Pentagon: Taliban 'Eviscerated,'" *Washington Post*, October 17, 2001.

Loeb, Vernon, and Marc Kaufman, "CIA Sent Aircraft to Rescue Slain Leader," *Washington Post*, October 29, 2001.

Loeb, Vernon, and Thomas E. Ricks, "Pressure to Curtail War Grows," *Washington Post*, October 30, 2001.

Loeb, Vernon, and Bradley Graham, "Navy Ordered to Block Any Bid by bin Laden to Escape by Sea," *Washington Post*, November 22, 2001.

————, "Seven U.S. Soldiers Die in Battle," *Washington Post*, March 5, 2002.

Martz, Ron, "Q&A with General Tommy Franks," *Atlanta Journal and Constitution*, April 7, 2002.

————, "From Tampa, Franks on Top of the War," *Atlanta Journal and Constitution*, April 18, 2002.

McManus, Doyle, and Robin Wright, "Broad New U.S. Strategy to Fight Terror Emerging," *Los Angeles Times*, September 16, 2001.

McManus, Doyle, and James Gerstenzang, "Bush Takes CEO Role in Waging War," *Los Angeles Times*, September 23, 2001.

Memmott, Mark, "Poll: Americans Believe Attacks 'Acts of War,'" *USA Today*, September 12, 2001.

Milbank, David, and Vernon Loeb, "'U.S. Employing Calm, Multi-faceted Response," *Washington Post*, September 24, 2001.

Miller, Judith, and Eric Schmitt, "Ugly Duckling Turns Out to Be Formidable in the Air," *New York Times*, November 23, 2001.

Mitchell, Alison, and Richard L. Berke, "Differences Are Put Aside as Lawmakers Reconvene," *New York Times*, September 12, 2001.

Mitchell, Alison, and Philip Shenon, "Work on $40 Billion Aid and a Military Response," *New York Times*, September 14, 2001.

Moniz, Dave, "In New Type of War, Public Will Receive Little News," *USA Today*, September 19, 2001.

———, "Soldiers Describe '18-Hour Miracle,'" *USA Today*, March 7, 2002.

Moore, Molly, and Kamran Khan, "Afghanistan: A Nightmare Battlefield," *Washington Post*, September 17, 2001.

———, "Big Ground Force Seen As Necessary to Defeat Taliban," *Washington Post*, November 2, 2001.

Moore, Molly, and Susan B. Glasser, "Remnants of al Qaeda Flee Toward Pakistan," *Washington Post*, December 17, 2001.

———, "Afghan Militias Claim Victory in Tora Bora," *Washington Post*, December 18, 2001.

Morin, Richard, and Claudia Deane, "Poll: Americans Willing to Go to War," *Washington Post*, September 12, 2001.

Mufson, Steven, and Alan Sipress, "Bush to Seek Nation's Support," *Washington Post*, September 20, 2001.

Mufson, Steven, and William Branigin, "U.S. Sets Stage for Offensive," *Washington Post*, November 2, 2001.

Myers, Steven Lee, "Marines Build Firepower in the South, Bolstering Their Patrols and Readiness," *New York Times*, December 3, 2001.

Myers, Steven Lee, and Thom Shanker, "Pilots Told to Fire at Will in Some Zones," *New York Times*, October 17, 2001.

Myers, Steven Lee, and Eric Schmitt, "Material Seized in U.S. Ground Raid Yields Few Gains," *New York Times*, October 30, 2001.

Myers, Steven Lee, and James Dao, "U.S. Stokes the Fire, Adding Gunships and More," *New York Times*, November 22, 2001.

Nichols, Bill, and Dave Moniz, "Experts Predict U.S. Will Fight First Extended Commando War," *USA Today*, September 17, 2001.

Pae, Peter, "U.S. Predicting Fight Will Last Until Well into Spring," *Los Angeles Times*, October 22, 2001.

———, "Future Is Now for Creator of Predator," *Los Angeles Times*, January 3, 2002.

Pape, Robert A., "The Wrong Battle Plan," *Washington Post*, October 19, 2001.

Perlez, Jane, "Powell Says It Clearly: No Middle Ground on Terrorism," *New York Times*, September 13, 2001.

———, "U.S. Demands Arab Countries 'Choose Sides,'" *New York Times*, September 15, 2001.

Perlez, Jane, David E. Sanger, and Thom Shanker, "From Many Voices, One Battle Strategy," *New York Times*, September 23, 2001.

Peterson, Scott, "A View from Behind the Lines in the U.S. Air War," *Christian Science Monitor*, December 4, 2001.

Priest, Dana, "Zinni Urges Economic, Diplomatic Moves," *Washington Post*, September 14, 2001.

———, "Team 555 Shaped a New Way of War," *Washington Post*, April 3, 2002.

Priest, Dana, and Bradley Graham, "U.S. Deploys Air Defenses on Coasts," *Washington Post*, September 12, 2001.

Pomfret, John, "Taliban Accepts Surrender Deal," *Washington Post*, December 7, 2001.

———, "Kandahar Bombs Hit Their Marks," *Washington Post*, December 12, 2001.

Pomfret, John, and Rajiv Chandrasekaran, "Taliban Faces Tribal Revolt," *Washington Post*, November 15, 2001.

Purdum, Todd, "Leaders Face Challenges Far Different from Those of Last Conflict," *New York Times*, September 15, 2001.

Rashid, Ahmed, "Al Qaeda Has Network of Sleepers Across North America," *London Daily Telegraph*, September 15, 2001.

———, "Taliban in Key Defeat as Rebels Turn to Ex-King," *London Daily Telegraph*, September 25, 2001.

"Rendezvous with Afghanistan," *New York Times*, September 14, 2001.

"Report of Air Force, Navy Wrangling Misses the Mark," *Washington Times*, November 13, 2001.

Revkin, Andrew C., "New Sensors Report, 'I Know They're In There, I Can See Them Breathing,'" *New York Times*, November 22, 2001.

———, "U.S. Making Weapons to Blast Underground Hideouts," *New York Times*, December 3, 2001.

Reynolds, Maura, "Russia Seeks to Unite Against a 'Common Enemy,'" *Los Angeles Times*, September 15, 2001.

———, "Russia Mulls Options to Help U.S.," *Los Angeles Times*, September 18, 2001.

Reynolds, Maura, and Paul Richter, "U.S. Opposes Any Deal with Taliban Forces," *Los Angeles Times*, November 20, 2001.

Richburg, Keith B., and William Branigin, "U.S. Jets Expand Afghan Strikes," *Washington Post*, October 29, 2001.

Richburg, Keith B., and Molly Moore, "Taliban Flees Afghan Capital," *Washington Post*, November 13, 2001.

Richburg, Keith B., and William Branigin, "Attacks Out of the Blue: U.S. Air Strikes on Taliban Hit Military Targets and Morale," *Washington Post*, November 18, 2001.

Richter, Paul, "Experts Weigh Risks of Air, Ground Campaigns in Afghanistan," *Los Angeles Times*, September 14, 2001.

Richter, Paul, and Peter Pae, "U.S. Concedes Taliban Battle Will Be Tough," *Los Angeles Times*, October 25, 2001.

Ricks, Thomas E., "Pentagon Issues Order to Elite Units in Infantry," *Washington Post*, September 17, 2001.

―――, "Warplanes Begin Deploying to Gulf, Central Asia," *Washington Post*, September 20, 2001.

―――, "Former Soviet Republics Are Key to U.S. Effort," *Washington Post*, September 22, 2001.

―――, "Land Mines, Aging Missiles Pose Threat," *Washington Post*, September 25, 2001.

―――, "Rumsfeld Confident of Use of Saudi Bases," *Washington Post*, October 4, 2001.

―――, "Next Phase to Include More Troops," *Washington Post*, October 9, 2001.

―――, "U.S. to Target Elite Taliban Assault Force in Next Phase," *Washington Post*, October 14, 2001.

―――, "U.S. Arms Unmanned Aircraft," *Washington Post*, October 18, 2001.

―――, "Target Approval Delays Cost Air Force Key Hits," *Washington Post*, November 18, 2001.

―――, "In the South, U.S. Faces a Guerrilla War," *Washington Post*, November 21, 2001.

―――, "Bull's-Eye War: Pinpoint Bombing Shifts Role of GI Joe," *Washington Post*, December 2, 2001.

―――, "Rumsfeld's Hands-On War," *Washington Post*, December 9, 2001.

―――, "A War That's Commanded at a Distance," *Washington Post*, December 27, 2001.

―――, "Battle Sends Broader Message of U.S. Resolve," *Washington Post*, March 5, 2002.

————, "In Mop Up, U.S. Finds 'Impressive' Remnants of Fallen Foe," *Washington Post*, March 20, 2002.

————, "Beaming the Battlefield Home," *Washington Post*, March 26, 2002.

————, "Un-Central Command Criticized," *Washington Post*, June 3, 2002.

————, "Errant U.S. Bomb Hits Civilians," *Washington Post*, July 2, 2002.

————, "War Plan for Iraq Is Ready, Say Officials," *Washington Post*, November 20, 2002.

Ricks, Thomas E., and Vernon Loeb, "Initial Aim Is Hitting Taliban Defenses," *Washington Post*, October 8, 2001.

————, "Special Forces Open Ground Campaign," *Washington Post*, October 19, 2001.

Ricks, Thomas E., and Alan Sipress, "Attacks Restrained by Political Goals," *Washington Post*, October 23, 2001.

Ricks, Thomas E., and Doug Struck, "U.S. Troops Coordinating Airstrikes," *Washington Post*, October 31, 2001.

Ricks, Thomas E., and Bradley Graham, "U.S. Special Forces on the Trail of Taliban Leaders," *Washington Post*, November 14, 2001.

Ricks, Thomas E., and Bob Woodward, "Marines Enter South Afghanistan," *Washington Post*, November 26, 2001.

Ricks, Thomas E., and Vernon Loeb, "U.S. Claims Advantage in Battle," *Washington Post*, March 7, 2002.

Ricks, Thomas E., and Bradley Graham, "Surprises, Adjustments and Milestones for U.S. Military," *Washington Post*, March 10, 2002.

Ricks, Thomas E., Kamran Khan, and Molly Moore, "Taliban Refuses to Surrender bin Laden; U.S. Develops Options for Military Action," *Washington Post*, September 19, 2001.

Robbins, Carla Anne, Greg Jaffe, and Robert S. Greenberger, "Small-Scale Steps Could Be Key in Military's Reaction to Attacks," *Wall Street Journal*, September 17, 2001.

Robbins, Carla Anne, and Jeanne Cummings, "Powell's Cautious Views on Quick Strikes and Faith in Coalitions Shape Bush Plan," *Wall Street Journal*, September 21, 2001.

Robbins, Carla Anne, and Alan Cullison, "U.S. Is Prepared to Support an Assault on Kabul by Northern Alliance Forces," *Wall Street Journal*, October 23, 2001.

Rose, Matthew, "News Media Showed Tendency to Misfire During Early Phase of War in Afghanistan," *Wall Street Journal*, December 24, 2001.

"Rumsfeld Warns Against Leaks," *Washington Times*, September 13, 2001.

Safire, William, "Inside the Bunker," *New York Times*, September 13, 2001.

Sands, David R., and Tom Carter," Attacks Change U.S. Foreign Policy," *Washington Times*, September 12, 2001.

Sanger, David E., "Bin Laden Is Wanted in Attacks, 'Dead or Alive,' President Says," *New York Times*, September 18, 2001.

———, "Bush Is Deploying Jet Bombers Toward Afghanistan," *New York Times*, September 20, 2001.

Sanger, David E., and Eric Schmitt, "U.S. Puts Afghan Strike Ahead of Full Plan," *New York Times*, September 22, 2001.

Sanger, David E., and Michael R. Gordon, "U.S. Takes Steps to Bolster Fighting Terror," *New York Times*, November 7, 2001.

Scarborough, Rowan, "Military Officers Seek Swift, Deadly Response," *Washington Times*, September 12, 2001.

———, "Officials Talk of Military Response," *Washington Times*, September 13, 2001.

———, "Intercepts Foretold of 'Big Attack,'" *Washington Times*, September 22, 2001.

———, "Rumsfeld Cautions Against Mass Strike," *Washington Times*, September 26, 2001.

———, "Bombing Plan Spares Civilian Structures," *Washington Times*, October 4, 2001.

————, "Pentagon Will Not Rush Manhunt," *Washington Times*, October 9, 2001.

————, "U.S. Gunship Attacks Taliban Troops," *Washington Times*, October 16, 2001.

————, "U.S. Splits Afghanistan into 'Engagement Zones,'" *Washington Times*, October 18, 2001.

————, "Pentagon Insiders Criticize Tactics, Missed Opportunity," *Washington Times*, November 1, 2001.

————, "Air Force Slow to Transfer Special Bomb Kits to Navy," *Washington Times*, November 7, 2001.

————, "Air Force Gets Use of Airfield in Tajikistan," *Washington Times*, November 10, 2001.

————, "Change of Target Saved Hundreds of Taliban Soldiers," *Washington Times*, November 21, 2001.

————, "Special Forces Get Free Rein," *Washington Times*, November 23, 2001.

————, "U.S. Rules Let al Qaeda Flee," *Washington Times*, December 21, 2001.

————, "Military Officers Criticize Rush to Use Ground Troops," *Washington Times*, March 7, 2002.

————, "Afghan Operation Termed a Success," *Washington Times*, March 12, 2002.

————, "Navy's P-3 Orion Aircraft Played Prominent Role in Afghanistan," *Washington Times*, April 2, 2002.

————, "'Friendly Fire' Judge's Memo Assailed," *Washington Times*, July 30, 2002.

Schmitt, Eric, "Generals Given Power to Order Downing of Jets," *New York Times*, September 27, 2001.

————, "Seeking a Blend of Military and Civilian Decisionmaking," *New York Times*, October 24, 2001.

————, "Improved U.S. Accuracy Claimed in Afghan Air War," *New York Times*, April 9, 2002.

———, "U.S. Raids Along Afghan Border Seen as Lasting Past Summer," *New York Times*, May 6, 2002.

Schmitt, Eric, and Thom Shanker, "Administration Considers Broader, More Powerful Options for Potential Retaliation," *New York Times*, September 13, 2001.

Schmitt, Eric, and Michael R. Gordon, "U.S. Dispatches Ground Troops and Top Officer," *New York Times*, September 21, 2001.

Schmitt, Eric, and Steven Lee Myers, "U.S. Steps Up Air Attack, While Defending Results of Campaign," *New York Times*, October 26, 2002.

Schmitt, Eric, and Thom Shanker, "Trouble in Deploying Commandos Is Said to Hurt U.S. Air Campaign," *New York Times*, November 2, 2001.

Schmitt, Eric, and Steven Lee Myers, "U.S. Escalating Efforts to Bomb Taliban Caves," *New York Times*, November 6, 2001.

Schmitt, Eric, and James Dao, "Use of Pinpoint Air Power Comes of Age in New War," *New York Times*, December 24, 2001.

———, "U.S. Is Building Up Its Military Bases in Afghan Region," *New York Times*, January 9, 2002.

Schmitt, Eric, and Thom Shanker, "Afghans' Retreat Forced Americans to Lead a Battle," *New York Times*, March 10, 2002.

———, "Taliban and al Qaeda Death Toll in Mountain Battle Is a Mystery," *New York Times*, March 14, 2002.

Schrader, Esther, "U.S. Keeps Pressure on al Qaeda," *Los Angeles Times*, January 8, 2002.

———, "War, on Advice of Counsel," *Los Angeles Times*, February 15, 2002.

———, "Simple Mission Became 18-Hour Fight," *Los Angeles Times*, March 8, 2002.

Schrader, Esther, and Paul Richter, "Fighter Jets Assume New Protective Role," *Los Angeles Times*, September 15, 2001.

Sciolino, Elaine, "Bush Tells the Military to 'Get Ready'; Broader Spy Powers Gaining Support," *New York Times*, September 16, 2001.

————, "U.S. Prepares to Brief NATO on Strategy to Fight bin Laden," *New York Times*, September 25, 2001.

Seper, Jerry, and Bill Gertz, "Bin Laden, Cohorts Are Top Suspects," *Washington Times*, September 12, 2001.

Shanker, Thom, "New Blueprint for Military Shifts Priority to U.S. Soil, Revising Two-War Strategy," *New York Times*, October 2, 2001.

————, "U.S. Tells How Rescue Turned into Fatal Firefight," *New York Times*, March 6, 2002.

————, "Addressing Worries, Pentagon Says It Can Fight Wider War," *New York Times,* March 29, 2002.

Shanker, Thom, and Eric Schmitt, "Rumsfeld Asks Call-Up of Reserves, as Many as 50,000," *New York Times*, September 14, 2001.

Shanker, Thom, and Steven Lee Myers, "U.S. Sends in Special Plane with Heavy Guns," *New York Times*, October 16, 2001.

————, "U.S. Set to Aid Afghan Rebels, Rumsfeld Says," *New York Times*, October 19, 2001.

————, "Rumsfeld Says Attacks Seek to Help Rebels Advance," *New York Times*, October 23, 2001.

Shanker, Thom, with Dexter Filkins, "U.S. Planes Hit Taliban Positions Threatening Rebels," *New York Times*, October 29, 2001.

————, "U.S. Commander, Saying Rebels Need Help, Hints More Troops," *New York Times*, November 9, 2001.

Shanker, Thom, and Steven Lee Myers, "Rapid Changes on the Ground Lead the Pentagon to Focus on Counterguerrilla Tactics," *New York Times*, November 15, 2001.

Shanker, Thom, and James Dao, "U.S. Ready to Send Additional Troops to Hunt bin Laden," *New York Times*, November 21, 2001.

Shanker, Thom, and Eric Schmitt, "Marines Advance Toward Kandahar to Prepare Siege," *New York Times*, December 5, 2001.

————, "Taliban Defeated, Pentagon Asserts, But War Goes On," *New York Times*, December 11, 2001.

Shanker, Thom, with Carlotta Gall, "U.S. Attack on Warlord Aims to Help Interim Leader," *New York Times*, May 9, 2002.

Shenon, Philip, and David Johnston, "U.S. Backs Away from Talk of More Attacks," *New York Times*, October 2, 2001.

Sipress, Alan, "U.S. Debates Whether to Overthrow Taliban," *Washington Post*, September 24, 2001.

Sipress, Alan, and Steven Mufson, "U.S. Lines Up Support for Strike," *Washington Post*, September 13, 2001.

Sipress, Alan, and Marc Kaufman, "Taliban Opponents Increase U.S. Contacts," *Washington Post*, September 22, 2001.

Sipress, Alan, and Thomas E. Ricks, "Military Strike Not Imminent, Officials Say," *Washington Post*, September 27, 2001.

Sipress, Alan, and Molly Moore, "Pakistan Grants Airfield Use; U.S. Pounds Taliban Bunkers," *Washington Post*, October 11, 2001.

Sipress, Alan, and Vernon Loeb, "U.S. Steps Up Strikes on Taliban Troops," *Washington Post*, November 1, 2001.

Smith, David R., "Iran Warns U.S. to Keep Warplanes Out of Its Airspace," *Washington Times*, October 2, 2001.

Smith, Michael, "Attack 'Could Come This Weekend,'" *London Daily Telegraph*, September 15, 2001.

————, "U.S. Aims to Take Vital Afghan Air Base," *London Daily Telegraph*, September 25, 2001.

————, "U.S. Special Forces Beat Retreat as Enemy 'Fought Back Like Maniacs,'" *London Daily Telegraph*, October 26, 2001.

Soriano, Cesar G., "Elite Marine Unit Makes First Strike on Taliban," *USA Today*, November 5, 2001.

————, "Allied Operations Said to Be Dwindling in Afghanistan," *USA Today*, May 9, 2002.

Spitzer, Kirk, "Green Berets Outfought, Outthought the Taliban," *USA Today*, January 7, 2002.

Stone, Andrea, ""Soldiers Deploy on Mental Terrain," *USA Today*, October 3, 2001.

————, "Pentagon Confirms Errant Bomb Strikes," *USA Today*, October 29, 2001.

Stout, David, "U.S. Bomber Crashes at Sea; Crew Members Are Rescued," *New York Times*, December 13, 2001.

Strauss, Julius and Dashti Qala, "Waves of Jets Herald the Start of Northern Alliance Offensive," *London Daily Telegraph*, October 29, 2001.

Struck, Doug, "Rebel Leader Claims to Be Guiding Air Strikes," *Washington Post*, October 24, 2001.

"Text of Bush Statement," *Washington Post*, September 13, 2001.

"Text of Joint Resolution," *Washington Post*, September 15, 2001.

Timburg, Craig, "Anxiety, Uncertainty at Norfolk Station," *Washington Post*, September 19, 2001.

"Top Brass: Military Spread Too Thin," *Washington Times*, March 21, 2002.

Tucker, Neely, and Vernon Loeb, "District, Nation Move to High Alert," *Washington Post*, September 15, 2001.

Tyler, Patrick E., "Bush Advisers Split on Scope of Retaliation," *New York Times*, September 20, 2001.

————, "U.S. and Britain Strike Afghanistan, Aiming at Bases and Terrorist Camps; Bush Warns 'Taliban Will Pay a Price,'" *New York Times*, October 8, 2001.

————, "After a Lull, Dawn Bombing Caps Night of Heavy Strikes," *New York Times*, October 9, 2001.

————, "U.S. Names Envoy to Rebels," *New York Times*, November 6, 2001.

Tyson, Anne Scott, "Why U.S. Is Moving So Deliberately," *Christian Science Monitor*, October 4, 2001.

————, "Al Qaeda: Resistant and Organized," *Christian Science Monitor*, March 7, 2002.

————, "Anaconda: A War Story," *Christian Science Monitor*, August 1, 2002.

"U.S. Grounds Spy Plane," *Washington Post*, July 13, 2002.

"U.S. Drops Bomb as Two Afghan Factions Clash," *Los Angeles Times*, July 19, 2002.

Vandehei, Jim, "Reluctant to Share Terrorist Evidence, Bush Retreats from bin Laden Pledge," *Wall Street Journal*, September 25, 2001.

Vick, Karl, "Marines Hunt for al Qaeda Materials," *Washington Post*, January 2, 2002.

Vick, Karl, and Bradley Graham, "Raid Finds Untouched al Qaeda Compound," *Washington Post*, January 3, 2002.

Vogel, Steve, "'They Said No. This Is Our Answer,'" *Washington Post*, October 8, 2001.

————, "Over Afghanistan, Gantlets in the Sky," *Washington Post*, October 29, 2001.

————, "Gas Stations in the Sky Extend Fighters' Reach," *Washington Post*, November 1, 2001.

————, "Al Qaeda Tunnels, Arms Cache Totalled; Complex Believed Largest Found in War," *Washington Post*, February 16, 2002.

Vogel, Steve, and Walter Pincus, "Al Qaeda Complex Destroyed; Search Widens," *Washington Post*, January 15, 2002.

Von Drehle, David, "Bush Pledges Victory," *Washington Post*, September 14, 2001.

————, "Senate Approves Use of Force; Military Patrols Cities and Ports," *Washington Post*, September 15, 2001.

Von Drehle, David, and Alan Sipress, "War Won't Be Short, Bush Says," *Washington Post*, September 16, 2001.

Wald, Matthew, "Pentagon Tracked Deadly Jet But Found No Way to Stop It," *New York Times*, September 15, 2001.

Walsh, Edward, "National Response to Terror," *Washington Post*, September 12, 2001.

————, "U.S. Campaign on Schedule, Generals Say," *Washington Post*, November 5, 2001.

Watson, Paul, and Norman Kempster, "Taliban Will Unravel If Key Players Gone, Experts Say," *Los Angeles Times*, September 20, 2001.

Watson, Roland, and Michael Evans, "America Turns Up the Heat," *London Times*, November 7, 2001.

Webster, Philip, "Blair Seeks United Democratic Response," *London Times*, September 13, 2001.

Weiner, Tim, "Rumsfeld Says Ramadan Won't Halt U.S. Attacks," *New York Times*, November 5, 2001.

Weisman, Jonathan, "Pentagon Denies Taliban Casualty Claim," *USA Today*, October 23, 2001.

———, "War's Deadliest Day," *USA Today*, March 6, 2002.

Weisman, Jonathan, and Andrea Stone, "U.S. Expects Longer War," *USA Today*, October 29, 2001.

Williams, Carol J., "Afghan Force Maintains High Profile Despite Risks," *Los Angeles Times*, May 16, 2002.

Wines, Michael, "Russia Faces Fateful Choice on Cooperation with U.S.," *New York Times*, September 21, 2001.

———, "Putin Offers Support to U.S. for Its Antiterrorist Efforts," *New York Times*, September 25, 2001.

Woodward, Bob, and Vernon Loeb, "CIA's Covert War on bin Laden," *Washington Post,* September 14, 2001.

Woodward, Bob, and Dan Balz, "At Camp David, Advise and Dissent," *Washington Post*, January 31, 2002.

———, "Combating Terrorism: 'It Starts Today,'" *Washington Post*, February 1, 2002.

Briefings

Deptula, Major General David A., USAF, "Operation Enduring Freedom—Highlights, Challenges, and Potential Implications: Some Observations from the First 60 Days," undated briefing charts.

Dunlap, Brigadier General Charles J., Jr., USAF, "Air and Information Operations: A Perspective on the Rise of 'Lawfare' in Modern Conflicts," presentation at a conference on Current Issues in the

Law of Armed Conflict, Naval War College, Newport, Rhode Island, June 2003.

Harward, Captain Robert S., USN, "Operation Enduring Freedom: Special Reconnaissance and Direct Action Operations in Afghanistan, October 6, 2001–March 30, 2002," Santa Monica, Calif.: RAND Corporation, August 19, 2002.

"Joint Air-Ground Operations: Operation Anaconda Background," undated briefing charts, Directorate of Plans and Programs, Headquarters Air Combat Command, Langley AFB, Virgina.

Martin, General Gregory S., USAF, "Operation Enduring Freedom: Humanitarian Relief and Force Sustainment Operations," Headquarters USAFE, Ramstein Air Base, Germany, September 24, 2002.

Wald, Lieutenant General Charles F., USAF, "Command Brief," Headquarters 9th Air Force, Shaw AFB, South Carolina, January 25, 2001.

———, "Enabling the PSAB CAOC Weapon System: Roadmap for the Future," undated briefing to Corona Top '02.

———, "Operation Enduring Freedom: The CFACC Viewpoint," undated briefing to the ACC [Air Combat Command] air commanders, 2002.

Miscellaneous

Arnott, Bob, "Electronic War in the Afghan Skies," MSNBC.com, March 11, 2002.

Barker, Major Kenneth, USAF, "The ASOC," unpublished paper, August 27, 2002.

Capaccio, Tony, "U.S. Pentagon Asks $19 Billion for Weapons, Intelligence," Bloomberg.com, September 19, 2001.

———, "Sixty Percent of Bombs Dropped on Afghanistan Precision-Guided," Bloomberg.com, November 20, 2001.

———, "Afghan Lessons Don't Apply to 'Axis,' Generals Say," Bloomberg.com, February 20, 2002.

Davis, Major Mark G., USA, "Operation Anaconda: Command and Confusion in Joint Warfare," unpublished thesis presented to the faculty of the School of Advanced Air and Space Studies, Maxwell AFB, Alabama, June 2004.

"Executive Summary of the Battle of Takur Ghar," Washington, D.C.: Department of Defense, May 24, 2002.

Fleri, Major Edgar, USAF, Colonel Ernest Howard, USAF, Jeffrey Hukill, and Thomas R. Searle, "Operation Anaconda Case Study," College of Aerospace Doctrine, Research, and Education, Maxwell AFB, Alabama, November 13, 2003.

Galaydick, Captain Scott J., USAF, "Bullet Background Paper on Space AOC Support for Operation Enduring Freedom," 614th Space Operations Squadron, Vandenberg AFB, California, March 19, 2004.

Grossman, Elaine M., "Operation Anaconda: Object Lesson in Poor Planning or Triumph of Improvisation?" InsideDefense.com, August 12, 2004.

McIntyre, Jamie, CNN report, March 19, 2002.

"Space Tasking Order (STO)," Doctrine Watch No. 21, Air Force Doctrine Center, Maxwell aFB, Alabama, provided to the author by the office of the Commander, 14th Air Force, Vandenberg AFB, California, n.d.

Stephens, Alan, "Afghanistan and the Australian Way of War," unpublished paper.

"Talking Paper on 3rd Aerospace Expeditionary Task Force Lessons Learned," Headquarters 85th Airlift Wing/XP, Ramstein Air Base, Germany, September 19, 2002.

"Talking Paper on Push and Pull Logistics Lessons Learned," Headquarters USAFE/LGXX, September 19, 2002.

"Talking Paper on Operation Enduring Freedom 3rd Aerospace Expeditionary Task Force A-4 and Logistics Readiness Cell Perspective," Headquarters USAFE/LGTR, September 20, 2002.

"USAF Talking Points: The War on Terrorism," SAF/PA, November 28, 2001.

"USAF Talking Points: The War on Terrorism," SAF/PA, January 16, 2002.

"USAF Talking Points: The War on Terrorism," SAF/PA, March 21, 2002.

Wald, Lieutenant General Charles F., USAF, "Memorandum for All USCENTAF Personnel, Subject: Commander's Intent," Headquarters U.S. Central Command Air Forces, Shaw AFB, South Carolina, May 18, 2000.